THE YOUNG EARL OF SOUTHAMPTON
Reproduced by permission of the Duke of Portland

SHAKESPEARE

AND THE

EARL OF

SOUTHAMPTON

G. P. V. AKRIGG

HARVARD UNIVERSITY PRESS
CAMBRIDGE MASSACHUSETTS
1968

Printed in Great Britain

TO

MARIAN, DAPHNE

AND

GEORGE

The web of our life is of a mingled yarn, good and ill together. Our virtues would be proud if our faults whipped them not, and our crimes would despair if they were not cherished by our virtues.

All's Well That Ends Well
IV, iii, 83–87

CONTENTS

PART ONE

THE PATRON

PART TWO

THE POET AND THE PATRON

LIST OF ILLUSTRATIONS

PREFACE

'Let us have the evidence first and let speculations—which of course may be very valuable and even necessary—be founded upon that.'

J. A. K. THOMSON, *Shakespeare and the Classics*

This is a book written in two parts. Part One is a biography of Shakespeare's patron. Here I have sought to record all that we know about Henry Wriothesley, third Earl of Southampton, that may relate to his influence upon Shakespeare and Shakespeare's work. In this portion of the book mention of Shakespeare is limited to listing his dedications to the Earl, along with those of other men. I have kept away from tendentious statements about Shakespeare being 'Southampton's poet'. Reading Part One, those who are intimately acquainted with their Shakespeare may find an incidental pleasure in spotting for themselves possible Shakespeare-Southampton connections, and in seeking to anticipate points that I shall make in Part Two.

My account of Southampton's life need not have extended beyond 1616 when Shakespeare died, or indeed beyond 1613 when *Henry VIII* closes the Shakespeare canon. Knowing that readers, once interested in Southampton, would want to follow his story to its end, I have continued his chronicle until his death in 1624, though I have dealt rather briefly with his later career. No doubt other pens will supply us with book-length studies of 'Southampton, Champion of Parliament' and 'Southampton and the Founding of Virginia'.

Part Two of this book is devoted to Shakespeare's work inasmuch as it *may* in places reflect Southampton's influence. Here we quickly pass beyond what little we know, and enter into realms of speculation. In the past an incredible amount of fevered thinking has gone into elaborate theories about Shakespeare's relations with Southampton. Much of what has been written is labyrinthine, improbable, and wildly partisan. Some of it is simply lunatic. But probability (even a strong degree of probability) supports some of the hypotheses that have been advanced. It is with the latter that I have concerned myself, adding at times some new ideas or pieces of evidence. Speculation, properly conducted, can be an exhilarating and exciting pastime. It can be knowledge in the making. Often it

stimulates us to fresh insights into Shakespeare's plays and poems. All
that is required is that neither author nor reader confuse speculation,
however interesting, with proven fact.

Unless otherwise noted, all dates in this book are Old Style, though
each New Year begins on January 1st not, according to the old fashion,
on March 25th. When quoting from sixteenth- and seventeenth-century
documents I have silently expanded abbreviations, and I have followed
modern usage for the letters 'i', 'j', 'u' and 'v'. When I have used the
Historical Manuscripts Commission's calendar of the Hatfield archives,
I refer to '*Salisbury MSS.*' When I have worked from photocopies of the
original documents, I refer to the '*Cecil Papers*'.

While working on this book I have been assisted with research grants
from my university. I must express gratitude to the Canada Council for a
grant to cover my travel expenses when I journeyed to England in 1964.

Sometimes, agonizing at my desk trying to work masses of recalcitrant
material into coherent chapters, I have suspected that only masochism
could drive one to authorship. The life however does have its compen-
sations. I recall my thrill when a chance remark in the Southampton
Borough Archives revealed that the Wriothesley family papers had survived and could be examined in the Hampshire Record Office at Winchester. Since that assiduous researcher Mrs. C. C. Stopes had not
found any family papers, it had seemed obvious that none could be extant.
But in Mrs. Stopes's day, almost fifty years ago, these papers were
stored away in wooden chests in the Chancery Lane Safe Deposit. Only
after 1930 were they taken to Welbeck by Mr. Francis Needham, then
librarian to the Duke of Portland, who calendared these papers before His
Grace deposited them in the Hampshire Record Office. Arriving at
Winchester, I was somewhat dashed to find that no personal correspondence had survived in the Wriothesley Papers, only the family's legal and
business records. However, even these proved interesting and useful.
Also at Winchester was the typescript of Mr. Needham's exemplary
calendar. In the person of Mrs. E. Cottrill, the County Archivist, the
papers have a most co-operative custodian, one who has cheerfully responded to my numerous requests for further information, xerox prints
and microfilms.

I have had other interesting and rewarding experiences while doing my
research for the present book. I recall a most enjoyable time spent in
Ireland, retracing the routes of Southampton and Essex, my wife beside
me gamely learning to drive on the left side of the road; I, with xeroxes of
Essex's journals in my lap, watching for landmarks. Or in England,
exploring the vicinity of Titchfield, carefully watching the odometer to
see how far the young Earl of Southampton must have travelled to visit the

fugitive Danvers brothers at Whitley, I remember being received at Whitley (now Whiteley) Lodge by Mrs. Somers who kindly took us into the house for tea.

Most of my research was, of course, of a more orthodox kind, and I must say a word of gratitude to those institutions in which I worked on this book—the Public Record Office, the British Museum, the Lambeth Palace Library, the National Library of Ireland, the Huntington Library, the Library of the University of California at Berkeley, and that of my own university. A special word of praise is due to the Public Record Office in London for its promptness and efficiency. It is a great thing for a scholar working on the west coast of North America to be able to send to the P.R.O. in London for a xerox of a much-needed document and to receive it on his desk within ten days.

Many individuals have helped me along the way. The Rev. Mr. N. A. L. Miller, the vicar of Titchfield, most kindly took his parish register up to Winchester for microfilming so that I could make a transcript of that portion extending from 1587 to 1625. Mr. T. Cottrell-Dormer of Rousham obligingly took to the Bodleian Library, for xeroxing, his letters written by Southampton's mother. Miss Clare Talbot, the Marquess of Salisbury's librarian, has been most helpful. The Folger Shakespeare Library (where I was once a research fellow) has assisted by supplying me with prints from its microfilms of the papers at Hatfield. My friends there, Giles Dawson and James McManaway, have helped me with my enquiries. In Ireland I was aided with information and advice by Professor Hayes-McCoy of the University College, Galway. In England the late Mr. L. W. Henry, in conversation, drew upon his extensive research into the life of Elizabeth's Essex. Others who have assisted me are Miss Alice Stanley of the Literary Department of the Principal Probate Registry, London; Messrs. G. P. B. Naish and J. Mundy of the National Maritime Museum, Greenwich; Mr. F. Puryer White, Keeper of the Records of St. John's College, Cambridge; Miss H. E. Peek, Keeper of the Archives, Cambridge University; Mr. L. H. Sidwell of the Holborn Society, Professor A. C. Hamilton, Dr. Mark H. Curtis and Mr. Michael Burn. I am obliged to the Duke of Portland for permitting me to reproduce in colour for the first time his portrait of Southampton during his youth. I am grateful for encouragement from Dr. John B. Macdonald during the stimulating years when he was President of the University of British Columbia.

My colleagues at U.B.C. have been generous with their help, especially in assisting me when my knowledge of foreign languages has proved insufficient. I wish particularly to thank Professors G. B. Riddehough, H. V. Livermore, J. A. McDonald, L. Jenaro-MacLennan, R. Giese, R. Holdaway, A. L. Farley, A. Busza and G. Creigh. I am particularly

grateful to Professor John Bosher of Cornell University for locating in
the Bibliothèque Nationale Beaumont's very important dispatch of 1604
and securing for me a microfilm of it.

I owe much to the helpful comments of Professor G. B. Harrison who
read over Part One for me, Professor G. A. Hayes-McCoy who read my
chapter on Southampton in Ireland, and my colleagues Professors R. W.
Ingram and J. A. Lavin who read Part Two. Needless to say, none of
these gentlemen is to be held responsible for anything in this book.

My chief acknowledgement is to my wife, Helen Manning Akrigg, my
research assistant and typist. My debt to her is very great indeed.

The Unversity of British Columbia   G. P. V. AKRIGG
Vancouver, Canada

PART ONE

THE PATRON

The Founders of His House

O F THE four Earls of Southampton of the Wriothesley line,[1] the first became Lord Chancellor and 'almost governed everything' in the later years of Henry VIII; the second was an unhappy man who never really found his stride in life; the third became Shakespeare's patron and distinguished himself in both war and peace; and the fourth became Lord Treasurer of England and one of the most respected counsellors of the realm under Charles II.[2] Although this record is on the whole a notable one, the family was not particularly illustrious in its origins. Its name of Wriothesley, probably pronounced Rýe-ose-ley but usually elided to Rise-ly,[3] was invented as an aristocratic-sounding name for his family by the second son of Sir John Writh, the latter being a Garter King of

---

[1] The one earlier Earl of Southampton was William Fitzwilliam, High Admiral of England and later Lord Privy Seal under Henry VIII. He received his earldom in 1537 but it became extinct when he died without issue in 1542. His estates passed to his half-brother Sir Anthony Browne, father of the first Viscount Montagu whose daughter Mary was to become the wife of the second and the mother of the third of the Wriothesley earls.

[2] The fourth earl having no male issue, the title became extinct upon his death. His estate passed to his daughters and, in the process of time, to the Dukes of Portland, Bedford, and Buccleuch, and to Lord Montagu of Beaulieu, the present continuators of the line.

[3] Thomas Heywood, who was at one time in Southampton's employment, has a couplet:

> Wriothesley was such, in all things striving
> To gaine a Name, by Artes, and Armes: surviving
> (*A Funeral Elegie upon King James*, London, 1625, sig. B6r.)

To get an equal number of feet in each line we have to read 'Rye-oath-ess-ly'. In actual informal practice the name seems almost invariably to have been contracted into three syllables at most, cf. the notice in the Titchfield parish register of the burial on December 28th, 1624 of 'Lord James wryosley'. The 'io' was usually reduced to a single vowel with most people, apparently, saying 'Risely' but with a few possibly saying 'Rosely'.

Among the pronunciations that have been championed are 'Wresley' (C. C. Stopes, *The Life of Henry, Third Earl of Southampton*, Cambridge, 1922, p. 12); 'Rosely' (Charlton Hinman, *T.L.S.*, October 2nd, 1937, p. 715); 'Wrisley' (A. F. Pollard, *T.L.S.*, October 9th, 1937, p. 735); and 'Wreesley' (E. I. Fripp, *Shakespeare: Man and Artist*, Oxford, 1938, I, 264). According to Hinman, G. L. Kittredge pronounced the name 'Riz-ly', and C. T. Onions reported that 'the name is pronounced "Rosely" by persons now living'.

Seeking a living Wriothesley who could tell me how he pronounces his name, Mr. Michael Burn most obligingly went through the telephone directories for the entire British Isles but found no Wriothesleys.

Arms who died in 1504. Sir John's elder son William followed him into
the College of Arms, made a middle-class marriage, and begat a large
family. His elder son Thomas was to become the first of our Earls of
Southampton.[1]

Young Thomas Wriothesley after his student years at Cambridge
returned to London, married Jane Cheney the daughter and heiress of
William Cheney of Chesham Bois in Buckinghamshire, and obtained a
minor post in the court of Henry VIII. A subsequent appointment as one
of the Joint Clerks of the Signet proved a stepping-stone to service on
missions to Brussels and Marseilles. Calculating that training in the law
would bring further preferment, young Wriothesley in 1534 secured
admittance to Gray's Inn.

With his further qualification, Wriothesley moved steadily ahead.
Renewed diplomatic service took him to the Continent to seek the young
widowed Christina, Duchess of Milan, as wife for King Henry. But his
master's way with wives was becoming notorious, and the lady herself
reputedly declined with a quip that, had she two heads, she would gladly
let the King of England have one of them.

Knighted in April 1540, Sir Thomas Wriothesley became that year one
of the King's two Secretaries of State and a member of the Privy Council.
He was now an important man, with a royal warrant to keep forty gentle-
men and yeomen wearing his badge or livery besides 'all such as did daily
attend upon him in his household'.[2] Skill in negotiating an alliance with
Emperor Charles V won him further advancement and, at a ceremonial
banquet at Hampton Court on New Year's Day 1544, he was created
Baron Wriothesley of Titchfield. On May 3rd, 1544, after several months as
Lord Keeper of the Great Seal, he was promoted to the full dignity of Lord
Chancellor of England. The following year he was made a Knight of the
Garter.

This swift ascent from obscurity to greatness was achieved with the
help of a powerful patron. Wriothesley had early attached himself to the
service of Thomas Cromwell, the man who to the profit of Henry and his
ministers attended to the spoliation of the English monasteries. Wriothesley was among the most ruthless of Cromwell's creatures. Descending
upon Winchester in September 1538, and going to work at three o'clock in

---

[1] For fuller information on the origins of the family see A. L. Rowse, 'Thomas
Wriothesley, First Earl of Southampton', *Huntington Library Quarterly*, XXVIII
(1965), 106–29. With a few minor changes this is reprinted as the first chapter of
Rowse's *Shakespeare's Southampton, Patron of Virginia* (London, 1965). Most of the rest
of the book is of little worth.

[2] *v. Wriothesley Papers*, *5M53/150*, in the Hampshire Record Office, Winchester.
Future citations to the Wriothesley Papers will use the abbreviation *W.P.* and omit
the 5M53, the H.R.O. call letters for the entire series.

the morning when they were least likely to be prevented by the outraged townspeople, Wriothesley and his officers entered the cathedral and demolished the shrine of St. Swithin. As for nearby Hyde Abbey, Wriothesley secured for himself a brief lease to the land and then proceeded to level the abbey, obliterating in the process the tomb of Alfred the Great, but no doubt making for himself a tidy penny out of all the stonework, carvings and tiles.

The dissolution of the monasteries proved a lucrative business for Wriothesley. In 1537 he acquired the lands of Quarr Abbey on the Isle of Wight and those of Titchfield Abbey, his future family seat in Hampshire. In 1538 he secured Beaulieu Abbey and its lands, and in 1539 the richest of the manors belonging to Hyde Abbey. Subsequent years brought further acquisitions. When, at the beginning of the reign of Edward VI, he secured letters patent confirming his possession of various estates obtained during the previous reign, the list included the manors of Upton and Ipley, Micheldever, East Stratton, West Meon, North Stoneham, and Abbot's Worthy, Popham Grange, and lands in the parish of St. Pancras Middlesex.[1] One way and another, Lord Chancellor Wriothesley had become a very rich man and a major Hampshire landowner.

What sort of a person was he? The cracked old portrait hanging to this day in the mansion house at Beaulieu shows him holding up his head with a sort of proud, challenging jauntiness. A notable gleam in his eyes suggests the ready emotionality which was so much a part of the make-up of both his son and grandson. He was sharp and shrewd. Colleagues thought him opiniated and overbearing. Certainly he could be ruthless and cruel. Poor Anne Askew, the pious Lutheran daughter of a Lincolnshire squire, tells how Lord Chancellor Wriothesley put his own hand to the rack when she was being tortured as a heretic.[2] When Anne was burned at the stake at Smithfield, Wriothesley was present to see the sentence performed.

Yet despite much that was unappealing, Wriothesley had his attractive side. John Leland the antiquary, a friend of his youth, tells us that he was always a friend to the Muses. Roger Ascham, who was not a man to indulge in empty flattery, sent Lord Chancellor Wriothesley a copy of his *Toxophilus* and an epistle describing him as 'a great patron of the University of Cambridge and of literature'. Wriothesley seems to have been sincere in his loyalty and devotion to Henry VIII. Incredible as it seems, he could hardly speak for tears when reporting to parliament the death of the old tyrant.

If anything in the history of the English peerage is to be regarded with

[1] *W.P. 995.*
[2] *Letters and Papers, Foreign and Domestic, of the Reign of Henry VIII*, Vol. XXI, Part I, p. 590.

suspicion, it is the process by which Thomas Wriothesley became Earl of Southampton. Shortly before the coronation of Edward VI, the governors of the boy king announced that, in compliance with the last wishes of Henry VIII as expressed on his death bed to Secretary Paget, they were to receive promotions in the peerage. Since nobody had the hardihood to question the veracity of Paget, the new honours were awarded in short order. One of the new creations was that of Thomas Wriothesley who on February 16th, 1547, received his patent creating him Earl of Southampton.

The ink on the new earl's patent was scarcely dry before disaster struck. Lord Protector Somerset and his allies, deciding that they could not count on Southampton, used a minor procedural slip on the part of the Lord Chancellor to deprive him of his office. Southampton helped the Earl of Warwick to overthrow Somerset in 1549, but Warwick too lacked confidence in Southampton and in February 1550 he secured his dismissal from the Privy Council.

By now Southampton was a sick man, deep in melancholy, and 'desiring to be under the earth rather than upon it'. In late June the Privy Council gave him permission to withdraw to Hampshire. Apparently he was too ill to do so for on July 30th he died in London. Four days later he was buried in the parish church of St. Andrew's Holborn, close to his London residence Southampton House.[1] He left numerous daughters[2] and one son, Henry, who now at the age of five became the second Earl of Southampton.

The new earl, being a minor, passed into the custody of the royal Master of Wards. The Master, to raise revenues for the Crown, customarily sold wardships to the highest bidders, who then set about administering their wards' estates in the manner which would yield them the highest returns on their investment. The purchaser of the wardship of young Henry Wriothesley, second Earl of Southampton, was a family friend, Sir William Herbert. It appears that the boy's mother, following a not uncommon practice, bought back from Herbert the wardship of her son.[3]

The widowed Countess of Southampton was a most devout Roman

---

[1] Southampton House stood south of Holborn and east of Chancery Lane, hence the name 'Southampton Buildings' for the edifice which now occupies part of this site.

[2] In 1545 he had arranged marriages for four daughters. Preserved in the Wriothesley Papers are the indentures for a marriage between Elizabeth and Thomas Radcliffe, Lord Fitzwalter, the son and heir of the Earl of Sussex (*W.P. 281*); between Mary and Richard Lister (*W.P. 932*); between Katherine and Matthew Arundell (*W.P. 933*); and between Anne and Henry Wallop (*W.P. 935*). Apparently the last two of these marriages were not carried through. Katherine married a Thomas Cornwallis, and Anne, it seems, died before she could be married to Henry Wallop. Another of the first Earl's daughters, Mabel, married Walter Sandes or Sandys.

[3] H.M.C., *Salisbury MSS.*, XIII, 27.

Catholic. During the five years of the restoration of Catholicism under Queen Mary, she had no trouble in seeing that her boy was brought up in the tenets of her religion. Matters became more difficult when Elizabeth came to the throne in 1558. The mother obviously did everything she could to protect the young earl from the influences of the Protestant court. Her tactics did not go unobserved. In December 1564 a letter was sent 'to the Countes of Sowthampton requiring her, in the Quenes Highnes' name, without furder delaye or protract of tyme, notwithstandinge her former excuses, to take order that the Earle, her sonne, may be here at Coourte before Candelmas Eve next comyng'.[1] By now however the Earl was nineteen years old and his character and convictions had been formed. To his dying day he was to remain fervently loyal to the Old Religion.

The Earl of Southampton's country seat at Titchfield became, like so many of the great houses of the Catholic English nobility, a bastion of Catholicism. Many a priest was harboured there before slipping away to the next such asylum, the magnificent mansion at Cowdray, across the border in Sussex, the home of Anthony Browne, first Viscount Montagu. Not surprisingly, when the Earl married on February 19th, 1566, his bride was Montagu's thirteen-year-old daughter, Mary. A note written in the new Countess of Southampton's prayer book provides an interesting detail about this marriage: it was 'solemnyzed att London in my Lord Montagew's howse by hys advise without the consent of my Lady, his [the young earl's] mother'.[2] Although the bridegroom's mother was hostile upon this occasion, more than a year before she had signed an agreement for this marriage.[3]

Once the Earl had celebrated his twenty-first birthday, he could 'sue for livery' (for his estates to be transferred from wardship to himself). He did so and belatedly, on February 7th, 1568, received letters patent from the Crown permitting him to enter upon 'all the honours, castles, manors' left by his father. Three days later he signed the deed of convenant transferring a number of these manors to his wife as her marriage settlement.[4]

With his estate thus settled, master of his own affairs and happily married, the young earl could look forward to a pleasant life. Unfortunately within a few months difficulties began to confront him.

The key to the unhappy life of the second Earl of Southampton is to be found in the fervour of his Catholicism. He was by no means unusual

[1] *Acts of the Privy Council of England, 1558–1570*, pp. 173–4.
[2] *Complete Peerage*, Vol. XII, Part I, p. 127.
[3] *W.P. 198*. This agreement, dated January 20th, 1565, had an expiry date of June 24th following, and so had lapsed when the marriage finally was solemnized.
[4] *W.P. 234* and *184*.

among the lords of England in maintaining his allegiance to this faith. A survey of 1567, preserved in the Vatican archives, found thirty-two of the English peers to be firm reliable Catholics, twenty others to be well affected towards Catholics, and only a little band of fifteen firmly committed Protestants.[1] Elizabeth and her councillors, knowing at this period that they could count upon only minority support among the peers in matters of religion, were not out to stir up trouble. Elizabeth herself did not believe she should 'make windowes into mens harts and secret thoughts'.[2] So long as her lords gave her their political loyalty, she was not too concerned with the form of the prayers that they heard in their chapels. Unfortunately Southampton was not one to settle for quasi-tolerance by a Protestant government.

First indications of the coming storm are found in a letter that the Earl of Sussex wrote to Sir William Cecil in February 1569. Southampton must have seriously offended the government, for the letter is a plea to Cecil for 'his helping hand for the young Earl of Southampton that he may be rather charitably won than severely corrected'.[3] The government seems to have adopted Sussex's suggestion for in the summer of this year Queen Elizabeth, in the course of her southern progress, honoured Southampton by being his guest one night at Titchfield. The gesture was wasted. In November came the Rebellion of the Northern Earls. Southampton and his father-in-law, Viscount Montagu, had earlier been associated in treasonable plans with the leaders of the rebellion. When it was obvious that the rebellion had failed they sought to flee England, and in mid-December they set sail for Flanders. Contrary winds forced Southampton and Montagu back to England where they were greeted with orders from the Queen to come immediately to court and explain their actions. Surely unaware that the two lords had consulted with the Spanish ambassador whether they should join in the rebellion at home or take service under the Duke of Alba on the Continent, the Queen and her ministers were anxious to come to an amicable arrangement with Southampton and Montagu. Things were smoothed over and Montagu was appointed a Joint Lord Lieutenant of his county as an evidence of royal trust. With Montagu these tactics succeeded. He kept his religion, but he never again conspired against the Queen. When in the Armada year Elizabeth reviewed her army at Tilbury:

> ... the first that shewed his bands to the Queen, was that noble, virtuous, honour-
> able man, the Viscount Montague, who ... now came, though he was very sickly
> and in age, with a full resolution to live and die in defence of the Queen and of his

[1] Cal. S.P. (Rome) I, Elizabeth, 1558–1571, pp. 265–6.
[2] T. Powell, A Welch Bayte (1603), sig. B3v.
[3] Cal. S.P. (Foreign), 1569–1571, p. 31.

country, against all invaders, whether it were pope, king, or potentate what-soever. . . .[1]

Southampton would have done well if he had followed his father-in-law in loyalty to the Crown. As it was, a time for decision was at hand for him and for all other English Catholics. In May 1570 John Felton pinned on the door of the Bishop of London's house a copy of the Bull of Pius V excommunicating Queen Elizabeth and ordering her subjects 'that they presume not to obey her, or her monitions, Mandates, and Lawes', under pain of similar excommunication. In this crisis the Earl of Southampton sought out the only available Catholic prelate, John Leslie, Bishop of Ross (the agent in London of Mary Queen of Scots, now in her English captivity). Southampton asked the Bishop whether he should or should not continue to serve his Queen. Although this interview took place secretly by evening in the seclusion of the Lambeth marshes, it was cut short by the arrival of the watch. None of the conversation had been over-heard, but the circumstances of the meeting could not but arouse sus-picions of treason. On June 18th, the Privy Council ordered Southampton arrested and confined incommunicado in the house of Beecher, one of the sheriffs of London.[2] On July 15th, still with only suspicions to proceed upon, the Council transferred him to the custody of William More at the latter's country home of Loseley, near Guildford. To make the Earl's detention spiritually profitable, the councillors instructed More to induce him to join in the household devotions using the Book of Common Prayer. Such participation would be construed as conformity with the Church of England. After some evasions, Southampton finally joined in the family prayers and in November was given his freedom.

If the Earl thought he was safely out of the woods, he was sadly mis-taken. In September 1571 the government learned the full scope of the Ridolfi Plot. This conspiracy, which had been simmering for a year, centred about the Duke of Norfolk, who was to raise an English Catholic army, release Mary Queen of Scots and then, with the aid of a Spanish invasion force, capture London and put Mary on Queen Elizabeth's throne. Almost as deeply involved in the plot as Ridolfi, the Florentine banker who had hatched the scheme, was the Bishop of Ross. Placed under arrest, Ross learned that he had been hopelessly incriminated by con-fessions made by Norfolk's secretaries. Told that he had no diplomatic immunity and threatened with the death upon the scaffold that awaited Norfolk, the bishop panicked and told all. Nor did he limit himself to the Ridolfi Plot. Eager to ingratiate himself with his captors, he spilled

---

[1] *Harleian Miscellany* (London, 1809), II, 76.
[2] *Salisbury MSS.*, I, 557–62.

the whole story of his meeting with the Earl of Southampton in the Lambeth marshes. He even reconstructed the questions that Southampton had put to him there:

> But I pray yow tell me, what think yow of this Bull, that is now publist abroad, whether yf the Subjects of this Land may, with save [safe] Conscience, obey the Quene as our Righteous Princess?

According to the bishop, Southampton had been greatly agitated by the prospect of risking excommunication himself if he continued to obey Queen Elizabeth:

> . . . he said it war better to losse all that he had, nor to lyve onder Cursing within this cuntrey, for then shuld he be in continual Feare of Conscience.[1]

The bishop said that he had assured Southampton he would not risk excommunication by continuing in his allegiance to his queen.

An English earl who had asked a Roman Catholic bishop whether or not he should obey the Queen had to be severely punished. Arrested at the end of October 1571, the second Earl of Southampton was packed off to the Tower of London. There he spent the next eighteen months. True, he did not lead the life of a felon wearing leg-irons in a dungeon. At his own expense he could maintain and furnish a chamber, and he could occasionally receive a licence for a visit by his kin, but it was a grim life all the same.

During his second year in the Tower, Southampton redoubled his efforts to secure his release. Writing to William Cecil, Lord Burghley, on February 13th, 1573, 'from my weriful prison', he begged him 'for God his sake to continue the same your honorable and charitable goodnes towardes me', and he enclosed a petition to the Queen, humbly requesting Burghley to amplify or diminish it in whatever way he saw fit and then to have it presented to Her Majesty. The next day Southampton wrote to the Privy Council assuring them that he was 'carefull and studious to leave no meane undune by all humble and therwith faythfull submission, and attestation of loiall obedience, to recover her Majesties good grace, opinion and favor toweardes me'.[2]

Finally the representations made by the Earl and his friends had their effect. On May 1st, 1573, the Privy Council released Southampton from the Tower and committed him again to the easy custody of William More at Loseley.

A more politic man, having secured partial liberty after so much suffering, would have conducted himself circumspectly and have caused not the

---

[1] William Murdin, *A Collection of State Papers Relating to Affairs in the Reign of Queen Elizabeth, from the Year 1571 to 1596* (London, 1759), p. 40.
[2] *Lansdowne MS. 16*, ff. 46r and 48r.

slightest trouble. Not so Southampton. With that soreheaded obstinacy which seems to have become a part of his character, he refused to pay the bill submitted by the Lieutenant of the Tower for his diet and 'for all extraordinarie charges that the Lieutenant hath ben at above his due allowaunce'.[1] Writing to the Privy Council, he fulminated against the Lieutenant for having outrageously overcharged him. Probably the Lieutenant had done so (he would have been an unusual Elizabethan official if he had not), but since in the shifting fortunes of his life Southampton might once again find himself the Lieutenant's prisoner, it was hardly the part of wisdom thus to antagonize him. And the Privy Council, though it conscientiously appointed a four-man commission to adjudicate the dispute, would hardly have been the better disposed towards Southampton for this additional trouble.

All things considered, Southampton was lucky that, on July 14th, the Council further enlarged his freedom by transferring him to the custody of his father-in-law at Cowdray, and allowing him an occasional overnight leave to supervise the building of his mansion at Dogmersfield. There was a compassionate reason for this further relaxation. The Countess was pregnant and the time of her delivery was drawing near. On October 6th, 1573, she gave birth to a son. The Earl, in a state of euphoria at having an heir to his title, sat down and wrote a letter to William More at Loseley, with whom, despite having twice been his involuntary guest, he was on warm terms. 'To my assured frend Mr William More, Esquire, Losly, geve thes' runs the inscription on the outside of the letter, and the contents read in part:

> Although yt is so happed by the sudden sickness of my wife, that wee coold not by possibility have her pressent as we desired, yet have I thought good to imparte unto you such comfort as God hath sent me after all my longe trubles, which is that this present morning, at iii of clok, my wife was dd. [delivered] of a goodly boy (God bless him!) the which, allthough yt was not without great perell to them both for the present, yet now, I thanke God, both are in good state. Yf your wife will take the paynes to visit her, we shalbe mighty glad of her company. . . . From Cowdray, this present Tuesday 1573.
>
> Your assured ffrend,
> H. Southampton.[2]

The babe was given his father's name of Henry. In time he would become the third Earl of Southampton. One of our two principals had made his entrance within the theatre that is this life. The other had made his nine and a half years earlier, and was now a schoolboy in Stratford-upon-Avon.

[1] *Acts P.C., 1571–1575*, p. 108.
[2] A. J. Kempe, ed., *The Loseley Manuscripts* (London, 1836), p. 240.

CHAPTER II

The Broken Home

THE FIRST six years of the future third earl's life were spent in a family where a certain amount of peace and security prevailed. An elder sister, Jane, died at some indeterminate period, perhaps even before young Harry (as he was called) was born, but he had another sister, Mary, a little older than himself, for a companion. The children must often have visited with their parents the great house of their Grandfather Montagu, set amid its open park and gently rolling woodlands at Cowdray. No doubt they were taken to see their grandmother, the Dowager Countess of Southampton, at Place (Palace) House, at Titchfield, the Premonstratensian abbey which her husband had converted into his country seat. But most of the time the children must have been at one of the houses which their father, careless of expense, maintained in various parts of Hampshire: Itchell, Beaulieu, Dogmersfield, Bull (or Bugle) Hall, the large town house that the Earl maintained in the city of Southampton itself. Occasionally their parents may have taken them up to London to the Earl's city residence, Southampton House in Holborn, or to Montagu House across the Thames in Southwark.

The half-dozen years after the birth of his heir were probably the happiest of the second earl's life. Queen Elizabeth, after ending his period of more or less nominal custody at Cowdray, was giving him small offices and other signs of favour to demonstrate that loyalty paid. In 1574 he was appointed to the Commission of the Peace for his shire, and joined in making a survey of its defences. In 1579 he served on a special commission for the suppression of piracy. The death of the Dowager Countess, in September 1574, augmented the second earl's means, but also encouraged him in his extravagances. We find him impoverishing himself, lavishing funds upon the building of his great new mansion at Dogmersfield and maintaining a retinue much larger than he needed. Years later Gervase Markham was to recall how the second earl's 'muster role never consisted of foure *Lackeys* and a *Coachman*, but of a whole troupe of at least an hundred well mounted Gentlemen and Yeomen'.[1] After his years of deprivation in the Tower the Earl was in a mood to deny himself nothing. In future years the third earl would nearly bankrupt himself trying to keep up something of his father's magnificence.

[1] *Honour In His Perfection* (London, 1624), sig. D2v.

The second earl's years of peace soon came to an end. His marriage was turning out to be an unhappy one. Tetchy, ill-tempered and proud, both weak and obstinate, he was no doubt something less than a perfect husband. His wife, no longer the demure young thing of her wedding portrait preserved at Worksop, was on her way to becoming the self-willed, self-pitying, sensuous woman of her middle years. She and her husband had their quarrels and reconciliations. The danger signals were plainly flying around 1577 when the Earl, upset at the intimacy of her friendship with a man named Donesame, 'a common person',[1] forbade her ever to see him again. The storm broke early in 1580 when the Earl learned that his wife had been seen with Donesame at Dogmersfield under circumstances which left him no doubt that the man was her lover. In his fury the Earl broke not only with her but with her family. An entry in the register of the Privy Council indicates that, as with the Montagues and Capulets, so with the Montagus and Wriothesleys, the servants took up the family quarrel:

> xxiii Februarij, 1579 [1580 New Style]
> This day Edmund Prety, servaunt to the Erle of Southampton was, for certain misdemeanours by him used against Mr. Anthony Brown, the eldest sonne of the Lord Montacute . . . committed to the Marshalsea.[2]

Light on the whole affair is cast by a letter of March 21st, 1580, written by the lady to her father. She was at this time apparently at one of her husband's Hampshire residences where, having forever banished her from his 'board and presence', he was keeping her under close surveillance and permitting her only occasional visits by carefully selected guests. Her father had written to her for a complete honest account of the situation and her letter, long, rambling and not always very coherent, was written in response to that request.

A number of things emerge in the course of this letter. The Earl apparently is dealing with her only through an intermediary, one Thomas Dymock, a gentleman of his bedchamber. The Countess is vehement against Dymock whom she views as 'the begynner & contynnuer of this dissention betwene us'. Contemptuously she observes, '. . . this howse is not for them that will not honor Dymocke as a god'. The Earl himself, she reports, stands 'so doubtfull and perplexed betwene hate & dread, as what to do he knoweth nott well'. She concedes that 'I rest condemned generally, though, I trust not so much of the better sorte, that knoweth me, as some could wishe I shoulde'. About two-thirds of the way through her very long letter, she comes to the adultery that has been charged against her. Her defence is a declaration of innocence, and a counter-charge that

[1] B.M., *MS. Titus B II*, f. 372r.
[2] *Acts P.C.*, *1578–1580*, pp. 396–8.

her enemies are perjuring themselves in order to ruin her. Perhaps it is only fair to give the lady's own account of the relationship with Done-same:

> . . . it may be my Lord will unripp olde matters, repented & forgotten longe since. if he do, well he may blame me of folly, butt never justly condemne me of falt. And as for the matter charged of Dogmarshefeilde, & donesame his cominge thether, he shall never prove it as he wolde, excepte he wynn some to perjure themselves about it. for by my truthe, in my liffe, did I never se him in that howse. neither I assure your Lordship since I was by my Lord forbydden his companye, dyd I ever come in itt. desyre I dyd to speake with him I confesse, & I tolde yow why and I wishe that the cause with my meaninge were uttered by the partie himself upon his conscience (if he have any) wherefore I coveted to speake with him. and then (I trust) I shoulde be acquited of greater evell, then overmuch follye, for desiringe or doinge that, which, beinge by my enemyes mistaken, doth brede this my sklander and dainger.

In conclusion, the Countess has one petition. Her husband has said that he will be reconciled with her only if the Queen herself instructs him to end their separation, and mockingly he has declared that Her Majesty will never open her mouth on his wife's behalf. Accordingly, the Countess begs her father to have some of the Privy Council give a secret hearing of her her case. She will submit to their verdict.

There is a postscript to the letter:

> That your Lordship shall be witnes of my desier to wyn my Lord by all such meanes as resteth in me, I have sent yowe what I sent to him by my litle boye. butt his harte was to greate to bestowe the readinge of it cominge from me. yett will I do my parte so longe as I am with him. butt good my Lord procure so soone as conveniently yowe may some end to my miserie, for I am tyred with this liffe.[1]

And so we have our first view of Henry Wriothesley, soon to become third Earl of Southampton, as a little boy of six coming into his father's presence with a letter from his mother which his father refuses to read. The emotional strains on the little boy must have been terrible. The father saw to it that, as long as he lived, the Countess would not see their son again.

Among those whom the Countess denounced as her enemies there is one notable omission—Charles Paget, brother of Lord Paget, whom two con-temporaries labelled as particularly responsible for setting the Earl against his Countess. One who made this charge was the Jesuit Father Parsons. Parsons, in later years writing of how quarrels among the leading English Catholics had weakened their position, noted:

[1] The original of this letter is in the British Museum (*Cotton MS. Titus B II*, ff. 370r–372v). It was printed in full, but with numerous misreadings by Mrs. Stopes (pp. 521–4). Mrs. Stopes believed the Countess's story. A. L. Rowse, *Shakespeare's Southampton, Patron of Virginia*, reproduces Mrs. Stopes's errors, without acknow-ledgement, citing only the original manuscript.

One thing also increased the difficulties of the Catholikes at this tyme, which was the falling out betweene the Earle of Southampton and the Lord Montacute [a common variant of Montagu] about the Earles wife, which was daughter to the Lord, and put away by the Earle, as suspected of incontinency, in which quarrell and dissention as also that of the Lord Pagett with his wife, [it] was then said in England that Mr. Charles Pagett brother to the said Lord had much falt.[1]

In July 1599 an English Catholic exile in Brussels, speaking of the same Paget, declared in a letter, 'I will overpass his youthful crimes, as the unquietness he caused betwixt the late Earl of Southampton and his wife yet living . . . .'[2]

Where so little evidence exists it is impossible to say whether or not the Countess had committed the adultery of which she was accused. The son probably believed his father was justified in his actions. When he reached manhood the third earl appeared to have had no great fondness for his mother. We find her, at the time of her son's own marriage in 1598, exclaiming that he 'never was kind to me'.[3] Presumably as a young boy in the company of his grim unhappy father, he had had burned into him a conviction of his mother's sin and shame. Worse still, brooding over his mother's alleged infidelity, he may have developed a distrust of all womankind which for years would make him look to men for love and loyalty.

The unhappy second earl had more than his wife's conduct to worry about. His intense devotion to the Roman Catholic faith was again leading him into troubled waters. According to Father Foley, the historian of the English Jesuits, Southampton was imprisoned in consequence of the antirecusancy act of January 16th, 1581.[4] Certainly he was in real trouble in August of that year when the authorities learned that the Jesuit martyr Edmund Campion (recently hanged, drawn and quartered) had been in communication with the Earl of Southampton by means of that Thomas Dymock so heartily detested by the Countess.

Probably the mounting strain of these difficulties, both domestic and religious, undermined the health of the second earl. In any event, on October 4th, 1581, two days before his son turned eight years old, he died at his house of Itchell, adjacent to Dogmersfield, in Hampshire.

That the Earl's health had been failing for some months before his decease is evident from his will, which he drafted three months earlier, 'notynge with my self the uncerteine state and condicion of mans ffrayle and decayable nature'. The original draft survives among the Wriothesley Papers.[5]

---

[1] 'A Storie of Domesticall Difficulties', Catholic Record Society, *Miscellanea*, Vol. II, p. 183.   [2] *Cal. S.P. (Dom.), 1598–1601*, p. 234.   [3] *Salisbury MSS.*, VIII, 379.
[4] Henry Foley, *Records of the English Province of the Society of Jesus* (London, 1877–1883), III, 659.
[5] *W.P. 936*. The probate copy is at Somerset House (P.P.C., Rowe 45).

The will is a long and complicated document but its clauses cast a flood of light upon the character of the second earl. In an early clause the Earl orders his executors to erect not one but two tombs in the chapel of the church at Titchfield. The first is to be made for his mother and father (the latter's remains being exhumed and brought from their burial place in London); the second is to be made for himself and, like the first, ornamented with effigies carved out of alabaster or similar material. The executors, economizing in view of the Earl's crippling debts, in fact built only one tomb for the three of them. This still stands in Titchfield parish church with a statue of a kneeling boy, the mourning third earl, among its 'portraitures'. Besides ordering these two sumptuous tombs, the Earl left instructions (never carried out) for the decoration of the chapel itself. An iron grille was to separate it from the body of the church. Its floor was to be newly paved, and new windows were to be set in the side wall. An ornate plaster ceiling was to be installed, with pendants 'sett full of my Armes', and the walls were to be 'playstered lyke my howse at Dogmersfeld'. This great house at Dogmersfield, whose building was to have been the great achievement of his life, was very much on his mind. In subsequent clauses he gives his executors eight years in which to see that this mansion be 'fully fynisshed and builded . . . according to the forme all redy begon and Modell made by Adam of Grenewich', and he gives them ten years in which to complete furnishing it. Here too the executors were to change things in consequence of the Earl's unrealistic view of his resources. They seem to have brought an end to the whole Dogmersfield project.

A great number of specific legacies are mentioned. Among these is a small annuity to old Alban Langdale, the priest who in happier days had disputed against Cranmer, Ridley and Latimer at Oxford, but now for years had been the family's Catholic chaplain. A rather odd clause provides for the education, until the age of twenty-one, of 'william my Beggers boye'. What really stands out in the will, however, is the extraordinary concern for 'my good & trustie servant Thomas Dymock'. Not only is Dymock named as one of the five executors but, either in association with Charles Paget[1] or alone if necessary, he is to rule on the interpretation of any disputed clause in the will. Clause after clause heaps praises and benefits upon Dymock. Like the other gentlemen of the Earl's bedchamber, he is to receive a legacy of £40. Over and above this he is to

---

[1] Also an executor. The others were Edward Gage of Bentley in Sussex, Gilbert Wells of Bambridge in Hampshire, and Ralph Hare, Bencher of the Middle Temple. The Earl of Northumberland, Lord Paget, and a brother-in-law, Thomas Cornwallis, were designated as the 'overseers' who were to make sure that the executors performed their trust.

receive a special legacy of £200. Because of the 'good opynion and faith-full trust' that the Earl has in him, he wants Dymock 'to be attendant and dayly about the person of my sonn'. To make Dymock the more careful of the son, and to keep him mindful of what a good lord and master the second earl has been, he is to get another £40 a year. (These sums were substantial: multiply by twenty at least for modern values.) Until the third earl is of age, Dymock is to have Whitley House, adjacent to Titch-field, for his own residence. He is authorized to keep stock in Whitley Park and in the great park at Titchfield. He is to be supplied with hay and fuel. On and on the special privileges continue. When the third earl comes of age he is to give Dymock or his children a twenty-one year lease to Bromwich farm. Dymock is given the Earl's black bay. The other execu-tors are not to do anything without the approval of Dymock. Obviously just as, in the years after his marriage, the second earl had depended on his father-in-law Montagu for guidance and support, so in his last years he was pathetically dependent upon Dymock. Guilty or not, the Countess had good grounds for her complaint that Dymock was regarded as a god.

The failure of the Earl's marriage and the bitterness that he felt towards his wife are reflected in the provision that he made for his surviving daughter, Mary. A legacy of £2,000 is to be paid to her when she comes of age. Until then, a sum of £60 (rising to £80 at the age of eleven) is to be paid annually for her upbringing. She is to be brought up in the home of her Aunt Katherine or of her great-aunt, Mistress Lawrence, or in 'som other good vertuose howse'. Moreover, 'because childhod is to be manteyned by mans authoritie and slipery and wavering youthe to be underpropped with elder councell', she is to be governed entirely by the executors in her choice of a husband. Then comes a culminating clause: she must never be in the same house as her mother. If she does not obediently live where the executors decide, she is to be cut off without a penny. There is no legacy or even an expression of regard for his father-in-law, the friend and counsellor of earlier years.

It is pleasant to record that a codicil attached to the probate copy of this will in Somerset House reveals that in the few remaining months of his life the Earl showed a more forgiving spirit. Noting that Dogmersfield, which would pass to his widow under her jointure, would be much too large a house for her, he instructed his executors to offer her in place of it an annuity of £80. Moreover, should she agree to this arrangement, he ordered that, as a demonstration to the whole world that he died in a spirit of perfect charity, his executors were to pay her a bequest of £500. Apparently there had been a reconciliation with the old viscount, her father—'And I gyve to my Lord Montague a George and a Garter [almost

certainly those of the first earl] of the value of ffourtie poundes in token of perfect love and charitie betwene us'.

The Earl did not pass to his grave unlamented by the Muse. John Phillips in a ballad entitled 'An Epitaph on the death of the Right honorable and vertuous Lord Henry Wrisley, Noble Earle of Southampton', mourned him in unabashed doggerel:

> Yet though he sencelesse lye, *South hamptons* Earle by name
> Yet death in him lyes dead no doubt, by means of noble fame.

Phillips seems to have been in the know about the Countess. Relentless couplets tell how children, friends, servants, tenants—in fact just about everybody except the wife—wept at the death of the good earl. One couplet, indeed, does seem to glance reproachfully in the Countess's direction:

> In wedlock he observed, the vow that he had made:
> In breach of troth through lewd lust, he ne would seeme to wade.[1]

Apparently the Southampton family scandal was fairly widely known.

The newly-widowed Countess was not appeased by her husband's codicil declaring that he died in perfect charity towards her. She saw various of the provisions of the will as intolerable affronts and she set about securing their cancellation. Her family was connected with the Earl of Leicester, the Queen's favourite. If anybody could do anything for her it was probably Leicester. Ten days after her husband died, she wrote a highly emotional and not very tactful letter to Leicester. In it she inveighed against Dymock as a person 'voyde of ether wytt, abelyte [ability] or honesty', and entreated Leicester to use his influence with Dr. Drury, before whom the probate was to be made, to nullify the Earl's will and turn over to herself the administration of her husband's estate. In a postscript she begged Leicester to keep confidential his receipt of this letter, declaring that she had made no creature privy to it.[2] Quite possibly she had not shown this letter to her father, but she is unlikely to have addressed Leicester without her father's consent. In any event, when Leicester replied he sent his letter not to her but to Viscount Montagu. That reply has been lost, but from the lady's next letter it is clear that Leicester was ready, within reason, to assist his kin. There was, however, one point on which Leicester wanted information. He had been informed that the youthful third earl was already a stalwart Papist who refused to attend the Church of England. In her reply the widowed Countess had no trouble exculpating herself in this matter. It was not her fault if her 'lyttyll sonne' refused to hear the Anglican service for she had not seen him for almost two years.[3]

[1] S.T.C. 19867: *Huth Ballads*, p. 262.   [2] *Cottrell-Dormer MSS.*, Letter XVII.
[3] *Cottrell-Dormer MSS.*, Letter V.

With Leicester working on her behalf, the Countess had considerable success in contesting her husband's will. A first victory was scored when on November 28th, two days before the belated but magnificent funeral of the second earl, a group of his servants rode over to Cowdray from Titchfield, bringing with them the Lady Mary who was turned over to her mother and apparently lived with her until her marriage four years later. On December 11th the Countess was able to write to Leicester that a final agreement had been reached with her husband's executors. It seems that under the terms of this agreement Thomas Dymock retained all the benefits conferred upon him, but upon condition that he permit another of the executors, Edward Gage, to take over administration of the late earl's estate.

Possibly Dymock was just as glad to be clear of any further responsibilities, for Montagu in a letter to Leicester reported that the provisions of the late earl's will had extended so far beyond the revenues left to the executors as to require extraordinary care and application in the administering of his estate. In fact the only person able to give the necessary time and attention was the foresaid Edward Gage. The trouble was that Gage, convicted as a recusant, would have to return to Marshalsea prison when a special leave of absence expired on Christmas Eve. Accordingly, Montagu asked Leicester for his 'helpinge hand for the Libertye of the said Edwarde gage'.[1] The helping hand was not refused. Successive extensions of the leave of absence from his imprisonment gave Gage almost a year to devote himself to sorting out the late earl's affairs.

For any Elizabethan family of substance and property the succession of an heir who was not yet of age created a very serious situation. The Tudor monarchs, in their quest for revenues, were unconscionably exploiting the archaic institution of royal wardship. In the Middle Ages each landowner had held his land in return for service to his lord in his wars. In those days the argument ran, not illogically, that when a man died and left a boy as his heir, the king was deprived of the fighting services of a man and therefore logically could resume possession of the man's land until his heir was of age to give the service which his father had owed. The practice under the Tudors was for feodaries, officers of the Master of the Wards, to keep a most vigilant watch for the death of any landowner holding even the smallest portion of his land from the Crown, and quickly to notify the Master when the heir was a minor. The Master would then, on behalf of the Crown, take over the wardship of the heir and his land, and sell this wardship to the highest bidder.

When the second Earl of Southampton died, the wheels began to turn. William Cecil, Lord Burghley, Master of the Wards, made a note in his

[1] *Cottrell-Dormer MSS.*, Letter XII.

almanac of the Earl's death.[1] Down at Alton in Hampshire, the feodary for the shire and the escheator swore in a jury of twelve men. On June 13th, 1582, they submitted their *Inquisition Post Mortem*, a detailed report listing all the dead earl's estates, noting how and under what terms he had come to possess them, and setting a value on each.

This 'inquisition' is valuable to us for it gives a clear statement of the heritage of the third earl. The estates left by the father are enumerated in three categories:

(1) The estates that now passed to the widow, for the rest of her life, under the terms of her marriage settlement:

> The following Hampshire manors:
> > Dogmersfield
> > Soberton
> > West Stratton
> > East Stratton
> > Crofton
> > Walsworth
> > West Meon
> > Botley
> > Farringdon
> > Swanwick
> Bloomsbury manor in Middlesex

These, with a few farms and granges, constituted the third of the value of the estate to which the widow was entitled under Elizabethan law. The annual worth of these was placed at £362 19s.

(2) The properties to which the Queen was entitled during the minority of the young earl. These properties would be turned over to the purchaser of his wardship, who would administer them to his own profit as long as his guardianship lasted. The 'Queen's third' included:

> The manors of
> > Charke Le Brutton
> > Bromwich
> > Newlands
> Portions of the manors of
> > Beaulieu
> > Segenworth
> > Long Sutton
> Lee ground at Titchfield
> Land at North Stoneham
> Ippely farm in the New Forest
> Rentals from properties in Southampton
> The late earl's 'creation money' (£20 annually payable out of the customs collected in Southampton)

The total value of the 'Queen's third' was given as £370 16s. per annum.

---

[1] *Salisbury MSS.*, XIII, 201. He got the date one day late, probably giving the day he received the news.

(3) The final part of the estate, that which the second earl had been free to use for the payment of legacies or to turn over to his executors to administer on behalf of his son. This included:

Southampton House in London
Bull (or Bugle) Hall in Southampton
The manors of
    Brodenhembury
    Woolverston
    Portsea
    Copnor
    Corhampton
    Hook
    Hook Valence
    Micheldever
    Marks Mirabel
    Titchfield
    North Stoneham
Portions of the manors of
    Beaulieu
    Segenworth
    Long Sutton

This final group of properties was valued at £363 11s. per annum.[1]

Adding these sums, we find that the total value of the second earl's estate was placed at £1,097 6s. per annum (something more than £20,000 per annum in modern values). Two observations need to be made however. Escheators and jurors, coming from the same district as a deceased land-owner, frequently did his family the kindness of making their appraisal fall far short of the real value, and there is evidence that this was done in the present case.[2] Secondly, though these are not mentioned in the inquisition, the second earl had left very large debts.[3]

Once the *inquisition post mortem* had been held and the appraised value set, the next step was to determine a price for the sale of the wardship of the young earl. In the past much uncertainty has surrounded the South-ampton wardship. The present writer has been successful, however, in finding in the records of the Court of Wards an entry showing that the Court accepted the inquisition's evaluation of the second earl's estate, and recording:

. . . the wardship and Marryage of the said Earles heres masclo [male heir] . . . I[s]

---

[1] Mrs. Stopes found the first and third sheets of this *Inquisition P.M.* in the Public Record Office (C142/196). I found the missing sheet in C142/404, but by now it should have rejoined its two companion sheets in C142/196.

[2] For example, the mansion, parsonage and farm at Beaulieu were valued at £6 per annum in the *Inquisition P.M.*, but two years later John Chamberlain was paying at least £30 for his occupancy of the parsonage and farm (*v. Lansdowne MS. 43*, f. 147r).

[3] For mention of the 'great detts by him owing', see P.R.O. *Wards 9/85*, p. 428.

solde to the Right honorable Charles Lord howard of Effingham Lord Chamber-
len to her majestye for one thowsand pounds.[1]

The inclusion of the marriage of the young earl reminds us that a
guardian had the right to arrange the marriage of a ward, and counted on
a substantial price from the bride's parents as part of his profits.

After Lord Howard of Effingham had received this grant of the
Southampton wardship from Lord Burghley, the Master of the Wards,
he entered into some further agreement, of which no documentation can
now be found, which transferred to Burghley personally the custody and
marriage of the young earl, but left Howard holding his lands.[2] Despite
the lack of official documentation, there is plenty of evidence that Lord
Treasurer Burghley did take over the care of the young earl. When,
around 1586, the Court of Wards decided that Southampton should have
an increase in the 'small exhibicion' the Queen allowed for his personal
expenses, it directed his father's executors to turn over to Burghley 'now
committie of the saide warde' several leases whose income would be
devoted 'to the use of the said yonge Earle'.[3] In after years Sir Henry
Neville, questioned in court as to the extent of his acquaintance with
Southampton, was to testify, 'I have never spoken with my Lord since
he was a child, in my old Lord Treasurer's house'.[4] It is to that house that
we must next follow young Harry Wriothesley.

[1] P.R.O. *Wards 9/157*, ff. 74v–75r. *W.P. 273* in the Hampshire Record Office is the
indenture of demise of June 28th, 1582, transferring the 'Queen's third' to Howard.
  [2] *W.P. 128.*
  [3] *Wards 9/85 (Entry Book of Decrees, 22–29 Elizabeth)*, pp. 427–8.
  [4] *Cal. S.P. (Dom.), 1601–1603*, p. 6.

Her Majesty's Ward

SOMETIME LATE in 1581 or early in 1582[1] the eight-year-old Earl of Southampton was delivered into the care of William Cecil, Lord Burghley, Master of the Wards and Lord Treasurer of England and, next to Queen Elizabeth, the most powerful person in the realm. The scene must have been like one out of an opening chapter by Dickens— young Southampton conducted by a kinsman or trusted servant to Cecil House, which rose on the north side of the Strand, 'verie fayre . . . raysed with brickes, proportionablie adorned with four turrets placed at the four quarters of the howse'.[2] Into whose presence was the boy first conducted? That of Lady Mildred, austere but kindly? Or that of the great Lord Burghley himself? The meeting of ward and guardian is not too hard to picture. The boy, lightly built, bright-eyed, and high-complexioned, stirred by inward fears and hopes, and facing him, white-bearded, rosy-cheeked, clad in his sober black with small ruff, a gold chain about his neck and perhaps his white rod in hand, the great Burghley, not tall but 'very straight and upright of bodye and leggs'.[3]

Burghley spent an arduous life amid the press of business—Privy Council meetings, foreign ambassadors, Parliaments, secretaries, finances, attendance on the Queen, and the administration of his own great wealth. Yet amid it all he was 'most patient in hearing, ready in dispatching, and myld in aunswering suitors'. In his leisure hours at Cecil House he loved to gather around him old acquaintances 'who co[u]ld discourse of thir yewth'. He partook of no physical games or exercise, though sometimes he would pause to watch men practising at the archery butts or playing on the bowling greens. His own great recreation was reading. One of the most brilliant students of his day at Cambridge, he had kept his love of learning. When he could snatch a day of surcease from the endless round of business, he enjoyed withdrawing to his nearby country seat of Theobalds

---

[1] The earlier date seems the more likely. With the attorney-general in December 1581 issuing a warrant to the Recorder of London, 'to resorte unto the Earle of Southampton's howse in Holborne, and there to make searche for the apprehending of one William Spencer . . . a very badd fellowe and practiser against the State', it seems unlikely that Burghley would lose much time in getting the boy removed from such an atmosphere. *Acts P.C.*, *1581–1582*, p. 298.

[2] *Harl. MS. 570*, quoted in H. B. Wheatley, *London Past and Present* (London, 1891), I, 343.   [3] Francis Peck, *Desiderata Curiosa* (London, 1779), p. 44.

where he would dwell not in his great mansion, which was one of the showplaces of England, but in a little lodge amid the quietness of his wooded walks. If he could not get away from London, he would take an hour or so of recreation in the widespread gardens of Cecil House, sedately riding side saddle on a little mule, and reading all the while. He had a standing rule that business must never be discussed at his table at meal-time. And here he had another pleasure, the company of children. The great man, ordinarily austere and reserved, found in children one of the joys of his life.

After Burghley's death an anonymous biographer, who had for twenty-five years been a servant in his house, left jottings recording the more human side of his master's personality:

> His kindnes most expressed to his children; to whom there was never man more loving nor tender harted.
> And yet with so wise moderation & temper as he was inwardly more kinde, then outwardly fond of them.
> And, which is ever a note of good nature, if he could gett his table sett round with his young, little children, he was then in his kingdome.
> It was exceeding pleasure; to heare what sport he would make with them.
> And how aptlie, & merelie, he would talk with them; and such pretty questions, and witty allurements, as much delighted himself, the children, & the hearers.[1]

Though Burghley's own children were grown to adult years when Southampton joined the household, it would be strange if some of this kindness had not remained to be shown to him.

The Elizabethans expected their statesmen such as Burghley to be 'sententious', 'full of wise saws and modern instances'. In his interviews with his guardian, and at the table, the young Southampton would have heard again and again the maxims which Burghley never tired of uttering —that in all things we must seek first the Kingdom of God; that our enemies can never do more than God will permit them; that it is the lot of those who govern to do good and to be badly spoken of; that virtue gets its reward in honour but it is a reward gotten with labour and held with danger. And ever and again, he would deliver a favourite maxim, spoken in the Latin which was the second tongue of his household, '*Prudens qui patiens*'—the wise man is the man who can wait.[2]

For the boy earl everything in Cecil House must have seemed curiously the reverse of what he was accustomed to. From a house where utter enmity separated husband and wife, he came to one where for thirty-five years a signally happy marriage had reigned. From a home where the Queen was regarded as a usurping heretic, he came to one where she was regarded with unshakable devotion and admiration, Burghley often declaring he did not believe there ever had been a wiser woman born than

---

[1] Peck, p. 36.   [2] Ibid., pp. 44–6.

Her Majesty. From a home where religious services were surreptitiously conducted by Catholic priests, he passed to one where twice daily, at eleven in the morning before the noontime meal and again at six o'clock before supper, the entire household went to the chapel for prayers. (No longer could his young lordship absent himself from Anglican devotions.) From a disorderly ill-managed household where an underling ruled, he passed to the machine-like good order of Cecil House. 'Drones hive not with me' might well have been Cecil's rule. Cecil House, with its staff of eighty servants, was a model of sobriety and industry.

Part of the credit belonged to the mistress of the house. After Burghley's first wife had died within fifteen months of their marriage, he had married Mildred Cooke. Judicious, firm yet kind, Lady Burghley was an intensely religious person, almost a Puritan in her personal theology. She was moreover a learned lady, for her father Sir Anthony Cooke had given her and her sisters an education far beyond that usually received by women even of the highest station. Typically, she had translated a work of St. John Chrysostom out of the original Greek.

Sharing her husband's love of learning, Lady Burghley joined him in benefactions to his old college at Cambridge. When Burghley was left a widower in 1589, he set down some recollections of his wife, 'written by me in sorrow', and recorded how after her death he discovered that she had secretly been carrying out her own benefactions to St. John's, in addition to his. Among the former were two scholarships endowed in perpetuity, and funds to provide fires in the college hall on winter Sundays and holidays, and also special stipends for sermons in the chapel of St. John's. With an amusing mixture of pride in his wife's goodness, and slightly abraded egotism since he had not been aware of what was going on, he recorded:

> And these distributions have bene made a long time, whylest she lyved by some of my servants, without gyvyn[g] me knolledg thereof; though in dede I had cause to thynk that she did sometymes bestow such kynd of alms.[1]

In view of the devotion to learning and the encouragement for scholars that Southampton was to display throughout his adult life, it is hard not to give to Lord and Lady Burghley credit for instilling a love of books into the boy whom they admitted into their home.

At Cecil House Lord Burghley superintended the best school for boys to be found in Elizabethan England, the tutors being distinguished scholars who served Burghley also as chaplains or secretaries. Membership in this very exclusive little academy was reserved for sons of noblemen. At least two motives had led Burghley to develop this school. One was simple

[1] Thos. Baker, *History of the College of St. John the Evangelist* (Cambridge, 1869), II, 594–5.

snobbery. Painfully aware of his own very humble beginnings, he had found compensation in marrying his children into the first families of the kingdom, and in bringing the sons of earls to live with him and serve at his table while receiving their education. Burghley's second motive related directly to his responsibilities as Master of the Wards. When Burghley took over this office, the deficiencies in the education of the English upper class were nowhere more apparent than in the upbringing of the royal wards. Many guardians grudged every penny they had to spend on the education of their charges. Some deliberately kept their wards half-illiterate so that they could encroach upon their privileges and marry them, to their own profit, to persons unfit either by breeding or intelligence. In 1561, a few months after Cecil had assumed his mastership, Sir Nicholas Bacon wrote him a very frank letter about the scandal that, though the Court of the Wards gave plenty of attention to the lands of the wards, it gave hardly any to their minds. In an age when the aristocracy was still expected to provide the political and military leadership of the country, the consequences could be serious when young lords advanced to privilege and office without having been properly educated. Sir Nicholas thought that a special school should be set up for the Queen's wards. Burghley's own solution was to superintend, under his own roof, the education of the most important of the wards. To the quality of that education Joel Hurstfield has paid an impressive tribute:

> There can be no doubt that, at Cecil House in the Strand, there existed the best school for statesmen in Elizabethan England, perhaps in all Europe. . . . It was a highly selective school to which only very fortunate young men gained admission . . . . Parents were well aware that entry into Cecil House meant not simply unique educational opportunities, but attractive prospects of advancement in later life. The quality of education—cultural and political—was beyond dispute.[1]

No information survives concerning the studies prescribed for Southampton at Cecil House. Probably these were much the same as those which Burghley had prescribed years earlier for the Earl of Oxford:

7 – 7.30	Dancing
7.30 – 8	Breakfast
8 – 9	French
9 – 10	Latin
10 – 10.30	Writing and Drawing
Then Common Prayers and so to dinner	
1 – 2	Cosmography
2 – 3	Latin
3 – 4	French
4 – 4.30	Exercises with his pen
Then Common Prayers and so to supper.[2]	

[1] *The Queen's Wards* (London, [1958]), p. 255.
[2] *S.P. (Dom.) Eliz.*, 26.50, cited by B. M. Ward, *The Seventeenth Earl of Oxford* (London, 1928), p. 20.

The kind of surveillance exercised over Southampton can be deduced from the experience of the Earl of Rutland. When Rutland asked leave to visit his mother in the country, Burghley agreed on condition that he take his tutor with him and keep up his studies since learning would serve him 'in all ages, all places and fortunes'. Burghley let Rutland join the Belvoir Hunt, but with heavy humour added a proviso that 'you will, whan you ar weary of huntyng, recontinew some exercise of huntyng in your book'.[1]

Chief among Burghley's wards when Southampton came to Cecil House was Robert Devereux, the second Earl of Essex. Fifteen years old, tall and handsome, Essex, who had just completed his studies at Cambridge, spent much of his time quietly at his own residence in Wales, and his visits to Cecil House cannot have been very frequent. Nevertheless it is entirely likely that Southampton first met Essex during such a visit. In the years that lay ahead Southampton was to form with him one of the closest friendships of his life. Six years later, when Essex was out in the great world and Southampton was at Cambridge, Roger Manners, the twelve-year-old Earl of Rutland, already at the same university, became another of Burghley's wards. Rutland formed a close friendship with Southampton and in time with Essex. Southampton was to marry one of Essex's cousins, and Rutland Essex's stepdaughter. Thus there emerged that circle centring around Essex and his two satellite earls, doomed to frustration and disappointment in the court of Queen Elizabeth.

At Cecil House Southampton would have met Burghley's sons. The elder of these, born of his father's first marriage and heir to his title, was Thomas Cecil, slow, well-meaning, not very intelligent. He was so much older than Southampton as to have little in common with him. Nearer in age was Burghley's special favourite, the little hunchback Robert Cecil, his son by Lady Mildred, who already at the age of nineteen was starting along the road to succession to his father's high offices. Southampton and Robert Cecil would be both adversaries and friends in the years that lay ahead. One day it would lie with Sir Robert Cecil whether or not Southampton should die with Essex on the scaffold.

An important event in young Southampton's years as a ward was the marriage of his sister Mary in June 1585 to Thomas Arundell. The two families had long been on a friendly basis. In fact the groom's father, peppery old Sir Matthew, had once been on the brink of marrying one of Southampton's aunts. Probably the young Earl was present when his sister was married in the chapel of Southampton House in Holborn. The newly-married couple seem to have set up residence at Itchell, in the country house where the bride's father had died a few years before.

[1] H.M.C., *Rutland MSS.* I, p. 274, p. 283.

In October 1585 Southampton turned twelve, an age at which some boys went to university. Lord Burghley, who among his other offices was Chancellor of Cambridge University, sent him to his beloved St. John's College there.[1]

Founded in 1511 by Lady Margaret Beaufort, mother of Henry VII, St. John's had been in its early days the chief centre of Renaissance New Learning in the university, though later it had sunk into mediocrity and discontent. Early in the reign of Queen Elizabeth a group of militant Puritans had secured control of St. John's, had introduced the Geneva Psalter in the college chapel, and had barely tolerated the wearing of surplices by the clergy taking the services there. John Still, the fourteenth master, was credited with rooting out puritanism, but his successor, Richard Howland, had to bring in a new set of statutes before he could establish 'tolerable order' within the college. In February 1586, a few months after Southampton became a student at St. John's, Howland was succeeded as master by Dr. William Whitaker. Of Whitaker the eighteenth-century historian of the college was to declare that he was 'one of the greatest men the college ever had',[2] and there can be no doubt that under his kindly rule St. John's experienced a sort of golden age.

We have no record as to who was Southampton's tutor during his Cambridge years. That tutor may well have been Whitaker himself. Certainly just as Whitgift when master of Trinity superintended the education of Essex at that college, so Whitaker would carefully have watched over that of Southampton at St. John's. Earls were treated with enormous deference in the Elizabethan age, and an earl whose guardian was the chancellor of the university could be sure of very special attention.

If Whitaker was Southampton's tutor, the lad's studies were directed by a man of enormous learning. So great was the erudition that went into Whitaker's polemics in defence of the Church of England that the mighty Scaliger, putting down one of his tomes, exclaimed, 'Whittakerus! Oh! Qu'il estoit bien docte!'[3] Aside from his learning, Whitaker was a kindly man with an attractive personality. Appointed to his post by Burghley and the Queen, who apparently negated the fellows' election of another master, he did the nearly impossible and, after initial difficulties with a recalcitrant faction, so won over the fellows that 'they were at last united in their affection to their master, and he had no enemies to overcome'. Whitaker was mildly sympathetic to the moderate Puritans, and while he was immersed in his studies he left much of the running of the college to his

---

[1] Southampton's admission in the college register is dated October 16th. Baker, I, 548. A set of rooms (I. 3) in the S.E. corner of the First Court at St. John's is still known traditionally as 'the Earl of Southampton's Chamber'. College records show that it had this name as early as 1614.   [2] Baker, I, 180.   [3] Ibid., II, 603.

assistant John Alvey, who was definitely in the Puritan camp. At Cecil House Southampton had learned to conform at least outwardly with the Church of England. At St. John's he may well have acquired the germ of the militant Protestantism of his later years. Certainly in later life he looked back with affection to St. John's and became in time one of its principal benefactors.

Southampton's studies at Cambridge would have consisted of the invariable rhetoric, logic and ethics, but we need to remember what Professor Curtis has pointed out, that the best tutors had their students reading both ancient and modern history, and sixteenth-century political theory as well, and even saw that they were informed of recent discoveries in mathematics, astronomy and navigation. St. John's had college lecturers in Greek, arithmetic, geometry, perspective and cosmography.[1] Education in the Cambridge colleges 'was not static and indeed was being adapted to changing intellectual currents as fast as public demand and interest required'.[2] Much of Southampton's education had, of course, a moral and even a theological tinge. Thus on Saturday afternoons he would be catechized in the chapel, as required by the decrees of his college. Training in the verbal presentation of argument was very important, and Dr. Whitaker was punctilious about being 'at his lectures in his chamber on Friday nights to hear his pupils declaim'.[3] The young Earl of Southampton, the protégé of Whitaker's own patron, must have received a good proportion of the Master's attention upon these evenings.

Summer vacations did not mean a holiday from studies for Southampton, for Burghley assigned him Latin themes to write, of which two survive. The first of these, submitted in June 1586, is on the subject, 'The arduous studies of youth are agreeable relaxations in old age'. The little essay is gracefully penned in a fine Italian hand and studded with quotations from Cicero. Apparently the young earl had difficulty finding much to say on the assigned subject, and a veteran marker of student themes reading it today feels an impulse to reach for the red ink and write 'Padding' and 'Irrelevant' at points along its margin. Manfully the lad begins, 'Since the subject on which I discourse seemed to me a worthy one, I am not loath to discuss it.' And then he launches into what is in effect a plea for freedom for youth, coupled with a declaration that seemly behaviour is necessary in old age:

> Often we see a man living wretchedly and an object of contempt in his old age who in his youth lived wantonly and wilfully. Yet young men may, with justice, relax their minds and give themselves up to enjoyment. But let them then beware

[1] J. B. Mullinger, *St. John's College* (London, 1901), p. 297.
[2] Mark H. Curtis, *Oxford and Cambridge in Transition 1558–1642* (Oxford, 1959), p. 116.   [3] Baker, I, 183.

of excess and be mindful of modesty. Cicero, however, says (in his speech in defence of M. Caelius) 'Let some allowance be made for a person's years, let youth be allowed greater freedom, let not everything be denied to the passions, let not that severe and unbending reason always prevail, let desire and pleasure sometimes triumph over reason.'[1]

Behind all the stilted phrasing, there seems to be a cry from the heart. One wonders how Burghley responded when he reached the final tremendous *non sequitur*, 'Therefore the arduous studies of youth are agreeable relaxations in old age'.

Writing next month on the theme, 'All men are spurred to the pursuit of virtue by the expectation of reward', the young earl gave a twist probably not anticipated by Burghley when he gave him that rather cynical text. The reward, according to Southampton, was 'praise and reputation'. Here was a subject to which a young Renaissance aristocrat could warm; and though Southampton dutifully noted that both the fairest virtues and the worst vices can spring from the desire for reputation, he became decidedly eloquent when declaring how every man 'burns with a certain boundless lust for fame'.[2] Sir Sidney Lee reading this essay thought it revealed 'a refinement most uncommon in boys of thirteen'.[3]

Fame and honour must have been much in the mind of the young earl in 1586, for this was the year when all the chivalry of England, or at least that part of it which could get the grudging permission of the Queen, were trooping off to the wars in the Low Countries under the command of the Earl of Leicester. Essex was with the army, and so were most of the men who were to be Southampton's close friends in the years that lay ahead—Sir Charles and Sir Henry Danvers, Sir Charles Blount (the future Lord Mountjoy and Earl of Devonshire), and a host of others. How the lad must have cursed that he had not been born three or four years earlier so that he too could be off on the great adventure. Perhaps his later devotion to the wars sprang from a need to compensate for this disappointment of his earlier years.

The Armada Year, 1588, came and went with Southampton still too young at fourteen to serve. The next year he finished his studies at Cambridge and took his M.A. after a public oral defence of his thesis.[4] (B.A.s

---

[1] *Lansdowne MS. 50*, f. 51r.

[2] *Cecil Papers*, 164, 82.

[3] *A Life of William Shakespeare* (New York, 1927), p. 657.

[4] The grace permitting him to receive the degree is preserved at Cambridge (*Liber Gratiarum* △, f. 158(a)). The evidence that Southampton was not one of the young noblemen who got themselves exempted from this defence of a thesis is supplied by *Harl. MS. 7038* (p. 77):

> Anno 1589: Jun: 6 Henricus Comes Southt: Coll: Jo: alumnus cooptatur in ordinem M:A: cum prius disputasset publice pro gradu.

were by-passed by noblemen as beneath their dignity.) As the next step in
the young man's education, Burghley had already secured for him admission into Gray's Inn.[1] As an owner of large estates who would be
involved in litigation, property settlements, transfers of land, and all the
accompanying intricacies of Elizabethan law, Southampton obviously
would benefit from obtaining at least a smattering of legal knowledge. One
hesitates to say more than a smattering, for the young noblemen who were
admitted to the Inns of Court used them more as gentlemen's clubs than
as colleges for the study of the law.

The throng of young men who studied law either nominally or in dead
earnest at the Inns of Court constituted the liveliest, brightest group to be
found anywhere in Elizabethan London. They prided themselves on their
manners, their breeding, their elegance of fashion and their wit. And they
were the especial patrons of the theatre, deeming themselves *cognoscenti*
of the stage. On high occasions they brought the actors to their own halls
to put on plays specially commissioned by them. Thomas Hughes' *The
Misfortunes of Arthur* was presented at Gray's Inn on the evening before
Southampton became a member of that society. On December 28th,
1594, Shakespeare's *Comedy of Errors* was produced at Gray's Inn. His
Twelfth Night was written for production at the Middle Temple in 1601.[2]
A little later his *Troilus and Cressida* was written almost certainly for one
of the Inns of Court. Often of an afternoon groups of young Inns of Court
men would head for the public playhouses in the London suburbs, where
a personal acquaintance with the players helped to distinguish the real
bloods among them. Probably it was on some such excursion that William
Shakespeare and the young Earl of Southampton first saw each other.

On October 6th, 1589, Southampton's birthday, Lord Burghley made
an entry in his diary concerning him and two other earls whom he was
bringing up:

> Oct. 6   Edw. [sic] Co. Southampton erat aetatis 16 annorum
>   Edw. Co. Bedford erat aetatis 15 annorum
>   Rog. Co. Rutland erat aetatis 13 annorum[3]

There was purpose behind the old man's methodical noting of these ages.
His wards were approaching marriageable years. And for Southampton
Burghley had a bride ready to hand. He would marry him to his own
granddaughter, Lady Elizabeth Vere, the nineteen-year-old daughter of
that Earl of Oxford who had been one of his earliest wards. The first

---

[1] He was admitted on February 29th, 1588. *Complete Peerage*, Vol. XII, Part I, p. 128.
[2] G. P. V. Akrigg, '*Twelfth Night* at the Middle Temple', *Shakespeare Quarterly*, IX
(1958), pp. 422–4.
[3] William Murdin, *A Collection of State Papers* (London, 1759), p. 792.

evidence that we have of Burghley's intentions is provided by a letter written to the old man by Sir Thomas Stanhope on July 15th, 1590. In it Stanhope urgently assured Burghley that he had not sought a match between Southampton and his own daughter, knowing of Burghley's own plans for the Earl and 'Lady Vayer'.[1] Only one barrier was blocking Burghley's design—the opposition of the groom-elect, who resolutely refused to marry the girl. When mounting pressures were brought to bear on Southampton, he remained obdurate. It was not that he disliked this particular girl. He simply was averse to marriage. Burghley, however, would not abandon his scheme. He wanted to get the girl looked after— her mother, Burghley's daughter Anne, had died a few years before and her father was neglecting her. Lady Burghley had died the previous year and without his wife's restraining counsel the old man was passing into the testy irritability, so alien to his earlier nature, that marked his final years. Persisting in seeking the match, he found allies in Southampton's mother and grandfather. After a meeting with Burghley at Oatlands, Viscount Montagu wrote to the impatient old man that, when South-ampton had recently visited him at Cowdray, he had discussed the whole matter of the marriage with him. All that Montagu had been able to get out of Southampton was 'this generall answere that your Lordship was this last winter well pleased to yeld unto him a further respitt of one yere to answere resolute[ly] in respect of his yonge yeres'.[2] To no effect had Montagu pointed out that the year of grace was almost expired. At the end of his letter Montagu informed Burghley that he and the lad's mother would be coming up to London in a few weeks and would then have a full discussion of the matter with him. He carefully reassured the great man that he would conduct himself to Burghley's liking in this business.

The situation was a serious one for Southampton's kin. Catholics them-selves, they laid themselves open to all sorts of reprisals if the irate old Lord Treasurer thought that they were not doing everything in their power to promote the match. As for the young man, he was almost cer-tainly putting himself in the position of having to pay a very large sum which the law would allow Burghley in compensation for the refused marriage.

The new year entered with Southampton much in his guardian's dis-favour. In various ways the young man was being pressured to accept Lady Elizabeth. No longer would Burghley concern himself to see that the South-ampton estates were properly administered. Thus, in 1592 we have an alarmed young Earl writing to Michael Hicks, Burghley's confidential servant, asking him to use his influence with Burghley to avoid 'the greate decay and daunger' which threatened much of his inheritance through lack

[1] Cal. S.P. (Dom.), 1581–1590, p. 680.   [2] S.P. 12/233/71.

of maintenance. It is with this background in mind that we must look at the first book to be dedicated to Southampton. The book was *Narcissus*[1] and the person who dedicated it to the young earl was John Clapham.

An elegantly printed little book, just fifteen pages in length, *Narcissus* relates in fluent Latin verse the old Greek legend of how a handsome young man perished from self-love. Somewhat surprisingly the scene has been transferred from ancient Greece to England, the fairest isle that 'Ocean batters with his cool waves', an island named 'Blessed', flourishing under the rule of a Virgin Queen, free from care and enjoying eternal peace. Here young Narcissus makes his way through a large forest to the Temple of Love where he finds depicted the ancient stories of those whom Love has conquered—Hercules, Hero and Leander, Hector, Paris and Achilles, the Scipios, Hannibal and Caesar. Venus receives Narcissus in her pleasant embrace and conducts him to the inner sanctuary of the temple. Here Love looses his arrow at the youth, who then declares himself Love's slave. Accepting his service, Love instructs him in the use of the Petrarchan conceits, cunning lies, and other aids to seduction, and he adds a brief lecture on female psychology. Then, oddly enough, Love ends up by saying that Narcissus will always be pleasing to himself.

He announces in fact that Narcissus is doomed to flatter himself until he is captured by his own reflection and blindly perishes by it. To make sure that his prophecy will succeed, Love sprinkles the youth with water from the river Lethe so that he will not know himself. Narcissus then mounts an untamable horse, called 'Lust', who bolts off with him, finally hurling him headlong into the spring Philautia (self-love). After drinking of this, Narcissus falls in love with his own image reflected in the pond, not recognizing it as his own. When night obliterates the reflection, the desperate youth falls headlong into the pond and drowns. Venus, lamenting, gives him a new life in the form of the flower Narcissus.

All this is pleasant, pretty, and vacuous enough until one catches the clue to the poem's significance by identifying the author. The John Clapham who wrote *Narcissus* was one of Burghley's secretaries.[2] Then one sees the point of it all. Narcissus is Southampton—that explains the careful identification of England as the land where this Narcissus dwells.

It is not hard to picture the scene which gave rise to *Narcissus*. We have old Burghley, angered by Southampton's refusal to marry his granddaughter, muttering perhaps that the young man is in love with himself, using possibly the very name of Narcissus for the narcissistic young man. Standing by, listening, is the bright young secretary who as a household jest, knowing it will do him no harm with his chief, writes a poem on

[1] The book was printed in London by Thomas Scarlet in 1591. S.T.C. 5349.
[2] v. Hurstfield, p. 267.

Narcissus and then dedicates this 'Short and Moral Description of Youthful Love and Especially Self-Love' to Southampton. The usual motive for a dedication, a handsome reward from the dedicatee, could not be looked for from seventeen-year-old Southampton, living on a pitifully small 'exhibition'. It would be Burghley, gratified at seeing the treatment given the wretched young nobleman, who would supply Clapham with his reward.

Once we look at *Narcissus* in this light we find extra meanings along the way. The bland Latin façade of the dedication itself is seen to conceal a taunting implication. 'Clarissimo et Nobilissimo Domino Henrico Comiti Southamtoniae: Johannes Clapham virtutis, atque honoris incrementum, multosque annos foelices exoptat.' Everything turns on the meaning of 'virtutis', which means not 'virtue' in the sense of our English word, but the old Roman 'virtus'—that which makes a man, let us call it 'vigour', 'manly excellence'. There is more than is apparent in this dedication to a rather effeminate young man: 'To the most distinguished and most noble Lord, Henry, Earl of Southampton, John Clapham wishes *increase of vigour* and honour, and many happy years.' The text of the poem contains further hints. Recalling the solid Catholicism of his ward's earliest education, Burghley must have chuckled when he read how Narcissus in his youth had been nurtured by Opinion 'with the warm milk of Error'. Southampton, on the other hand, must have felt hurt and affronted.

Resuming the chronicle of the events of 1591, we must first note a journey that Southampton did not make. For many years persons writing about Southampton have reported that in this year the Earl visited the Continent. As evidence they have cited a letter of his written to Essex from Dieppe on March 2nd. However the letter in question was almost certainly written in 1598[1] and, in the complete absence of any other

---

[1] It is not generally known that various of the documents at Hatfield have had conjectural dates written on them. A prime offender according to Miss Clare Talbot, the present librarian of the Marquess of Salisbury, was a Mr. Stewart, who made a calendar of the papers about 1859.

The letter now before us, beginning 'Though I have nothinge to write' (*Cecil Papers*, 168, 8), has an original subscription 'Diep the 2 of March', but contains within itself no evidence as to the year in which it was written. Scrawled on the reverse in pencil is the date '1591'. A similar incorrect date (1599) in pencil is to be found on 179, 88. Miss Talbot thinks that both these inscriptions are of comparatively recent date, and are probably in Stewart's hand. One can only conjecture that whoever put '1591' on the letter did so because he knew that Essex himself was in the area in the summer of this year, and assumed that Southampton had preceded him there. The Historical Manuscripts Commission editor who catalogued this letter apparently accepted this hypothetical and almost certainly incorrect date, for he dated the letter as '[1590-1] March 2' (*Salisbury MSS.*, IV, 96). Logically, if he accepted as original the incorrect date on the back, he should have entered the year as 1591-2. For the evidence that the letter probably dates from 1597, see p. 69 *infra*.

evidence, we must conclude that this French trip never took place, even though one author has eloquently told us how, to escape the pressures to marry Lady Elizabeth Vere, 'the badgered young Earl, taking matters into his own hands, fled across the Channel to Dieppe to escape commands and exhortations'.[1]

We have some indication of Southampton's whereabouts later in 1591. In June that year a letter to the Countess of Rutland contained the information that her son, the young Earl, would be staying on at Cambridge a little after Commencement, 'because my Lord of Southampton sent word that he would come and see my Lord'.[2] Later that summer Southampton must have been on hand when Queen Elizabeth, in her summer progress through the shires, was a guest at Titchfield. Her previous stop was at Cowdray, where from August 15th to 21st she was sumptuously entertained by old Viscount Montagu. At her arrival a porter clad all in armour, a club in one hand and a gold key in the other, delivered a typically Elizabethan allegorical speech of welcome. In her reply the Queen declared that she would take her oath that she had no man more faithful to her than Montagu. Towards the end of her stay, after all the hunting and the pageants and the banqueting, there was 'a pleasant daunce' put on by the country people with tabor and drum in which, to the delight of all the beholders and the Queen's own 'gentle applause', old Montagu and his lady had joined in. When Elizabeth left, she showed her favour to her host by creating six new knights, among them George Browne, one of the sons of the house, and Robert Dormer, Montagu's son-in-law.

Though we have surviving a very full account of the royal visit to Cowdray,[3] we know practically nothing of the day or two she spent at Titchfield. Burghley was with her and addressed a letter from there on September 2nd. Possibly his guardian, seconded by the Queen, once more pressed Southampton to go through with the marriage to Lady Elizabeth Vere.

By now Southampton was spending a good part of his time in attendance at the Court. Thus we find him in attendance when Queen Elizabeth visited Oxford late in September 1592.[4] The university subsequently published a Latin poem by John Sanford commemorating the royal visit. Sanford's verses are full of the flattery that the Elizabethans customarily lavished upon their notables. Nonetheless his description of Southampton

[1] Barbara A. MacKenzie, *Shakespeare's Sonnets: Their Relation to His Life* (Cape Town, 1946), p. 2.
[2] H.M.C., *Rutland MSS.*, I, 293.
[3] See *The Honorable Entertainment given to the Queenes Majestie in Progresse, at Cowdray in Sussex* (London, 1591), printed in the second volume of John Nichols, *The Progresses and Public Processions of Queen Elizabeth* (London, 1788–1821).
[4] *Alumni Oxonienses 1500–1714*, ed. Joseph Foster (Oxford, 1892), IV, 1689.

is worth the quoting. At the end of a fulsome description of Essex and his virtues, he came to Southampton: 'After him there follows a lord of lofty line whom rich Southampton claims in his own right as a great hero. There was present no one more comely, no young man more outstanding in learning, although his mouth scarcely yet blooms with tender down.'[1]

In October 1592 old Viscount Montagu died at his manor house at West Horsley in Surrey. Presumably Southampton accompanied his mother to the funeral at Midhurst. By and large the old man seems to have had a kindly influence on the boy and his emotional, somewhat irresponsible mother. He was succeeded in his title by a grandson, Southampton's cousin, Anthony Maria Browne, a fantastic young nincompoop who immortalized himself by the grandiose 'Book of Household Rules' that he drew up for the servants, in which he included the clause that none should be guilty of the unseemliness of turning his back upon a roast while it was being cooked for his Lordship's table.

An indication of Southampton's growing prominence at Court is found in a rumour, circulating in May 1593, that the young earl was to be created a Knight of the Garter.[2] George Peele, writing The Honour of the Garter this year, made a non-existent Earl of Southampton an original member of the Order and then worked in a smooth compliment to 'Gentle Wriothesley, South-hamptons starre'. Southampton did not get the Garter at this time, but he received a much more dazzling honour. William Shakespeare, publishing his Venus and Adonis this spring, dedicated it to him. The following year, when he published his Lucrece, he dedicated it also to the young earl.

It is about this time that Southampton became acquainted with a very unusual person, the renegade Antonio Perez, a former Secretary of State to King Philip II of Spain, who had fled his homeland and in the spring of 1593 arrived in the English court.

Witty, urbane, cunning and ingratiating, Perez had been in the complete confidence of King Philip and had shared his secrets until His Majesty discovered that Perez, to dispose of a man dangerous to him and his close friend the Princess of Eboli, had misused Philip's permission to arrange what seemed to be a needed political assassination. Philip had imprisoned Perez but the latter had made his escape, finding safety finally in the court of Henri IV of France. Consulting with Henri and drawing upon his detailed knowledge of Spain's military strengths and weaknesses, Perez had elaborated a plan for a joint campaign against Spain to be waged

[1] Apollinis et Musarum Euktika Eidyllia (Oxford, 1592), reprinted by Charles Plummer in Elizabethan Oxford (Publications of the Oxford Historical Society, VIII, 294).   [2] H.M.C., Seventh Report, p. 522.

by England and France. To advance these plans, Henri sent Perez over to England. Here he was enthusiastically received by the Earl of Essex, who had already adopted his policy of war with Spain, opposing the Cecils who wanted England's military undertakings kept minimal.

An ageing gallant in his fifties, surrounded by a vague aura of homo-sexuality, Perez when he arrived in England impressed many people as opinionated, affected, pompous and pedantic. But he had a very shrewd knowledge of human psychology and usually could charm when he wished. He was, declared a shocked nineteenth-century historian, 'one of the most diabolically false, vain, fascinating scoundrels that ever dis-graced and bewitched humanity'.[1] The full force of that charm was turned on Essex during the two years that Perez remained in England, and Essex responded warmly. When, in 1593 or 1594, Perez published his *Relations*, or autobiography, under the pen name of 'Raphael Peregrino' (Raphael the Wanderer), he dedicated his book to Essex, and made a point of presenting copies to all the leading members of the Essex group. Thus it happened that Southampton received a copy of 'Peregrine's' book with a special commendatory letter.[2] We do not know if Southampton was taken in by Perez as much as Essex was. Certainly Perez seems to have still been high in Essex's favour when he returned to France in August 1595, but when he briefly revisited England in 1596, he apparently found that Essex, finally aware of his unreliability, was no longer interested in him.

Shakespeare was not the only person to dedicate a book to the Earl of Southampton in 1593. Another was Thomas Nashe who had been at St. John's College in Southampton's time and must have got to know him there. In the winter of 1592–93 Nashe was down in Southampton's part of the country, being a guest of Sir George Carey, the Captain of the Isle of Wight, at Carisbrooke Castle. He may well have taken the oppor-tunity to drop around at Titchfield and renew acquaintance with South-ampton. In any event, when in June 1593 Nashe finished writing *The Unfortunate Traveller, or the Life of Jacke Wilton*, he dedicated it to the young earl.[3]

Nashe was a mad, wild wit, and his *Unfortunate Traveller* is a strange work indeed. In the main it is a picaresque novel embellished with mur-der, rape and seduction, but it is also in part a jest book and in part an anti-Puritan treatise. The best of Nashe's works, it is still read, even if

[1] M. A. S. Hume, 'Antonio Perez in Exile', *Transactions of the Royal Historical Society*, New Series VIII (1894), p. 107.

[2] Perez, *Obras* (Geneva, 1631), p. 531.

[3] There can be no question that Shakespeare was the earlier in seeking Southampton as patron. *Venus and Adonis* was entered in the Stationers' Register on April 18th, 1593, and *The Unfortunate Traveller* on the following September 17th.

only by students in English Honours. In his lively dedication to Southampton, Nashe speaks merrily of the reception that poets are finding at
the Earl's hands:

> A dere lover and cherisher you are, as well of the lovers of Poets, as of Poets
> themselves. Amongst their sacred number I dare not ascribe my selfe, though now
> and then I speak English.[1]

The plural reference to 'poets' is explainable by the fact that in 1593, very
soon after *Venus and Adonis*, Barnabe Barnes had published his collection of poems entitled *Parthenophil and Parthenophe*[2] which, though not
dedicated to Southampton, contained a commendatory sonnet addressed
to him. Presumably Southampton generously rewarded both Shakespeare
and Barnes. He may have aided various other poets but, if he did, all
record of these benefactions has been lost.

Nashe's exclusion of himself from the company of poets must not be
taken too literally. At some unknown time he wrote a pornographic poem
entitled 'The Choosing of Valentines', of which a few manuscript copies
survive.[3] In it an unidentified speaker goes into considerable detail about
his experiences when he tracked down a mistress of his who had shifted
her abode to a bawdy-house. For meticulous erotic detail, 'The Choosing
of Valentines' is quite the match of *Fanny Hill*. The poem begins and
ends with sonnets to 'Lord S'. Sir Sidney Lee and J. Q. Adams thought
Southampton was probably the Lord S. in question; however, E. K.
Chambers favoured Lord Strange while R. B. McKerrow seems to
have wavered between the two.[4]

Some of the literary men who sought Southampton's patronage as he
approached his coming of age may have over-estimated the estate that he
would inherit. That estate probably yielded the Earl an annual income of
about £3,000.[5] In the light of Elizabethan values this figure seems very
impressive. On the other hand, these estates may still have been partly
encumbered with debts of the second earl. Moreover, Southampton, when
he came of age, was confronted with two major expenses which must have

---

[1] *The Works of Thomas Nashe*, ed. R. B. McKerrow (London, 1910), II, 201. Nashe's
dedication to Southampton does not appear in the later editions of the book, an omission which has led to speculation that Nashe was disappointed in Southampton's
response to his bid for patronage.

[2] Barnes' book was entered in the Stationers' Register on May 10th, 1593, about three
weeks after *Venus and Adonis*.

[3] McKerrow printed it only in the subscribers' copies of his magisterial edition of
Nashe. Indicative of an altered moral climate, F. P. Wilson had it in all copies of his
1958 reprint of McKerrow.

[4] *v*. ed., *Nashe*, IV, 255 and V, 141.

[5] Lord Howard of Effingham seems to have erred on the high side when, in January
1583, he estimated that 'at full age' Southampton would receive £4,000 per annum
(*Lansdowne MS. 37*, f. 66).

absorbed most of his revenue for the next few years. One was the very large fee which the Crown, giving a final squeeze, exacted for the legal transfer of his lands back to him.[1] The other was a staggering fine of £5,000 that he had to pay Burghley for refusing to marry the bride that the latter had chosen for him.

Tenacious to the last, Burghley had kept his granddaughter unmarried and available as long as Southampton was his ward. In January 1595, finally conceding defeat, he married her to the Earl of Derby. Commenting upon the Derby match, Father Garnet, in a manuscript preserved in the archives of the English Jesuits at Stonyhurst, noted, 'The young Erle of Southampton refusing the Lady Veere payeth 5000^{li} of present payment.'[2] Garnet's note is our only source for this information, and it has been discounted by some modern historians. There is, however, no real reason for not believing it to be correct. If any would discount Father Garnet, the Superior of the English Jesuits, as an untrustworthy informant, let them turn to Philip Caraman's recent biography of Garnet in which, after fourteen years of study of his life and writings, he can speak of the 'sense of accuracy in statement that is marked throughout his long correspondence'.[3] As for the amount of the fine, it is outrageously but not unbelievably high. Lord Sandys we know had to pay £2,000 because he refused, while a minor, a proposed marriage. And Burghley was just the man to exact a scandalously large sum. Joined to hurt pride at the young puppy having refused his own granddaughter was that love of money for which Burghley was notorious.

As Master of the Wards, Lord Treasurer Burghley was in a position to see that the highest possible damages were charged on his behalf against his former ward. The law in this matter was plainly on his side: 'If an heir, of what age soever he be, will not marry at the request of his lord, he shall not be compelled thereunto; but when he cometh to full age he shall give to his lord, and pay him as much as any would have given him for the marriage.'[4] The really shocking aspect of the whole business is Garnet's mention of *present* [immediate] payment. With a sum as great as this the normal decent thing, even by Elizabethan practice, would have been to allow Southampton to pay in annual instalments. By making him pay this great sum in one payment, Burghley probably forced Southampton to go to the moneylenders.

To us, one of the most admirable things in Southampton's whole life

---

[1] *v. Salisbury MSS.*, VI, 553. On the extent of these fees charged when a former ward 'sued for his livery', see Hurstfield, p. 179.

[2] *Stonyhurst MSS., Angl.* Vol. I, n. 82. This letter is endorsed November 19th [1594], about six weeks after Southampton turned twenty-one.

[3] *Henry Garnet 1555–1606 and the Gunpowder Plot* (London, 1964), p. 7.

[4] Statute of Merton (1236), quoted by Hurstfield, p. 142.

was his refusal, no matter what the price, to marry where he could not love. A lesser man would have capitulated, have married Lady Elizabeth, kept away from her bed, and have provided himself with a mistress in her stead. Southampton could easily have followed the tactics of Lady Elizabeth's father, the Earl of Oxford, who, dragooned by Burghley into marrying his daughter Lady Anne Cecil, had made her life such a living hell that her early death came as a merciful relief. But Burghley had no understanding or sympathy for Southampton's refusal. Marriage was a matter of money. In the maxims which he drew up to guide his son through life, his counsel was to marry where there was money. 'Let her [your bride] not be poore, how generous [nobly born] so ever. . . . Gentilitie is nothing but ancient Riches.'[1] In collecting such large damages from Southampton, Burghley was only running true to form. And thanks partly to him, the Earl of Southampton entered into his own already seriously in debt.

[1] *Certain Precepts, or Directions for the Well Ordering and Carriage of a Man's Life* (London, 1617), sigs. A5v–A6v.

A Melodramatic Interlude

O N OCTOBER 6TH, 1594, Burghley tersely noted in his diary—
'The Erl. of Suthampton at full age'.[1] Traditionally a coming of
age called for a round of celebrations, tenants pressing in with their
congratulations and respects, hospitality for all, and a general gathering
of relatives and friends. Southampton was at his family seat of Titchfield
for the great day but no record survives of any festivities that may have
marked it. His mother seems not to have been with him. She was probably
in London with the new husband that she had married the preceding May,
old Sir Thomas Heneage, Queen Elizabeth's Treasurer of the Chamber,
Vice-Chancellor of the Household, and Chancellor of the Duchy of Lan-
caster. It was as well if she was not at Titchfield for the occasion. Her son
had a murderer, Sir Henry Danvers, in hiding a couple of miles from his
house and was busy arranging to get him safely out of England.

The Danvers, or Davers, were a Wiltshire family with which Southampton probably became acquainted through his Arundell kin,[2] and the two
sons of the house were his close friends. The elder, Sir Charles, about five
years older than Southampton, was an experienced courtier—witness his
rueful quip, 'I have, to my friends' cost, lived in Courts'. Early in life he
had made a tour of the Continent; he had been M.P. for Cirencester; and
had received his knighthood while serving under Lord Willoughby in the
Low Countries. Sir Charles was a man of educated taste. A list of some
two hundred books that he imported from Venice in 1593 includes a copy
of Petrarch's poems along with a commentary, Montemayor's *Diana*, and
a treatise on Dante's *Inferno*, though the vast majority of the books are
military, historical or geographical.[3] In his combination of military and
literary tastes he was clearly a man after Southampton's own heart.

We know rather less about the character of the younger brother, Sir
Henry, the fugitive murderer. Like his brother, Sir Henry had served in
the Low Country wars, where he had been a page to Sir Philip Sidney. At
the age of eighteen he had commanded a company of foot. He too had
won his knighthood in the field, receiving it from Essex at the siege of

[1] *Salisbury MSS.*, XIII, 508.
[2] Both the Arundells of Wardour Castle and the Danvers of Dauntsey were 'county
families' in Wiltshire. In 1584 Sir Matthew Arundell purchased the manor of Sock
Denys from Sir John Danvers. [3] *Cecil Papers*, 170, 2.

Rouen. Sir Henry, who was the same age as Southampton, seems to have been his particular friend. Not everybody, however, considered him the better of the two brothers. A few years later a French correspondent writing to the Earl of Essex pointedly remarked: 'The two Davers have suddenly gone towards Italy. The elder is a most excellent man.'[1]

Behind Sir Henry's killing of Henry Long lay a feud between the Danvers family and the Longs. We do not have the Longs' version of the fatal quarrel, but we do have one drawn up by the Danvers matriarch after the murder, one which her family obviously regarded as the definitive statement of their position.[2] According to Lady Danvers, everything was the fault of the Longs. Her worthy husband, Sir John, as a conscientious Justice of the Peace had discovered two robberies and a murder committed by servants of Sir Walter Long. The consequence of his labours had been that 'Sir Walter Longe his Brothers & followers by manie Insolent behaviors & termes provoked & moved quarrel againste the said Sir John Danvers'. Members of the Long faction had murdered one of Sir John's men, dangerously wounded another and, breaking into the house of one of Sir John's tenants, thrown a glass of beer 'in the face of the principall officer of the said Sir John Danvers: Saying in derision They had nowe doubbed him a knight allsoe.' These outrages had led to a heated exchange of letters. In one of these Henry Long told Sir Charles Danvers that 'Wheresoever he mett him, he would untye his points & whip his etc with a Rodd: calling him Asse, Puppie, ffoole & Boy.' Obviously a gentleman could not endure such insults and Sir Charles went, with a small company, into an 'ordinary' [an inn serving meals] and, finding Henry Long there, gave him a cudgelling to teach him a lesson. The matter thus tidily looked after, Sir Charles turned to withdraw but made a distressing discovery—somebody had locked the door and he could not get out. Long then drew his sword on Sir Charles, who was 'daungerously wounded in vij severall places'.[3] To save his brother, Sir Henry discharged his pistol.

For the consequence of the pistol shot, we may turn to the report of a coroner's jury convened the next day. This jury found that, on the morning of October 4th, 1594, in the town of Corsham in Wiltshire, Sir Henry Danvers and Sir Charles Danvers and two assisting yeomen, not having the fear of God before their eyes, but being seduced by the devil, had with divers weapons attacked Henry Long, and that Sir Henry Danvers, holding in his right hand a pistol loaded with powder and a lead

[1] *Salisbury MSS.*, VI, 489.
[2] Two identical copies, in the same hand, have ended up in the Public Record Office, *S.P. 12/219/78* and *S.P. 12/251/123*. Each has had the final section carefully clipped off.   [3] *S.P. 12/219/78.*

bullet did shoot the said Henry Long, the bullet striking him beneath the left breast, passing right through his body, and killing him instantly.[1] The jury added that the murderers had fled.

They had fled, in fact, to the Earl of Southampton at Titchfield. What happened in the vicinity of Titchfield during the next few weeks is of decided interest and gives us an opportunity to see the scale on which the Earl lived in his part of the country, the influence he exerted there, and the degree to which he would engage himself in the service of his friends.[2]

We begin on October 5th, the day after Henry Long was murdered. The scene was Whitley Lodge, owned by the Earl of Southampton and a little less than two miles from his mansion at Titchfield. Whitley Lodge was still occupied by Thomas Dymock under the provisions of the second earl's will. About nine o'clock in the morning Sir Charles and Sir Henry Danvers, with their servant John, arrived there and were given shelter in the house. Sir Henry Danvers had been at Titchfield only a few days earlier, at which time one of the grooms, Thomas Dredge, had noticed Sir Henry's handsome maidenhair-coloured velvet saddle. Dredge now saw Dymock and Francis Robinson, the Earl's gentleman of the horse, quarrelling over the possession of this same saddle which appeared to be 'all bluddie'.

Sunday, October 6th, was the Earl's twenty-first birthday. No doubt festivities at Titchfield marked the occasion. We know that Southampton's sister and her husband, Thomas Arundell, were guests there. The Danvers brothers remained quietly at Whitley all this day. On the following afternoon Southampton mounted horse at Titchfield and rode over to Whitley. There he dined with his friends and stayed for the night.

On Tuesday, October 8th, shortly before sunrise, Southampton, Dymock, Sir Charles and Sir Henry Danvers, and two or three others rode westward to Bursledon ferry. Here the brothers entered a boat owned by Henry and William Reed, who were instructed to carry them across Southampton Water to Calshot Castle. Southampton then rode home to Titchfield.

Landing at Calshot, the Reeds found that James Honyng (or Hunning) the Earl's steward, who had preceded them thither, had negotiated in vain with Nicholas Caplyn, the deputy commanding the Castle in the absence

---

[1] Sir Edward Coke, *Reports* (London, 1826), III, 246.

[2] For the events now to be outlined, see the examinations of witnesses before the commission composed of the Earl of Hertford, Sir Thomas West and William St. John, which subsequently investigated the escape of the Danvers brothers (*Salisbury MSS.*, V, 84–89). Also useful is a contemporary account, largely based upon these examinations, entitled 'A lamentable discourse taken out of sundrie examinacions concerning the willfull escape of Sr Charles and Sr Henrie Danvers'. (*Lansdowne MS. 827*, ff. 22r–25r.)

of Captain Thomas Perkinson. While clearance was awaited from Perkinson in his home in Southampton, the Reeds' boat cruised between the coastal forts of Calshot and St. Andrew's, which faced each other on opposite shores of Southampton Water. At the end of the day the Reeds anchored close to St. Andrew's Castle.

The next day Dymock brought word to the Danvers brothers that Captain Perkinson had agreed to let them use Calshot Castle as a hideout. Crossing Southampton Water again, they and their little company came ashore at the Castle. Unfortunately Perkinson's message had not yet reached the little garrison of four soldiers there (Calshot was only a small coastal fort, one of a chain of blockhouses that Henry VIII had built along the Hampshire coast). Kitch, the master gunner, who was temporarily in command, knew however that the hue and cry was up for the arrest of Sir Charles and Sir Henry Danvers. Accordingly he arrested them, disarmed them, and locked them up in the deputy's chamber. Fortunately for the prisoners, Caplyn, the deputy, arrived an hour or so later with the belated message from the captain. Caplyn released the knights and dined with them in his quarters. Sir Charles and Sir Henry were observed to be very sad. They had more reason than they knew for their sadness. That afternoon Lawrence Grose, the sheriff of Southampton, while in the vicinity of St. Andrew's Castle on private business had learned that the wanted men had almost certainly crossed to Calshot in the Reeds' boat. Grose had headed to Southampton to inform the mayor and arrange for their capture.

On Thursday, October 10th, Sir Charles and Sir Henry rested quietly at Calshot. A surgeon dressed Sir Charles' hand. Their respite was brief. The next morning a local justice of the peace, Sir Thomas West, received a letter from the Privy Council ordering the arrest of the fugitives. He passed on these instructions to the unfortunate Captain Perkinson, who does not seem to have stirred all this while from Southampton. Perkinson immediately dispatched a subordinate to Calshot Castle with an urgent warning to the fugitives to resume their flight. He also sent a message to the Earl's contact man in Southampton, Payne, the keeper of his lordship's wardrobe, to get word to Titchfield that the Danvers were having to move. Finally, having allowed ample time for his secret messages to be delivered, Perkinson did his duty and sent another message to Calshot, this one ordering the arrest of the knights who had, of course, fled hours before.

When Perkinson's clandestine warning arrived at Calshot, the knights and their company, 'hastelie shouldering one another' in their panicky flight, almost swamped the boat in which they recrossed Southampton Water. Coming ashore at Bald Head (modern Hill Head), which lies only

TITCHFIELD AND ENVIRONS

From Saxton's map of Hampshire, 1575

a couple of miles from Titchfield, they asked Dymock if he knew the way thither. Concerned to protect the Earl, Dymock replied that he would not until midnight. He seems to have taken Sir Charles and Sir Henry back to Whitley Lodge and then, in the secrecy of the night, to have conducted them to the Earl of Southampton's mansion at Titchfield.

Apparently Sir Charles and Sir Henry remained in hiding at Titchfield on Saturday and Sunday, October 12th and 13th. About this time their Scottish servant Gilbert was travelling to and from London with secret letters concealed within the lining of his cap. One humorous little interlude enlivened the weekend. John Florio, the Earl's hot-tempered Italian language teacher, travelling on the Itchen–Southampton ferry with a certain Humphrey Drewell,[1] found on board Lawrence Grose, the sheriff of Southampton, and his wife. Remembering how Grose had helped raise the hue and cry, Florio 'threatned to cast him the saide Grose overboord and saide they woulde teache him to meddle with his fellowes, with many other threatening wordes'.[2] The Earl's other servants showed comparable loyalty. Once Southampton took the very risky step of taking the fugitives under his own roof, the trail went cold. Only one servant, the stable groom Thomas Dredge, blabbed; and all that Dredge could subsequently tell the investigating commission was that on the evening of Monday, October 14th, Robinson, the gentleman of the Earl's horse, had told him and his fellow grooms to saddle up seven horses and leave them ready in the stable; and that another groom had told him that one of the Earl's gentlemen, Arthur Broomfield, had led off these horses about midnight. Broomfield returned to Titchfield about dawn on Thursday, October 17th, with four of the horses. Dredge was then told that the Earl would take the horses up to London with him as soon as they had been fed. A few hours later Southampton's barber came around and had a heart-to-heart talk with Dredge, who must already have been causing some concern because of his volubility. He asked Dredge who had told him that Sir Henry Danvers had been at Whitley Lodge. When Dredge gave his answer, the barber 'sware deeplie by Gods woundes, and charged him uppon payne of his lyfe, not to speake any more of itt, for that it was his Lordes will and pleasure that the saide Sir Henrie Davers should be there at Whitley Lodge'.[3] And here the records cease. The next that we hear of Sir Charles and Sir Henry Danvers, they are in France at the court of Henri IV.

Appended to a contemporary account of the flight of the Danvers from Titchfield, one which Mrs. Stopes reasonably enough conjectured to have

---

[1] Drewell was a close friend of Thomas Arundell. In 1596 he was knighted by Essex at Cadiz.

[2] *Lansdowne MS. 827*, f. 24v.

[3] Loc. cit.

been drafted by Sir Walter Long's attorney,[1] is a list of the possible witnesses, servants of the Earl of Southampton, who had not been called by
the investigating commission. Heading the list is Honyng, the Earl's
steward. There may have been a good reason why the commissioners had
cut short their investigation. As things were, they had unmistakable evidence that the escape of the Danvers brothers had been engineered by the
Earl of Southampton. The calling of further witnesses would probably have
put the authorities in a position where they could not avoid taking action
against Southampton. That no such action was taken must have been the
result of a deliberate decision by the Queen's advisers. One cannot help
wondering, however, if the enormous damages so soon afterwards given
to Burghley for Southampton's failure to marry Lady Elizabeth Vere may
not have been, in part, a disguised fine. Part of an understanding may have
been that if the Earl paid up without complaint, the investigation into the
escape of the Danvers brothers would not be pushed beyond a certain
point.

[1] *Lansdowne MS. 827*, ff. 22r–25r. For Mrs. Stopes's view of this document, see
p. 80 of her life of Southampton.

CHAPTER V

Family Problems

FROM THE ACCOUNTS of the Danvers escape, it is clear that Southampton, when he attained his majority, was already maintaining a rather extensive retinue. In view of the very large sums he was going to have to pay to Burghley for the refused marriage, and to the Crown for the transfer of his estates out of wardship, one might have expected him to be keeping a more modest establishment. Presumably he, like his father, was determined to live like an earl.

One concession appears to have been made to economy. His lordship decided not to go to the expense of maintaining Southampton House, his London residence. In November 1594 the porter's lodge there, together with various other buildings, rooms, lofts and garrets, were leased out to a certain John Bellingham.[1] At about the same time, following a common practice, Southampton signed a deed of uses, vesting in a trust the formal title to all his manors with their thousands of acres of arable land, meadow, pasture, marsh, woodland, furze and heath. For his trustees, the young earl chose two of the persons who had figured in the Danvers drama— James Honyng, his steward, and Arthur Broomfield, one of his gentlemen.

The year 1595 saw the handsome young Earl of Southampton emerging at the court of Queen Elizabeth as a budding favourite who might well replace Essex, whose open displays of bad temper and petulance were causing Her Majesty a good deal of annoyance. According to Sir Henry Wotton (at one time a secretary to Essex), Sir Fulke Greville, seeing in the Queen '. . . some weariness . . . or perhaps some wariness' towards Essex, 'almost superinduced into favour the Earl of Southampton'.[2] Tying in with Wotton's report is a letter written from the court at the beginning of October in this year:

> My Lord of Essex kept his Bed all Yesterday; his Favour contineus. . . . Yet my Lord of Southampton is a carefull Waiter [attendant] here, and *sede vacante* [Essex's place being vacant] doth receve Favors at her Majestyes Handes; all this without Breach of Amity between them.[3]

[1] For the lease to Bellingham, see *W.P. 267*. For the deed of uses see *W.P. 224* (letters patent under the great seal, dated December 2nd, 1594), *W.P. 335* (their exemplification enrolled in the Court of Common Pleas, February 12th, 1595).

[2] 'Parallel Lives of Essex and Buckingham', *Reliquiae Wottonianae* (London, 1672), p. 165.

[3] Arthur Collins ed., *Letters and Memorials of State (The Sidney Papers)* [1746], II, 62.

47

The period of Southampton's favour with the Queen was not to endure much longer however. Only a few weeks later, the same correspondent was to report:

> My Lord of Southampton offering to help the Queen to her horse, was refused, he is gone from the Court, and not yet returned.[1]

He was back by November 17th, the anniversary of Elizabeth's accession to the throne, and found sufficient acceptance to be allowed to joust in the ceremonial tournament which traditionally marked 'The Queen's Day'. George Peele, writing a fine Spenserian poem upon the occasion, gave high praise to 'younge Wriothesley' whom he found 'gentle and debonaire'.[2] Gentle and debonair he may have been, but we never again hear of Southampton being high in the graces of Queen Elizabeth.

The reason for the Queen's rebuff may have been female jealousy at finding that the resplendent young lord was giving more attention to one of her maids of honour than to herself. The maid in question was Essex's cousin, Elizabeth Vernon. Born on January 11th, 1573, she was about Southampton's own age. Demure in appearance, and almost doll-like in her prettiness, she was highly strung and notably emotional. She was a very feminine lady, and she had made a great impression upon the Earl of Southampton. Passing on the gossip of the court late in September, Rowland Whyte, from whose correspondence we have been quoting, noted:

> My Lord of Southampton doth with to[o] much Familiarity court the faire Mistress Vernon.[3]

The over-familiarity shown towards Mistress Vernon sounds a little ominous. In an age when the marriages of earls were dynastic alliances and the bride's dowry a major element in the negotiating, Elizabeth, one of the numerous daughters of a recently deceased country squire, Sir John Vernon of Hodnet in Shropshire, could not hope for such a match. Only the fact that her mother was Essex's aunt had secured her the post of a maid of honour. Financially she seems to have been dependent on Essex who paid her an allowance of £50 per annum, which he supplemented with various gifts.[4] Mistress Vernon would be lucky if she picked up a knight for her husband. Her friends might well warn her that Southampton

---

[1] H.M.C., *De L'Isle MSS.*, II, 176.

[2] v. *Anglorum Feriae*, ll. 226–35.

[3] Collins, I, 348.

[4] E. M. Tenison, *Elizabethan England* (Royal Leamington Spa, 1933–60), X, 473. Tenison gets this information from the unpublished Devereux MSS., Vol. III, at Longleat.

For the Vernon family tree see *Publications of the Harleian Society*, Vol. 29 (1889), p. 474.

was indeed 'a prince, out of thy star'. His ardent and all too obvious attentions could only detract from her reputation and spoil her chances of making a reasonably good match elsewhere.

The autumn of 1595 presented other problems for Southampton besides his growing involvement with Elizabeth Vernon and the Queen's display of disfavour. His mother was waging feuds which must have been troublesome to her son. In October of this year her second husband, Sir Thomas Heneage, died. We find quite a light thrown on Southampton's volatile and difficult mother in the letters that she sent to Lord Burghley and his son Sir Robert Cecil reporting the stages of Heneage's final sickness. Writing to Sir Robert on July 29th, she sent her regards, with heavy coyness, to a lady friend of his:

> I pray you commend me to that wicked woman that loves you and likes me. They call her Lady Katherine.[1]

Two weeks later something had angered the lady and she wrote furiously to Cecil:

> We hold it a great infortunite for us that any occasion moved her Majesty to speak of us to so great an enemy as we esteem yourself to be to us both, assuring ourselves you took the present occasion to pour forth your malice, which we must bear and desire no better.[2]

The dowager Countess could hardly do herself or her family any good by writing in this manner to one of the most powerful men in the kingdom. In his will Heneage testified to the loving care that he had received from his wife, but she seems to have been a tactless and stupid woman, no matter how kind her heart.

The arrangements for Heneage's funeral got his widow into a blazing row with Richard Fletcher, the Bishop of London, who had sent one of his officers to collect the fee due to him for the use of St. Paul's Cathedral. From the unhappy and apprehensive letter that the Bishop wrote to Cecil about the business, we gather that the lady was going around slanderously declaring that Fletcher had spoken dishonourably of both the deceased and Cecil.[3]

Heneage's death left Southampton's mother a major financial problem. This arose from the practice, freely indulged in by various royal treasurers, of drawing in advance funds payable to their office, then using these to their own profit until such time as the money had either to be spent in the payments for which it was intended, or be remitted to the Crown. This way of making an interim private profit often left Elizabethan officials substantially in arrears in their accounts. Such proved the case with

---

[1] *Salisbury MSS.*, V. 294. In 1589 Cecil had married Elizabeth Brooke, daughter of Lord Cobham.

[2] Ibid., V, 309.   [3] Ibid., V, 475.

Heneage. In 1596 his widow, as executrix of his estate, was presented by the Queen's auditors with a statement showing that Heneage had died owing the Crown just over £12,000 and that, although she had made two substantial payments, there was still more than £7,800 to be paid.[1] Heneage had been generous to his wife in his will but the payment of this very large debt may have forced her to dip into her own resources. It is worth noting that in 1596 Southampton gave his mother permission to sell one of the Wriothesley manors, Faringdon, which she held as part of the jointure settled on her by his father.[2]

If Southampton's mother was having problems at this period, so was his sister Mary. Her husband, Thomas Arundell, was gifted and scholarly, sensitive and courageous. However, handicapped by being a fervent Roman Catholic, and by having a hostile irascible father, who grudged him any money, he had failed to find any career for his talents and had sunk into a melancholic existence as a semi-pensioner, living a 'studious solitary life' either at one of the Wriothesley estates in Hampshire or in an apartment reserved for the family in Southampton House. At length his father let him have enough money to leave England and serve in the war that was being waged by the Emperor Rudolph against the Turks, who were still a grave menace to Christian Europe.

Thomas Arundell presented himself at the imperial court, was gladly received and entered into the life of action and honour for which he craved. Unfortunately his wife, deprived of his company, grew unhappy and began to urge him to come home. Old Sir Matthew Arundell became highly indignant when he learned what she was up to, and used all his influence to get the Queen to appoint his son to some service abroad that would effectively keep him from returning to his wife. The Arundells and the Cecils were related, and in November 1595 Sir Matthew wrote to Sir Robert Cecil soliciting his support:

> [My daughter-in-law] looking no further than to a desire of her husband's company, or at least a seeming thereunto, seeks his return by all means she may before the next spring's war be growen to an end, neither regarding his reputation nor my great charge of setting him forth . . . let the love poor W. Arundel bore you, besides the service that Thomas himself may hereafter do you, win so much from you that he may be someways employed for her Majesty's service for trial of his loyalty and wit, and to deliver him from the scandal that either he durst not tarry [remain at the war] or he undertook the journey to cosen [trick] his father of all his horses and £1,100.[3]

[1] P.R.O., *A01/33/386*. This document contains in identical form the entry concerning payments to Kempe, Shakespeare and Burbage to be found in *E.351/542*, f. 107b. For a moment when the present writer saw the name 'Shakespeare' in the Audit Office manuscript, he had his heart in his throat and a bemused feeling that he really had struck gold.

[2] *Victoria County History, Hampshire*, III, 20.   [3] *Salisbury MSS.*, V, 480.

Sir Matthew's artful little manoeuvre failed. Far from waiting until the end of the coming spring campaign, Thomas Arundell took his leave from the Emperor in mid-December of this same year. During his service with the imperial forces Arundell had shown great valour, in one engagement wresting from the Turks their banner with his own hand.[1] In recognition of the Englishman's services, Rudolph conferred upon him the title of Count of the Holy Roman Empire. His letters patent, given at Prague on December 14th, note that Arundell traces his descent from the royal blood of England, that he has travelled in many different cities in foreign countries and has furnished his mind with 'knowledge of all good and useful Literature'; then they recite his recent military services:

> . . . you have come at so great a Distance into Hungary at your own Expense (excited thereto by a singular and unusual Zeal to bear Arms under us in this sacred War, which we wage against the Turk the common Enemy of the Christian Name); and have behaved yourself with such undaunted Bravery, both in the open Field, and in besiegeing Cities and Camps, as to be held in general Admiration. . . . [2]

Proudly the new nobleman set off for home.

Approaching England, Arundell's ship was caught in a great storm and wrecked near Aldeburgh on the Suffolk coast. Count Arundell lost everything that he had with him, and was lucky to stand at last 'extreamely cold & wett upon the shore'.[3] At the beginning of February he wrote to Cecil informing him of his arrival and assuring him that he had neither been to Rome nor associated with the Popish or Spanish faction. Proudly he reported that 'The honour which the Emperor hath done me, having made me an Earl of the Empire, may in part witness of my good desert at the camp'.[4] When Cecil passed on the latter news to Queen Elizabeth, she was furious. What did the Emperor mean by giving Arundell such a title? How could Arundell have had the audacity to accept it? She, and only she, was the fountain of honour for her people. Things would become absolutely impossible if her Catholic gentry could slip away to Catholic courts and return calling themselves earls. She sent Burghley to question Arundell, and Burghley packed Arundell off to the Fleet prison. From the Fleet the unhappy count wrote letters full of arguments why the Queen should not carry out her threat to make him renounce his title. He also set forth grandiose schemes for advancing the profit of England if he were released:

[1] Sir William Dugdale, *The Baronage of England* (London, 1676), II, 422.
[1] John Pym Yeatman, *The Early Genealogical History of the House of Arundel* (London, 1882), p. 275.
[3] Peck, ed., *Desiderata Curiosa*, p. 282.
[4] *Salisbury MSS.*, VI, 43.

My intention is to the East Indias where there are many kings so great as that they can bring into the field a hundred thousand or two hundred thousand men apiece, viz. the king of Bengala, the king of Pegu, the king of Sumatra, the Emperor of China, the king of Giava, Presbiter Ihon, &c. If it please the Queen to let me have her letters to some of these, I will not doubt to conclude such an amity and intercourse of traffic as shall much weaken the Spanish strength in those parts, shall much enrich our merchants and by consequence the Queen, and greatly increase her Majesty's customs.[1]

In the end the Queen wrote a letter to Rudolph in which, after giving His Imperial Majesty a firm little sermon on why he should not give titles to other monarchs' subjects, she blandly thanked him for the honour shown Arundell—she could see that it was really 'an overt testimony of your love and kindness to ourself'. Since there was no point in quarrelling with the Emperor, she had given him a face-saving way out. She was not so quick to forgive Arundell. Although she had informed Rudolph that she had imprisoned his new count only 'for a shew of correction', she took her time about letting him out of prison. Not until mid-April was Arundell brought before Burghley, told that he was free, but forbidden to appear at Elizabeth's court. In a not unkindly fashion Burghley broke to Arundell the news that he must not use his imperial title in England. He explained that it was really impossible to let Arundell go around styling himself an earl, especially since 'stranger Earls have by courtesy a place above the Earls of this land'.

In the months that followed, Arundell sent off unavailing letters begging restoration of the Queen's favour and permission 'to kiss those sceptre-bearing hands'. Contemplating the sad truth that at the age of thirty-seven he was still without prospects or a career, he sank deeper and deeper into depression. Adding to his cares was the feud being waged between his wife and his father. When in July Sir Matthew grudgingly permitted his son and his family to come to live with him at Wardour, he made one exception: he would not have his daughter-in-law in his house. Writing to Sir Robert Cecil, Mary Arundell implored him to intercede on her behalf, promising that she would be kind and respectful to tempestuous old Sir Matthew. We do not know the outcome of this appeal. Certainly Cecil and his father, Lord Burghley, must by now have been thoroughly tired of their Arundell kin.

As for Master Thomas Arundell, when he found that repeated propitiatory letters to the Cecils had failed to gain him readmission to the Court, or even the return of the seized letters patent given him by Rudolph he finally blew sky-high and wrote a furious letter to Sir Robert:

If you take me for an enemy, why do you not proclaim your anger and the cause? If for a friend, why do you use me thus? Have I not already suffered crosses

[1] *Salisbury MSS.*, VI, 128-9.

enough, my shipwreck, my imprisonment, my disgrace, known to all men, my father's disinheriting of me and the general malice that is borne me, but that yourself (the only person of honour by whom I hoped to receive comfort) must not only forsake but persecute me?[1]

And here, for a while, Thomas Arundell fades from our ken. We may note, however, that he was finally able to use the style of a nobleman in England for King James I in 1605 created him Lord Arundell of Wardour, but his descendants had to wait until the reign of James II before they could use in England their inherited dignity of Count of the Holy Roman Empire.

We have no evidence as to how Southampton viewed his brother-in-law's difficulties. We do not know if he was amused or offended when rumour said that his sister was claiming for herself the precedence of a countess. One thing seems obvious: because of the Earl of Southampton's own conduct, that of his mother, of his brother-in-law and possibly of his sister, he and his family cannot have been regarded at this time with any enthusiasm by either the Queen or her closest advisers.

The literary men, meanwhile, were keeping a thin trickle of dedications and commendatory verses coming Southampton's way. On March 2nd, 1596, the bookseller Edward Blount made an entry in the Stationers' Register reserving for himself the right to publish 'a most copious and exacte Dictionarye in Italian and Englishe made by JOHN FFLORIO dedicated to the right honorable the E[a]rle of SOUTHAMPTON'.[2] The mention of the dedicatee in such an entry is most unusual. Often not even the name of the author is given. 'Resolute John Florio', sometime tutor of Italian to the Earl, must have been making a great deal of his patronage. Actually, Florio's Italian-English dictionary was not published until 1598 and then Southampton had to share the dedication with the Earl of Rutland and the Countess of Bedford. In his dedication Florio paid glowing tribute to the 'most noble, most vertuous, and most Honorable Earle of Southampton, in whose paie and patronage I have lived some yeeres', and he declared that his lordship, while living in England, had become so complete a master of Italian as to have no need of travel abroad to perfect his mastery of that tongue.[3]

When in 1597 Henry Lok published his *Sundry Christian Passions*, two hundred colourless religious sonnets, he printed with them a commendatory sonnet addressed to Southampton. Perhaps we should not attach much significance to this, however, since Lok had fifty-nine other

[1] *Salisbury MSS.*, VI., 358

[2] Edward Arber, *A Transcript of the Registers of the Company of Stationers of London, 1554–1640* (London, 1875–94), III, 60.

[3] *A Worlde of Wordes or Most Copious and Exact Dictionarie in Italian and English* (London, 1598), sig. A3v.

commendatory sonnets to other people who he hoped would reward him for his pious but mediocre labours.

Probably more to Southampton's taste was a highly spiced amatory romance dedicated to him in this same year by William Burton. *The Most Delectable History of Clitophon and Leucippe*, to give the full title of Burton's work, is a free translation of a romance written by Achilles Tatius, an Alexandrine Greek, near the end of the second century A.D. Fairly widely read in the Renaissance, the tale had previously been translated into French and Italian. When framing his dedication to Southampton, the English translator apparently had his eye on Shakespeare's dedication of *Venus and Adonis* for just as Shakespeare made the promise, if his poem pleased, of presenting Southampton with 'some graver labour', so Burton assured the Earl that, should *Clitophon and Leucippe* prove acceptable, it would be followed by 'some matter of greater import, then [than] a superficiall toy'.

Tatius's romance is, in its English form, a fluently and gracefully written book, and decidedly readable except towards the last when it rather bogs down. It tells how young Clitophon, in the face of his father's stern resolve to make him marry his half-sister, elopes with the fair Leucippe and with her is wrecked on the shore of Egypt. Various fantastic adventures follow. Abductions, an attempted seduction of Clitophon, and seeming deaths of Leucippe (at one point Clitophon believes he is embracing her headless corpse), are only a few of the incidents. At the end everything ends happily at Ephesus with a final reunion of Clitophon and Leucippe at the temple of Diana. Their marriage occurs in the presence of Leucippe's father who, in a dream, has been told by Diana that he will find his daughter in Ephesus.

There are unpleasant passages in *Clitophon and Leucippe*. Some relate to the homosexual Clinias and his boy Charicles. Charicles, when his father seeks to marry him to an unattractive woman, laments that he is doomed to a double hell 'for since a faire wife is a great trouble, how can it otherwise be, but that an ill favoured one must needs be twise worse'. Clinias then launches into a catalogue of the miseries that women have brought upon men. Urgently he begs Charicles not to permit 'so deformed a Gardener croppe so fayre and sweete a Rose'.[1] In a debate as to which most merits love, a woman or a boy, the last word is given to the homosexual Menelaus. A decidedly unpleasant erotic sadism enters into the account of one of the supposed slayings of Leucippe:

> Then one of the men which lead her . . . bound her fast to the table whereon shee lay, after the same maner as Marcyas was bound to a tree, when Apollo did

---

[1] *The Loves of Clitophon and Leucippe*, ed. Stephen Gaselee and H. F. B. Brett-Smith (Oxford, 1923), pp. 8–10. Despite the altered title, this is a reprint of Burton.

flea [flay] the skin from his body: and thrusting in his sworde at the lower end of her belly, ript her up to ye heart, wherwith instantly her bowels fell forth of her belly.'[1]

This is strong stuff and one scholar has surmised that the reason why only one copy of *Clitophon and Leucippe* survived into our century could be that the book may have been one of those burned by order of the Archbishop of Canterbury.[2] What is interesting is that Burton chose Southampton as the dedicatee for his work. Presumably he thought the Earl would like it.

[1] *Clitophon and Leucippe*, p. 58.
[2] *The Times Literary Supplement*, February 10th, 1905, p. 50.

To the Wars at Last

D URING THE MONTHS when Arundell was off on his adventures abroad, his brother-in-law, young Southampton, probably became the more impatient to travel himself, to see the world, and to win honours in battle.

In March 1596 it appeared that Southampton would soon receive his initiation into the wars. A project was under way to send a fleet under Lord Admiral Howard, and an expeditionary force under the Earl of Essex, to capture the Spanish naval base at Cadiz. Southampton seems to have participated in the planning for this expedition, for in mid-March we find him at Dover attending a conference with his former guardian, the Lord Admiral, aboard the *Due Repulse*,[1] which would carry Essex on this expedition. Clearly Southampton was expecting to take part in the Cadiz expedition that summer. Then a sudden development brought the prospect of almost immediate action against the Spaniards.

At this period Henri IV of France was England's ally in her war with Spain. While besieging La Fère, Henri received news that the Cardinal-Archduke Albert, governor of the Spanish Netherlands, had taken to the field and was about to attack Calais. Unable to bring his army to the rescue of Calais, the French king desperately appealed to Elizabeth for help. In the Queen's court at Greenwich, where men could hear the reverberations of the Spanish guns cannonading Calais, instant action was looked for. Sir Conyers Clifford, making a reconnaissance on April 3rd, found that the Spanish had already captured the fort that commanded the approaches to Calais harbour. At Dover, Essex hourly awaited instructions to sail with a hurriedly assembled force and save the city. Unfortunately Queen Elizabeth postponed action while she tried to extort from the French the highest possible terms for her aid. On April 13th Essex was given his commission to take six thousand soldiers to Calais, but only if the French would undertake to hand over the city to the English. This commission empowered Essex to take certain noblemen over to France but specifically instructed him not to take the Earls of Derby and Southampton.[2] South-

---

[1] *Salisbury MSS.*, VI, 102.

[2] *Cal. S.P. (Dom.), 1595–97*, p. 203. Derby and Southampton appear to have been rather close friends at this period. See *Salisbury MSS.*, VI, 158, for a cryptic reference to some venture in which the two earls were partners in this same month.

ampton must have been a bitterly disappointed man. However he had lost nothing for two days later, just when Elizabeth had sent Essex authorization to sail, word arrived that the citadel at Calais had surrendered.

Preparations for the Cadiz expedition went forward with increased vigour. The establishment of a Spanish naval base directly across the Straits of Dover had badly shaken English morale and a vigorous counterstroke was needed. On June 1st Howard and Essex sailed from Plymouth with 48 warships, 100 transports and victuallers, and an army of about 10,000 men. Despite disagreements among the commanders, the expedition was a brilliant success. The English sailed into the inner harbour of Cadiz, utterly defeated the Spanish naval forces and captured two great galleons. Then the troops were successfully landed. Essex and his men, mounting the walls of Cadiz, hoisted the flag of St. George and took the city at a cost of only some two hundred lives. The next day the citadel surrendered. A humane truce allowed the inhabitants of Cadiz to evacuate their city. Then the troops were turned loose for two weeks of pillaging. Despite some missed opportunities, the campaign was a notable victory and Essex returned to England at the height of his reputation.

For some reason Southampton was not among the thousand gentlemen 'covered with feathers, gold, and silver lace' who set out with Essex and returned with glory, together with rich ransoms from Spanish officers as well as plate, carpets, tapestry, sugar, quicksilver, and butts of wine as their share of the pillage. No doubt Southampton had greatly desired to sail with Essex. One person, at least, was under the false impression that he had sailed. Thomas Wilson, travelling on the Continent, had made a translation of Jorge de Montemayor's enormously popular pastoral romance *Diana*, 'transplanting vaine amorous conceits out of an Exotique language'. This translation survives in a manuscript captioned:

> Diana de Montemayor done out of Spanish by Thomas Wilso[n] Esquire, In the yeare 1596 & dedicated to the Erle of Southampto[n] who was then uppon ye Spanish voiage wth my Lord of Essex.[1]

But the evidence is clear that Southampton was not on this Spanish voyage for on July 1st, when Essex and his army were exulting in captured Cadiz, Southampton was in London signing a letter of attorney.[2] We can only conjecture as to why Southampton, contrary to expectation, had not sailed with Essex. Presumably the Queen's prohibition barring Southampton from the projected French expedition of the previous April had

---

[1] *Add. MS. 18638*, f. 2r. A subsequent dedication to Sir Fulke Greville was apparently added some years later by Wilson. For a letter written to Southampton from Cadiz, by Sir George Gifford, see *Salisbury MSS.*, XIII, 577–79.

[2] This document, seen by Edmond Malone, has apparently been lost. For Malone's reference to it, see the 'Third Variorum' edition of Shakespeare (1821), XX, 438.

been extended to his participation in the Cadiz venture. Once more Southampton had been kept from the martial glory for which he yearned.

The February of the following year saw Southampton involved in a quarrel with Essex's brother-in-law, the Earl of Northumberland. For an account of this we have a letter sent by Northumberland to his friend Anthony Bacon.[1] Northumberland reported that, angered by certain words allegedly spoken by Southampton, he had given him the lie. Southampton had then sent a gentleman with a challenge 'stuffed with strange circumstances'. Thus, although men customarily fought with a rapier in the right hand and a dagger in the left, Southampton had asked that they fight with rapiers only, alleging that he had recently injured his arm playing 'balloon' (a game using a heavy inflated ball and a wooden bracer attached to the arm). Northumberland had contemptuously replied that he knew that Southampton did not play with his left arm, and he had offered to wait until his arm was healed. Northumberland had scarcely got off this answer when a message arrived from the Queen summoning the two earls to Court. Here the lords of the Privy Council assured Northumberland that Southampton had not spoken the words which had started the quarrel. Southampton withdrew his challenge and peace was restored.

One of Southampton's friendships was with Sir Robert Sidney, the younger brother of the famous Sir Philip Sidney. On March 1st Southampton was the godfather at the christening of Sir Robert's daughter, Bridget. A little later we hear for the first time of a possible third marriage for Southampton's mother. For some years one of the friends of the family had been a certain William Harvey. Much younger than the Countess, Harvey was the kind of man that Southampton himself liked, a traveller and a soldier who had served in the Low Countries. Our earliest mention of the possible marriage comes in a letter sent to Sir Robert Sidney by Rowland Whyte in May 1597.[2]

What little evidence we have suggests that Southampton had been living very lavishly since his coming of age in 1594. By 1597 he was deep in financial difficulties. On February 11th of the latter year, noting that he 'stood indebted to divers persons in great sums of money, for payment of which he and sundry his friends stand bound', he transferred the entire administration of his estate to three attorneys. The persons to whom the Earl turned over this sorry mess were Ralph Hare and Edward Gage, both of whom had been executors administering his father's estate, and William Chamberlain, whose family had long been in the service of the

---

[1] Lambeth MSS., *Bacon Papers*, Vol. IX, f. 78. The letter is endorsed on the reverse, 'Letter le Comte de Northumberland le 8ᵐᵉ de feavrier 1596'. This, I assume, despite the French, to be an Old Style dating.

[2] Collins, II, 53.

ROBERT DEVEREUX, EARL OF ESSEX
National Portrait Gallery

Wriothesleys, and whose own long and faithful service would end only with his own death and burial in Titchfield Church. The Earl made only one stipulation in the deed appointing these administrators of his estate—they must not sell the manors of Titchfield, Beaulieu, North Stoneham, Micheldever, Ewshott or Long Sutton. The next day he signed a covenant with his mother and his friend Lord Mountjoy, promising to keep these manors and to leave them, and whatever other estates his attorneys did not dispose of, to his own future issue or, should he have none, to his sister, 'the Lady Mary, wife to Thomas Arundell and their right issue'.[1]

Arundell himself was in new trouble in 1597. Smallman, a messenger by whom Arundell had sent a message to the Emperor, was suspected of being a member of an underground Catholic espionage network. The authorities failed at first to catch Smallman, but they arrested Sir Humphrey Drewell[2] on suspicion of helping him elude capture, and they arrested Arundell as well. Searching the latter's chamber, they found nothing more incriminating than an account of England written in Italian and a memorandum on novel military devices, which showed Arundell to be interested in the possibility of germ warfare:

> Learn of Mr. Platt his way to poison air and so to infect a whole camp.[3]

In June, partly because Arundell's wife, 'a sick and weak woman', was faltering under the strain, and partly because they could prove nothing criminal against him, the Council discharged Arundell to the custody of his father. The latter at first vehemently protested against having to receive his son, and then insisted on behaving as his jailer, until he was transferred elsewhere.

As far as Southampton was concerned, the great event of 1597 came when, at long last, he went to the wars. The occasion was 'The Islands Voyage', the expedition made by the Earl of Essex to the Azores in the summer and autumn of this year. During the months following Essex's triumph at Cadiz, intelligence had trickled into England revealing that the Spaniards, determined to avenge their recent humiliation, were outfitting a fleet at Ferrol and Corunna, and mustering an army for an invasion of England. The Queen and her Privy Council were well along with their plans for meeting this attack when further news arrived that a great storm had shattered the Spanish fleet at Ferrol and that sickness had ravaged the Spanish regiments, setting back by months the invasion schedule. Under the altered circumstances, the English decided to continue mustering their forces but to use them for a new attack on Spain.

---

[1] For the deed of attorney and the covenant, see *W.P. 580, 580.1* and *169*.
[2] *Vide supra*, p. 45.   [3] *Salisbury MSS.*, VII, 167.

This new English offensive was to be based on the highly successful Cadiz operation, but this time the attack would be made against Ferrol, where the fleet of the Adelantado of Castile, preparing against England, would be finally destroyed. Should the Spanish fleet have left Ferrol, the English ships were to seek it out and force it to action. They would then proceed to a further operation—sailing westward to the Azores and there intercepting the 'Flota', the Spanish treasure fleet which, sailing under convoy from Havana once every year, brought King Philip the gold and silver from his mines in America. The English also hoped to seize and garrison the island of Terceira, where Angra, the main Spanish stronghold in the Azores, was situated.

On July 10th the English set sail from Plymouth with 'a wind both fresh and large'. Essex, the commander-in-chief, had for his flagship the *Merhonour*. Immediately under his command was a squadron consisting of six warships of the Royal Navy, six armed merchantmen and ten transports. His vice-admiral, Lord Thomas Howard aboard the *Due Repulse*, had in his squadron seven warships, one armed merchantman and twelve transports. Sir Walter Raleigh, the rear-admiral aboard the *Warspite*, had six warships (one commanded by Sir William Harvey, Southampton's future stepfather), an armed merchantman and ten transports. Besides these ships, which constituted the official strength of the expedition, there were numerous other vessels, such as Raleigh's 'twenty voluntary barks of the west country'. There was also a Dutch squadron, commanded by Essex's close friend Jan van Duyvenvoord, this being made up of ten warships and fifteen transports.[1]

Crowded aboard the transports were 5,000 soldiers, including 1,000 English veterans brought back from the Low Countries by Sir Francis Vere, who was smarting at the indignity of being given only the third position (that of Marshal) in the chain of military command. The position of Lieutenant-General, second only to that of Essex himself, the Queen had given to another of her gilded court favourites, Charles Blount, Lord Mountjoy, not yet the famous soldier he was to become. Besides those appointed to commands, some five hundred other lords, knights and gentlemen went along as volunteers at their own expense and served directly under Essex, the general. Among them were the Earls of Southampton and Rutland, and the Lords Audley, Grey, Rich, Cromwell and Windsor.

As, with the sounding of trumpets, shrilling of whistles, and firing of cannon, the hundred and fifty or more ships of Essex's fleet put out from Plymouth Sound, the Earl of Southampton stood on the deck of the

[1] *The Naval Tracts of Sir William Monson*, ed. M. Oppenheim (The Navy Records Society, 1902), II, 38–40.

Garland, which had been placed under his command, though its actual management was entrusted to a veteran captain named Troughton or Traughton. The *Garland*, commonly miscalled the *Guardland*, was a fine and comparatively large ship. Her normal complement consisted of 190 mariners, 30 gunners and 80 soldiers. For armament she carried 16 brass culverins, 12 brass and 2 iron demi-culverins, 2 brass and 2 iron sakers, 2 brass fowlers and 2 brass portipieces.[1] Southampton must have felt elated as his ship moved out to the open sea. Not that he was under any illusions about his crew. Earlier that day, writing to Cecil, who had secured the Queen's permission for him to go on this expedition, he had mentioned that most of the seamen rounded up for the *Garland* by the pressmasters had proved quite unsuitable:

> I have already been driven to set 30 sick men on shore, besides some that have run away, and those that remain are for the most part unable to perform any labour that belongs to them.

All the same, Southampton had ended on a resolutely cheerful note: 'I verily believe a willinger company never undertook any journey.'[2]

Disaster was not long in overtaking the English fleet. On the second day out, the fresh wind that had been blowing from the north-east mounted to a gale in which Raleigh and four of his ships were separated from the fleet. This gale abated but was followed by a great tempest which struck from the south-west. Life became an agony for those caught in these little Elizabethan ships, top-heavy with ordnance, reeling before the force of a full Atlantic storm. Masts snapped, seams opened, and in Raleigh's ship the bricks in the galley were pulverized into dust, as the tiny ships madly gyrated and pounded up and down in the enormous seas. Seasickness was an agony which some men did not survive. John Donne, who was on this expedition, has left some account of the suffering:

> Lightning was all our light, and it rain'd more
> Then if the Sunne had drunke the sea before.
> Some coffin'd in their cabbins lye, equally
> Griev'd that they are not dead, and yet must dye;
> And as sin-burd'ned soules from graves will creepe,
> At the last day, some forth their cabbins peepe:
> And tremblingly, aske what newes . . .
> *(The Storme*, ll.44–49)

Well might Donne conclude, 'Compar'd to these stormes, death is but a qualme'. Once the storm had blown itself out, most of the dispersed fleet headed for the nearest port to recover from the mauling. Essex limped into

---

[1] M. Oppenheim, *A History of the Administration of the Royal Navy 1509–1660* (London, 1896), p. 157.

[2] *Cal. S.P. (Dom.)*, *1595–1597*, pp. 456–7.

Falmouth harbour, the *Merhonour* a wreck which had to be sent to Chatham for rebuilding.

Not all the English ships were routed by the storm. The *Garland* and a few others managed to ride out the tempest. On July 20th Southampton and the captains of the other surviving ships came aboard the flagship of Lord Thomas Howard the vice-admiral, who informed them of his intention to proceed to the North Cape and await Essex at the pre-arranged rendezvous there. Off the Spanish coast they deliberately gave the enemy 'a fair sight' of them, vainly hoping to provoke the Spaniards to put out and fight them. In the end, they received orders from Essex to return home, and on July 31st entered Plymouth harbour where the rest of the fleet was undergoing repair.

Essex now faced a serious situation. Not all his ships could be refitted in time for a renewed attempt this summer. His soldiers, landed from the transports, were eating up the rations grudgingly granted by a penurious Queen for the few precious months allowed for the expedition. Sickness and desertion were taking their inevitable toll. Nor were desertions limited to the common soldiers. Many of the gallants who had been so resplendent in plumes and satins and gorgets embellished with silver and gold were slipping away, having learned that 'the boisterous winds and merciless sea had neither affinity with London delicacy or court bravery'. 'This storm hath killed the harts of many voluntary Gentlemen', observed Sir William Browne, commander of the *Mary Rose*, and young William Slingsby, in a letter to his father, a Yorkshire squire, gave a fuller picture of the deteriorating situation:

> . . . dayly our fleete growes les and les, our vittayles spending, and our Soldyers Sycke and weake; some crave leave to go for there infermyties, and some go wythout leave indispyte of all proclamations prohibiting them: many of the Gentylmen adventurers alredy gone, some for sea sicknes discoradged by the last storme, some out of a more base disposytion hopeles now to make profytt of the vieadge [cf. the Cadiz loot of the previous year], for whych end only they undertooke the Jorney, & som for want, long synce spent to the uttermost.[1]

It is gratifying to note that Slingsby, even though by his own account the most seasick of the six hundred men aboard his ship, did not pull out. Neither did the Earl of Southampton.

The day after Howard returned with his ships, Essex, followed soon after by Southampton, hastened to Court to consult with the Queen and her Privy Council. A drastic revision of plans was agreed upon. Essex at his return dismissed all his troops except Vere's thousand professionals, consolidated his remaining supplies in a much-reduced train of victuallers,

[1] Daniel Parsons, ed., *The Diary of Sir Henry Slingsby . . . and Extracts from the Family Correspondence* (London, 1836), pp. 250-1.

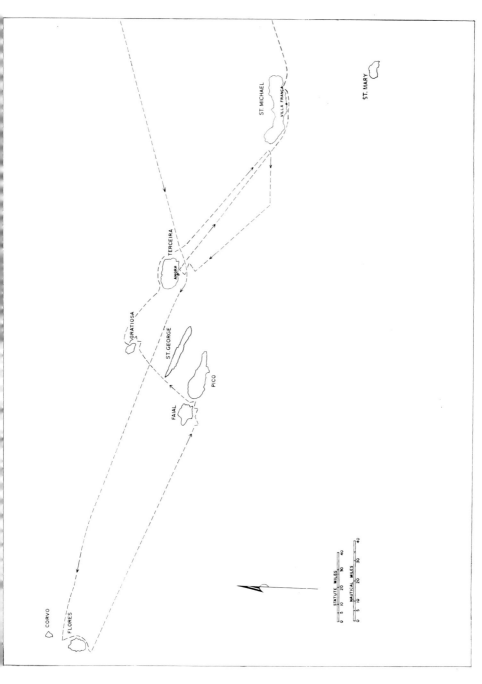

THE EARL OF ESSEX'S COURSE ON THE ISLANDS VOYAGE OF 1597

and abandoned all hope of capturing Ferrol. Instead he set out, on August 17th, to see if with the aid of fireships he could destroy the fleet in Ferrol harbour before heading to the Azores in quest of the plate fleet.

Once again the fleet ran into bad weather. Shortly before dawn on August 24th the *Saint Matthew*, a former Spanish galleon and one of the largest ships in the fleet, lost her bowsprit and foremast. As the *Saint Matthew* was wallowing in her distress, the *Garland* was seen in the early morning light coming to her assistance. Southampton could not possibly take on board the seven hundred men on the larger ship, but he sent his pinnace to bring off its commander, Sir George Carew, with whomever he might select out of his company. Despite repeated urgings from Southampton, Carew, 'having a more tender care of the losse of his Honour, then of the hazard of his life, would not forsake the Ship',[1] and the *Garland* sailed on. A few days later at a council of war Essex and his chief officers decided to abandon the fireship raid on Ferrol. When, soon afterwards, one of Raleigh's captains arrived with word from a Plymouth pinnace that the Adelantado's warships had sailed from Corunna and Ferrol and were making for the Azores to convoy home the treasure fleet, Essex, completely believing a false report, ordered his own fleet to follow.

En route to the Azores, the English fleet was totally becalmed in tropic waters. John Donne has left us a vivid account of how the ships stood, rooted as still as the Islands they sought. In the 'calenture' the pitch ran from the seams, and the crews sweltered miserably:

> And on the hatches as on Altars lyes
> Each one, his owne Priest, and owne Sacrifice.
> *(The Calme,* ll.25–26)

When the English fleet reached Flores, the most westerly of the islands, Essex, had he been wise, would have adopted the tactics recommended by his naval advisers. Spreading his ships in a broad screen north and south, he would have sailed westward to meet the Spanish plate fleet, which was in fact already nearing the Azores. Unfortunately, the men closest to Essex were soldiers not sailors, and had no taste for days of dull patrolling and seasickness in mid-Atlantic. Hostile to what they termed 'the idolatry of Neptune', they longed for action on land. Accordingly, when the English caught a pinnace sailing in advance of the plate fleet, the military men eagerly swallowed the fiction (invented by the Spaniards to save their comrades) that the plate fleet might not be sailing that year and that, in any event, it would by-pass the Azores and take a more southerly route. Eagerly the military men urged Essex to leave just a few nimble vessels

---

[1] Sir Arthur Gorges' account of the Islands Voyage in *Purchas His Pilgrimes* (Glasgow, 1907), XX, 51.

scouting in case the flota did show up, and to let them get on with the attractive job of plundering the islands. Essex yielded to their urging. While the Dutch ravished the island of Pico, the English sailed eastward and, after defeating the Spanish garrison at Fayal, went on to Gratiosa.

Here Essex learned that a 'great ship' had been sighted coming in from the West Indies. Ordering his ships to sea, he assigned to each of his squadrons a different route in a skilful plan to intercept the flota and deny it sanctuary under the guns of the fort at Angra. These plans had scarcely been made and the orders given, however, when word came that the great ship had proved to be a small English bark. Countermanding his orders, Essex instructed his fleet to sail southward to the island of St. Michael which he hoped to take from the Spaniards. Apparently this change in instructions failed to reach four of the warships which that night sailed well west of Terceira while the rest of the fleet held their course east of that island.[1] One of these four detached warships was the *Rainbow*, commanded by that veteran seaman Sir William Monson.

About midnight Monson encountered twenty-five ships heading eastwards. There was hardly any wind and Monson, getting into his ship's boat, was able to have himself rowed up to the strange ships. His hail revealed that they were Spanish. He had encountered the elusive treasure fleet. Sensibly refusing Monson's challenge to fight, the Spaniards with their precious freight made for Angra. Monson fired off cannon and lit signal fires on the *Rainbow*, desperately hoping to engage the attention of the twelve English ships which he believed to be following him.

When daylight came, Monson found himself a little over two miles behind the plate fleet. Behind him was a Spanish straggler, a frigate, and in the distance beyond it was the *Garland* with the Earl of Southampton. Coming up with the frigate, Southampton ordered the *Garland*'s guns brought into action, captured and looted her, took off her crew as prisoners and left her ready to sink. Looking over the frigate's sailing instructions, the English discovered that if only Essex had maintained his patrol off Flores he would inevitably have encountered the plate fleet there. Meanwhile two more sail had come into view, and these Southampton's prisoners declared to be Spanish. The Earl in great excitement prevailed upon a sceptical Monson[2] to abandon the pursuit of the twenty-five known Spanish ships and join him in engaging the newcomers, which

[1] Discrepancies and contradictions are to be found among the contemporary accounts of what happened at Gratiosa and how these four ships happened to be where they were. I have followed Sir Julian Corbett, *The Successors of Drake* (London, 1916), pp. 202-3, in accepting the version in Essex's official account of the Islands Voyage. (v. *Purchas His Pilgrims*, XX, 28-9.)

[2] Monson, *Naval Tracts*, II, 27-9.

turned out to be the *Mary Rose* and the *Dreadnought*, the last two of the four English warships on the westerly course. These had heard Monson's cannon during the night and had been steering in the direction of the sound. Although reinforced, Monson had by now no chance of overtaking the Spaniards. Essex had not detached ships to block the approach to Angra harbour, and the treasure fleet slipped into safety under the protection of the guns of the Spanish forts.

Furious at the escape of this enormous prize, Southampton and the other captains came aboard the *Mary Rose* for a council of war summoned by Sir Francis Vere, the senior officer present. Here they decided that once night fell they would send in their small boats, cut the cables of the nearest Spanish ships, and get them out to sea with the help of the strong off-shore wind. Despite the darkness the Spanish, alert in their watch, saw the English coming and frustrated the attempt.

Essex had not yet landed his troops at St. Michael when a pinnace brought him news that the treasure fleet was at Angra. Hastening thither with all his forces, he had the good fortune to intercept a rich galleon which, with its two escorting warships, had left Havana a day after the treasure fleet. These he captured. Later it was claimed that the value of these prizes did more than 'countervail the expense of the whole voyage', but the profit was as nothing compared with the silver, valued at ten million pesos,[1] which now lay at Angra. Arrived there, Essex found the galleons unloaded and close warped under the forts which had been strengthened with men and cannon landed from the fleet. In their councils of war the English frantically considered one scheme after another for getting at the treasure. Common sense finally convinced them that none of their projects had any likelihood of success. Angra, one of the strongest of King Philip's bases, was too strong for the English. In the end, the fleet simply sailed away. Juan Gutierrez de Garibay, the Spanish commander, could thank his luck or his saints that he had reached Terceira safely. Sir Richard Hawkins, a prisoner on one of the Spanish ships, later told Essex that his fleet had been strong enough to have overwhelmed the Spanish if he had engaged them at sea.

Back at St. Michael, the English military men, dropping their plans to seize the capital of the island, contented themselves with taking Villa Franca, 'a pretty neat town' some distance down the coast where they took 'tolerable Booty'.

Autumn was now far advanced, and the English were low in provisions and morale. Reluctantly they faced the fact that there was nothing for

---

[1] Monson, op. cit., II, 66-7. Over the years various English squadrons attempted to capture the plate fleet. None of them succeeded. When, in 1628, the Spanish luck ran out, the winner was a Dutch admiral, Piet Heyn.

them to do but to head home. Essex ordered Villa Franca evacuated. When Sir Francis Vere still had about five hundred of his soldiers to embark, he found a Spanish force approaching. In his *Commentaries* Vere has left us a vivid little picture of how, warned of possible trouble, Essex came riding into the market-place accompanied by Southampton and other lords and gentlemen on foot, and took tobacco there while mulling over the situation. As things turned out, the threatened battle did not occur. After some skirmishing the Spaniards retired and let the English complete their withdrawal.

It was customary at the end of a campaign to award honours. Essex, aware that his expedition had on the whole been decidedly inglorious, was less lavish than usual and conferred only about half a dozen knighthoods at St. Michael. One of the new knights was the Earl of Southampton.

On October 15th, just one month after their arrival at Flores, the English sailed from St. Michael to the sound of an ironic salute from the Spanish guns. On their way back to England they ran into a tempest which left them limping into port 'scarcely two ships in company'. Essex should have been grateful for this storm, however, for it inflicted much greater damage on the Adelantado who, informed that Essex was in the Azores, had sailed from Ferrol with the double intent of making a landing near Falmouth and of lying in wait for the returning English ships. Caught off the Scilly Islands by this storm, eighteen of the Spanish ships were lost and others saved themselves only by putting into English ports and surrendering.

Essex returned from the Azores stripped of the prestige that he had won at Cadiz. But the English, hungry for anything that looked like a victory, made much of Southampton's successful encounter with the Spanish frigate. Writing to Sir Robert Sidney, Rowland Whyte enthusiastically reported: 'My Lord of Southampton fought with one of the Kings great Men of Warre, and suncke her.' Over the years the tale improved with the telling. In 1624 Gervase Markham gave the following glorified account of the episode:

> This brave *Southampton* light upon the King of *Spaines* Indian Fleete laden with Treasure, being about foure or five and thirty Saile, and most of them great warlike Gallioons; they had all the advantage that sea, winde, number of ships or strength of men could give them; yet like a fearefull heard [herd] they fled from the fury of our Earle; who notwithstanding gave them chase with all his Canvase; one he tooke, and sunke her, divers hee dispierst which were taken after, and the rest he drave into the Iland of *Tercera*, which was then unassaileable.[1]

[1] Collins, II, 72; *Honour in His Perfection*, sig. D4R.

Marriage

W HILE SOUTHAMPTON was away on the Islands Voyage Elizabeth had summoned one of her infrequent parliaments. It was
the first to have been called since the young earl had come of age
and he made his initial appearance in the House of Lords on November
5th. Somebody, perhaps Lord Burghley, took pains to draw Southampton
into the business of the House, and he was appointed to no less than six
committees, including those for the increase of mariners, the relief of the
poor, and the defence of the realm. If Burghley had hoped that these
appointments would make a diligent Parliament man out of Southampton
he was disappointed. Southampton became a chronic absentee. He was
present for only one of the twelve sittings of the Lords after the Christmas vacation.[1]

Personal problems may have contributed to Southampton's frequent
absences from Parliament. He had returned from the Azores to find that,
despite the endeavours of his attorneys, his finances were still critical.
Surveying the situation, he decided to live quietly abroad for a few
years. To pay off the most pressing of his debts and to raise money
for his travels, he resorted to the last expedient of a lord nearing bankruptcy—he began selling land. Late in 1597 and early in 1598 he sold
his manors of North Stoneham, Portsea, Copnor, Corhampton and
Bighton.[2]

Travel on the Continent was regarded as part of the education of
Elizabethan noblemen and Southampton, with his mastery of Italian and
French, was well equipped for what would become in time the Grand
Tour. Moreover, a particularly good opportunity had presented itself.
Sir Robert Cecil was being sent to France to try to keep Henri IV from
making peace with Spain. In Cecil's company, Southampton would have
an easy entrée into the French court.

One unhappy consequence attended this highly sensible decision to
spend a couple of years abroad—Southampton would be separated from
his mistress. Elizabeth Vernon was quite unable to conceal her anguish.
On January 14th Rowland Whyte wrote Sir Robert Sidney:

[1] For the record of attendance see *Journals of the House of Lords*, II, 192 ff.
[2] *v. W.P. 225* and *V.C.H., Hampshire*, III, 39, 192, 248, 479.

> I heare my Lord *Southampton* goes with Mr. Secretary to France, and soe onward on his Travels; which Cours of his, doth extremely grieve his Mistres, that passes her Tyme in weeping and lamenting.[1]

Further complicating Southampton's life at this time was a quarrel with Master Ambrose Willoughby, one of the Queen's gentlemen who, in the course of his duty, had evicted the Earl from the Presence Chamber. In another of his invaluable newsletters to Sidney, Rowland Whyte reported the incident thus:

> The quarrell of Lord Southampton to Ambrose Willoughby grew upon this: that he with Sir Walter Rawley and Mr. Parker being at primero in the Presence Chamber, the Queen was gon to bed, and he being there as squier for the body, desired them to give over. Anone after he spake to them againe, that if they wold not leave, he wold call in the gard to pull down the bord; which Sir Walter Rauley seing, put up his money and went his wayes. But my Lord South Hampton tooke exceptions at hym betwen the tennis court wall and the garden, strooke hym, and Willoughby puld of some of his locke. The Queen gave Willoughby thanckes for what he did in the Presence, and told hym he had done better yf he had sent hym to the porter's lodge, to see who durst have fetcht hym out.[2]

There may have been more to the incident than the Queen knew. Writing a few days earlier, Whyte had mentioned that 'unkindness' had arisen between Southampton and his mistress 'occasioned by some Report of Mr. Ambrose Willoughby'. Whyte had added that it seemed to him that Southampton was 'full of discontentments'. Poor devil, near bankruptcy, having an emotional crisis with Elizabeth Vernon, and out of favour with the Queen, he had plenty of reasons for being unhappy.

In consequence of the Willoughby trouble, the Queen for a short while forbade Southampton to present himself at her court. He was allowed back by the end of the month, when Whyte reported that Southampton, Lord Compton, Lord Cobham and Sir Walter Raleigh had complimented Cecil on the eve of his embassy with 'Plaies and Banquets', an interesting first direct linking of Southampton with the players.

At the beginning of February Whyte reported that Southampton was still having difficulties with the two women, his sovereign and his mistress:

> My Lord of *Southhampton* is much troubled at her Majesties straungest Usage of hym. Some Body hath plaied unfriendly Partes with him. Mr. Secretary hath procured hym Lycense to travell. His faire Mistress doth wash her fairest Face with many Teares. I pray God his Going away, bring her to no such Infirmity, which is, as yt were, hereditary to her Name.[3]

In another letter Whyte mentioned that there were secret reports that Southampton was about to marry his 'faire mistress'.

Contributing to Southampton's moodiness and irritation was the Queen's delay in granting him permission to leave England. Finally on

---

[1] Collins, II, 81.   [2] H.M.C., *De L'Isle MSS.*, II, 312.
[3] Collins, II, 87.

February 6th, just four days before Cecil was to set out, she gave Southampton her licence to travel beyond the seas for two years, taking with
him ten servants, six horses, and £200.[1] That same day Southampton
purchased a letter of credit from Humphrey Basse of London for 1,000
crowns in gold or silver, payable to him in Rouen. The next day, hastening
to get everything in order before his departure, Southampton signed a new
power of attorney which freed Hare, Gage and Chamberlain from the
restrictions in the earlier deed and, significantly, left them free to sell any
of his estates.[2] There was also a final leave-taking with Essex. Two days
after Cecil set out on his embassy Whyte wrote to Sidney:

> My Lord of *Southampton* is gon, and hath lefte behynd hym a very desolate
> Gentlewoman, that hath almost wept out her fairest Eyes. He was at *Essex* House
> with 1000 [Whyte's code number for the Earl of Essex], and there had much
> privat Talke with hym for two Houres in the Court below.[3]

Since Essex was Elizabeth Vernon's cousin and had secured her position
as a Maid of Honour, the lady's highly compromised position no doubt
occupied a large part of the conversation between the two earls.

Crossing together in the *Vanguard*, Cecil and Southampton landed at
Dieppe on February 15th. Writing from there on February 19th Cecil
recounted something of the hardships of their passage:

> I passed very well, but the Vanguard will roll. I could come no nearer [to
> Dieppe] in her than four leagues, which gave us a great row. Young Norris was
> very sick, as were Ch. Blount, Vane, Tufton, Cope, Wotton, and others in the
> Crane and Quittance. I only fear lest Sir Thos. Wilkes prove worse. . . .[4]

The worsening condition of Cecil's fellow ambassador, Wilkes, in fact
detained the whole company until March 2nd when he died at Rouen. It
seems highly likely that Southampton, whiling away the time, that day
sent off from nearby Dieppe the letter of compliment to Essex which we
noted earlier as wrongly assigned to 1591.[5] Resuming their journey, Cecil
and his company reached Paris on March 6th. From there they proceeded
to Angers to see Henri IV. Reporting to the Privy Council on his first
meeting with the French king, Cecil mentioned that at its conclusion he
begged Henri 'to permit me to present to him the Count of Southampton,
who was come with deliberation to serve him'. When next morning Cecil
presented Southampton to Henri, the King 'very favourably embraced
and welcomed the Earl'.

In April when Cecil returned to England, his mission a failure, the Earl
of Southampton remained at the French court where one of the attractions
was the company of the fugitive brothers, Sir Charles and Sir Henry

[1] *Cal. S.P. (Dom.)*, 1598–1601, p. 19.   [2] *W.P. 582* (see p. 58 *supra*).
[3] Collins, II, 90.   [4] *Cal. S.P. (Dom.)*, 1598–1601, p. 30.
[5] *v.* p. 34 *supra*.

Danvers. After peace had been made with Spain, Henri IV no longer needed the services of such English military adventurers at his court. Accordingly Southampton and the Danvers decided to leave France and visit Italy. The decision had hardly been made when it was laid aside because of good news from England. Ever since their flight three and a half years earlier, the Danvers brothers had assiduously sought their pardon so that they could return home to England. Sir Henry had paid a fine of £2,000 levied against him. Sir Charles had made himself useful to Cecil by sending him intelligence from the Continent. Commendatory letters had been secured from the French king and English notables such as the Earl of Shrewsbury visiting his court. Their widowed mother was said to have married the Queen's kinsman Sir Edmund Carey only in order to secure pardons for her sons. At last, all of these efforts had their reward. At the end of June Sir Charles and Sir Henry received their pardons upon condition that they paid £1,500 damages to Sir Walter Long, brother of the murdered man. In Wiltshire the bells rang for joy in the parishes where the Danvers had their estates, and in Paris the brothers prepared to go home. An illness of Sir Henry's delayed their departure, but in mid-August they were on their way. With them they bore a letter to Cecil from Southampton, in which the Earl said that he was postponing his departure for Italy until one of the brothers (apparently Sir Henry), having attended to necessary business at home, could accompany him thither.[1]

On August 30th John Chamberlain, the letter-writer, noted that Sir Charles and Sir Henry Danvers had arrived in London. The date is significant for at this very time the Earl of Southampton, in complete secrecy, also returned to England. Indeed, it is quite possible that he crossed in the company of the Danvers brothers, perhaps passing as their servant. The letter to Cecil, which was a little late in being delivered, may have been only a blind to cover his surreptitious journey.

The reason for Southampton's return was sufficiently scandalous. At some date, now quite impossible to determine, he had learned that as a consequence of one of their last meetings, Elizabeth Vernon was pregnant. In similar imbroglios with Maids of Honour, Raleigh earlier had married Elizabeth Throckmorton, and the Earl of Pembroke later was to refuse to marry Mary Fitton. Southampton had to decide what his own course would be. Two considerations must have made Southampton

---

[1] *Salisbury MSS.*, VIII, 313. For the identification of Sir Henry see Stopes, p. 121. For evidence of Southampton's whereabouts the previous month we have a letter from the English ambassador at Paris to Sir Robert Sidney forwarding 'certain Songes', which were delyvered me by my Lord of Southampton' with a message, 'His Lordship commendeth himself most kindlie to you, and would have written to you yf it had not ben for a little Sloathfullness.' Collins, II, 102.

ELIZABETH, COUNTESS OF SOUTHAMPTON

By permission of the Duke of Buccleuch

incline towards marriage: his feelings for the girl, and his friendship for
her kinsman Essex. Over against these was the compelling fact that, if
ever there was a nobleman who needed for his wife a wealthy heiress
whose fortune would repair his finances, it was Southampton. Poor
Elizabeth Vernon could bring him hardly anything. Probably the decision
went first one way and then the other. What is clear is that late in August[1]
he arrived in London and sent the following letter to Essex:

> The chief cause of my coming to this town is to speak with your Lordship. If you
> will be therefore pleased to give me assignation of some time and place where I
> may attend you to find you alone, so that I may come unknown, I will not fail
> to perform your appointment.
>   I beseech you to let me know your will by this bearer, either by letter or word
> of mouth, and bind me so much unto you as not to take notice of my being here
> to any creature till I have seen you.[2]

What happened at this interview we do not know, but about this time, at
some unknown place, Southampton married Elizabeth Vernon.

On September 3rd, after Southampton had started back to Paris, Queen
Elizabeth learned of his secret marriage. Since she had never had any
great liking for Southampton and fornication with the Maids of Honour
always hit her on a raw nerve, her response was predictably vehement.
Immediately she had a letter sent to Sir Thomas Edmondes, her ambassador in Paris, ordering him to seek out Southampton and instruct him to
return to England at once.[3] By the same post Cecil sent his own letter to
Edmondes with a friendly warning that Southampton would only make
matters worse if he did not return promptly.[4] He also wrote directly to the
peccant Earl, officially informing him of the Queen's commands:

> I am grieved to use the style of a councillor [of a member of the Privy Council
> acting in a disciplinary role] to you, to whom I have ever rather wished to be the
> messenger of honour and favour, by laying Her Majesty's command upon you;
> but I must now put this gall into my ink, that she knows that you came over very
> lately, and returned again very contemptuously; that you have also married one
> of her maids of honour, without her privity, for which, with other circumstances
> informed against you, I find her grievously offended; and she commands me to
> charge you expressly (all excuses set apart) to repair hither to London, and adver-
> tise [make known to her] your arrival, without coming to the Court, until her
> pleasure be known.[5]

Meanwhile there was the new Countess of Southampton to be punished.
For news here we have a letter of September 7th:

> ... the Queen was informed of the new Lady of Southampton and her adventures,
> whereat her patience was so much moved that she came not to the chapel. She
> threateneth them all to the Tower, not only the parties but all that are partakers
> of the practice [plot]. It is confessed that the Earl was lately here and solemnized
> the act himself and Sir Thomas German [Jermyn] accompanied him in his return

[1] N. E. McClure, ed., *The Letters of John Chamberlain* (Philadelphia, 1939), I, 44.
[2] *Salisbury MSS.*, VIII, 373.   [3] *Stowe MS.*, *167*, f. 40r.
[4] Ibid., f. 38r.   [5] *Cal. S.P. (Dom.)*, *1598–1601*, p. 90.

to Margate. . . . I now understand that the Queen hath commanded that there shall be provided for the novissima countess the sweetest and best appointed lodging in the Fleet [prison].[1]

Back in Paris and presumably unaware that his secret was already known, Southampton wrote to Cecil telling him of his marriage and asking him 'to find the means to acquaint Her Majesty therewith, in such sort as may least offend'.[2] Any hopes he might have nurtured that Cecil could save him from the Queen's anger ended a few days later when he received Cecil's letter giving him the Queen's orders to return, and a visit from Edmondes with the same message.[3]

At this point Southampton had to make an important decision. Should he hasten to England, make the fullest possible demonstration of his obedience, and cast himself upon the Queen's mercy even though her anger was still fresh? Or should he find excuses for delaying his return, and hope to slip back into England unheeded when his trespass had been largely forgotten? His friends in England were clear that his better course was the former. He would only harden the Queen's hostility if he disobeyed her direct command. Unfortunately Southampton was not ready to face the music. Instead of returning, he wrote to Cecil begging him to tell the Queen that he could not possibly return until he had received some money, now due to him, which would enable him to pay for his passage back to London. Southampton might solemnly declare 'this is unfeignedly true'[4] but, if it were, all he had to do was to inform Edmondes of his destitute condition and ask him to ship him home with his next courier going to England. In a letter to Essex, who seems to have been paying for the maintenance of the new Countess of Southampton in the Fleet,[5] her husband enlarged on the subject of his poverty:

> I protest unto your Lordship I scarce know what course to take to live, having at my departure let to farm that poor estate I had left for the satisfying my creditors and payment of those debts which I came to owe by following her [the Queen's] court, and have reserved only such a portion as will maintain myself and a very small train in the time of my travel.[6]

Late September and October found Southampton at the lowest point that his fortunes had yet reached. Ignoring warnings from his friends that

---

[1] *S.P. 12/268/50.* I have modernized the spelling.

[2] See his letter of September 9th to Essex, *Salisbury MSS.*, VIII, 353.

[3] Writing to Essex on September 12th, Southampton told him of receipt of Cecil's letter. On September 13th Edmondes wrote to Cecil, telling of his interview with the Earl and reporting the latter's great grief at having incurred Her Majesty's anger. *v. Salisbury MSS.*, VIII, 357–8 and *Stowe MS., 167*, f. 46r.

[4] *Cal. S.P. (Dom.), 1598–1601*, pp. 100–1.

[5] I take this to be the significance of an item among Essex's disbursements for 1598 of an unspecified amount paid by Essex on warrant for 'the Countess of Southampton', *Salisbury MSS.*, VIII, 554.

[6] *Ibid.*, VIII, 357.

his continued absence from England would only exasperate the Queen, he hung around Paris wasting his money gambling. One of Cecil's agents informed him that Southampton was losing money at such a rate (the Marshal of Biron had alone won 3,000 crowns from him in a few days) that if he did not quickly leave France he would find himself without estate or reputation both there and in England.[1]

Things could not long continue in this fashion. On October 6th Southampton finally wrote to Essex that he had decided to make his submission to the Queen 'as soon as I can with conveniency leave this country'.[2] A couple of weeks later Edmondes informed a correspondent that Southampton was on the point of departure. At the beginning of November Southampton was back in London, lodged in the Fleet prison. About a week later John Chamberlain wrote to his friend Dudley Carleton, 'The new Countess of Southampton is brought a bed of a daughter.'[3] The babe was christened Penelope after Lady Penelope Rich, Essex's sister. Essex sought to get the father released as speedily as possible, but Southampton did not secure his freedom until the end of the month.

During his weeks in prison, Southampton fretted over a crisis with his mother. She had long been on intimate terms with Sir William Harvey, terms so intimate that rumour frequently had them married. Southampton asked Essex to make enquiries. Essex was already going through an abrasive experience trying to get the Dowager Countess to accept her new daughter-in-law. (Only a few weeks before he had received an emotional, half-incoherent letter from Southampton's mother, fairly wallowing in self-pity and complaining of her son's unkindness.[4]) Essex however undertook to interview both Southampton's mother and Harvey about their situation and plans. He told the Dowager Countess of the 'discomfort and discontent' that she was causing her son, and warned her 'how dangerous and miserable a life she was like to lead' if she persisted in alienating herself from Southampton. Speaking to Harvey, Essex warned him that he risked making an enemy of himself as well as of Southampton and assured him that any marriage with the dowager would be a 'mischief' to the son.[5]

At some point in these proceedings the serpentine Lord Henry Howard,

---

[1] *Salisbury MSS.*, VIII, 358.

[2] Ibid., VIII, 392. Rowse in his *Shakespeare's Southampton*, p. 127, has Southampton make a non-existent second secret crossing to England in late September, but this is the consequence of his failure to take proper heed of a question mark set before '1598' by the H.M.C. editor when printing a letter from Essex to Southampton bearing only the date '25th of Sept.' (*Salisbury MSS.*, VIII, 557). The letter was in fact written in 1600. *vide infra*, p. 107, footnote 1.

[3] Chamberlain, *Letters*, I, 52.   [4] *Salisbury MSS.*, VIII, 379.

[5] Ibid., XIV, 79–81.

who enjoyed a reputation as a smooth negotiator, was brought in to recon-
cile mother and son. An undated report from Howard to Essex survives.
Written in Lord Henry's characteristically over-elaborate style, it is
larded with unctuous compliments to Essex and exhibits such super-
abundant tact as never to mention the lady by name, referring to her
simply as 'my honourable friend'. Howard had been assured by his
honourable friend that she was not married, but she had spiritedly added
that she 'would ever reserve her own liberty to dispose of herself where
and when it pleased her'. She said also that 'she hoped that her son would
look for no account of her proceedings in the course of marriage that
made her so great a stranger to his own'. Finally she said that, if there was
to be a marriage, Harvey would discuss the matter with Southampton
first—that is, unless she decided to forbid him to do so.[1]

In the end Southampton apparently agreed to his mother's remarriage.
After all he had no reason for not thinking well of Harvey. The marriage
occurred early in the next year. On January 31st, 1599, John Chamberlain
reported to his friend Carleton, 'Sir William Harvies marriage with the old
countesse of Southampton that have lien smothering so longe, comes now
to be published.'[2] Shortly afterwards, as a sign of his good will, Southampton granted Harvey and his wife permission to cut timber on the lands
which his mother held during her lifetime under the jointure made by
his father.[3]

---

[1] *Salisbury MSS.*, VIII, 371–3.   [2] Chamberlain, *Letters*, I, 67.
[3] *W.P. 1000*, February 20th, 1599.

CHAPTER VIII

A Sometime General of the Horse

IN THE SPRING of 1599 the Earls of Essex and Southampton, landing in an Ireland of which less than one-twentieth remained under English control, brought with them the largest army that Queen Elizabeth had ever sent beyond the borders of her England. The events that had led to the dispatch of this expedition were rooted in recent Irish history.

Early in 1593, old and worn out, Turlough O'Neill, head of one of the greatest of the Irish tribes, had surrendered his chieftainship to his cousin Hugh. Seated on a stone throne in an open field in Ulster, then the most Gaelic portion of Ireland, Hugh had been invested with the title of 'O'Neill', (or 'The O'Neill' in English usage). The new chieftain had been educated in England and had received from Queen Elizabeth the title of Earl of Tyrone. For twenty years he had been one of the most valued of the chieftains through whom England maintained some kind of rule over the wild Irish who dwelt beyond the five anglicized counties that lay within the English Pale. Provided by England with 'butter captains' to train his soldiers, Tyrone had been the trusted mainstay of the English authority in northern Ireland. That situation now changed. Tyrone, advanced by his people to the chief position among them, was determined to end English encroachments. Secretly he entered into a confederacy with the other great northern chief, The O'Donnell. Young, but already the inveterate enemy of the English, Hugh Roe O'Donnell became much more dangerous now that he was allied with one of the great men of Irish history. Tyrone at the time of his defection was in his mid-forties. To O'Donnell's vehemence and single-minded hate he added patience, foresight and authority, providing effective leadership for the Irish rebels not only in Ulster but in the other provinces of Connaught, Munster and Leinster. He was, says Cyril Falls, 'the chief who ruled, the politician who understood, the strategist who planned, the tactician who commanded'.[1] In 1595 he openly took the field against the English, who in June issued a proclamation in the name of Queen Elizabeth declaring him a traitor.

Tyrone's great achievement was the forging of something approximating a contemporary European army out of the wild sporadic levies used in native Irish warfare. Admittedly Tyrone's cavalry, still using stirrupless

[1] 'Hugh O'Neill the Great', *The Irish Sword* (Winter, 1963), VI, 97.

cushions for saddles and hence incapable of mounting massed charges like the heavier English horse, were comparatively ineffective. But it was a different story with his infantry. Taking his native Irish kerns and his mercenaries (both 'redshanks' imported directly from Scotland, and 'gallowglasses' recruited from warrior Scottish families that had settled in Ireland), Tyrone formed them into companies on the English model, disciplined and even uniformed them. Aided partly by a thin trickle of gold and weapons from Spain, he armed many of them with pikes and muskets instead of the traditional battle-axes of the gallowglasses and the darts, bows and arrows of the kerns. Thus Tyrone supplied himself with a mobile professional army, ready to move to any part of Ireland, far more dangerous than the local levies which served only in their home areas. The English soon realized that a new kind of enemy confronted them. Not long after Tyrone defected, Sir Henry Wallop reported to Cecil that the Irish were no longer limited to ambushes and hit-and-run tactics, but could face the English in open battle, well-armed and well-trained.

Tyrone reaped the reward of years of painstaking preparation when, on August 14th, 1598, he won a great victory which set the church bells pealing in Spain and confronted Queen Elizabeth and her Privy Council with a major crisis. What happened that day was that Tyrone and O'Donnell, turning aside from their siege of an English fort on the banks of the Blackwater River, fell upon an English relief column as it approached under the command of Tyrone's brother-in-law but inveterate enemy, Sir Henry Bagenal. Bagenal had almost 4,000 foot, among them 600 veterans who had served in the Low Countries, and 300 horse. The rebels had a force which was rather larger. English mistakes, and the terror among them when some of their gunpowder exploded, brought disaster upon their army. Considerably fewer than half the English regained the safety of Armagh from which they had set out that morning. Bagenal and thirty of his officers lay dead on the battlefield. It was the greatest victory that the Irish had ever achieved over the English.

The effects of the Battle of the Yellow Ford were predictable. The rest of Ireland, which had been comparatively quiet following the suppression of earlier rebellions, flared into revolt. The whole of Ulster was lost to the English almost at once. Connaught burst into flame. The Leinster rebels went right into the English Pale, burning and slaying within sight of Dublin. The Irish in Munster rose in support of a column of 4,000 men that Tyrone dispatched into their country. The English president of the province, Sir Thomas Norris, retired within the walls of Cork leaving the rebels to 'Kill murther, ravish and spoil without Mercy'. Typical was the experience of the poet Edmund Spenser who found his home, Kilcolman Castle, set ablaze in the night. With the surviving members of his

family he fled destitute, joining the torrent of terrified English colonists heading for Cork. When winter set in, the English had in fact lost control of Ireland and were holding out only in a few cities and castles and their immediate vicinities. All that was needed to end completely the English occupation of Ireland was for King Philip of Spain, who had already sent officers to survey possible invasion ports, to land a force equipped with the artillery that Tyrone lacked.

Elizabeth and her ministers energetically set themselves to re-establish their rule over Ireland. They realized that an all-out effort was required, no more the 'softe kind of warre, that hath bin to, to long used in this Realme'.[1] That winter the instructions went out to the muster-masters in the shires to raise the largest army ever assembled for the Irish wars. Speculation centred about who would be appointed Lord Lieutenant of Ireland and charged with ending the rebellion. Success would bring fame and glory; but Ireland, that 'moist rotten country', was notorious as a place where English forces decayed and English governors lost their reputations. Various possible commanders were suggested at meetings of the Privy Council, only to be declared unsatisfactory by Essex. In the end, Essex reluctantly agreed to head the army of reconquest himself. After the semi-fiasco of the Islands Voyage he had failed to re-establish himself as the Queen's favourite, and Sir Robert Cecil and his allies were effectively keeping him from political power. To Essex, the only career that seemed open to him was that of England's leading soldier. Hence he accepted the post despite the warnings of his wiser friends.

As 1598 drew to its close, London was full of rumours as to whom Essex would appoint as his principal officers. On December 8th John Chamberlain wrote that the Earl of Southampton was to be Essex's General of the Horse. The report was premature to say the least. A few months later, in a private interview at Richmond, the Queen told Essex that she did not want Southampton to have any command in the army preparing for Ireland. Seeking to comfort a sorely disappointed Southampton, Essex wrote that he had not argued the matter with the Queen since, once he had his commission, he would be empowered to appoint his own officers anyway, and 'then if she quarrel with me, her wrong is the greater and my standing upon it will appear more just'.[2] A more fatuous course, and one more sure to anger the Queen, could hardly be imagined. Essex's relations with his sovereign were in fact already getting worse. Though at times she could be gracious and kindly to Essex, she was more often nagging, suspicious and shrewish.

[1] John O'Donovan, ed., 'Docwra's Relation of Service Done in Irelande', *Miscellany of the Celtic Society* (Dublin, 1849), p. 200.
[2] *Salisbury MSS.*, XIV, 107.

On March 12th, 1599, Essex received his commission appointing him viceroy and commander-in-chief in Ireland. Although this commission gave him very extensive powers, among them the anticipated privilege of appointing his own officers, the Queen could not refrain from continued interference and needling. When Essex asked that his stepfather, that experienced soldier Sir Christopher Blount who was to be marshal of the army, be given a place on the Council of Ireland, the Queen refused. When Essex, angered, said that in that case he would not use Blount's services at all, she commanded him to take Blount as marshal but not as councillor. With things going this way it is little wonder that Essex regretted that he had ever accepted the Irish command, and termed it mere 'banishment and proscription to the cursedest of all islands'.[1]

On March 27th the new viceroy set out from London for Ireland. With him he took the Earl of Southampton, the Lords Grey, Audley and Cromwell, and several hundred other gentlemen volunteers who hoped to win honour amid the Irish bogs. Essex might no longer be cherished by the Queen and a good part of her court, but he was still the darling of the Londoners. The citizens thronged the way for miles to cheer him as he and his brilliant entourage rode forth towards St. Albans, the first stopping-place on their journey. But right at the outset there was an ill omen:

> . . . when hee and his companie came foorth of London, the skie was very calme and cleere; but before hee could get past Iseldon [Islington] there arose a great blacke cloude in the northeast and sodainely came lightening and thunder, with a great shower of haile and raine; the which some helde as an ominous prodigie.[2]

A few days later he was writing a letter to the Privy Council, full of complaints and self-pity, to advise their lordships they 'might rather pity me than expect extraordinary success from me'.

Arrived in Wales, Essex and his officers were magnificently feasted at Mostyn Hall. Here Southampton had perhaps his first real contact with the Celtic world when the family bard sang in Welsh a song he had composed honouring 'Earl Essex, an Earl above all other commanders'.[3] There were disappointments as well as festivities at Mostyn. Essex found that part of his army assembled there was not yet ready to embark, and headwinds prevented his own departure. Frustrated, he headed for the splendid Edwardian castle at Beaumaris, arriving at dead of night after riding at low tide across the shallow straits separating the Island of Anglesey from the mainland. A few days later the Queen's ship Popinjay after a rough and dangerous passage brought him to Ireland.

On April 15th, 1599, the Earl of Essex received the sword of state in

---

[1] Nichols, The Progresses of Queen Elizabeth, II, 701.
[2] Ibid., II, 702.   [3] Tenison, Elizabethan England, XI, 44.

Dublin. With that ceremony his commission came into effect. The same day, using the powers he now enjoyed, he appointed Southampton his General of the Horse. To Southampton's friend Sir Henry Danvers he gave the rank of Lieutenant of the Horse. The young Earl of Rutland, who had slipped out of England despite the Queen's orders to remain at home, was given the rank of Lieutenant-General of the Infantry. Calling for a report from the Council of Ireland, Essex received the next day a detailed table showing that there were exactly 19,997 rebels in Ireland. A second survey prepared independently a few days later set the figure however at 29,352.[1] Nobody can say that the Elizabethans did not seek for exact figures in their statistics.

In Ireland the Earl of Southampton was in a country very different from England. Riding out from Dublin, he would see for the first time the Irish peasants clad in their saffron-dyed tunics, and their long Irish cloaks. In remoter areas he would see them still wearing their hair in the traditional 'glyb' or massive roll over the forehead. He would find them amid the bogs passing with their strange three-pegged pattens over terrain impassable for other men. Perhaps he would have his ear assaulted by the howling of a wake, so unnerving an uproar that a stranger 'at the first encounter would beleeve that a company of *Hags* or *hellish Fiendes* were carrying a dead body to some infernall Mansion'. Some Irish ally of the English may have taken the English lords to an Irish banquet or 'coshering' where they would hear 'their lowsie Bardes and Rythmers' sing songs (fortunately in unintelligible Irish) 'usually in commendation of Theft, or Murther, of Rebellion, of Treason . . . making repetition how many Cowes they [had] stolen, how many murthers they had committed, how many times they had rebeld against their Prince, and what spoiles and out-rages they had done against the English'. Perhaps in some field he would see a peasant in his poverty still following the practice of hitching his plough to his horse's tail rather than fashioning a harness. He would be shocked to see the dirty Irish, with their superstition that it was unlucky to wash a milking vessel, using milk pails 'furred halfe an inch thicke with filth'.[2] Probably he ended up, like Barnaby Rich, wondering how the Irish 'invironed with England, Scotland, France and Spaine' could remain 'more uncivill, more uncleanly, more barbarous and more brutish in their customes and demeanures, then [sic] in any other part of the world that is knowne'.[3]

Before leaving England Essex had shared with the Queen and Privy

---

[1] v. *Cal. S.P.* (*Ireland*), *1599-1600*, p. 14, and John Dymmok, *A Treatice of Ireland* (Dublin, 1842), pp. 27-30.

[2] Barnaby Rich, *A New Description of Ireland* (London, 1610), *passim*.

[3] Barnaby Rich, *A Short Survey of Ireland* (London, 1609), sig. B1.

Council a beautifully simple plan for his military operations in Ireland. Since the rebellion had its source with Tyrone, that egregious traitor would be crushed first. Speedily leading his 16,000 foot and 1,300 horse into Ulster, Essex would attend to Tyrone. Then he would restore order in the rest of Ireland.

In Dublin Essex found that matters were not quite so simple. Up in the north there would not be forage for his cavalry until June. Moreover, the supplies of food and the transport needed to put so large a force into the field had not been acquired. Beleaguered English garrisons in Leinster and Connaught were desperately appealing for relief. Much of his army needed seasoning. The Council in Dublin was unanimously against taking the army north. Under the circumstances Essex concluded, probably rightly, that the first thing was to 'settle Leinster in some reasonable state', and while doing so to travel to the border of Munster and confer with the English president of that province. After sending a full report on the situation that he had found in Ireland, Essex received the approval of the Queen and her councillors for his altered course of action. Reinforcing the garrisons that guarded the Ulster border, Essex prepared for a campaign in the south.

On April 28th a list was drawn up of the cavalry officers who were to serve in the coming campaign under the command of the Earl of Southampton, the General of the Horse. They were Sir Henry Danvers, Lord Mounteagle, Sir J. Leigh, Sir William Warren, Captain Garret Moore, and Captain Fleming.[1] Since they were to take with them only selected squadrons of light horse out of their companies, Southampton had a mere 160 English horsemen at his disposal. Even his own company did not go with him on this expedition. Left stationed at Carrickmayne, five miles from Dublin, it later proved notably unsuccessful in heading off a rebel raid that left Carrickmayne in ashes. Along with his small force of English cavalry, Southampton had with him in the field about 300 Irish horsemen, useful chiefly for reconnaissance and light skirmishing.

On May 9th Essex, accompanied by the English cavalry, set out from Dublin for Naas where over 2,000 English infantry had already been mustered. After reviewing his little army Essex proceeded to a rendezvous with the Earl of Ormonde, who brought with him almost a thousand of his Irish. At Athy the blockhouse-type castle, set at one end of the bridge across the Barrow, surrendered after a mere show of resistance and the army, having crossed unmolested, headed north to revictual the beleaguered garrison at Maryborough (Port Laoise). Travelling from Athy through country firmly held by the rebels, Southampton had his first encounter with the enemy:

[1] *Salisbury MSS.*, IX, 145.

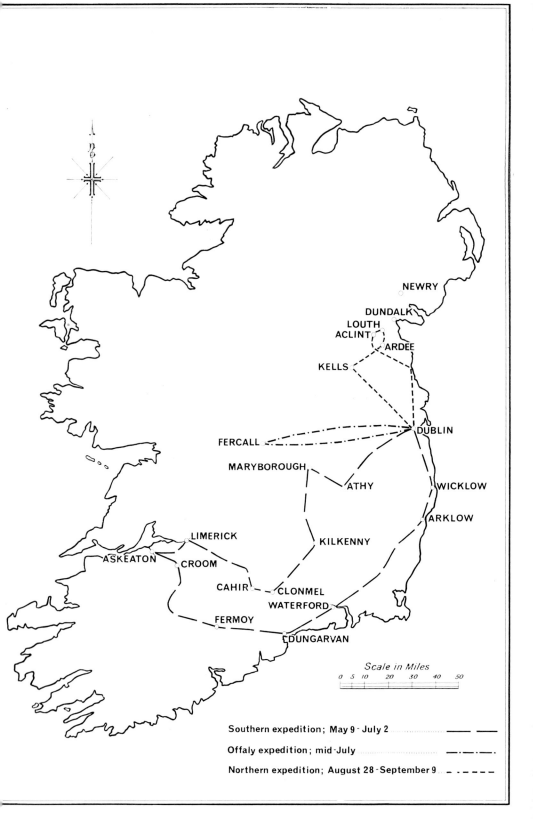

NEWRY

DUNDALK
LOUTH
ACLINT
ARDEE

KELLS

FERCALL

DUBLIN

MARYBOROUGH

ATHY

WICKLOW

ARKLOW

LIMERICK

ASKEATON
CROOM

KILKENNY

CAHIR
CLONMEL
WATERFORD

FERMOY

DUNGARVAN

Scale in Miles
0 5 10 20 30 40 50

Southern expedition; May 9 - July 2 .... —— ——

Offaly expedition; mid-July .... —·—·—·—.

Northern expedition; August 28 - September 9 .. –·–––––

THE JOURNEYS OF THE EARLS OF ESSEX
AND SOUTHAMPTON IN IRELAND IN 1599

... the rebell presented himself about 200 stronge, in the sight of the Castle Reban (a howse of Capt. Leas, a myle from the armie), whiche, upon sighte of the Earle of Sowthampton, who hasted towardes them in moste soldierlike order, withe a small troope of horse and foote, retyred themselves to theire bogges, and from thence to theire woodes.[1]

During this operation a most unfortunate incident occurred. Some of the cavalry were under the command of the high-spirited young Lord Grey of Wilton who, carried away by excitement, pursued the retiring rebels some distance into the adjacent woods after Southampton had ordered him to turn back. Grey's impetuosity and disobedience could have played into the hands of the rebels, who habitually tried to lure the English into the bogs or forest where they fought at a disadvantage. Southampton, moreover, saw Grey's act as a challenge to his own authority. Discipline had to be maintained and Essex, when Southampton laid a charge of disobedience against Grey, felt that he could not ignore the incident. He made the punishment as minimal as he could, sentencing Lord Grey to a single night spent in the custody of the Marshal of the Army (Sir Christopher Blount) who was charged with policing the camp; but Grey never forgave either Essex or Southampton the humiliation. In the next few years this enmity was to have dangerous consequences for both the earls.

Having reinforced and resupplied Maryborough, the army moved southward through country firmly held by the rebels who showed themselves in great numbers on the flanks of the slow-moving English army. Near Ballyknockan the English found themselves marching down a road with a steep, densely-wooded hill on one side and a boggy valley on the other. It was one of those 'passes' where an army could not have its usual protective screens of soldiers out on each of its flanks, but had to move forward in a long cramped column. Trouble was always to be expected in such places and, sure enough, the rebels launched an attack while the long train of English supply wagons was lurching through the defile. The chief brunt of the fighting fell on Sir Henry Danvers who, with thirty horsemen, covered from the rear the main body of the army. Two English officers were killed and two others wounded in this engagement. Essex, in his dispatches, put his losses among his common soldiers at only three or four slain and six or five wounded, and he claimed to have inflicted much greater losses upon the rebels. The Irish told a somewhat different story:

Owny O'More with 500 foot met him [Essex] in Leinster as he was leading his army through a narrow pass and routed his reaguard and killed some soldiers and officers and carried off some spoils amongst which were many helmet plumes, whence the place is to this day called the Pass of the Plumes.[2]

[1] Sir John Harington, *Nugae Antiquae* (London, 1804), I, 270–1.
[2] Matthew J. Byrne, trans., *Ireland Under Elizabeth . . . being a portion of the history of Catholic Ireland by Don Philip O'Sullivan Bear* (Dublin, 1903), p. 124.

Without further molestation the army continued southward, into the safety of the Earl of Ormonde's country. Here, while the soldiers rested for a few days at Clonmel, 'after their toyles and weerynes caused as well by theire daylie marches, as allsoe by the fowlenes of the weather',[1] Essex and his staff were Ormonde's guests in his castle at Kilkenny. Hither Essex summoned Sir Thomas Norris, president of adjacent Munster, to report on conditions in that province. Norris painted such a dismal picture of the situation of the English there that Essex was persuaded to extend his march into Munster.

Moving westward into Norris's province, Essex made first for Cahir Castle, one of the strongest fortresses in Ireland, which was held by the rebels. Negotiations failed to persuade the garrison to surrender but permitted Sir Henry Danvers, one of the emissaries, to make a useful survey of the castle's strength. Essex moved up his army and commenced a siege.

For a while everything went wrong for the English. Negligently, much of the equipment and supplies needed for a siege had been left in Waterford. The Irish managed to slip a new force into the castle and greatly strengthen the small garrison there. When Essex's two small pieces of artillery belatedly arrived and were installed on the east bank of the River Suir, opposite the island on which the castle stood,[2] the one was soon out of action with a broken carriage and the other 'cloyed with a bullet'. Essex himself was racked with sickness, suffering from a chronic bowel complaint which he blamed on constant worry about the hostility of the Queen and the intrigues of his enemies back in England.

The Irish had their troubles, too. One of the worst of their mistakes was allowing the English to establish a force in the orchard which lay south of the castle on the same small island in the river. Although one of Tyrone's allies, a claimant to the earldom of Desmond known to his enemies as the 'Sugan [straw rope] Earl', arrived with considerable forces on the west bank of the river, he completely failed to raise the siege. In the end, just when the English were ready to launch a three-pronged assault against the castle, the Irish abandoned it, seeking to slip away unobserved in the night. Their movements were spotted by an English sentry and murderous fire at short range massacred the defenders as they cast themselves into the river and sought to swim to safety.

We do not know what role Southampton played at the siege of Cahir, though assuredly he must have been present. His young friend the Earl of Rutland received his knighthood from Essex the day after the castle

---

[1] Lambeth Library, *Carew Codex 621*, f. 126r. The *Calendar of the Carew Manuscripts* (London, 1869) omits much that is interesting in this journal of Essex's expedition.

[2] For a drawing made at the time of the siege, showing the location and layout of the castle and the placing of the English forces, see Tenison, *Elizabethan England*, Vol. XI, Plate 8. The original is at Hatfield.

was taken. This was probably given him as a consolation for being sternly ordered home by Elizabeth who was angry at his surreptitious crossing to Ireland.

The capture of Cahir Castle, an action whose importance seems to have been unappreciated in England, was the main achievement of the campaign. Some indication of the effect on rebel morale is provided by the fact that when Edmund FitzGibbon, a principal rebel known as the White Knight, heard of the fall of Cahir, he abandoned and ruinated his own castle at Balliboy and took to the forests and bogs rather than risk such a siege himself.

Moving on from Cahir through tempestuous rains, the English repaired the broken bridge at Golden and travelled down a broad rich plain past Tipperary, and arrived at last at Limerick, one of those cities which, with a small adjacent area, had remained in English hands. Here Essex was received with welcoming orations and an appeal for help from the Queen's garrison besieged in the large and important castle at Askeaton. Pausing a few days to rest his troops, Essex plunged even farther westward to the relief of Askeaton. At Adare, amid some of the loveliest countryside in all Ireland, Essex found the Sugan Earl with ensigns flying and more than 2,000 Connaught men and mercenaries set to block his advance. However, because of either treachery or incompetence (the Irish themselves could never decide which), their carefully prepared assaults were not carried through. The English pushed on with minimal losses. On June 10th Essex was at Askeaton, his farthest point west, watching the long-delayed supply boats coming up the river. That same day in England the Privy Council dispatched to Essex a letter so devastating in its effect upon him and Southampton as to require quotation in full:

> Her Majesty having of late received certain knowledge that your Lordship hath constituted the Earl of Southampton General of the Horse in Her Majesty's army under your charge, with which she is much displeased, hath given us commandment to signify her mind in that behalf, and to let your Lordship understand that she thinketh it strange, and taketh it offensively, that you would appoint his Lordship to that place and office, considering that Her Majesty did not only deny it, when she was here moved by your Lordship to that purpose, but gave you an express prohibition to the contrary, that he should not be appointed thereunto. This commandment being (as Her Majesty saith) so precisely delivered unto you, and the same being now so manifestly to the world to be broken, hath moved Her Majesty to great offense in that respect. And therefore Her Majesty's pleasure is, that you do no longer continue him in that place and charge of General of the Horse, but to dispose of it to some other, as you shall think good, Her Majesty esteeming it a very unseasonable time to confer upon him any so great place, having so lately given her cause of offence towards him. This being Her Majesty's direction and commandment unto us, we do deliver it by this our letter as from herself, wherein having discharged our duties, we are sorry for the occasion.
>
> The Court at Greenwich, 1599, June 10.[1]

[1] *Cal. S.P. (Ireland), 1599–1600,* p. 62.

The Queen must have known for over a month of Southampton's appointment. She cannot have been pleased with it, but she had not made an issue of it. There can be no doubt as to what caused her action at this late date: news had reached her of Lord Grey's punishment for disobeying Southampton's orders. No doubt Grey's friends presented this to her in a light very disadvantageous to the General of the Horse. At the end of June George Fenner writing to Venice passed on the news: 'The Earl of Southampton is not commanded to return, but only to leave his office of general of the horsemen, by means of a quarrel between him and Lord Grey.'[1]

Unaware of the bad tidings en route to them, Essex and Southampton with a weary dispirited army began a long circuitous march back to Dublin. The very first day of their homeward journey found the English engaged in extensive skirmishing with the rebels. The fighting reached a climax after Lord Grey, commanding the cavalry in the vanguard, raced off several miles in pursuit of some rebels who had shown themselves. The vanguard thus drawn off, the Irish swarmed out of a great forest that lay to the right of the English army, bearing down on the screen of musketeers that guarded the main column on that side. Fighting off the Irish, Essex managed to get his baggage train safely into open country. Then, the rebels persisting in their attack, he called for a charge by his cavalry. When Sir Henry Norris riding at the head of his troop was mortally wounded, his place was taken by the Earl of Southampton who all this day had been 'in much daunger whiles he expected [awaited] in the head of his troopes (all the tyme of the skirmysh) opportunyty to charge the rebells'.[2] Southampton's charge having driven the Irish back into the forest, the English continued without further molestation to Croom, where they camped that night.

Onward the little English army held its way. Leaving Fermoy behind, it headed towards the Sugan Earl's stronghold at Conna, which Essex intended to storm. Approaching Conna, Sir Henry Danvers became a casualty in one of the intermittent skirmishes along the way. John Dymmok, who seems to have been on this expedition, gives us an account of the incident:

> . . . Sir Henry Danvers, endeavouring to save certen stragglers which had indiscreetly ingaged themselves, was shott in the face, the bullet passing to the roote of the lefte eare, where yt still resteth, but without any anoyance, he beinge allreadye perfectly recured.[3]

As it turned out, Essex had no occasion to stop at Conna, for the Sugan Earl, having no taste for siege like that at Cahir, abandoned and burned his castle at Essex's approach.

[1] *Cal. S.P.* (*Dom.*), *1598–1601*, p. 225.
[2] Dymmok, *A Treatice of Ireland*, p. 37.   [3] Loc. cit.

Late in June the army reached Waterford, where several days were spent getting the army across the inlet, its wagon train being 'farre greater then ever heretofore in this Countrey followed so fewe fighting men'.

From Waterford, Essex and his army slowly worked northward past Enniscorthy and Fernes. Once again they were entering country held by the rebels. These hung on their flanks but avoided battle while the English ravaged the countryside, burning all the villages that lay in their way. On June 30th there was a running fight as the English drew near to the fortified town of Arklow, held by forces loyal to the Queen. At a ford about three miles from Arklow two hundred of Essex's 'olde Irish souldiers' got so deeply engaged with the rebels that Essex had to send in Southampton with some cavalry to extricate them. After this little action, the Irish ceased their attacks and the English, with Arklow in sight before them, began to relax the discipline of their march, their long column straggling out at excessive length and, though in 'no disorder, yet in some unreadiness'. The result was almost fatal for Essex. His route northward to Arklow led across firm open ground which gradually sloped upwards to a wide hollow between two rounded hills. Riding with his staff to the eastern one of these, Essex saw a spectacle which must have almost unnerved him. Beyond this open valley his route lay down a bush-covered escarpment and then opened on to the seashore, the beach serving as a road for the last half-mile to the gates of Arklow. Along this stretch of shore Essex's vanguard, completely out of touch with the main body of the army, was racing happily towards the gates of the town. Meanwhile some eight or nine hundred rebels, who had lain hidden in the woods inland from the beach until the vanguard had passed, were now emerging to attack Essex's wagon train and its escort of some fifty foot soldiers as it came down from the higher ground. Looking northward, Essex could see where 'our poore men stood amazed at the gaze, ready to be cutt in peeces'.[1]

Confronted with this crisis, Essex sent a rider galloping southwards with orders to the officer commanding the rearguard to hasten to the rescue with all his cavalry and three hundred of his light infantry. Meanwhile, moving forward with the available infantry, Essex sent Southampton, with the little group of mounted gentlemen who comprised his own staff, down the descent that led to the seashore. On the level land below, Southampton was to interpose his little squadron between the rebels and the English wagon train as it continued towards Arklow. Unfortunately, once Southampton had taken up his position with the sea on his right

[1] *Carew Codex 621*, f. 138r. This manuscript, a copy of Essex's own dispatch recounting the fight near Arklow, is confusing in some of its topographical references. In what follows I have done my best to explicate matters in the light of a visit that I made to Arklow in 1964, when I viewed the scene with Essex's account in my hand.

hand, he found a bog lying between himself and the woods on the left from which the rebels were attacking. Essex, advancing meanwhile by a more inland route, came down from the heights with his small force of foot and took up a station a few hundred yards east of Southampton.

The rebels, seeing the English general facing them with only some eighty foot soldiers, raised their screeching war-cry and launched an attack. Southampton, realizing Essex's peril, threw caution to the winds and ordered his horsemen, about twenty-four in number, to charge across the bog. Attacked thus unexpectedly on their flank the Irish withdrew with casualties to the safety of the woods. Southampton then swung his horsemen around and rode back to the safety of firmer ground, only to discover that he had left three of his gentlemen mired in the bog. Gallantly he repeated his charge in an attempt to rescue them before the Irish kerns could move in and cut their throats. One of the three, a Master Cox, had in fact already received mortal wounds. Another, Captain Constable, was severely wounded, and Robert Vernon, a kinsman of Southampton's wife, had been caught beneath his fallen horse. Among those who rode with the Earl of Southampton that day were Lord Mounteagle, Sir Thomas Jermyn, Sir Alexander Radcliffe, Sir Thomas Egerton, Captain Poolye, Master George Manners, Master Carew Reynolds, Master Heydon, Master Thomas West and Master Bellingham.

The worst of the crisis was now over, for sixty mounted men from his rearguard had reached Essex. Thirty of these horsemen were at once sent to reinforce Southampton. Some serious fighting had still to be done —Essex had to repel an attack by the Irish cavalry, and Southampton had to make another charge when the Irish infantry attempted to mount an attack against him. Southampton had just successfully completed this charge when the Earl of Ormonde, the delinquent commander of the vanguard, aware at last that the main army was in trouble, arrived from Arklow with some of his troops. The Irish saw that their opportunity had passed and broke off the engagement.

Back in Dublin two days later, Essex was confronted with a difficult decision concerning Southampton. The Queen's orders for the dismissal of Southampton from his post as General of the Horse had been received, and Essex was strongly inclined to disobey them. After all, Southampton had given him devoted service in a long and difficult campaign, service that had been climaxed by his bravery and initiative in the fight outside Arklow. Moreover, the Queen's belated opposition to Southampton's appointment was indirectly the result of the disciplining of Lord Grey for disobeying Southampton's orders, and Essex knew that (no matter what Grey's friends had told the Queen), Grey was guilty of insubordination. Southampton had received a letter from Lord Henry Howard, putting all

the blame on the Grey faction and mentioning that for five days Secretary Cecil had held up the dispatch of the Queen's orders, hoping that she would change her mind. Howard said that the feeling at court was that Essex would not dismiss Southampton pending an appeal to the Queen on his behalf.[1] Essex followed just this line. On July 11th he wrote to the Privy Council asking for the revocation of Southampton's dismissal. Some of his arguments were a bit specious, as when he declared that the Queen had not forbidden him to give Southampton his post but had only 'shewed a dislike of his having any office'. He was on stronger ground when he pleaded that to be successful in Ireland he must be free to choose his own instruments. With more honest indignation than tact, Essex mentioned what he took to be the real reason for the Queen's hostility towards Southampton:

> Was it treason in my Lord of Southampton to marry my poor kinswoman, that neither long imprisonment, nor no punishment besides that hath been usual in like cases, can satisfy or appease; or will no punishment be fit for him, but what punisheth not him, but me, this army, and poor country of Ireland?[2]

On July 19th the Queen, determined to have Southampton stripped of his command, wrote a stinging personal reply to her viceroy. After disposing of Southampton as 'one whose council can be of little, and experience of less use', and recalling the 'old lively arguments' Essex had once used against Southampton, she expressed her amazement that Essex should:

> ... dare thus to value your own pleasing in things unnecessary, and think by your private arguments to carry for your own glory a matter wherein our pleasure to the contrary is made notorious.[3]

Essex responded in typical fashion. After relieving Southampton of his duties, he abolished the post of General of the Horse.

When Southampton left for the Irish war he had lodged his wife and daughter at Essex's Staffordshire home of Chartley, in company with the latter's sister, Lady Penelope Rich. Four of the Countess's letters to her husband in Ireland have survived[4] and these leave no doubt that Elizabeth

---

[1] *Salisbury MSS.*, IX, 340–2.

[2] W. B. Devereux, *Lives and Letters of the Devereux, Earls of Essex* (London, 1853), II, 45.　　　　　　　　　　　　[3] *Cal. S.P. (Ireland), 1599–1600*, pp. 100–1.

[4] These are now in the Cecil Papers at Hatfield (Vol. 100, items 61, 91 and 116; Vol. 101, item 16). Also at Hatfield are two letters written to Southampton at this time by Lady Rich (Vol. 99, item 167, and Vol. 101, item 25). The dates of these letters are limited to the day of the month. Some of these letters have been subsequently endorsed, apparently in the last century, with the date '1603'. This dating is obviously in error since in one of the Countess's letters mention is made of Lady Rich writing to her brother, Essex, who died in 1601. In one of her letters, dated July 9th, Lady Rich writes, 'I am sorry for Sir Hary Davers hurte, though I hope so littell will not marr his good face.' Clearly she is referring to the wound Sir Henry had sustained near Conna. All these letters will be found calendared, though under the wrong year, in *Salisbury MSS.*, Vol. XV. The correct dating was first established by Mrs. Stopes (p. 156).

Vernon had turned into a most loving wife. Written in her large schoolgirl hand and filled with strange spellings, these letters breathe the very accents of devoted love. All have the same opening, 'To my deare lorde and only Joye of my life', but the expression was much more than a stereotype. For Bess, Southampton was the man 'whom I do and ever wil most infinitly and truly love'.[1] Both of them eagerly desired a son to succeed to the family title. Apparently Bess believed that she was pregnant when her husband left for Ireland, and she was a most unhappy woman when she had to tell him that they had entertained false hopes. When his kindly reply was received, all Bess's love burst forth:

> . . . my longing to heare of you was never mor, nor my desir infiniter to have from your selfe sartain knolige that you weare parfitly wel in the Jurney which I harde you wear gone [the Leinster–Munster expedition], and I protest unto you the assurance your letter givefs me, that you ar so is the nues that my harte only delites in, and which caries as much contentment unto it as it can posabelly injoye whilst you ar from me whom I far dearlier love then it is posabel with any wordes to expres, the witnis you give me in your letter that you ar not trobelt for my not being as I protest unto you I infinitly desirde to have bin is much to my content, and though I be not nowe in that happi state yet I doute not but that in good time and for the infinit confort of you and my selfe god wil bles me with bering you as many boayes as your owen harte desirs to have. . . . [2]

Thus the Countess in a letter of June 11th. A month later she was writing about a difficulty that had arisen at Chartley. Lord Rich was becoming insistent that his wife return to him, and Lady Rich felt that she would have to go by St. Bartholomew's Day (August 24th) at the latest. Reluctant to leave the Countess without her company, Lady Rich had invited her to accompany her to Lord Rich's country house at Lees in Essex. Anxiously Bess asked for her husband's instructions, declaring 'wher you likedest i shulde be that plas shal be most pleasing to me and all others to be in most hatful to me'. What Southampton's answer was we do not know, but probably he approved the move. Let us return to Ireland and his adventures there.

Essex, having rested his troops after the southern campaign, set out in mid-July on a tour through Offaly and West Meath, accompanied as always by Southampton. There was skirmishing in which Southampton saw more action, but little was achieved. In the area of Fercall,[3] Essex and Southampton met with Sir Conyers Clifford, the President [governor]

---

[1] This phrase occurs in a totally undated letter, outside the Irish group, written by the Countess at a time when her husband was expected to visit her shortly. (*Cecil Papers*, 109/31; *Salisbury MSS.*, XV, 203–4.) Mrs. Stopes assigned this to March or April 1599, but I find it hard to accept this date.

[2] *Cecil Papers*, 100/91.

[3] Dymmok, p. 43. Gervase Markham in his panegyric of Southampton in *Honour in His Perfection Riding* (sig. D4v) declares Southampton 'reduced the Country of Fercall'.

of Connaught, who had reached the rendezvous only after some savage fighting. To reinforce Clifford, Southampton's company of a hundred horsemen was attached to him, apparently under the command of Sir Griffith Markham. Southampton himself remained with Essex and was not present on August 5th when the rebels in the Curlew Hills routed the little army, slaying both Clifford and his second-in-command, Sir Alexander Radcliffe. What honour the English won that day fell to Markham, 'who chardging the pursewers in the head of my Lo: Southampton's troope gave securitie to this ignominious flight'.[1]

Back in Dublin, Essex gave way to desperation and despair when he received the news of Clifford's disaster. Well he might. His Offaly expedition had resulted in nothing more than the capture of 500 cows and 60 'garrans' [small Irish horses]—he, the resplendent English viceroy, had been reduced to the level of a raiding Irish chieftain. Sir Christopher Blount, his stepfather, detached to revictual Maryborough once more, had been very seriously wounded in that operation. He had failed to keep for his friend Southampton his now thoroughly deserved command of the cavalry. Cahir Castle, whose capture had been the most notable achievement of his long southern campaign, had been retaken by the rebels and its English garrison slain.

The Queen, who even before this loss had regarded the long Leinster–Munster journey as quite unjustified, was reportedly saying that she had paid £1,000 a day so that Essex could 'go in progresse'. Meanwhile Lord Grey had arrived back in the English court to join the host of enemies whom Essex saw poisoning the ears of his sovereign with slanders against him and his army. As for the attack against Tyrone in his Ulster fastness, Essex knew that he simply did not have the resources to carry this through to success. Worst blow of all, the Queen, to goad him into undertaking that campaign, had written him that 'till the northern action be tried' she was cancelling his permission to return to England whenever he saw fit, for personal consultation with Her Majesty.

Bogged down hopelessly in Ireland, denied access to the Queen while his enemies flocked to her court, Essex turned madly to thoughts of rebellion. The wounded Sir Christopher Blount had been carried to Dublin Castle, where Southampton had turned over his own quarters to him. Here, in the latter part of August, Blount was visited by Essex and Southampton. In 1601, after the failure of the Essex Rebellion, Blount gave an account of what transpired at that meeting. Essex had announced his decision to sail for Wales with between 2,000 and 3,000 of his best troops. Landing at Milford Haven, he would be joined by other forces and march on London. Leaving Blount to think things over, Essex withdrew.

[1] Dymmok, p. 47.

When he came for his answer the next day, Blount told him that since the enterprise would cost much blood he could not approve of it. He advised Essex to lay aside all thoughts of an invasion army and, if he had to return to England, to take with him only sufficient of his friends to protect him from his private enemies.

Southampton, according to his testimony in 1601, had heard nothing of this rebellious scheme until Essex broached it to Blount, and he too urgently dissuaded him from it:

> . . . Sir Chr. B. being hurt and lying in the Castle of D. in a chamber which had been mine, the Earl one day took me thither with him, where being none but we three, he told us he found it necessary for him to go into England, but, doubting [considering] there the power of his enemies, he thought it fit to carry with him for his security as much of the army as he could conveniently transport, to go ashore with them in Wales, and there to make good his landing with those, till he could send for more, not doubting but that his army would so increase within a small time that he should be able to march to Lond. and make his conditions as he desired. To which project I answered, that I held it altogether unfit. . . . [1]

Thus counselled, Essex put by his plans for invading England instead of Ulster.

We have no evidence concerning Southampton's own mood during this summer of 1599. He must have been angered by the Queen's action in stripping him of his generalship. Probably his temper was little improved by a letter from Sir Charles Danvers intimating, as tactfully as possible, that he could thank his own stiff-necked attitude for much of his trouble with Her Majesty. Urging Southampton to petition the Queen on his own behalf, Danvers expressed the hope that:

> . . . you would be moved to use your own pen in such a style as is no less fit for this time than contrary to your disposition, it being apparent that her Majesty's ill conceit is as much grounded upon the sternness of your carriage as upon the foundation of any other offence.[2]

With the idea of rebellion laid aside, Essex decided at least to go through the motions of mounting a campaign against Tyrone in the north. Even though eighteen colonels and captains, including Southampton, had signed a letter protesting the unfitness of his army, Essex set forth from Dublin on August 28th. Travelling through weather 'so monstrous wet as the like hath not been seen', he rendezvoused on August 31st with his sodden little army of about 2,700 foot and 300 horse in the vicinity of Kells.

From here Essex had intended to strike north-west and take in Cavan. Intelligence that Tyrone and his army were poised north-east of there, ready to sever Essex's lines of communication and march on Dublin,

---

[1] *Salisbury MSS.*, XI, 72–3. For Blount's account see ibid., XI, 48.
[2] *Ibid.*, IX, 246.

ended this scheme, and Essex turned in Tyrone's direction, apparently intending to base himself near Louth. Arrived at 'Ardolph' [Ardee?] on September 3rd, he found Tyrone and his forces in the woods outside that town. Skirmishing began when the English sent out working parties to fetch firewood. The next day, shadowed by the rebel army, Essex moved north to Louth, where he established his camp and awaited a victualling train from Drogheda. The day following, Essex sent one of his officers, Sir William Warren, into Tyrone's camp to negotiate for the release of a captain whom the Irish had recently captured in Offaly. Warren may have had additional matters to discuss with the Irish because about this time Thomas Lee, another of Essex's captains, had brought word from Tyrone that 'if the earl would be guided by him, he would make him the greatest man in England'.[1]

This same day Tyrone's trusted lieutenant, Henry O'Hagan, rode over to the English and announced that Tyrone wished to meet Essex for a parley. If Essex, now confronted by a rebel army more than double the size of his own, was ready to reach an accommodation with Tyrone, he at least behaved in public in a manner worthy of an English general. He told O'Hagan that if his master wished to meet him he would have his opportunity on the morrow when he would find him in the field at the head of his army. The next morning Essex marched his army out from their quarters and stationed them in formal battle array on the brow of a nearby hill. Only the slightest of skirmishing occurred, however, in which one of the gentlemen in Southampton's troop of horse was wounded. Tyrone, who knew his Irish were best at guerrilla warfare, was too wary to meet the English in their sort of battle on a battlefield of their own choosing. Essex, on the other hand, knew that it would be suicidal to try to fight his way into Ulster with Tyrone using every wood and bog and glen to harass and destroy him. The next morning, September 7th, he faced the inevitable, turned his army around and marched off in the direction of Kells.

Essex had not travelled more than a mile from Louth when O'Hagan once more made an appearance. Riding up to where Essex was travelling in company with Southampton and the rest of his staff, O'Hagan declared that Tyrone desired the Queen's mercy and begged Essex to turn aside from his route of march and meet him at the ford of Bellaclynthe which lay to the right of his route. Essex accepted the invitation, and so began the train of events that led finally led to his ruin.

Today Aclint bridge over the River Lagan, some six miles north-west of Ardee, stands where once travellers crossed by the ford of Bellaclynthe. Two gently rising hills face each other on either side of the shallow valley through which the Lagan winds. The southern side still has, hidden within

[1] Thomas Birch, *Memoirs of the Reign of Queen Elizabeth* (London, 1754), II, 493.

the trees which crown its summit, a deep circumambient trench, a defence-work dating from an earlier age. Arriving with a troop of his cavalry at this hilltop, Essex saw a rebel company on the brow of the northern hill and Tyrone, alone on horseback, stationary in the stream which lapped up to his horse's belly. Charging the faithful Southampton to see that no man came within hearing of their conference, Essex, unaccompanied, rode down to the water's edge and for the greater part of an hour[1] conversed in secret with the man he had been sent to destroy.

Later Essex acquainted Southampton with what passed in that parley and Southampton in 1601 recorded what he had been told:

> For his conference with Tyrone, I saw it with many more, but heard it not, he having commanded me, whom I was then to obey, to stay myself and hinder all others from approaching him. Afterwards he told me that the rebel in his discourse did blame him for following the war in her Majesty's service, inciting him to stand for himself and he would join with him. Which offer, he told me, he utterly rejected and did confirm it to me afterwards; otherwise, I protest before God, I determined presently [immediately] to quit him, my heart did abhor to think of such villainy. . . . [2]

At the end of their conversation the two leaders rejoined their retinues. Their parting was only brief, however, for shortly Con O'Neill, a bastard of Tyrone's, rode over with word that his father desired a further conference, one attended by some of the principal men on either side. Accordingly Essex rode down with Southampton and Sir Henry Danvers, Sir George Bourchier, Sir Warham Saint Leger, Sir Edward Wingfield and Sir William Constable. They remained on the bank while Tyrone, his brother Cormack, two of his sons-in-law, his secretary, along with a MacMahon chieftain from Monaghan, and Richard Owen, a liaison man with Spain, rode out into the river to come within speaking distance. Tyrone made a great show of his respect for the English, speaking with his hat off as a sign of deference. At this second conference it was decided that each side should appoint commissioners to meet on the morrow and conclude an armistice.

The next day Essex's representatives met Tyrone and his commissioners at another ford, close to Garrett Fleming's castle. The truce which was made there gave Tyrone everything he could have hoped to achieve under the circumstances. The rebels were to remain in possession of whatever they now held. No new garrisoned posts were to be set up. A very explicit time limit was set on the peace: it was to last by renewable six-week periods only until May 1st. A provision for its termination at any time upon fourteen days' notice played completely into Tyrone's hands. He was expecting an expeditionary force to arrive from Spain to assist him.

[1] Sir James Perrott, *The Chronicle of Ireland 1584-1608* (Dublin, 1933), p. 172.
[2] *Salisbury MSS.*, XI, 73.

Once it arrived, he could attack the English almost immediately without violating the oath which he now swore to keep the truce.

With the conclusion of this sorry bargain Essex, whose health was once more faltering, dispersed his army and headed to Drogheda to put himself under the care of his physicians. He must have felt sick at heart. Only ten weeks earlier he had proudly told Phelim MacFiach, when the latter sought to negotiate terms after the fight outside Arklow, 'hee would never suffer his Commission to be dishonored by treatinge or parling with rebbells'.[1]

On Sunday, September 16th, one of Essex's captains arrived at the English court with dispatches reporting the meeting with Tyrone, but not the terms of the subsequent truce. The next day Queen Elizabeth sent him back to Ireland with a blistering letter telling Essex just what she thought of his interview with Tyrone. She was amazed, she said, that he had not arranged things better than to spend half an hour in secret conversation with a traitor. She feared that, after all the great expense of sending Essex and his army to Ireland, his conduct of those forces would prove not only dishonourable and wasteful, but 'perilous and contemptible'. She informed him that, unless any terms arrived at with Tyrone provided for the stationing of English garrisons throughout his territory, she would think Essex had only pieced up a 'hollow peace'. And she ended with an absolute command that Essex was not to issue any pardon to Tyrone or enter into any terms with him until he had submitted the proposals to her in writing and had received her warrant to proceed with them.[2]

Essex's response to this letter was dramatic and dangerous. Falling back on the second of the two plans that he had discussed with Southampton and Blount the previous month, he assembled a troop of his captains and friends as a sort of personal bodyguard and with them embarked for England on September 24th. Just one hour before he sailed he met with the Council of Ireland, told them of his decision, handed over the sword of state to the joint custody of Archbishop Loftus and Sir George Carey, and transferred the command of the army to the mediocre but serviceable Earl of Ormonde. With Essex when he embarked were the Earl of Southampton, Lord Dunkellin, Sir Henry Danvers, Sir Christopher St. Lawrence, Sir Henry Docwra and a number of other knights and captains. For the most part they were desperate men, constantly exciting each other's fears and apprehensions, and ready for almost any kind of action.

[1] *Carew Codex 621*, f. 140v.   [2] Devereux, II, 73–5.

CHAPTER IX

Season of Discontent

TRAVELLING AT A CLIP which must have come near to setting a
record for the journey from Dublin, Essex seems to have reached
London late on Thursday, September 27th. Early the next morning he set out on the last lap of his journey to Nonsuch where Elizabeth
was residing with her court. He no longer had Southampton with him,
thinking no doubt that the presence of his erstwhile general of the horse
would do nothing to help him with the Queen.

Such was the desperate haste of Essex and the half-dozen followers
with him that, as soon as they had been rowed across the Thames to Lambeth, they commandeered horses which they found tethered by the
landing there, and at once started south towards Nonsuch. Lord Grey
was only a short distance ahead of them on the road. In all likelihood he
had learned of Essex's arrival in London and was bent on getting to the
Court ahead of him and alerting Secretary Cecil. On the road Essex was
overtaken by Sir Thomas Gerard. Gerard, aware that Grey was ahead,
sped on and asked him if he would not pull up and exchange greetings
with his former commander. When Grey refused, alleging he had business
at Court, Gerard frankly begged him to let Essex 'ride before, that he may
bring the first Newes of his Return hymself'. Grey asked if this request
was made by Essex himself, to which Gerard made the spirited but tactless reply, 'No, nor I thincke will desire nothing at your Hands.'[1] At this
Lord Grey resumed his dash towards Nonsuch.

When Gerard reported his failure, Sir Christopher St. Lawrence, a
ruffian whom we find involved in various challenges and affrays, offered
to take off after Grey, murder him on the spot, and then go on to Nonsuch
and murder Cecil. Fortunately Essex had enough sanity left to refuse the
offer.

Fifteen minutes behind Lord Grey, Essex with his followers galloped
up to Nonsuch. Spattered from head to foot with mud, he marched
straight to the royal apartments. Grey must have gone in search of Cecil,
for no word had yet reached the amazed attendants that Essex was back
from Ireland. No one tried to stop him as he strode through the Presence

[1] Letter of Rowland Whyte, September 29th, 1599, Collins, II, 128. Later Camden
in his *Annals* was to give another version, that Grey overtook Essex on the road and
'passed by him without any compliment'.

94

Chamber, through the Privy Chamber, and into the Queen's Bed Chamber. For months Essex had been persuading himself that all his troubles were due to enemies, led by Secretary Cecil, who while pouring their own slanders into her ears had kept him from seeing the Queen. He had convinced himself that if he could only see her alone and explain everything he would regain her favour. Now he had achieved the meeting he desired and stood in the presence of his startled sovereign, who had not yet completed her toilette and stood with her hair still hanging down from her head. For an account of what followed we are indebted to Rowland Whyte, who wrote the next day to his friend Sir Robert Sidney:

> ... he kneeled unto her, kissed her Hands, and had some privat Speach with her, which seemed to give him great Contentment; for coming from her Majestie to goe Shifte hymself in his Chamber, he was very pleasant, and thancked God, though he had suffered much Trouble and Storms Abroad, he found a sweet Calm at Home. 'Tis much wondred at here, that he went so boldly to her Majesties Presence, she not being ready, and he soe full of Dirt and Mire, that his very Face was full of yt. About 11 he was ready, and went up againe to the Queen, and conferred with her till half an Howre after 12. As yet all was well, and her Usage very gracious towards hym. He went to Dinner, and, during all that Tyme, discoursed merely [entirely] of his Travels and Journeys in *Ireland*, of the Goodnes of the Countrey, the Civilities of the Nobility that are true Subjects, of the great Intertainment he had in their Houses, of the good Orders he fownd there. He was visited franckly by all Sortes here of Lordes and Ladies, and Gentlemen. Only strangeness [coolness] is observed between hym and Mr. Secretary, and that Party. . . . Then he went up to the Queen, but found her much changed in that small Tyme, for she began to call hym to question for his Return. . . . [1]

This was, in fact, the last time that Essex was ever to be in the presence of Elizabeth. Her mind was hardening against him, and late that night she ordered him confined to his quarters.

The next morning the Privy Council considered the problems posed by Essex's unauthorized return to England. When they adjourned for dinner at noon, court observers were swift to mark how the division into two factions was signalled by who dined with Cecil and who dined with Essex. Those who went with Mr. Secretary were the Earls of Shrewsbury and Nottingham, Lord Thomas Howard, Lord Cobham, Lord Grey and Sir George Carew. Those who went to Essex's table were the Earl of Worcester and the Earl of Rutland, Lord Mountjoy, Lord Rich, Lord Henry Howard, Lord Lumley, and a number of knights.

At two o'clock that afternoon the Privy Council reconvened. Essex, brought before it, was required to answer to six charges:

> (i) His contemptuous disobedience to Her Majesty's instructions in returning to England
> (ii) His presumptuous letters written from time to time

[1] Collins, II, 127.

(iii) His proceedings in Ireland, contrary to the course agreed upon in England before he went there
(iv) His rash manner of coming away from Ireland
(v) His overbold intrusion the previous day into Her Majesty's bedchamber
(vi) His creation of an inordinate number of knights [more than seventy] while in Ireland.

After Essex left, the privy councillors talked things over for fifteen minutes and then went to the Queen to deliver their verdict. Elizabeth took a day to think things over. Then, on Monday, October 1st, she announced her verdict. She had decided against Essex. That afternoon he was sent to London, there to be a close prisoner in the Lord Keeper's residence, York House, forbidden even to walk within the walled precincts of its garden.

At York House Essex sank into a profound melancholy. He refused to open letters that arrived for him from Ireland. He announced that he would see no visitors except those sent to him by the Queen. And he became intensely religious. To Southampton, who jointly with Lord Mountjoy was administering his affairs, he wrote a long moralistic letter. After saluting Southampton as 'my friend, whose honour, whose person, and whose fortune is dear unto me', he gave a sermon on how Southampton must regard himself as accountable to God for all he possesses and how if he persists in serving his own worldly delights he will be guilty of perfidious treachery to God. Earnestly Essex besought Southampton to harken to 'the admonition of your truest friend', to keep better company, and not to dismiss these spiritual exhortations as the 'vapor of melancholie, and the stile of a prisoner'. In his conclusion, Essex grew more and more eloquent:

> It was just with God to afflict me in this world, that he might give me joy in another. I had too much knowledge when I performed too little obedience, and was therefore to be beaten with double stripes; God grant your lordship may feel the comfort I now enjoy in my unfaigned conversion. . . .[1]

Southampton and his wife meanwhile set up residence in Essex House. After about ten days the Countess of Southampton, to discourage the stream of visitors who called around to show their sympathy for Essex, headed off to the country, accompanied by Lady Rich. As for Southampton, Rowland Whyte reported that he and his friend Rutland 'pass away the tyme in London merely in going to plaies every Day'.[2] Essex's wife had given birth to a daughter and in intervals of play-going Southampton found time, along with the Countesses of Rutland and Cumberland, to be a godparent at the christening of the babe. It is indicative of Elizabeth's

---

[1] *A Collection of Scarce and Valuable Tracts . . . in . . . Public as well as Private Libraries, particularly That of the late Lord Somers*, 2nd ed. (London, 1809), I, 504.
[2] Collins, II, 132.

bitter feelings that when Essex's mother-in-law petitioned her to let Essex write a letter of comfort to his wife after her delivery, she refused the permission.

October was an uneasy month in London, for while Essex prayed and moped and sank deeper into sickness at York House, 'all Sortes of Knights, Captens, Officers, and Soldiers' who had followed him home from Ireland, filled the town, brawling in the taverns, loudly declaring their allegiance to their chief, and posing a threat of which the authorities were fully aware. Finally the Queen had Lord Dunkellin, Sir Christopher St. Lawrence, and the rest of them present themselves at court, spoke to them very graciously, but shortly thereafter ordered all the captains back to Ireland. About the same time she told Mountjoy that she intended to send him to Ireland, as the new Lord Deputy, to save the situation there. Matters being thus settled, the Privy Council petitioned the Queen to give Essex his liberty. Elizabeth rejected this request.

We come now to the problem as to why, month after month, Elizabeth kept the hapless Earl, miserably ill and unconvicted by any court, the prisoner of an increasingly impatient Lord Keeper Egerton. Essex's friends declared that it was all Cecil's doing. They pictured the little hunchback as a malevolent Machiavellian inspired by hateful jealousy for the magnificent Essex. In the reign of James I, the poetaster Robert Pricket gave a doggerel statement of the Essexian view of Cecil and his supporters:

> Then in that time an undermining wit,
> Did closely frame all actions jumply fit,
>   Molehills were to mountain raisde,
>   Each little fault was much dispraisde.
>   . . .   .
> Herein lay the secret ill,
> She sought to chide, they sought to kill.[1]

The truth was quite different. Cecil was an utterly devoted royal servant and one of the best administrators of the age. He understood men, and he knew that Essex, unstable and emotional, unorganized and unreliable, was not qualified for the positions of real political power which he so greatly desired. Cecil would have been criminally negligent as a royal counsellor if he had not made this conviction of his clear to Queen Elizabeth. On the other hand, he was not unappreciative of Essex's winning qualities of candour and generosity, gallantry and courage. He was quite prepared to let him cut a figure at court as the Queen's fancy man, or to exercise in positions of military command his modest talents in that area. All the evidence indicates that, if Essex had been able to see himself

---

[1] *Honors Fame in Triumph Riding*, sigs. B2v and B3r.

realistically and to accept the roles for which he was fitted, Cecil would have been glad to follow a policy of live and let live. However when Essex, egged on by his military bravados, decided that Cecil was his implacable enemy and began to plot his destruction, Cecil was simply following the course of self-preservation when he sought to terminate the Earl's career at Court, a course in which he was abundantly assisted by Essex's stupidity.

Ironically what chiefly kept Essex a prisoner in York House was the indiscretion of his own followers. Whenever the Queen appeared inclined to give him his freedom, some fool among his followers created a scene in a tavern, circulated a libel in the court, or got out a book with covert pro-Essex overtones, actions which threw Her Majesty into renewed anger and ended any impulse towards mercy.

With the Queen determined that Essex remain a prisoner, and with intermittent rumours that he was due to be transferred to the more secure custody of the Tower, Essex's friends began to consider ways of rescuing their chief. Sir Charles Danvers, coming to town at the beginning of November, found Southampton and Mountjoy debating whether to arrange Essex's escape to France, to raise a rebellion on his behalf in Wales, or to attempt by a sudden coup to secure control of the court. Southampton told Danvers that he himself was ready both to risk his life for Essex and to go into banishment with him. When Southampton asked Sir Charles how much he would venture in the cause, Danvers, mindful of how Southampton had stood by him after the Long murder, told him that he would venture 'the life he had saved, and my estate and means whatsoever'.[1] Sir Charles made only one stipulation, that he not be required to do anything against the person of Cecil, to whom he was much beholden.

As it turned out, Sir Charles was not yet required to risk his life for Essex. Southampton and Mountjoy finally decided that Essex's best course was to break out from York House and make for France. Southampton got this message through to Essex, along with a promise that he and Sir Henry Danvers would accompany him in his flight. The prisoner's reply was decisive: 'if they could think of no better course for him than a poor flight, he would rather run any danger than lead the life of a fugitive'. This reply expressed in part the lassitude of ill health. Even in Ireland Essex had not been a well man. Years of court intrigue and rivalry, and his constantly worsening relations with the Queen, had probably produced ulcers. To make matters worse he had contracted in Ireland the persistent dysentery known as the 'Irish flux'. At York House, weighed down with worry and despair and denied all forms of exercise, he began to sink into a

[1] Birch, *Memoirs of Queen Elizabeth*, II, 471-2.

really serious condition. At the end of November the Essex womenfolk returned to Essex House, probably to be on hand should they be required for a deathbed parting. Watching from afar with growing concern was Queen Elizabeth. On December 8th she sent eight physicians to examine the unhappy man and make recommendations. The medical men reported that 'they fownd his Liver stopped and perished; that his Intrailes and Guttes were exulcerated'. Sensibly they suggested Essex needed peace of mind, rest and recreation. Pensive and grieved, Elizabeth received the report and sent Doctor James to the apparently dying man with some broth and a very conditional promise 'that she wold, if she might with her Honor, goe visit hym'. Bystanders observed that she had tears in her eyes. The message brought some comfort to the Earl, but a week later he was still so weak that he had to be lifted from his bed in a sheet when his attendants came to change his linen. However, with hope renewed, Essex gradually improved. By January 1600 he was evidently on the mend. Ironically it would have been best for everybody if he had not regained his health, for he recovered only to perish on the headsman's block fourteen months later.

With Essex's recovery, the government resumed plans for his trial, and his friends schemes for his rescue. Probably such schemes were discussed when Southampton met Sir Charles Danvers at Ramsbury in mid-January. The key man in the Essex faction was now Lord Mountjoy, who had not yet taken up his command in Ireland. Essex's friends were counting on him, once he had the Irish army at his disposal, to carry through the invasion plans discarded by Essex the previous summer. After securing oaths from Essex, and apparently from Southampton,[1] to do nothing against the Queen's person or sovereignty, Mountjoy agreed to bring over four thousand men from Ireland. He stipulated, however, that James VI of Scotland, whom the Essex faction regarded as the legitimate successor to the ageing Elizabeth, would have to agree to the scheme. To clear the matter with King James, Mountjoy sent up to Scotland a trusted follower, Henry Leigh. Unfortunately King James took so much time deciding to be non-committal that Leigh was still with him when, on February 7th, Mountjoy set out in state for Dublin. The day after his departure was that scheduled for the trial of Essex on various counts of disobedience during his Irish governorship. However, when the spectators queued up for admission to the hall that morning they learned that the trial had been cancelled. The ostensible reason was that Essex, at the urging of Secretary Cecil, had written a submissive letter begging Her Majesty to spare him the shame and ruin of a public trial, and that the Queen, presented with

[1] Birch, II, 471–2. Mountjoy said he received this oath, 'as I remember from my lord of Southampton'.

this letter by Cecil, had at the last moment turned merciful and cancelled the Star Chamber proceedings. What the real reasons were is another matter. Possibly the Crown had misgivings about the strength of its case. There may have been last-minute qualms that the trial would provoke riots by the London crowds, who still regarded Essex as their darling. There may even have been some sort of deal made with Mountjoy before the latter's departure.

Whatever its causes, the abandonment of proceedings against Essex produced enormous rejoicings among his followers, who decided that their hero was finally in the clear. Southampton and Essex's mother (the Countess of Leicester) with a group of friends got access to a house that overlooked York House garden and exchanged salutations with Essex. News of this demonstration was received with cold disapproval at Court. On February 22nd John Chamberlain wrote to his friend Dudley Carleton:

> You left us here with so faire weather and with so confident an opinion that all shold go well with my Lord of Essex, and that we shold see him a cockhorse again, that I know yt wilbe straunge newes to you to heare that all was but a kinde of dreame, and a false paradise that his frends had fained to themselves, geving theyre hopes and discourses libertie to outrun theyre wit, for the bright sunshine that seemed so to dasell them, was indeed but a glimmering light, that was sodainly overshadowed again, and the skie as full of cloudes as before. . . .[1]

Nevertheless, hopes soared again at the beginning of March when word leaked out that Essex was to be released from York House and sent back to his home. The Countess of Leicester, the Countess of Southampton, and Essex's sisters the Countess of Northumberland and Lady Rich moved into Essex House ready to welcome the Earl when he crossed the threshold. The outcome was far different from their expectations. The Queen ordered them all to leave and, when Essex returned to his home, he was under the custody of two keepers, Sir Dru Drury and Sir Richard Berkeley, who had orders to allow no one to speak with him without the Queen's express permission. Essex had merely been transferred from one place of imprisonment to another. Passers-by found the gates in front of Essex House kept closed, and caught no sight of the Earl who was kept incommunicado in the great house.

The Earl of Southampton had been expected to return to Ireland with Mountjoy when the latter crossed in February. Two things, however, had postponed his return. One was the Queen's distrust. For a long time she seems to have been unwilling to let Southampton serve again in Ireland. The other was his own intense desire not to leave without a reconciliation

---

[1] Chamberlain, I, 86.

with the Queen. He knew now the crippling consequences of his sovereign's dislike, and was determined, if he could, to achieve a rapprochement. Repeatedly he sought permission to present himself before Queen Elizabeth and kiss her hand, permission that would signal that he was once more a person in good standing in her court. However, even with the support of old Lord Treasurer Buckhurst,[1] all that Southampton could gain was permission to depart, along with a message that the Queen 'very graciously wished him a safe Going and Returninge'. Making the best he could of this, Southampton started for Ireland on April 21st, accompanied as far as Coventry by Sir Charles Danvers.

The Earl left London too early to receive a copy of the one book dedicated to him this year. This was *The Historie of the Uniting of the Kingdom of Portugall to the Crowne of Castill*, an English translation of a book by Conestaggio. Since the work was a defence of the Spanish conquest of Portugal in 1581, Sir Robert Cecil obviously had some doubts about letting it be published and referred it to Sir Walter Raleigh for an opinion before licensing it. Why Edward Blount, having entered the work in the Stationers' Register on April 14th, printed it with a dedication to Southampton is a complete mystery. A dedication to Cecil, who was trying to improve relations with Spain, would have made some sense; but Southampton was a leader of the party which was clamouring against any peace with the Spaniards.

As Southampton travelled along the road to Liverpool, his port of embarkation, he had more on his mind than the opportunities that Ireland would offer him to redeem his fault and do his country service. For one thing, he carried with him letters from Essex calling upon Mountjoy to invade Wales as a means of forcing his own release. For another, Southampton had disquieting fears that the government might by now know how far he himself had already dabbled in treason. Henry Leigh had at long last returned from Scotland, but only to be arrested by the English government whose spies may well have kept him under surveillance all the while. Southampton knew of Leigh's arrest, and fear that Leigh might tell too much was probably one of the reasons why Southampton had remained around London no longer but was heading for Ireland where he would be safe among friends. Actually Leigh revealed nothing damaging. All that Cecil seems to have learned from him concerning Southampton was that King James had heard that Southampton was friendly with the Earl of Bothwell while in France in 1598, and that the King had asked Leigh about the quarrel between Southampton and Lord Grey.[2]

The quarrel between Southampton and Grey had not yet run its

---

[1] *Salisbury MSS.*, X, 86.
[2] *v.* Birch, II, 471, and *Cal. Border Papers*, II, 654.

course. Only a few months before, Lord Grey had formally challenged Southampton to meet him in a duel before returning to Ireland. On January 24th, 1600, Rowland Whyte reported Southampton's response to Grey's letter:

> My Lord *Gray* hath sent hym a Challenge, which I heare he answered thus. That he accepted yt; but for the Weapon and Place, being by the Lawes of Honor to be chosen by hym, he would not preferr the Combat in *England*, knowing the Danger of the Lawes, and the litle Grace and Mercy he was to expect, if he ran into the Danger of them. He therefore wold lett him know, er yt were long, what Tyme, what Weapon, and what Place he wold choose for yt.[1]

Southampton's letter appointing a place still survives. After pointing out that, under the code of honour, he was not bound to reply to a challenge that arose 'abought a commande of mine when I bare a place in an armye above you', he declared that should he go to Ireland he would gladly meet Grey in any port there that the latter might choose. Should he not go to Ireland, he would meet Grey in any French port of the latter's choosing.[2] Lord Grey replied that Ireland was not an acceptable place—'how disadvantagious to mee, the partiality of the deputy, the comand, and adherents yow possess, doth demonstrate'.[3] He was ready, however, to meet Southampton in France and desired him to get in touch with him at Dover. Southampton countered with another letter, expostulating that his offer to go to France was conditional upon his not going to Ireland. Since he was bound to follow Mountjoy to Ireland, the duel would have to be fought there.[4] When Mountjoy departed unaccompanied by Southampton, Lord Grey sent the Earl a third letter. Once more he urged that they go to France for their duel, but he declared that if Southampton was in haste to leave for Ireland he would meet him at his port of embarkation, cross to Ireland with him, and fight him there. Grey concluded by saying he did not see what more he could possibly offer. He added that if Southampton did not accept this time, he would clear his own reputation by making public the letters that had passed between them.[5] Grey must have been filled with contempt when he got his answer. Completely ignoring Grey's very specific proposal, Southampton blandly declared that he had already offered more than enough to satisfy any reasonable creature. Grey might still feel dissatisfied but, concluded Southampton, 'I will leave to thinke farther of this business, referringe to your choice the publishinge of what hath past which I am sure is not such as I shall ever blush to heare it

---

[1] Collins, II, 164. For Grey's challenge see *Cecil Papers*, 76/27; *Salisbury MSS.*, X, 263.

[2] *Cecil Papers*, 76/26; *Salisbury MSS.*, X, 263.

[3] *Cecil Papers*, 68/56; *Salisbury MSS.*, X, 54.

[4] *Cecil Papers*, 68/57; *Salisbury MSS.*, X, 34.

[5] *Cecil Papers*, 98/108; *Salisbury MSS.*, XIV, 147.

repeated.'[1] Perhaps Southampton had some very good reason for his evasive final letter, but one is left with an uneasy feeling that he may have ignominiously shirked Grey's challenge. Southampton must have decided subsequently that he could not thus coolly walk away from the whole imbroglio. A few days after he finally left for Ireland, Rowland Whyte, who seemed to know just about everything going on in the Court, wrote to Sir Robert Sidney:

> My Lord *Southampton* upon his going away, sent my Lord *Gray* Word, that what in his first Lettre he promised, he was now ready in *Ireland* to performe, and if he wold send him Word of his being in any Post Town, he wold not faile to come unto him, and soe it restes.[2]

Grey, however, must have had second thoughts about Ireland, for he made no move to follow Southampton thither.

On the evening of May 16th Lord Mountjoy in his camp at Newry received word that the Earl of Southampton had arrived at Dundalk with reinforcements. He at once dispatched Captain Edward Blaney with 500 foot and 50 horse to support Southampton's little force as it travelled through the Moyry Pass, where rebel ambushes could always be expected. Riding into Dundalk next morning, Blaney found Southampton had with him forty mounted gentlemen volunteers, and two companies of foot under the command of Sir Oliver Lambert and Sir Henry Folliott. Taking command of Blaney's men as well as his own, Southampton deployed his troops for the march through the dangerous pass. For his vanguard he used Blaney and 250 of the latter's veterans. Behind Blaney he placed the wagon train with supplies, and behind it he stationed the cavalry which he kept under his own direct command. He had the rest of Blaney's foot and Lambert's and Folliott's infantry march as a rearguard.

Travelling north the column soon found bodies of rebels on its flanks. At the Four Mile Water, half way to Newry, they discovered the enemy on the farther side ready to prevent their crossing. Blaney was about to launch a frontal attack across the water when he saw a most encouraging sight. Mountjoy, with the prescience that marks a first-rate field commander, had marched his army south from Newry, and his vanguard was already coming into sight behind the enemy. Frustrated, the rebels yielded the crossing and concentrated their fire upon the rear of Southampton's column. Here they attacked so fiercely that the English rearguard was about to break when Southampton, seeing the danger, launched

---

[1] *Cecil Papers*, 68/58; *Salisbury MSS.*, X, 34–5. It will be noted that the preceding letters, all of which are undated, are not in proper sequence either in the volumes of the Cecil Papers or in the Historical Manuscripts Commission calendar. The credit for putting them in their correct order belongs to Mrs. Stopes (pp. 165–7).

[2] Collins, II, 192.

a charge and with only six or seven other horsemen to support him drove the rebels back to where Tyrone himself stood with his reserves watching the skirmish. Writing to Cecil a few days later, Mountjoy declared, 'I protest he saved our honour.'[1]

Triumphantly Southampton joined up with Mountjoy's army and continued unmolested to Newry. The English losses had been very slight, only two men slain and six wounded, though one of the latter was Captain Aderton, Southampton's lieutenant. However, if Mountjoy had not made his timely appearance, a dangerous situation could have developed.

Conferring with Mountjoy, Southampton found that the Lord Deputy was not in the least inclined to turn aside from the campaign which in the next few years would win him an earldom and a lasting place in the military history of his country. Mountjoy could see no reason for rebelliously taking his army to Wales now that Essex was obviously in no danger of his life.

Southampton seems to have settled down to soldiering. He got his reward when Mountjoy nominated him for the vacant governorship of Connaught. The actual granting of the post, however, could only be made by the Queen. For weeks Southampton anxiously awaited the decision. At last it arrived. Just as she had refused Essex a generalship for Southampton, so she now refused Mountjoy a governorship for him. It was an unfortunate decision. Given the appointment, Southampton would probably like Mountjoy have diverted all his energies to Ireland, have given the Queen good and faithful service, and never have joined Essex in rebellion. At the receipt of the news Southampton, bitterly disappointed, decided to shake the mud of Ireland off his shoes. On July 22nd he wrote to Cecil:

> ... since I have here nothing to do but as a private man, which condition cannot afford me means to perform aught worth the thinking of . . . I do intend, God willing, to go hence into the Low Countries, to live the rest of this summer in the States' army, where perhaps I may see somewhat worth my pains. . . . [2]

Leaving his troop of a hundred horse behind him, he forthwith sailed for the Continent.

Southampton's choice of the Low Countries was not surprising. A major Dutch campaign against the Spanish forces was in prospect, and various English lords and gentlemen, impatient for military glory, were heading for the Continent. In mid-June Sir Henry Danvers writing in jocular vein had reported, 'The famous Earls of Rutland and Northumberland, moved with the Low Country honour, are embarked thither.'[3] A little earlier Sir Robert Drury and Lord Grey had crossed over to serve

[1] *Cal. S.P. (Ireland), 1600,* p. 191 and p. 224.
[2] *Cal. S.P. (Ireland), 1600,* p. 329.
[3] *Salisbury MSS.,* X, 182.

with the Dutch. Drury, fed up with Grey's ego, had written from the Low Countries to Southampton:

> I shold have great cause to be gladd to see you here. And . . . to be revenged of my lord Graye, who overtopps us with a Barronny, we shold be very gladd that you wer here, to shadowe him with your Earldome. . . . [1]

Under the circumstances, especially since Southampton had unfinished business with Grey, the invitation was irresistible.

When the Privy Council learned that Southampton was en route to the Continent, it moved promptly to prevent a probable consequence. On August 3rd letters were dispatched to Southampton and Grey sternly forbidding any duel. In their letter to Southampton the councillors, after noting that it was public knowledge that there was 'unkindness and heart-burn' between the two men, came directly to the point:

> It hath pleased hir Majestie from hir owne Mouthe, to give expresse direction unto us to commaunde your Lordship in hir Name (uppon your Alledgieance) in no sort to offer, accept, or harken to any challendge or meeting with the Lord Grey.[2]

We have no indication as to when Sir Robert Drury, the Council's messenger, delivered these letters to Southampton and Grey. Delivered they were, however, for Southampton, in replying to an undated letter from Grey inviting him now he was on the Continent 'to right mee and your former letters', wrote:

> . . . you are acquainted with the comandement I have receaved, which forbiddes mee to answer you, which howsoever you respect not, I must obay, & therfor doe directly refuse your chalenge.

But the letter does not end here. Having by this declaration carefully put himself on the windy side of the English law, Southampton proceeded to give Grey his opportunity if he really was bent on a duel:

> I will to morrow in the morninge ride an English mile out of the portes, accompanied with none but this bearer & a lackay to howld my horses, who shall beare no weapons, I will beare this sword which I now send you, & a dagger which you shall see before my goinge, when you shall know the way I intend to goe, where I will attend [await] you 2 houres, if in the mean time I meet you, you may doe your pleasure, for I will quitt no ground but defend my self with the armes I carry whatsoever you shall offer.[3]

After this we hear no more of Southampton until late September when he arrived back in England. The Earl's biographers have been left to

[1] *Lansdowne MS. 107*, f. 143r.
[2] *Cecil Papers*, 81/10; *Salisbury MSS.*, X, 262.
[3] *Cecil Papers*, 76/25; *Salisbury MSS.*, X, 262–3.

make their own deductions as to whether or not Southampton and Grey, sword in one hand and dagger in the other, fought each other that morning. A. L. Rowse in his life of Southampton declares, 'Nothing seems to have transpired.'[1] Mrs. Stopes earlier had arrived at the opposite conclusion. The present writer believes that Mrs. Stopes has the right of the matter. Supporting her view is a letter that Lord Grey wrote to the Privy Council from 'Berges' on August 12th. This begins:

> May it pleas your Lordships: I assure my self yow either are, or will shortly bee infourmed of my disobedience. . . .

In tangled sentences and chaotic spelling Lord Grey attributed his disobedience to the failure of a letter addressed to him at Middelburg to reach him there. Pleading, 'How, if in time delivered[,] your Lordships letter would have swayed, my future conformity unto your pleasure shale best demonstrat', he urgently begged the councillors to seek his pardon from the Queen.[2] It would seem obvious that the letter to which Grey refers is that forbidding him to duel with Southampton, and that his disobedience consisted of failure to heed that prohibition. Grey's excuse should not be taken at face value. As we have just seen, Southampton in his letter arranging a meeting had noted that Grey had received the Council's commands against a duel.

Mrs. Stopes believed that, though Southampton and Grey fought, 'no wounds seem to have been received on either side'.[3] There is, however, a strong possibility that Southampton was seriously hurt in the duel. When Rowland Whyte reported to Sir Robert Sidney the Earl of Southampton's return to England, he noted, 'he hath bene extreme sicke, but is now recovered'. The 'extreme sicke' was in all likelihood a fiction invented to account both for the period when Southampton was recovering from his wounds and for his subsequent wan appearance'.[4]

Back in London on September 22nd,[5] Southampton lost no time in hastening to Lees, the country home of Lord and Lady Rich, where his loving 'Bess' was staying. Essex in a welcoming letter of September 25th

---

[1] Rowse, *Shakespeare's Southampton*, p. 151.

[2] *Cecil Papers*, 180/146; *Salisbury MSS.*, X, 273.

[3] Stopes, pp. 183-4 (also see p. 170).

[4] Collins, II, 216. The friends of both Southampton and Lord Grey would of course be busy denying that they had duelled in defiance of the Queen's orders. One who seems to have been persuaded by their disavowals is John Chamberlain who on October 12th belatedly reported, 'The erle of Southampton and the Lord Gray are come out of the Lowe Countries unhurt, though it were constantly reported they had fought and spoyled [wounded] each other.' (*Letters*, I, 107.) Presumably Cecil, who as Secretary would have opened Grey's panicky letter confessing disobedience, had done him and Southampton the kindness of suppressing its contents.

[5] Collins, II, 216.

told Southampton that he was sending his secretary Cuffe to attend upon him but longed for a personal meeting. He added a half-jocular comment, 'I did allso note down of your being so good a husband as to make a jorney downe to Leaze.'[1]

It was Essex, in fact, who was chiefly responsible for Southampton's return to England. Freed from house arrest only the previous month, but already toying once more with thoughts of rebellion, Essex had sent a follower, John Littleton, to summon Southampton home for consultations. At the call of his friend, Southampton had laid aside his plans for rather extensive travel on the Continent and had sailed for England.[2]

Among the worries tormenting Essex at this time were his finances. When Essex's father had died, he had left his son no great estate to sustain the title that then passed to him. To an extent unusual among the nobility, Essex had become dependent upon the largesse of the Queen. Chief of the gifts that he had received from her in happier days was the farm of the duties levied on all the sweet wines entering England. This was now coming up for renewal at Michaelmas 1600. If it were not renewed, Essex would become practically bankrupt. To Sir Charles Danvers, Essex confided that he regarded the Queen's decision at Michaelmas as a decisive indication of her future treatment of him. Seeking once more to ingratiate himself with the Queen, Essex sent her humble submissive letters, and these Elizabeth received sometimes with kindness but more often with cynicism. Michaelmas came and went without any decision. Essex, forbidden to appear at Court, sweated out the days at Essex House. At last, at the end of October, he received his answer. The Queen had decided not to renew his grant. For a few weeks more Essex persevered in seeking to regain the Queen's favour but when, in mid-November, his letter congratulating Elizabeth upon the forty-second anniversary of her accession went unanswered, he gave way to complete despair. His enemies had, he believed, completely poisoned the Queen's mind against him. Force would have to be used if he was to do himself right. Sir John Harington

---

[1] This letter (*Cecil Papers*, 179/88) is dated only September 25th and lacks the year. It may be confidently assigned to 1600, however, since the reference to Southampton joining his wife at Lees is paralleled in a letter of Lord Lumley's dated 'this last of September, 1600', which reads in part, 'My Lord of Southampton is returned out of the Low Countries, and is with his Lady, at my Lord Riche's in Essex.' Edmund Lodge, *Illustrations of British History* (London, 1838), II, 545. The H.M.C. editor who calendared Essex's letter (*Salisbury MSS.*, VIII, 557) attributed it, incorrectly, to 1598, but put a warning question mark beside that date. For Rowse's mistaken use of this letter see p. 73, footnote 2.

[2] *v.* John Bruce, ed., *Correspondence of King James VI of Scotland with Sir Robert Cecil and Others in England during the Reign of Queen Elizabeth*, Camden Society, Vol. 78 (London, 1861), pp. 87–104 *passim*.

has left a brief description of an interview he had with Essex at this time:

> . . . he uttered strange wordes borderinge on suche strange desyns, that made me hasten forthe and leave his presence. . . . His speeches of the Queene becomethe no man who hath *mens sana in corpore sano*.[1]

Essex and Southampton were well along the road to their great catastrophe.

[1] *Nugae Antiquae*, I, 179.

CHAPTER X

Rebellion

STRANGE SCENES were enacted at Essex House in December 1600
Essex and his friends were recruiting supporters, and malcontents
of all sorts thronged to the great Thames-side mansion—unemployed
captains who had served under Essex in Ireland, disgruntled lords and
knights who blamed Cecil for their disappointments at Court and were
determined to oust him, wild profligates and rakehells like Sir Edmund
Baynham and Captain Orrell, indignant Puritans and conspiratorial
Catholics drawn alike by Essex's declaration that there should be religious
toleration in England. Helping to attract the crowds to Essex House were
the sermons preached there by a number of Puritan clergymen. Transported by their zeal, some of these preachers said dangerous things. One
declared that, at times, it might be needful for great men in the state to
compel the sovereign to take the courses necessary for the good of the
commonwealth. Perhaps this was the time that Essex, speaking ever more
wildly, said of the Queen that her mind was as crooked as her carcass. Spies
employed by Mr. Secretary brought word of such utterances back to the
Court. Men began to wonder how long the Queen and Cecil would permit
this brazen anti-Court to flourish. Some believed that they simply dared
not move against Essex, the darling of the soldiers, of the Puritans, and of
the Londoners.

A frequent visitor to Essex House was the Earl of Southampton, full of
discontent and emphatic in his statements about the wrongs that had been
done to his friend. Closeted within the house, Southampton conferred
with Essex and Sir Charles Danvers. Part of their conversation turned
about a wild fiction which they had persuaded themselves was an established truth. Quite incapable of realizing the common sense of Cecil's
policy of seeking peace with Spain, they read the darkest meanings into
the unsuccessful negotiations that had been held at Boulogne the previous
summer by English and Spanish representatives. They had convinced
themselves that the unshakeably Protestant Cecil, his brother-in-law Lord
Cobham, and Sir Walter Raleigh were plotting to make the Spanish
Infanta the successor to the English throne. Essex and his friends regarded
James VI of Scotland as the proper heir, and saw themselves as his cham-
pions. The time had come, they decided, to oust from the Court the

'Spanish faction', King James' enemies and their own, and to force the Queen to recognize the Scottish king as her heir.

On Christmas Day 1600 Essex dispatched to King James a long detailed letter which he had drafted with the aid of Southampton, Sir Charles Danvers and Henry Cuffe. It is a very significant document. In it Essex enumerates all the wrongs that Cecil and his faction have done against him: they have corrupted servants of his, stolen papers belonging to him, suborned false witnesses, and employed forged documents against him. They have sought to suppress 'all noble, virtuous, and heroical spirits'. They have conspired with the Spanish Infanta and have made 'devilish plots with your Majesty's own subjects against your person and life'. Then Essex announces to James that he will try to wrest control of the government from these monsters:

> Now am I summoned of all sides to stop the malice, the wickedness and madness of these men, and to relieve my poor country that groans under her burthen. Now doth reason, honor, and conscience command me to be active. Now do I see by God's favor the fairest and likeliest hopes that can be of good success.[1]

Essex added that James was the first person to whom he was revealing his decision. He added a request that James send down the Earl of Mar by February 1st to be his representative during the coming coup.

The New Year saw active planning for the coming rebellion. Thus the dispatch by Southampton of one of the Earl of Rutland's servants to France about the beginning of January almost certainly ties in with the arrival, just a little too late in February, of a French bark 'laden with saddles, arms and such necessaries' consigned to Rutland.[2]

Around Christmas Essex and his friends were agitated by a court rumour that Southampton was to be arrested. The expected arrest did not occur, but on January 9th as Southampton, accompanied only by his horseboy, was riding in the vicinity of Raleigh's residence, he was viciously attacked by Lord Grey and a band of his followers. Southampton held off the attackers until help arrived, but his boy had one of his hands lopped off. The Queen swiftly punished Grey, committing him to the Fleet prison, but in Essex House a new fantasy crowded into the fevered minds of Essex and his coterie—their enemies, afraid to proceed against them by due course of law, were out to murder them. When Grey was given his release on February 2nd, Essex, Southampton and their friends took it as proof that the law would no longer protect them from their enemies.

Preparations for the coming coup were proceeding apace. In late Janu-

---

[1] *Add. MS. 31022* printed by Helen Georgia Stafford in her *James VI of Scotland and the Throne of England* (New York, 1940), p. 215.

[2] *Cal. S.P. (Dom.), 1598–1601*, pp. 552–3, and *Salisbury MSS.*, XI, 44.

ary Essex sent letters to his stepfather, Sir Christopher Blount, his sometime Marshal of the army in Ireland, and to Sir Ferdinando Gorges,
summoning them to London. When Gorges arrived, Essex asked him to
serve with Southampton, Sir Charles Danvers, Sir John Davies and John
Littleton on a committee that would do the necessary staff work in planning the coming action. The probable reason why Blount was not put on
the committee was that Essex knew of the dislike which Blount had for
Southampton. On February 2nd and 3rd members of the committee met
at Drury House, the London residence of Sir Charles Danvers.[1] Southampton, who seems to have acted as chairman, was present on both
occasions.

For the consideration of the committee Sir John Davies produced two
documents in Essex's own handwriting. One was a list of 120 noblemen,
knights and gentlemen who Essex believed could be counted upon in the
action which lay ahead. The other document was a list of points on which
Essex desired the committee's advice:

> (i) Should simultaneous attempts be made to seize both the Court and the Tower
> of London? How many men would be needed for the double enterprise?
> (ii) If the attack were to be launched only against the Court, what places in it
> should be first possessed, by what persons and with what numbers?
> (iii) Where, with least suspicion, could Essex assemble with those who were to
> accompany him when he himself came into the Court? (It was noted that a num-
> ber of the faction would infiltrate the Court in advance.)
> (iv) Should the Lord Admiral (Nottingham), Mr. Secretary (Cecil) and the
> Captain of the Guard (Raleigh) be detained as prisoners? If so, by whom?

At the second meeting at Drury House it was decided not to attempt
the Tower of London but to concentrate upon seizure of the Court at
Whitehall. Accordingly, Sir John Davies wrote down a list of the key
points in the palace and a tentative assignment of the persons to whom
their capture was to be entrusted. No sooner had he done this than there
was an outburst from Sir Ferdinando Gorges, who subsequently testified:

> I utterly disliked that course, as besides the horror I felt at it, I saw it was
> impossible to be accomplished. . . .
> As I would not condescend to that course, my Lord of Southampton said in a
> passion, 'Then we shall resolve upon nothing, and it is now three months or more
> since we first undertook this'; I said this was more than I knew, and advised his
> Lordship to try his friends in the city, by whom he had been so well assured;
> but this was so evilly liked, that we broke up, resolved upon nothing, and
> referred all to the Earl of Essex himself.[2]

Thus ended the second and last of the Drury House meetings.

---

[1] Rowse is mistaken (p. 155) in thinking that Drury House was Southampton's
residence. For evidence of Danvers' tenancy see *Salisbury MSS.*, XI, 45.

[2] *Cal. S.P. (Dom.), 1598–1601*, pp. 577–8.

Essex meanwhile had been holding separate consultations with Sir Christopher Blount. When he learned of the irreconcilable split in his Drury House committee, he drew up his own plan for his most trusted men to seize Whitehall. Sir Christopher Blount with his band would capture the Great Court Gate on the palace's northern side. Sir John Davies would occupy the Hall. Sir Charles Danvers, charged with getting possession of the Presence Chamber, would act in conjunction with Davies in seizing the all-important Guard Chamber. Apparently the royal guard had no guns, only halberds, which were usually piled against the wall. The plan called for Essex's men to seize these halberds before the guards could arm themselves with them. Part of the guard, having served under Essex in their time, were counted upon to defect.

This plan having been finally settled upon, preparations were accelerated. Essex's steward, Sir Gelly Merrick, unable to provide lodgings for all those coming into London ready for the action, 'with great heat and violence displaced certain Gentlemen who were lodged in a House close by *Essex-House*, and there posted divers of my Lord *Essex's* Followers and Accomplices'.[1]

If Essex felt any complacency at the progress of his preparations, that complacency ended on Saturday, February 7th. On that day the government, alerted by its informers, sent John Herbert, the second Secretary of State, to Essex House with a summons for the Earl to attend forthwith a meeting of the Privy Council at which he would be instructed how he should conduct himself. Essex, fearing imprisonment, refused to leave Essex House, making an excuse that ill health kept him from attending.

That night Essex supped with his sister Lady Rich, his stepfather Sir Christopher Blount, one of his cousins Sir Robert Vernon, and also Sir Charles Danvers and the Earl of Southampton. The little group consulted anxiously as to what Essex should do now that the Queen and Cecil had taken the initiative. Probably the best advice given was that of Sir Charles Danvers, who urged Essex to 'fly with some hundred gentlemen to the sea side, or into Wales, where he might command some ports'.[2] Essex, however, had dispatched a secretary, Temple, to the City and an unidentified messenger had brought assurances that Essex could count upon support there—apparently that of Sheriff Smith, who had a thousand men of the London militia under his command. Convinced that the City would support him, Essex decided against flight.

Before the first light of dawn on Sunday, February 8th, messengers were out summoning the supporters of Essex and Southampton to Essex

[1] Francis Hargrave, ed., *A Complete Collection of State Trials* (London, 1776), I, 210.
[2] *Cal. S.P. (Dom.), 1598–1601*, p. 580.

House. Old Lord Sandys, Southampton's kinsman[1] and Hampshire neighbour, was aroused by a messenger soon after six o'clock. At about the same time the Earl of Rutland started for Southampton's lodgings, apparently to join with him in mustering forces for the coming struggle.

While the company was assembling at Essex House, a message arrived from Sir Walter Raleigh that he wanted Sir Ferdinando Gorges to come over to talk with him. Distrustful, Essex and those about him would only let Gorges go out in a boat and meet Raleigh 'on the Water upon equal Terms'. Gorges seems to have been running with the hare and hunting with the hounds that day. When he returned, he said that Raleigh had tried to persuade him that he would be ruined if he remained at Essex House but that he had rejected his overtures. According to Raleigh's own subsequent testimony, Gorges had revealed to him that Essex was arming his friends.[2]

As the morning wore on, some three hundred armed men assembled in the courtyard of Essex House. Many of them did not know why they had been summoned hither, and these were given the explanation that Essex's life 'was practised to be taken away by Lord Cobham and Sir Walter Raleigh, and as he was sent for by the Council, he meant, by the help of his friends, to defend himself'.[3]

The first significant event of the day came about ten o'clock with the arrival of four emissaries from the Court. There were Sir Thomas Egerton (Lord Keeper of the Great Seal), Sir William Knollys (Comptroller of the Queen's Household), Lord Chief Justice Popham and the Earl of Worcester. They found Essex Gate closed when they arrived but Sir William Constable, who commanded the halberdiers on guard there, admitted them through a 'wicket' which was immediately closed, cutting them off from their attendants. William Camden has left a picture of the scene which faced the Queen's messengers:

> The Court-yard was fill'd with a confus'd Rabble, and in the midst was *Essex* himself, with *Southampton*. . . . [4]

When the emissaries declared that the Queen had sent them to learn the causes of Essex's discontents and why he had thus assembled these men, Essex declared in a very loud voice 'that his life was sought, and that he should have been murdered in his bed'. When the Privy Councillors

---

[1] One of Southampton's aunts, Mabel, was Lord Sandys' sister-in-law.
[2] Hargrave, *State Trials*, I, 202.
[3] *Cal. S.P. (Dom.), 1598–1601*, p. 552.
[4] *The History or Annals of England* in White Kennet's *A Complete History of England* (London, 1706), II, 631.

promised that Essex should receive a full hearing and justice, Southampton put in that he himself had already been attacked by Lord Grey. Pausing only to remind Southampton that Lord Grey had been punished for this assault, Chief Justice Popham suggested that they go into the house and confer in private. At this there was a great clamour raised by the crowd: 'Away, my Lord!' 'They abuse you!' 'They betray you!' 'They undo you!' 'You lose time.' The Lord Keeper, who out of respect for Essex had taken off his hat, replaced it as a sign that he now spoke for the Queen, and cried out, 'I command you all upon your allegiance, to lay down your weapons, and to depart.' His action was the Elizabethan equivalent of reading the Riot Act. Essex said nothing, but put on his hat and marched into the house. The Lord Keeper and his colleagues followed amid cries of 'Kill them', and a derisive shout, 'Cast the Great Seal out of the Window.' When Essex and the Queen's messengers entered the back chamber which served as Essex's study, the Earl, acting on the advice of Southampton, Blount and Davies, ordered that they be locked up in the room. Taking his leave of them, Essex begged them to be patient, and promised to return as soon as he had made his arrangements with the Lord Mayor and aldermen of London.[1] Essex left Sir John Davies in charge of his prisoners, with orders not to release them until he himself returned. To make sure the prisoners did not break out, men with loaded muskets and fire ready to ignite them were stationed in the next room, under the command of Owen Salisbury.

If Essex had been wiser, he would have abandoned his London project and at once have launched an attack against Whitehall, only twenty minutes' distance away. The government had seriously underestimated the threat posed by Essex and had failed to muster yet the trained bands of London and the adjacent shires. The only military force available was the royal guard (which at full force numbered only two hundred men), augmented by whatever courtiers and servants could be mustered at the moment. If Essex had headed for Whitehall with his three hundred desperadoes,[2] he might just possibly have succeeded with his coup. A few days later Master Vincent Hussey wrote of Essex:

> It is a blessed thing that he failed in judgment and attempted London first, for had he gone straight to Court, he would have surprised it unprovided of defence, and full of his wellwishers, before the world had notice of his treasons.[3]

Four earls, Essex, Southampton, Rutland and Bedford, travelled with the company of about one hundred and fifty men that now set out from

[1] Hargrave, *State Trials*, I, 201.
[2] This figure was given by Attorney-General Coke at Essex's trial.
[3] *Cal. S.P. (Dom.), 1598–1601*, p. 551. On the other hand, William Camden reports that the rebels lacked arms and believed the guard at Whitehall had been doubled.

Essex House for the home of Sheriff Smith in the adjacent City of London. A fifth earl, Sussex, was expected to join them momentarily. As the company moved down Fleet Street, they met Lord Cromwell who was persuaded to join Lord Sandys and Lord Mounteagle, who already were accompanying Essex and his fellow earls.

Apparently Essex originally intended to arrive at St. Paul's churchyard in time to address the great throng of Londoners that would be assembled there for the morning sermon. Precious time had been lost, however, in dealing with the Queen's emissaries, and Cheapside was thronged with people returning home after the sermon as Essex and his adherents pressed through the street on their way to Sheriff Smith. As the Essexians pushed eastward they spread word that a dastardly attempt at murder had been made by Raleigh and Cobham. There were confused cries of 'Murder! Murder!' and 'God Save the Queen!' Amid this hubbub Essex received word that the authorities were beginning to act. The Earl of Cumberland had been to Ludgate and had ordered a chain drawn across the passage through the city walls at that point.

Essex's chief concern now was to secure firearms for his followers who, forced into this premature action, had little more than rapiers and daggers for the coming fight. When, dripping with sweat, Essex arrived at Sheriff Smith's house in Fenchurch Street, he shouted that he had to have muskets and pistols since England had been sold to the Spaniards. Smith must have been extremely unhappy to find Essex on his doorstep demanding arms. He, with Sir William Rider, the Lord Mayor of London, and the aldermen had just a little while before been summoned from the sermon at St. Paul's by a messenger with orders from the Queen to put the city in arms and to dispatch a force to assist in the defence of Whitehall where an attack was awaited. A barricade of coaches was already being strung across the street at Charing Cross to block Essex's anticipated march on the palace.

Smith seems to have played for time. While his servants provided Essex's followers with beer, he headed off to the Lord Mayor with Essex's request that he come to him. A neighbouring armourer heard 'a tall, dark man', whom he understood to be Sir Christopher Blount, order his men to carry off half a dozen old halberds which he had in his shop.

While Essex was achieving little or nothing at Sheriff Smith's house, word came that Cecil's brother, Lord Burghley, was at hand with a herald and a dozen horsemen. Despite Lord Mounteagle's frantic orders to stop the herald's throat, Garter King of Arms read the Queen's proclamation declaring Essex a traitor. Too late, Mounteagle's men drove away Garter King, Lord Burghley and their escort. The damage had been done. In vain Essex declared that it was all a trick played by his enemies, that for

two shillings a herald would say anything, and that it was he who stood for the good of the Queen and of London. The first defections were already occurring. The Earl of Bedford had seized the opportunity of a side street to head for home. Now Lord Cromwell, learning of the proclamation, made his departure.

Seeing the Londoners making no move to join him, Essex headed westward, possibly hoping to seize one of the fortified gates of the city, but probably intent chiefly on getting home. Accompanied by Southampton, Rutland, and the rest of those still adhering to him, he turned down Lombard Street and Cheapside, descended the hill beyond St. Paul's and, at about two o'clock in the afternoon, came to Ludgate. The Earl of Cumberland had posted there a rapidly assembled company of pikemen and halberdiers and had entrusted their command to a veteran captain, Sir John Leveson. At Essex's approach Leveson adamantly refused to withdraw the chain set across the road and so to permit passage for him and his followers. Sir Ferdinando Gorges, after fruitless attempts to negotiate with Leveson, asked Essex to let him release his hostages and travel with them to Whitehall, there to secure the best terms he could before any blood was shed. Essex saw some merit in the plan but sent off Gorges with authority to release only one of his prisoners, Chief Justice Popham.

We have Leveson's own account of what happened after Gorge's departure:

> . . . one of the Earl's side cried, 'Shoot! shoot!' and then the pistols were discharged at us within a three quarters pike's length of us, and they were answered again by such shot as we had, and forthwith Sir Christopher Blount charged with his sword and target and came close to the chain and cut off the head of sundry the pikes, and with him divers other of the Earl's company, of which some got between the post and the chain and let drive among our pikes and halberts; and in this encounter Sir Chr. Blunt was hurt, first by a thrust in the face, and then felled by a knock on the head. Upon the sight whereof and the fall of young Mr. Tracy, the Earl's page, our company coming upon them put them back, which the Earl perceiving called them off and so departed from us.[1]

During the fighting Leveson's second-in-command, Waite, had been slain. Essex himself had come close to death, amid the cross-fire two bullets passing through his hat.

With Blount left behind a prisoner, Essex and Southampton retreated eastward, their force reduced to about fifty as one man after another slipped away, seeking to escape the coming vengeance of the law. Beyond the Gothic pile of old St. Paul's Cathedral, the little company turned down Friday Street where Essex 'beeing faynt' (probably in a state of shock), desired drink which was brought for him. Here the Londoners held up the

---

[1] *Salisbury MSS.*, XI, 59–61.

chain that had closed off this street, and Essex and Southampton and their remaining followers made their way to the river front at Queenhithe where boats were secured for the leaders. In the scramble to board the boats Lord Mounteagle fell into the Thames and almost drowned.

If Essex and Southampton had had time for clear thought, they would have realized that their cause was now hopeless, would have ordered the boats to turn downstream, and would have begun their flight to the Continent. Essex however believed he had still one card to play. With the Lord Keeper, the Earl of Worcester, and Sir William Knollys still his prisoners, he believed he could force the Queen to negotiate. He ordered the boats to turn upstream to the water stairs of Essex House. He landed to find that Gorges had left fifteen minutes earlier, taking all four hostages with him to Whitehall.

The brief siege of Essex House now began. The time was somewhere around four o'clock. In command of the loyalist forces was the Lord High Admiral of England, the Earl of Nottingham. On the landward side of Essex House, along the Strand, the Lord Admiral posted companies of cavalry and infantry under the command of the Earl of Cumberland, the Earl of Lincoln, Lord Thomas Howard, Lord Burghley, Lord Compton, and Southampton's old enemy, Lord Grey, The Lord Admiral himself, with his son Lord Howard of Effingham, Lord Cobham, Sir John Stanhope, Sir Fulke Greville, and Sir Robert Sidney, established other forces in the spacious garden on the river side of the great mansion. Within the house, Essex was burning papers which he thought might incriminate him or his friends.

The assault began. Lord Burghley broke down the gates and, with the loss of two of his men, won possession of the courtyard at the front of Essex House. The defenders lost men also. One of Southampton's footmen was slain and Captain Owen Salisbury was mortally wounded by a shot through a window. To defend themselves from such fire, the defenders jammed the casements with books taken from Essex's study. The Countess of Essex, Lady Rich, and their female attendants were within the house and, amid the volleying of guns and the flowing of blood, the women panicked and 'fill'd the Place with their Shrieks and Cries'. Their hysterics must have had a bad effect on Essex's already frayed nerves.

The Queen's forces were now bringing up artillery from the Tower of London, but before beginning the carnage of an artillery cannonade, the Lord Admiral ordered his men to hold their fire and sent forward Sir Robert Sidney, long a friend of the Essexians, to persuade them to surrender peacefully. Southampton came out on the roof of Essex House to reply to Sidney's overtures. Insisting that Essex and the rest of them had taken up arms only to defend themselves from their enemies, and that

they meant no harm to the Queen, Southampton said that they were ready to present themselves before Her Majesty if the Lord Admiral would give hostages to guarantee their safe return. Sidney's reply was that subjects must not seek to bargain with princes, and he reminded Southampton that Essex House was not so strongly built that it could hold out against the Lord Admiral's cannon. To this Southampton retorted that the rebels would rather die like men, with swords in their hands, than end their lives in ten days' time on a scaffold.[1] Essex had by now joined Southampton on the roof. He declared that he would have done God and his country good service by rooting out from England those 'Atheists and Caterpillars' who were his enemies. He said that he shared Southampton's resolution to die and accounted it the greatest punishment that God had ever laid upon him that He had not suffered him to die during his sickness of the previous year.

Obviously the negotiations were getting nowhere. Sidney reported back to the Lord Admiral, who of course refused to give the hostages which the rebels were in no position to demand. He did, however, offer to hold off his attack long enough for the women to be evacuated from Essex House. To this gesture Southampton, who seems largely to have taken over from the distracted Essex, replied that the defenders had laboured hard to barricade the doors and that if they now unbarred them to let the women depart, they would have to be given an hour in which to refortify them. To allow this time, the Lord Admiral Nottingham agreed to a two-hours' truce.

Once the brief cease-fire came into effect, argument broke out among the defenders of Essex House. Although Essex had told Sidney that the Lord Admiral's artillery could only blow him and his followers to Heaven, not all of them were ready to die. Counselling Essex to hold by his resolve to perish fighting, old Lord Sandys declared that it was 'more commendable for Men of Honour to die by the Sword, than by the Ax or the Halter'.[2] In the end, sanity won out over Lord Sandys' 'honour' and from the roof of Essex House it was announced that the rebels would surrender upon three conditions. First, the Lord Admiral must give civil treatment

---

[1] Stopes, p. 193.

[2] Camden, *Annals*, in Kennet's *Complete History*, II, 632. We have conflicting evidence as to Southampton's position in this debate. Dr. Hamey, a Flemish surgeon resident in England, writing to a friend on the Continent soon after the rebellion, declared, 'At length he [Southampton] gave way to his [Essex's] entreaty that he should not by his pertinacity sweep away so many innocent people in one final ruin.' (John J. Keevil, *Hamey the Stranger* (London, 1952), p. 78.) On the other hand, one of the accounts of Essex's trial informs us, '. . . the Erle of Essex heere confessed that he was perswaded to yeild by the Erle of Southampton and Ruttland for he thought not so to have done. . . .' H. L. Stephen, ed., *State Trials Political and Social*, Second Series (London, 1902), III, 73.

Sweet hart I doute not but you shall
heare ere my ~~letter~~ come to you of the
misfortune of your frendes, bee not so
apprehensiue of it, for gods will must bee
donn, & what is allotted to us by destiny
~~& ~~cannot bee auoyded; beleeue that in this
time there is nothinge can so much comfort me ~~as~~ to thinke you are well & take
patiently what hath happened, & contrarywise
I shall ~~—~~ liue in torment if I find you
~~soe~~ vexed for my cause, dout not but I
shall doe well, & please your self with the assurance ~~that~~ that I shall euer remayn

Your affectionat husband
H S SOUTHAMPTON

SOUTHAMPTON'S LETTER TO HIS WIFE AFTER
THE FAILURE OF THE ESSEX REBELLION
By permission of the Marquess of Salisbury

to Essex and his friends; second, the rebels must be given a fair and impartial trial; and third, Essex must be allowed the spiritual ministrations of Ashton, a clergyman in whom he had especial faith. These conditions being accepted, the doors of Essex House were unblocked. Essex and Southampton and their unhappy followers, going down on their knees, handed over their swords to Lord Admiral Nottingham. The time was ten o'clock. Essex's Rebellion had lasted just twelve hours. The good news was carried in haste to Whitehall where Queen Elizabeth had sworn she would not sleep until she knew that the rebels had been captured.

Though the night was dark and stormy, the authorities dared not lead their prisoners through the streets to the Tower for fear of demonstrations along the way. On the other hand the 'shooting' of London Bridge, required for a river journey, was dangerous also. In their quandary their captors decided to keep Essex and Southampton overnight in the Archbishop of Canterbury's palace at Lambeth. The Queen, however, would not be content until they were safely within the high walls of the Tower, and at three o'clock in the morning on February 9th, Essex and Southampton with the chief of their supporters were brought into the Tower.

Either at Lambeth or in the Tower, Southampton wrote the following letter to his wife:

> Sweet hart I doute not but you shall heare ere my letter come to you of the misfortune of your frendes, bee not to[o] apprehensive of it, for gods will must be donn, & what is allotted to us by destiny cannot bee avoyded; beleeve that in this time there is nothinge can so much comfort mee as to thinke you are well & take patiently what hath happened, & contrarywise I shall live in torment if I find you vexed for my cause, dout not but I shall doe well & please your self with the assurance that I shall ever remayn
>   Your affectionat husband
>   H. Southampton[1]

[1] *Cecil Papers*, 183/121; *Salisbury MSS.*, XI, 35. The letter was addressed simply 'To my Bess'. Miss Tenison was probably right when she thought that, since the letter ended up in the Cecil archives, it was probably never delivered to the wife. (*Elizabethan England*, XI, 432.)

CHAPTER XI

The Trial

URING THE DAYS after the collapse of the Essex Rebellion, London had the appearance of an armed camp as a thoroughly alarmed government assembled its forces. Five hundred men levied in Middlesex were brought to Charing Cross, four hundred men from Essex were assembled close to the capital, three hundred men levied by the Deputy-Lieutenants of Surrey were stationed in Southwark and Lambeth, four hundred Hertfordshire men marched into Holborn. A company of soldiers was stationed in St. Paul's churchyard. Two companies were posted at the Exchange. The government's apprehensions were not unfounded. One of Essex's captains, Thomas Lee, was found to be plotting to seize the Queen and force her to sign a warrant for the Earl's release. Lee was swiftly arrested and joined the ninety or so of Essex's followers imprisoned in the Tower, Newgate, the Marshalsea, the Fleet, Ludgate, the White Lion and the two 'compters'. When, one week after the failure of the rebellion, Londoners came to St. Paul's Cross for the Sunday sermon and the preacher (carefully briefed by the government) launched into denunciations of Essex, five hundred armed men stood by in case the sermon provoked demonstrations on Essex's behalf.

With the situation as tense as this, the Queen's ministers moved swiftly to bring the leaders of the revolt to trial. On February 13th the Privy Council dispatched letters to the peers whom it had chosen to hear the charges against the Earls of Essex and Southampton. These letters promised their lordships that they 'shalbe further acquainted with all the particularities not only of their secrett practises of treason againste this kingdom but of their actuall rebellion within the citty of London, where they assembled great forces on Sonday laste and killed divers of her Majesty's subjectes'.[1] The government was obviously not risking any verdict of 'Not Guilty'.

Meanwhile, although as the Attorney-General later boasted, no torture was used or even threatened, two of the conspirators, Sir John Davies and Sir Ferdinando Gorges, were ready to talk. Even without their testimony the government had little trouble in building up a damning case against Essex and Southampton. On February 17th indictments were produced charging Essex with an attempt to usurp the crown, and Essex, Southamp-

[1] *Acts P.C., 1600–1601*, p. 150.

ton, Rutland and Sandys with having conspired to depose and slay the Queen and to subvert the government. The next day the Queen signed a commission temporarily appointing Thomas, Lord Buckhurst, to the position of Lord High Steward, so that he could preside in that capacity at the trial of the Earls of Essex and Southampton. The trial was held the next day, February 19th, in Westminster Hall. For once nobody could complain of the law's delay.

During this time of danger Sir John Peyton, normally in command of the Tower of London, had been superseded by Lord Thomas Howard with a special appointment as 'Constable of the Tower'. Early on the morning of February 19th, Howard, Peyton, the two earls, 'those private gentlemen that do attend them', and their guard embarked on three barges and travelled up the river to Westminster. To prevent any attempt at a rescue, Sir John Brodie and a force of musketeers travelled as a convoy in other barges.

At Westminster Hall everything was in readiness for the trial. At the head of the hall a high canopied chair of state had been set up for the Lord High Steward. Ranged below him were eight justices, headed by Sir John Popham, Lord Chief Justice of the Queen's Bench, and Sir Edmund Anderson, the Lord Chief Justice of Common Pleas. These would rule on points of law. At a table in front of the row of justices sat the Clerks of the Crown. To left and to right, facing each other in parallel rows, were the nine earls and sixteen barons who would deliver the final verdict. Farther down the hall, facing the Lord High Steward and the justices, were the Queen's Counsel charged with prosecuting the case—the Attorney-General (Sir Edward Coke), the Solicitor-General (Sir Thomas Fleming), the Queen's Serjeant (Henry Yelverton), the Recorder of London (John Croke), two serjeants-at-law (Heale and Harris) and Francis Bacon.[1] Behind them, separated from the court by a long bar, were ranged the spectators.

It was nearing nine o'clock that morning when the Lord High Steward, preceded by seven sergeants-at-arms bearing maces, entered the court and took his place on the chair of state. Garter King of Arms stood on one side of him, and a gentleman usher bearing a white rod of office on the other. Also in attendance was Sir Walter Raleigh, Captain of the Queen's Guard, with forty of his yeomen.

The Lord High Steward's commission was read, and the Constable of the Tower was called upon to produce his prisoners. Preceded by the Gentleman Porter bearing an axe whose blade was turned away from them, Essex and Southampton came before the Lord High Steward and

[1] For a reproduction of the contemporary diagram of the arrangement of the court, preserved at Alnwick, see Tenison, *Elizabethan England*, XI, Plate 31.

'meeting within the barr kissed their hands and imbraced each other'.[1] Essex was attired in black. Southampton wore a dark-coloured suit and over that a cloth gown with long sleeves in which he kept his hands most of the day. 'The Erle of Essex, his Countenance was all that daye verie cheerfull and confydent. The other Erles somewhat sadd, but without dismay.'[2]

The Constable, having presented his prisoners, took his place among the lord jurors. These now answered to their summons as their names were called in order of seniority. On the list was Lord Grey. When Grey's name was called, Essex laughed and twiched Southampton's sleeve. During the reading of the indictments, Essex was observed to smile, to lift his eyes to Heaven, and make other gestures of incredulity. Then he and Southampton entered their separate pleas of 'Not Guilty' and the trial began.

The prosecution opened with a long speech by Serjeant Yelverton, who enlarged upon the indictments that had just been read. In the ornate rhetoric of the period, he likened the treason of Essex to that of Catiline. He was followed by Attorney-General Coke, who set forth for the lord jurors the law as it applied to the case now before them:

> He that raiseth power and strength in a settled government the lawe doeth construe it highe treason
> He that doe usurpe upon it, the lawe doeth intend that he purposeth the destruction of the Prince
> He that assembles powers, if the kinge doeth comand him uppon his allegiaunce to desolve his company, and he contineweth it without any question it is highe treason[3]

Borne on the full tide of his eloquence, Coke passed from the manner of the late rebellion to the nature of the persons now on trial. Speaking of the many offices and benefits that the Queen had showered on Essex, he upbraided him with his ingratitude. Turning to Southampton he claimed, with considerably less accuracy, that the latter had received diverse favours from the Queen even though his misdemeanours had caused her to think poorly of him. Building up to a fine climax, Coke declared that if Essex, who now stood before them attired in black, had had his way he would have worn 'a gown of blood', but it had pleased God that he who

---

[1] *S.P. 12/278*, f. 186v. Many manuscript reports of this trial survive, varying considerably in detail and in the order of the events they record. Some of them (e.g. *Harl. 2194*) are so full of errors as to be of little use. I have depended chiefly upon the account in the Public Record Office from which I have just quoted. This seems to have been the basic text used for the fullest of the printed accounts of the trial, that given by David Jardine in his *Criminal Trials* (London, 1847), I, 310–66. Useful, too, is the Helmingham manuscript account printed by H. L. Stephen in the Second Series of his *State Trials* (London, 1902), III, 3–87.

[2] Stephen, III, 17. [3] *S.P. 12/278*, f. 188r.

had sought to be Robert the First of England should be Robert the last of his earldom. According to one of the reports of the trial, Essex at the end of Coke's tirade expostulated:

> Mr. Attorney playeth the orator and abuseth your Lordships' ears with slanders against us. These are the fashions of orators in corrupt states, and such rhetoric is the trade and talent of those who value themselves upon their skill in pleading innocent men out of their lives. . . . [1]

After the opening oratory, the prosecution was ready for the presentation of its evidence. This consisted chiefly not of producing witnesses available for cross-examination but of reading statements and confessions secured from prisoners by the officers of the Crown. The practice was customary, but it was open to enormous abuses. Usually the documents produced and read in court had been carefully edited to exclude everything that did not support the case being presented by the prosecution. At times witnesses did take the stand and deliver their testimony in person. Thus when Essex, having heard Sir Ferdinando Gorges' evidence read in court, begged that he might confront him face to face, the Crown, feeling sure enough of Gorges, produced him and let him answer Essex's questions.

One piece of direct testimony was given under unexpected and highly dramatic circumstances. To justify the declarations he had made on the day of the rebellion that a plot existed to let the Spanish Infanta inherit the English crown, Essex testified that he had been told by a member of the Privy Council that Sir Robert Cecil himself had informed him that the Infanta's claim to the succession was as good as any other's. At this point Cecil, who had been listening to the proceedings from a place of concealment, stepped forth and demanded that Essex name the privy councillor who had told him this. For what happened when Essex refused to do so, we may quote, in modernized form, from one of the numerous contemporary accounts of the trial:

> 'Then,' quoth Mr. Secretary, 'It must be believed to be a fiction.'
> 'No!' quoth the Earl, 'It is not, for the nobleman that standeth by me heard it, and it was told jointly to us both.'
> Then Mr. Secretary said to the Earl of Southampton in effect as followeth: 'If it be so, then my lord I conjure you by all the love and friendship that hath been betwixt us, and as you are a Christian, by the honour of your name and house and whatsoever else you hold honourable, as I protest I hold you severed from him [Essex] in impudency, that you name here the councillor to whom I should speak it.'
> The Earl of Southampton answered that he referred himself to that honourable court whether it were fit for him, in the case he now stood in, to name him. 'I refer me,' quoth he, 'to yourself, sir, and if you will say upon your honour that it were fit I did name him, I will.'

[1] Jardine, I, 321.

'I protest,' quoth Mr. Secretary, 'before God and Heaven, that you should do your prince and country a most acceptable service, for I were a very unworthy man to hold that place I do in the state, if I were to be touched in that sort.'

Then the Earl of Southampton named Sir William Knollys to be the councillor.[1]

A messenger was sent to Whitehall to fetch Sir William. Knollys, when he arrived, testified that Cecil had never expressed the opinion attributed to him. He added that Cecil, speaking to him about a seditious book written by a certain Doleman (a name used by Robert Parsons, the Jesuit), had told him that its author said that the Infanta's claim to the crown was as good as any one's.

The lord jurors had made light of Essex's charge but Cecil, experienced in the jungle world of the royal court, knew that a report of this kind, touching so sensitive a matter as the royal succession, must be refuted at once if possible. He must have felt grateful to Southampton for giving him the means to end the matter so effectively. Probably Southampton saved his life by answering as he did.

The trial resumed with Coke and Bacon interjecting speeches of denunciation and horror amid the reading of the examinations of Rutland, Cromwell, Sandys, Danvers, Davies and Blount. In vain Essex protested that the examiners could easily have edited these examinations so as to make them all tell the same story 'were they never so far distant'. He could have pointed out another disadvantage under which he and Southampton laboured. The day had not yet come when men accused of criminal offences could produce their own witnesses, or engage lawyers to plead their cases. The two earls had to conduct their own defence.

Essex's defence was a simple one. Seizing upon the Elizabethan commonplace that man is governed by three laws, those of Nature, Reason and God, Essex asserted that everything he had done had been in compliance with the 'law of nature' (self-preservation), since he had known that his enemies were out to destroy him. He had intended nothing against the Queen, and had sought access to her only to present his case. He said that he locked up her emissaries that fateful Sunday morning because he wanted to protect them from the fury of his followers, who were no longer under his control. As for his failure to comply with the royal proclamation read in London by Garter King of Arms, he maintained that he 'could not beleeve that he had authority to doe that he did, beinge a man of noted dishonesty and once burnt in the hand'.[2] Essex's defence was weak and it is hard to see how, even with expert lawyers to defend him and all the

---

[1] *S.P. 12/278*, ff. 212v–213r.

[2] *S.P. 12/278*, f. 194. Dethick, the herald in question, had in fact been branded for a felony, and in 1594 Essex had cited his criminal record when trying to prevent his appointment to the College of Arms.

safeguards of twentieth-century British justice, Essex could have hoped for acquittal. In fact, he knew that he had no chance and, in the midst of defending himself, talked of going to his death with a courageous and cheerful heart.

Southampton's defence lay along different lines. He denied Coke's claim that he was one of a group of Catholic malcontents:

> And where as you charge me to be a Papist I protest most unfainedly that I was never conversant with any of that sort only I knewe one Wilde a Priest of that sort that went up and dowen the towen but I never conversed with him in all my lief.[1]

He was equally concerned to refute the charge, contained in the Earl of Rutland's examination, that he had long been discontented and had stirred up Essex to his rebellion. He declared that he had acted only out of loyalty to Essex, to whom he was related by marriage, and out of gratitude for the many benefits which Essex had conferred upon him. Speaking of the conferences at Drury House, Southampton did not deny that, had the plans discussed there been carried out, the conspirators would indeed have been guilty of treason. But they had not carried out these plans. Here Southampton sought to use for his own advantage a point which Coke made earlier, that the law takes cognizance not of intents but of deeds. Southampton said that when he came to Essex House that Sunday morning he had known nothing of any plan to march on London. He added that, despite charges to the contrary, he had brought to Essex House with him only ten or twelve of his usual attendants, and had carried no arms other than the sword which he habitually wore. He had not heard the Lord Keeper order those assembled at Essex House to depart. As for accompanying Essex when the latter led his force into London, Southampton protested that he had meant only to defend his friend from his private enemies. He said that in proceeding thus he was totally unaware that he had broken the law. Ignorance of the law is never a good defence, but this in essence was the plea of the Earl of Southampton. To particular points he had his answers:

> . . . when I was in London I heard not the proclamation, for I was not near by the length of a street. Let my Lord Burghley speak (I know him honorable) if he saw me in London. I never drew my sword all the day. I am charged to have carried a pistol. I carried none out with me, but being in the street I saw one having a pistol. I desired it and had it, but it had no stone [flint] nor could it hurt a fly. At my return to Essex House I did there what I could to hinder their shooting, and to that end sent Captain White about the house to stay them. From this, I hope, can be gathered no treason. And therefore I beseech you, my Lords, censure me not according to the strict letter of the law but as in your own consciences you are persuaded. . . .[2]

[1] *S.P. 12/278*, f. 198r. In various other accounts of the trial the priest's name is given as 'Wright' or as 'White'.

[2] *S.P. 12/278*, f. 192v. I have modernized the spelling and punctuation.

Such was the defence of the Earl of Southampton, pleaded with considerable eloquence, some naïveté, and more than a little disingenuousness.

At last, sometime between six o'clock and seven, the long day's trial drew to its close, Monsieur de Boissise, the ardently pro-Essex French ambassador, was probably the author of a highly coloured account of how the lord jurors concluded their business:

> Shortly afterwards, the Counsel ended their pleadings, and the Peers their biscuits and beer. For while the Earl and the Counsel were pleading, my Lords guzzled as if they had not eaten for a fortnight, smoking also plenty of tobacco. Then they went into a room to give their voices; and there, stupid with eating, and drunk with smoking, they condemned the two Earls.[1]

The lords having declared their verdict, the two convicted earls were asked what they had to say before the Lord High Steward passed sentence. Essex used the opportunity to declare his Protestantism, his penitence and his humility. His request for mercy from the Queen was almost incidental. Southampton was less resigned to his fate:

> I pray you truly to inform the Queen of my penitence, and be a means for me to her Majesty to grant me her gracious pardon. I know I have offended her; yet if it please her to be merciful unto me, I may, by my future service, deserve my life. I have been brought up under her Majesty, I have spent the best part of my patrimony in her Majesty's service, with frequent danger of my life, as your Lordships well know. . . . But since I am found guilty by the law, I do submit myself to death, yet not despairing of her Majesty's mercy; for I know she is merciful, and if she please to extend mercy to me, I shall with all humility receive it.

It remained only for the Lord High Steward to pass the terrible sentence required by the law in such cases:

> . . . you both shall be led from hence to the place from whence you came, and there remain during her Majesty's pleasure; from thence to be drawn upon a hurdle through the midst of the City, and so to the place of execution, there to be hanged by the neck and taken down alive,—your bodies to be opened, and your bowels taken out and burned before your face; your bodies to be quartered,—your heads and quarters to be disposed of at her Majesty's pleasure, and so God have mercy on your souls.[2]

Then the guard led the two condemned earls back to the Tower, the Gentleman Porter now bearing the axe with the blade towards them.

Among the spectators that day at Westminster Hall was John Chamberlain. Writing to Dudley Carleton a few days later, he gave his opinion of how Southampton had carried himself at his trial:

> The earle of Southampton spake very well (but me thought somwhat too much . . .) and as a man that wold faine live pleaded hard to acquite himself,

---

[1] *Memorials of Affairs of State . . . Chiefly from the Original Papers of the Right Honourable Sir Ralph Winwood* (London, 1725), I, 299; trans. Jardine, *Criminal Trials*, I, 361.

[2] Jardine, op. cit., I, 363–5.

but all in vaine for yt could not be, wherupon he descended to intreatie, and moved great commisseration, and though he were generally well liked, yet me thought he was somwhat too low and submisse, and seemed to loth to die before a prowde ennemie.

John Speed, a contemporary historian, records that the 'sweet temper' exhibited by Southampton 'did breed most compassionate affections in all men'.[1]

Back in the Tower of London, Essex sank into a mood of piety and contrition not unlike that which he had experienced late in 1599, when imprisoned because of his conduct of affairs in Ireland. Two days after his conviction, at Essex's own request, Lord Treasurer Buckhurst (who had presided at his trial), Lord Keeper Egerton, Lord Admiral Nottingham, and Secretary Cecil came to see him at the Tower. To them he made some sort of confession, apparently admitting that he and his accomplices had intended to force their way into the Queen's presence, 'and use her authority to change the government and call a Parliament, condemning their opponents for misgoverning the state'.[2] In the course of this interview Essex named, as chief persuaders to 'this great offence', his stepfather Sir Christopher Blount, his own secretaries Cuffe and Temple, and those who had participated in the Drury House conferences.

At the end of the interview, according to Sir Robert Cecil, Essex petitioned that he might die privately. The request was granted, and the manner of his execution changed to beheading. Between seven and eight o'clock on the morning of February 25th, Essex was led from his chamber to a scaffold erected on the green within the precincts of the Tower. About a hundred nobles and gentlemen were on hand to witness the execution. To them Essex spoke with dignity and composure admitting, in the words of one report, 'this my last sin, this great, this bloody, this crying, this infectious sin, whereby so many have for love of me been drawn to offend God, to offend their Sovereign, to offend the world'.[3] He insisted, however, that he had never intended violence or death for the Queen. Kneeling, he put his head upon the block and commenced his final prayer. The headsman bungled his job. The first blow struck Essex on the shoulders, the second on the head. Only the third finally severed the head from the neck. There was still plenty of sympathy for Essex in London, and when the

[1] Chamberlain, *Letters*, I, 20; John Speed, *The History of Great Britaine* (London, 1623), p. 1213.

[2] This confession has not survived. All that we have is a very brief account of the interview signed by Egerton, Buckhurst and Nottingham (*S.P. 12/278*, f. 228), and an account of the confession, passed on to Mountjoy in Ireland by Cecil in a letter of February 26th (*Cal. S.P. (Dom.), 1598–1601*, p. 598). The quotation just given comes from this letter.

[3] Jardine, I, 378.

headsman left the Tower he was so beaten by the mob that the sheriffs had to come to his rescue before he was murdered.

On March 5th Essex's stepfather, Sir Christopher Blount, his steward, Sir Gelly Merrick, his secretary, Henry Cuffe, whom he had accused of chiefly leading him astray, Sir John Davies and Sir Charles Danvers stood their trial for high treason. All were found guilty. Davies was reprieved but on March 13th Merrick and Cuffe were taken to Tyburn and there publicly put through the whole appalling course of being hanged, drawn and quartered. It seemed for a while that Sir Charles Danvers, who had offered to pay £10,000 in lieu of his life, would have his offer accepted. Danvers, however, had angered the authorities by resolutely keeping silent under examination until he had been shown the confessions extracted from his fellows. On March 18th he and Blount were publicly beheaded on Tower Hill. In his speech from the scaffold Danvers, turning to where Lord Grey sat on horseback near by, declared that he had been ill-inclined towards him, '. . . not from any Injury he had suffer'd from him, but purely on the *Earl* of *Southampton's* account, to whom the Lord *Grey* profest an absolute Enmity'.[1] Earlier Danvers had declared to the authorities that:

> The principal motive that drove [him] into this action was the great obligation of love and duty, in respect of many honourable favours done to him by the Earl of Southampton.[2]

Danvers met his death bravely:

> . . . though the flesh of his cheekes trembled, . . . [he] put off his Gowne and Doublet in most cheerefull manner, rather like a Bridegrome, then a prisoner appointed for death . . . his head was cut off at one stroke, saving a little which an officer cut off with his knife.

He was followed on the scaffold by Sir Christopher Blount. Before the headsman's axe ended his life, Blount conceded what the Crown had all along contended:

> I know, and must confess, if we had failed of our Ends, we should (rather than have been disappointed) even have drawn Blood from herself [the Queen].[3]

Meanwhile, what of the Earl of Southampton? If anybody could save him it was Cecil. After the failure of the rebellion his wife wrote a desperate letter of appeal to Master Secretary. On the day of the trial, as soon as she learned of the verdict returned by the lords, she wrote again to Cecil:

---

[1] Hargrave, *State Trials*, I, 211.

[2] Examination of February 16th. *Cal. S.P.* (*Dom.*), *1598–1601*, p. 571.

[3] John Stow, *Annales or A Generall Chronicle of England* (London, 1631), sig. XXXIr; Hargrave, *State Trials*, I, 212.

The woeful news to me of my Lord's condemnation passed this day makes me in this my most amazed distress, address myself unto you and your virtues as being the only likely means to yield me comfort. Therefore I do beseech you and conjure you by whatsoever is dearest unto you that you will vouchsafe so much commiseration unto a most afflicted woman as to be my means unto her sacred Majesty that I may by her divine self be permitted to come to prostrate myself at her feet, to beg for mercy for my Lord. Oh! let me, I beseech you, in this my great distress move you to have this compassion. . . . I restlessly remain the most unhappy and miserable Elizabeth Southampton.

Reinforcing the wife's appeal was one from the mother, for the Dowager Countess wrote also:

God of heaven knows I can scarce hold my hand steady to write, and less hold steady in my heart how to write, only for what I know, which is to pray mercy to my miserable son.

Thus she began her letter. Continuing in disjointed fashion, she said what little she could in palliation of her son's great offence:

It appeared to me many times his earnest desire to recover her Majesty's favour, his doleful discontented behaviour when he could not obtain it, how apt despair made him at length to receive evil counsel and follow such company. . . .

She had a point there. If Queen Elizabeth had not so relentlessly maintained her dislike of Southampton, denying him access to her Court, and refusing him first the generalship of the horse in Ireland and then the governorship of Connaught, Southampton might never have turned to treason. Cecil was a fair and just man, and he may have nodded assent when, reading Southampton's own appeal to him, he found him protesting that, if the Queen had occasionally allowed him access to her, this disaster could never have overtaken him.[1]

Counting against Southampton was a treacherous letter that his brother-in-law Arundell sent to Cecil. Since this has never been printed before, it seems proper to give it here in its entirety, though with modernized spelling and punctuation:

Right Honourable,
    I cannot choose but manifest unto yourself how much I am aggrieved for the fall of the Earl of Southampton, & am more than ashamed at the foulness of his fault. His honestest friends had often told him that his great expenses could not but bring him to great need, & *dura necessitas cogit ad turpia*. But his ears were hardened against wholesome counsel, for which I thought good to estrange myself from him, which strangeness yourself (by such speech as you had with me concerning him) could not but find, & all that know us perceived it, for that I saw him but once this two year. Yet can I not but grieve for being allied to one that hath so foully blotted his allegiance, & that to such a princess, under whom I presume he might have lived happy many years, had not the devil owed him a shame.
    I humbly desire that my unspotted faith to my ever reverenced princess may, by your favour, be recommended. The venture of my life & my poor ability shall

[1] For the text of this, and the preceding letters, see *Salisbury MSS.*, XI, 70–3.

be ever ready to do her faithful service against whatsoever traitor earl or earls. I thought it not good in these troublesome times to come up unsent for, though I shall be glad of any occasion to show my zealous heart to do her service. God, I beseech him, long to direct & prosper her.

Shafton, this 18th of February.

Your Honour's ever faithful kinsman,

Tho: Arundell

With this letter Arundell enclosed a statement, in his own handwriting but without his signature:

I cannot but write what I think may avail you, so doth my love manifest my folly. There is one Cuff, a certain Puritan scholar, one of the hottest-headed of my Lord of Essex his followers. This Cuff was sent by my Lord of Essex to read to my Lord of Southampton in Paris, where he read Aristotle's *Politics* to him, with such expositions as, I doubt [think] did him but little good. Afterwards he read to my Lord of Rutland. I protest I owe him no malice, but if he should be faulty herein, which I greatly doubt [think], I cannot but wish his punishment, *verbum sapienti*.

I do truly love you & therefore wish that every man should love you, which love in these troublesome discontented times is sooner won by clemency than severity. I would willingly tell you somewhat by word of mouth. If it please you to send me word by this bearer that I may come, I will be presently with you.

I love much, & therefore I presume much. The matter is this. If Her Majesty shall think my Lord of Southampton a fit man to receive life & mercy, God forbid but I should desire it & be glad of it. But if he must needs die & forfeit all, then my request is that by your favour the fee farm of that little land which he is now possessed of may be granted to myself at such a reasonable rent as you shall think good of. He hath sold the better half of what he had. The remainder (his mother's jointure being excepted) is not great. Yet this being the only means whereby I may be benefitted by your favour, who never expect any office in Court or reward for attendance, & seeing that my sons are his next heirs male, & seeing that here you may pleasure me without prejudice to any, or hurt to Her Majesty, I desire it as far forth as you shall allow of, without whom I will neither do nor desire anything. I am wholly yours & as so favour me & use me.[1]

Fortunately for Southampton, others were more mercifully inclined towards him. Public opinion favoured clemency. 'The Erle of Sowthampton is much pitied',[2] reported Thomas Screven a few days after the trial. Writing to Southampton's friend Mountjoy, Cecil, partly for politic reasons, permitted himself an expression of this widely held feeling, '. . . the man that grieveth me to think what may become of him, is the poor young Earl of Southampton. . . .'[3] Cecil must have felt the more kindly disposed to Southampton because of the way in which the Earl had helped him to refute Essex's allegations at the trial. Moreover, it is likely that after Essex had been executed the government felt that mercy to the other earl might help to conciliate public opinion. On the other hand, Southampton's role in the rebellion, especially at the Drury House con-

[1] Bodleian Library, *Ashmole MS. 1729*, ff. 189r–190r.
[2] *Rutland MSS.*, I, 367.   [3] *Cal. S.P. (Ireland), 1600–1601*, p. 201.

ferences, told terribly against him. As late as March 25th spectators came to Tower Hill, drawn by a rumour that Southampton was to be executed there that day. They were disappointed. The decision had already been made to commute his sentence to imprisonment.

In the Tower Southampton had little to congratulate himself upon, other than the reprieve of his life. His health was poor, and he was receiving the ministrations of Dr. Paddy both for a quartain ague and a swelling in his legs and other parts of his body. His earldom had, of course, been lost through his attainder, and he was now plain Henry Wriothesley. Although the lands which he had transferred to trustees by a deed of uses were apparently beyond the reach of the Crown,[1] all his other possessions were forfeit. Lord Burghley wrote to his brother, Sir Robert Cecil, to ask if he could have a bay horse and a black mare that had belonged to the fallen earl. Down to Titchfield that April came Sir Thomas Fleming, the Queen's Solicitor-General. With his clerks he trooped about the great mansion, through the entrance gate flanked by its four lofty towers and into the Fountain Court that lay beyond, up the handsome stairs that on the opposite side led up to the hall beyond, and so on to all the other parts of the great mansion: the gallery, the great dining-room, the little dining-room, the ladies' gallery, the music gallery, the earl's apartments, and those of his countess. On they went into the Kitchen Court and all the multiple offices that lay around it, the servants' hall, the still room, the kitchen, the wet larder and the dry larder, the small beer cellar and the strong beer cellar, and the arched wine cellar, everywhere from the Jericho Porch to the Audit Room.[2] As they went, they took inventory:

> In the great chamber
> One large Turkey carpett
> One large foote Turkey carpett
> Twoe chaires of crimson velvet
> vi high stooles of crimson
>
> . . .   . . .
> In the longe Gallery
> old mappes[3]

[1] *The Secret Correspondence of Sir Robert Cecil with James VI, King of Scotland* (London, 1766), p. 69.

[2] Since there is no evidence of any major structural changes at Titchfield during the seventeenth and early eighteenth centuries, I am assuming that in Southampton's day the layout of the house was essentially that shown in the only surviving plan of Titchfield House, or Place [Palace] House, that made in 1737 and now among the Wriothesley Papers on deposit in the Hampshire County Archives, *W.P. 1557–1558*. In 1786 the house was visited by Thomas Warton who wrote a rather brief description of it, printed in the Third Variorum (1821) edition of Shakespeare, XX, 434. Soon after Warton's visit the house was dismantled, and now only ruins remain.

[3] The single stained and faded sheet of this inventory that survives in the Public Record Office (E154/6/50) is in such poor condition that even under the ultra-violet lamp most of it remains tantalizingly illegible.

One must not think of Southampton as spending his days in the Tower in some dank dungeon. Like most political prisoners, he had chambers of his own and, judging from the rent of £9 a week[1] that he paid the Lieutenant of the Tower, they were probably fairly capacious and well furnished. His confinement, however, was initially very strict, and small events must have loomed large in a monotonous life. In June 1601 Captain Hart, who had been Southampton's keeper, finding his job no better than imprisonment for himself, handed over to an unknown successor. In July Lord Cromwell was released from the Tower, and in August Lord Mounteagle and Lord Sandys. Nobody could hope for similar leniency for Southampton, but in this latter month the Privy Council, taking note of Southampton's 'long sicknes (which he hath had before his trouble)', finally permitted him to be visited by his mother and those others 'that were putt in trust with his estate'. In October, having learned that Southampton had 'of late growne very sickly', the Privy Council permitted his wife 'at convenyent tymes to repayre unto him'.[2] He was also, for the first time, allowed to leave the confines of his chambers and walk in the fresh air on the leaden roof above them. By the end of the year Southampton was receiving visits in his lodgings from his old friends of the Essex faction,[3] the 'Octavians' as they were now known in consequence of the events of the ill-starred February 8th.

It is not surprising if Sir John Peyton, the Lieutenant of the Tower, and others treated Southampton with as much consideration and gentleness as they dared. They knew that the old Queen could not live for ever, and that her probable successor, James VI of Scotland, would almost certainly release Southampton and give him a position of power and influence. King James was in fact already regarding the prisoner with a solicitous eye. Writing from Scotland to the Earl of Northumberland, he spoke feelingly of 'poor southamtoune, who lives in hardest cais', and added, 'If in any sort your means may helpe to procure hem forder libertie or easier ward, pitie would provoke me to recommend it unto you.'[4]

In his long periods of loneliness Southampton had for his companion a cat, one which later tradition reported had been a favourite of his in more fortunate days and, finding its way to the Tower, had reached him by coming down the chimney into his quarters.[5]

---

[1] *Publications of the Catholic Record Society*, Vol. IV (London, 1907), p. 236.

[2] *Acts P.C., 1601–1604*, p. 175 and p. 256.

[3] *Secret Correspondence of Sir Robert Cecil*, pp. 34–35.

[4] John Bruce, ed., *Correspondence of King James I with Sir Robert Cecil and Others*, Camden Society (London, 1861), p. 71.

[5] Thomas Pennant, *Of London* (London, 1790), p. 272. Leslie Hotson (*Mr. W.H.*, London, 1964, pp. 207–8), has suggested that the cat is merely an iconographical symbol saying 'Give me back my freedom'.

IN VINCVL
INVICTVS

FEBRVA: 8: 160
602: 603: AP

SOUTHAMPTON IN HIS CAPTIVITY IN THE
TOWER OF LONDON, 1601—1603

By permission of the Duke of Buccleuch

Despite its small ameliorations, Southampton's life during his years in the Tower was a miserable one. For evidence we need only look at the portrait which, as a memorial to his long suffering, he had painted when he at last won his release. In the foreground stands Southampton, all in black, his features drawn and woebegone. By his right hand sits his cat and beside it, another diversion of his solitude, a book bearing the Wriothesley arms.[1] In the upper right-hand corner of the picture is a miniature representation of the Tower, his place of imprisonment. Beneath is lettered a motto: *In vinculis invictus* ('Unconquered though in chains'). Below that is the chronology of his imprisonment according to the Old Style dating, 'Februar: 8: 1600: 1601: 1602: 1603 Apri.'

April 1603! Queen Elizabeth had died on March 24th of that year. Her hostility could not reach beyond the grave. One of the first acts of King James, the new sovereign, was to order Southampton released.

[1] Azure, a cross or, between four falcons close argent.

CHAPTER XII

The Favour of King James

ON APRIL 5TH, 1603, James VI of Scotland, at last by the Grace of God also James I of England, set out on the long journey to London. One of his last acts before leaving Edinburgh was to send ahead an order for the release of Southampton. With that order he sent a letter addressed to the Privy Council and nobility of England in which he explained that he was acting out of concern for Southampton's health, and made it plain that he wanted Southampton on hand when 'that bodie of state nowe assembled' should greet him at the end of his journey:

> At which tyme wee are pleased hee shall allso come to our presence, ffor as yt is on us that his onlie hope dependeth, soe wee will reserve those workes of farther favor untell the tyme hee beehouldeth our owne eyes, whereof as wee knowe the comfort wilbee greate to him, soe yt wilbee contentment unto us, to have opportunitie to declare our Estimation of him.[1]

On April 10th, the royal warrant having arrived, the Lieutenant of the Tower freed Southampton and his fellow Essexian prisoner, Sir Henry Neville. Two weeks later, not waiting for the formal reception of the King by the Privy Council at Theobalds, Southampton arrived at Lord Burghley's mansion at Burghley-by-Stamford, and was ushered into the presence of King James. Essex had always maintained that James was the rightful heir to the English throne, and James regarded Essex as his 'martyr'. He was resolved to bestow upon Essex's friend the benefits which that unhappy man had not lived to receive.

The anticipated rewards and favours poured forth. On May 16th Southampton received a royal pardon for his offence committed in Elizabeth's time. The Earl's own copy of this deed survives to this day. Set forth in splendid calligraphy on two enormous vellum sheets, the plangent Latin sentences detail the King's clemency. At the head of the first sheet, under an emblazoned floral and armorial border and set beside the initial letter of the text, is a portrait of James enthroned in majesty under a canopy whose fringe bears the legend VIVAT REX JACOBUS.[2] On July 9th Southampton was installed as a Knight of the Garter, the fourth of the new reign, the first three being Prince Henry (the heir to the throne), the King of Denmark (brother to the new queen), and the Duke of Lennox (the kinsman who had come south with King James). When in July

[1] *Add M.S. 33051*, f. 53r.   [2] *W.P. 1001.*

fourteen courtiers were granted the privilege of access to the King's Privy Chamber, Southampton was on the list. On July 21st King James created his first English earls, the list being headed by Henry Wriothesley, formally again made Earl of Southampton but with the precedence of his former creation. Among the other creations was that of Southampton's old friend Mountjoy who, fresh from his subjugation of Ireland, was made Earl of Devonshire. The new barons included Sir Henry Danvers, now created Baron Danvers of Dauntsey.

Titles are all very well, but money is important too. Southampton, as we have seen, was practically bankrupt even before the disaster of the Essex Rebellion. Now, in splendid fashion, King James rehabilitated him financially. Writing to Lord Treasurer Buckhurst on August 20th, James instructed him to make over to Southampton that farm of the sweet wines which had provided Essex with most of his wealth. True, Southampton had to pay the Crown £6,000 per annum for this farm and bear the costs of collection, but since he apparently took in some £8,500 per annum in import duties paid by the wine merchants, the royal grant gave him an annual profit of about £2,000 (possibly as much as £40,000 in modern values).[1]

In September, in consequence of the death of George Carey, Lord Hunsdon, the Earl of Southampton was appointed Captain of the Isle of Wight.[2] The post was no sinecure. Because of its position the Isle of Wight was vulnerable both to enemy invasions and pirate raids. Only after the defeat of the Armada did the men of the Island cease evacuating their families to the mainland in time of war. Southampton, who always regarded himself as a soldier, entered with enthusiasm upon his captaincy. Periodically he took up residence in Carisbrooke Castle, and superintended the Island's defences, even advancing money out of his own pocket for the repair of the lesser castles at Sandown and Yarmouth. Like the benevolent monarch of a little kingdom, he exercised a calm Saturnian reign, later to be looked back upon with nostalgia by the Island gentry.

[1] For quietuses granted to Edward Gage of Bentley, William Chamberlain of Beaulieu, William Heynes of Chessington and Arthur Broomfield of Allington, in connection with this farm, see *W.P. 973* and *974*. In 1607, when the wine merchants appealed to the Lord Treasurer to change their allowance for leakage from the 10 per cent allowed them by Southampton to the 20 per cent that they had been allowed under Elizabeth, Southampton wrote to Cecil pointing out not only that 20 per cent was much too large but that the higher exemption would reduce his collections 'from 700l. to 1000l. a year'. When the Crown resumed this farm, Southampton was given a pension of £2,000 per annum in compensation (*Salisbury MSS.*, XIX, 374), (*Cal.S.P. (Dom.), 1611-18*, p. 40. No wonder Southampton subsequently wrote that without the sweet wines farm he would be enforced to live in a very mean fashion, *Cecil Papers* 125/169.

[2] Southampton had been granted the reversion of the post for life on July 7th, 1603 (*W.P. 968*). Hunsdon died September 8th.

Sir John Oglander would recall how every Tuesday and Thursday, when the Earl was at his bowling on St. George's Down, thirty to forty knights and gentlemen would join him, eating together and playing both bowls and cards.[1]

Probably the Earl could not spend as much time on his island as he might have desired. His own country seats at Titchfield and Beaulieu on the mainland required his presence part of the time. Much time, too, had to be spent at the royal court, of which he was one of the ornaments in the years which lay ahead.

Although Southampton, after the auspicious beginning, kept the friendship of the King and was one of the persons whom King James liked to have around him, he never became the royal favourite. That position, with its indefinable overtones, was reserved for handsome younger men, better suited to supply the emotional needs of the King. The unstable young Southampton of 1593 might have made such a favourite, but not the mature Southampton of 1603 who, his wilder years left behind, was increasingly interested in raising his family, starting an ironworks at Southampton, planting orchards, and reclaiming land at Titchfield. The King found Southampton an agreeable companion, but he became neither a royal favourite nor a royal crony. If Southampton's relations with James were cordial, so were his relations with Anne of Denmark, the new queen. We do not know when he first met Anne. Probably the occasion was on June 27th when the Queen, following her husband south, arrived at Easton Neston to be received there by James and his new court. Lady Anne Clifford mentions that among 'many great ladies' who met the Queen there was 'my Lady Southampton'.[2] Presumably her husband was with her. In the succeeding months Queen Anne must have found Southampton agreeable and attractive for when, in October, she was provided with a court establishment with her own Lord Chamberlain, Chancellor, Master of Requests and the like, Southampton was on the list as Master of the Queen's Game with direction over all Her Majesty's forests and chases.[3]

Only one incident briefly imperilled the Earl's relations with the Queen. One evening late in June the Queen, chatting with Southampton at Windsor, expressed amazement that at the time of Essex's Rebellion, 'so many great men did so little for themselves'. Southampton had a ready reply: they had had no choice but to yield, since their sovereign had sided with their enemies. He added that without Queen Elizabeth's support none of the private enemies of Essex and himself would have dared to oppose

[1] The Oglander Memoirs (London, 1888), p. 23.
[2] The Diary of Lady Anne Clifford (London, 1923), p. 10.
[3] W.P. 122.

them. At this Lord Grey, who was standing by, declared that he and his friends could have done much more than the Essexians. To end the unseemly quarrel that then erupted the Queen dismissed the disputants to their lodgings, where they were soon after put under guard. The next day the Privy Council decided to send them both to the Tower. Fortunately for Southampton and Grey, King James, playing his cherished role of peacemaker, stepped in and, forgiving them the 'wrong and disgrace done to her Majesty', secured some sort of reconciliation and set them free.[1]

Grey was not to trouble Southampton much longer. Two weeks later he was arrested for involvement in the Bye Plot. When Grey stood trial on December 7th, Southampton was on the jury. Remembering how Grey had been a juror at his own trial less than four years earlier, Southampton must have relished the reversal of roles. Lord Grey was found guilty and, after a last-minute commutation of the death sentence, was sent to the Tower to rot there until he died ten years later, leaving no son to continue his ancient line.

With Southampton so obviously enjoying the favour of the new king, he was sought after as a friend and a patron. Hardly was he out of the Tower when that adroit opportunist Francis Bacon sent a smooth note announcing that, in consequence of the accession of the new king, he could now safely show himself what he had always truly been—Southampton's humble and much devoted servant.[2] Sir John Davies, whose confession had been so useful to Bacon and the rest of the prosecutors during the trial of the two earls, began the difficult process of persuading Southampton that he had acted without falsehood or malice.[3]

Men of letters, who had ceased all dedications after Southampton's ruin, again sought him as a patron. Probably the first in the field was Samuel Daniel. Daniel, addressing to King James a *Panegyrike Congratulatorie* upon his accession, published along with it a fifty-six line poem praising Southampton for having used his misfortunes to demonstrate a heroic stoicism:

> How could we know that thou could'st have indur'd
> With a reposed cheere, wrong and disgrace,
> And with a heart and countenance assur'd
> Have lookt sterne Death, and Horror in the face?
> How should we know thy soule had bin secur'd
> In honest councels, and in wayes unbase?
> Hadst thou not stood to shew us what thou wert,
> By thy affliction, that descride thy heart.

John Davies of Hereford, publishing his long pedantic poem *Microcosmos*, not only worked an allusion to Southampton into his versified preface but

[1] John Nichols, *The Progresses, Processions, and Magnificent Festivities of King James the First* (London, 1828), I, 198.
[2] *Sloane MS. 3078*, f. 39r.   [3] *Salisbury MSS.*, XV, 84–5.

printed a congratulatory sonnet to him at the end of his book. This latter begins with the felicitous lines:

> Welcome to shoare unhappy-Happie *Lord*
> From the deepe Seas of danger and distresse . . .

Southampton might have been more impressed by this offering had not Davies, looking for largesse in every possible quarter, included thirty-three other sonnets addressed to everybody from sundry Scots who had come south with their king, to the Earl of Pembroke (who rated two sonnets); and from the Dean of Windsor to Magdalen College, Oxford. Francis Davison, publishing a sheet of verses[1] based on Latin anagrams of the names of court notables, contrived to wrestle an uncouth HENRICUS URIOTHESLEUS into THESEUS NIL REUS HIC RUO. In the accompanying verses he explained that because of a false charge brave Theseus (Southampton) had come to grief though not a criminal. Last of these literary tributes of 1603 was a strange concoction entitled *A Welch Bayte to Spare Provender*. On the reverse of its title page is printed:

> A Prelude uppon the name of
> Henry Wriothesly Earle of
> South-hampton
> Ever
> Whoso beholds this Leafe, therein shall reede,
> A faithfull subjects name, he shall indeede:
> The grey-eyde morne in noontide clowdes may steepe,
> But traytor and his name shall never meete.
> Never

There follows the dedication in routine form, along with six stanzas of limping commendatory verses, the whole closing with the subscription:

> Your Lordshippes
> In all the nerves of my ability,
> THO: POWELL

The book consists of three sections. The first gives an account of Queen Elizabeth's policies in matters of religion. The second tells of the feelings of unrest as the anxious city watchmen walked the streets of London on the night of her death. The third and concluding section, entitled 'The Scottish Englishing', expatiates on the rightness of a union of the two kingdoms. Powell declares that the purity, firmness and solidity of the Scottish language will 'delight the English Orator', a somewhat interesting claim in a book dedicated to Shakespeare's patron. We do not know how Southampton responded to Powell's hope that he might bask in his

---

[1] *Anagrammata T. Egertoni* (S.T.C. 6165).

'beames of Patronage'. We do know that the dedication did not save Valentine Simms from being fined for publishing the book without a licence.

The succeeding year, 1604, brought further dedications. Robert Pricket, who had served under Essex in the wars, published his doggerel *Honors Fame in Triumph Riding, or the Life and Death of the Late Honorable Earle of Essex*, and dedicated it to the Earls of Southampton and Devonshire, and to Essex's uncle, Lord Knollys. Possibly because of an insulting reference to Lord Henry Howard[1] the book was called in and the publisher interrogated.

Two other dedications of 1604 may belong to an earlier date. The first is that of John Hind's *The Most Excellent Historie of Lysimachus and Varrona, Daughter to Syllanus, Duke of Hypata*. This is a simple-minded little Arcadian romance. The careful parallelisms, the alliterations, and antitheses all proclaim the euphuistic style made popular years before by John Lyly. The author admits the Lylyian influence when he confesses that his gentlemen readers may censure him for being 'engulphed in an Ocean of conceit'. But nobody was writing euphuistic romances in 1604. By then the whole fashion was hopelessly *passé*. Accordingly it seems a reasonably safe supposition that behind Thomas Creede's edition of 1604 stands a lost earlier edition, published somewhere around 1594, a date that would accord better with both the nature of the book and the evolving taste of the dedicatee. The other work published in 1604 with a dedication to Southampton that may be of an earlier date is Thomas Wright's *The Passions of the Minde*. This is a substantial Elizabethan psychological treatise running to some four hundred pages of solid print. It was, in fact, an augmented and corrected second edition that came out in 1604. The first edition had appeared, without any dedication, in 1601. Mrs. Stopes may be right when she comments, 'If there had been a Dedication intended, it was probably suppressed because of Southampton's trouble.'[2] On the other hand, Wright in his dedicatory epistle clearly indicates that the 1601 edition had been printed without his surveillance or knowledge.

For Southampton there were things of more importance in 1604 than the appearance of these books. There was, for instance, King James' state procession through London. Because of the plague which had ravaged the city at the time of James' coronation in July 1603, this procession had been postponed until March 15th of the following year. Among those who walked in the enormous glittering train, through triumphal arches gorgeous with obelisks and symbolic shows, past singing boys and musicians and applauding crowds of citizenry, was our Earl of Southampton and his mother. His wife was not there and for an excellent reason. She expected

[1] See p. 142 footnote 2.   [2] p. 415.

any day the birth of a child, perhaps the male heir which she so longed to present to her lord.

The child was born a few weeks later. It proved to be another daughter. The Queen agreed to be a godmother to the babe, who was baptized with Her Majesty's own name of Anne in the Chapel Royal.

On March 19th King James opened his first parliament. Almost all the peers of England were present for the occasion, Southampton among them. When the session settled down to its business he proved one of the more faithful of the members of the House of Lords, attending 46 of its 69 sittings. When he was not present there was some good reason for his absence. Thus we learn that on March 26th:

> The Lord Chamberlain signified unto the House, That the Earls of *Southampton* and *Pembrook* were to be excused, for their Absence from the Parliament, for some Time; for that they were commanded to wait upon the King in his Journey to Roiston.[1]

The King's journey to Royston was for hunting, the pastime to which James was so addicted that his new subjects were soon complaining that His Majesty devoted himself more to the chase than to the government of his kingdom. Southampton was often to accompany the King on his extended visits to Royston, and acquired his own Cambridgeshire residence, a tidy little Italianate villa at nearby Shelford Parva. He must have proved an attractive companion for the King, witty, well-informed, wearing lightly at the table his considerable learning, and showing himself in the field an excellent horseman.

Various signs of continued royal favour came to Southampton in early 1604. On the anniversary of the monarch's accession he was one of the noblemen chosen to ride in the ceremonial tilting at Whitehall which traditionally marked the occasion. We are told that the Earls of Southampton and Cumberland were the two who 'ran with greatest commendation'.[2] A few weeks later he and his friend the Earl of Devonshire were appointed joint Lord-Lieutenants for Hampshire.

Suddenly the even happy flow of Southampton's career came to a halt. Late on the evening of June 24th he was arrested, along with Lord Danvers (his old friend Sir Henry), Sir Henry Neville (the Essex sympathizer who had shared his imprisonment in the Tower), Sir Maurice Berkeley (a fellow member of Queen Anne's council) and Sir William Lee. Southampton's papers were seized and scrutinized. He himself was interrogated. According to the French Ambassador, King James had gone

---

[1] *Lords Journals*, II, 266. During Southampton's absence, the Lords passed an act confirming the royal restitution of Southampton's titles.

[2] Foley, *Records of the English Province of the Society of Jesus*, I, 59.

into a complete panic and could not sleep that night even though he had a guard of his Scots posted around his quarters. Presumably to protect his heir, he sent orders to Prince Henry that he must not stir out of his chamber.

Next morning, while the Privy Council was examining its prisoners, wild rumours swept through the Court. Some men said that a plot had been discovered against the King and the Prince. Some maintained that the conspirators had planned to massacre the Scots who had flocked south with their king, with Sir George Home, the Lord Treasurer of Scotland, heading the list of intended victims. Others declared that not the Scots but the Howards were the intended victims, that the survivors of the Essex Rebellion had meant to assassinate various of the family and to force King James to remove their allies from the Privy Council. Still others affirmed that the whole matter had been trumped up by a faction in the English court inimical to Cecil and friendly to Spain—that since Southampton was now the close friend of Cecil, these devious pro-Spaniards had sought to weaken Cecil's hand in the peace negotiations now under way with Spain by striking at him through his friend. The most piquant of the reports was that politics were not involved and that the simple truth was that the King had learned that the Queen was having an affair with her Master of the Game.

Southampton was quickly found innocent of whatever charges had been brought against him. According to both the Venetian and French ambassadors, he was released on June 25th, the day after his arrest.

Probably we shall never know the nature of the charges brought against Southampton. No documents that relate to this episode survive in either the Public Record Office or in that other great depository of state papers of the period, the Cecil Papers at Hatfield. Probably King James, embarrassed by what had occurred, ordered that all the papers be destroyed. Certainly a determined effort seems to have been made to hush up the whole affair. For our knowledge of the incident we are dependent almost entirely upon the remarkably full report sent to Henri IV by the Comte de Beaumont, his ambassador in England, and a much shorter account sent home by the Venetian envoy.[1]

---

[1] For the French account, which has been my chief source for the preceding, see *Manuscrit Français 15983*, ff. 313r–314v, in the Bibliothèque Nationale. Dated July 5th N.S. (June 25th O.S.), this report notes 'ce Jourdhuy le Conte de Southanton a este non seulement mis en Liberte. . . .' For the Venetian references see *Cal. S.P. (Ven.), 1603–1607*, pp. 165 and 168.

Sir Anthony Weldon in his scandal-mongering *Court and Character of King James* (London, 1650), p. 41, says that Cecil, to prevent Southampton becoming the royal favourite, played on the King's jealousy. In referring thus to Cecil, Weldon must be mistaken.

If the charges are unknown to us, so too is Southampton's accuser. King James, though clearing Southampton, refused to divulge to him the identity of the informer. When Southampton, meaning to challenge his accuser to a duel, demanded to be told his identity, the King gave him only 'fair words'. Beaumont in his dispatch says that Southampton was accused by 'quelques uns Catholicques',[1] but indicates later that the chief accuser may have been either Sir George Home or that tortuous old conspirator, Henry Howard, Earl of Northampton. The latter, an ardent Catholic and sometime spy for Spain, seems the more likely candidate.[2]

That Southampton was completely exonerated and restored to favour there can be no doubt. In July, possibly to compensate for the humiliation and shock which he had endured, the King granted him the manor of Romsey in Hampshire, the manor of Compton Magna in Somerset, the manor of Dunmow in Essex, and the grange of Basilden in Gloucester.[3] In August, when the Constable of Castile came to England for the formal signing of a peace treaty, Southampton played a prominent part in the ostentatious ceremonies with which the English received the Spanish grandee. He ushered the Constable to court when he first arrived, and escorted him to Gravesend on the first stage of his journey home. The Spaniard noted that at the ball given on August 19th, it was Southampton who led the Queen in the opening 'brando', and danced with her the 'corrento' that closed the festivities.[4]

Southampton was back in favour, but he had received a jolting reminder as to how treacherous were the waters through which one sailed at court.

[1] MS. Fran. 15983, f. 313r and 314r.
[2] The only contemporary English notice of the affair to survive is to be found in a letter written by Francis Morice to Sir Bassingbourn Gawdy (H.M.C., Gawdy MSS., p. 92, where the letter is inexplicably dated June 7th, almost certainly in error of June 27th). Morice says that upon the arrest of Southampton and the others, a certain John Sharpe, 'sometime a chaplain to my late Lord Essex but now a chaplain to the King', went around London seeking to recruit gentlemen of 'special worth and ability', Papists and Puritans excluded, to come to the Court to defend the King's person. The Privy Council sent Sharpe to the Tower for his pains. In this same letter of Morice's we have our only reference to the suppression of Pricket's poem on Essex dedicated to Southampton (v. p. 139 supra). There may be some connection between Pricket's poem and Southampton's arrest. Some of Pricket's invective against the 'Most grosse ingendred flux' if a 'rhetoricall politician' who figures among Essex's detractors might very well point to Northampton (v. Pricket, f. A2v).
[3] Salisbury MSS., XVI, 187; Cal. S.P. (Dom.), 1603–1610, p. 137.
[4] W. B. Rye, England as Seen by Foreigners in the Days of Elizabeth and James the First (London, 1865), p. 123.

CHAPTER XIII

The Peaceful Years

> My Lady Southampton was brought to bed of a young Lord upon St. David's-
> day in the morning; a Saint to be much honored by that howse for so great a
> blessing, by wearing a leeke for ever upon that day.

S O WROTE THAT indefatigable correspondent Rowland Whyte in a
letter of March 4th, 1605.[1] The hopes of Bess had at last been ful-
filled. She had presented her earl with a son who could be the
continuator of his honours and line. Like his sister a year before, the babe
was baptized in the Chapel Royal.[2] The King's singing men were in
attendance and His Majesty stood as a godfather, giving the babe his own
name of James. The other godfather was Robert Cecil, recently created
Viscount Cranborne. A second son was born three years later. He was
given the name of Thomas at his christening in the little parish church
near his father's hunting lodge at Shelford Parva.

With the succession to his title assured, Southampton entered upon a
long sequence of happy, sunny years. He was one of the magnates of the
kingdom and he lived as befitted a lord. When he was in London he dwelt
part of the time in Southampton House, no longer leased out for the extra
revenue once so urgently required.[3] He had also a suite in the palace at
Whitehall. An amusing incident arose concerning these lodgings. In
December 1608 when Prince Henry complained that he was without
chambers of his own in Whitehall Palace, King James told him to take
over any that he wanted. The fifteen-year-old Henry then told the Earls
of Southampton and Pembroke to remove their households and horses
since he was taking over the quarters that they occupied. They refused to
move whereupon, according to the Venetian ambassador, the Prince 'had
them removed by his people to the indignation of these gentlemen, who
are of very high rank'.[4]

---

[1] Nichols, *Progresses of James I*, I, 497.

[2] E. F. Rimbault, *The Old Cheque-Book or Book of Remembrance of the Chapel Royal*,
Camden Society (London, 1872), pp. 173-4.

[3] We do not know when the Earl took over Southampton House. Presumably he
did so as soon as possible after he obtained the necessary means. A letter of his of
November 11th, 1604, is addressed from 'Southampton House in Holburne'. (*Salisbury
MSS.*, XVI, 353.) Sometime around 1617 King James extended the liberties of
Southampton House from Holborn Bars to the Rolls in Chancery Lane.

[4] *Cal. S.P. (Ven.), 1607–1610*, p. 206.

As one of the grandees of the English court, Southampton played his part in its gorgeous ceremonies, so meaningful in prestige for the participants and so utterly lacking in significance for us. Thus in January 1605 Southampton bore the coronet at the investiture of the four-year-old Prince Charles as Duke of York. In May he was an officer for the installation of the Duke of Holstein as a Knight of the Garter. In August he carried the sword of state in front of King James during his visit to the University of Oxford. The succeeding years brought like distinctions. In 1610 when the heir to the throne first displayed his prowess with the pike at 'Prince Henry's Barriers', Southampton was one of the six challengers who joined the Prince in successively encountering the fifty-six respondents. When, a few months later, Henry was formally created Prince of Wales, Southampton was the Prince's carver at the banquet, and the Earls of Pembroke and Montgomery His Highness's sewer and cup-bearer. On New Year's Day 1611 when Prince Henry honoured his father with the masque of *Oberon* and led out the Queen to begin the evening's dancing, it was Southampton who followed with his sister Princess Elizabeth.

Much of Southampton's time was spent of course in the usual pastimes of the court. There were cockfights to be attended in the Cockpit at Whitehall. Much of the excitement there lay in the betting, and Southampton was among those putting up money to back his fancy. On one occasion we find him a principal better at a match where £50 (about £1,000 in modern values) was staked on each battle.[1] With his fondness for the game, he must often have joined in the bowling, in fine weather on the green at Whitehall, in rainy weather in the big echoing Bowls House.

Sometimes Southampton left the court to dispense hospitality in his country houses at Titchfield and Beaulieu, or to hold his little court at Carisbrooke Castle. On various occasions his sovereign was his guest, not at Titchfield which James apparently never visited, but at Beaulieu which the King found conveniently close to the New Forest, for centuries one of the royal game preserves. James first visited Beaulieu ('Bewley' to use the phonetic spelling found in the accounts of the Royal Treasurer of the Chamber)[2] late in the summer 1606, when Southampton received him with 'great entertainment' which included military exercises by the militia of the Isle of Wight. His Majesty was back for his hunting the next summer, having in the interim appointed Southampton Keeper of the New Forest despite the counter-claims of the Earl of Pembroke. On August 5th, 1609, King James celebrated at Beaulieu the anniversary of his escape

---

[1] Edward Lodge, *Portraits of Illustrious Personages of Great Britain* (London, 1850), Vol. III (p. 99 of the 'Unpublished Papers' added at end of this volume).
[2] *AO 1 43/388*, f. 16r.

from the Gowrie Plot. The occasion may have triggered some neurosis in
the King for suddenly the mayor and burgesses of Southampton found
themselves confronted with a demand from Sir John Drummond, the
King's gentleman usher, for twenty-four 'able and sufficient men' to
guard His Majesty at Beaulieu. Not knowing what to make of so extraordinary a demand, the citizens got in touch with the Earl, who undertook
to supply the needed men out of the forces of the shire. Other royal visits
to Beaulieu came in 1611, 1613, 1618 and 1623.

In Southampton's day the social life of the English aristocracy was
beginning to fall into the pattern that it would hold until our own time.
Prominent in that pattern was the house party, an almost foreseeable consequence of the building of the immense 'progidy houses' of the sixteenth
century. Surviving in the Huntington Library in California is an amusing
little flirtatious memento of such a party.

The scene is Althorp, the great Northamptonshire home of Lord
Spencer. The date is uncertain, but probably some time after the marriage
of Southampton's eldest daughter, Penelope, to the Spencer heir. Among
the guests are Southampton and a certain Anne Uvedale, in all likelihood
the wife of Sir William Uvedale, one of Southampton's Hampshire neigh-
bours who lived at Wickham, only four miles from Titchfield.[1] The
weather is foul and Southampton sends a little note to his friend the Earl
of Huntingdon,[2] making the bad weather his excuse for not coming to see
him before returning to London. Apparently by the same messenger,
Anne Uvedale sends the following little note to the Countess of Huntingdon:

> Madam
>   If it weare not for the ill manners of my Lord of Southampton I had written to
> you with my owne hand, but within a few dayes you shall have one of a whole
> sheet of paper in the mean time I crave your pardon & will ever be
>   Your la: most humble servant
>   Ann Uvedale

[1] The Harleian Society's editor of the registers of Westminster Abbey appended
to the entry, November 30th, 1614, of the baptism of 'William, son of Sir William
Udall' the following note: 'Eldest son of Sir William *Uvedale*, the younger, Kt., of
Wickham, Hants., by his first wife Anne, dau. of Sir Edward Cary, Kt., third son of
Henry, Lord Hunsdon.' *The Marriage, Baptismal, and Burial Registers of the Collegiate
Church or Abbey of St. Peter* (London, 1876), Harleian Society, Vol. 10, p. 64. 'Udall'
is a very common spelling of 'Uvedale'.
    In 1605 when the Uvedales were deprived of two-thirds of their lands for recusancy,
Widley and other manors belonging to the family were granted to Southampton. It
seems obvious that Southampton was in fact doing an act of friendship and only
nominally taking over the property until the storm had blown over. In 1607 the Uvedales were back in possession. *v. Victoria County History of Hampshire*, III, 171.
[2] The two earls were closely associated in the business of the Virginia Company.
In 1621 Huntingdon named Southampton as one of his parliamentary proxies.

Below this, on the same sheet, is written a second note:

> Madam though this woman lay this fault uppon mee it is only her owne laziness
> & not my ill manners who you know to bee very civill & your la: humble servant.
> H. Southampton?[1]

Tours on the Continent were coming into vogue, especially trips to Spa, in the Low Countries, to take the waters. Southampton first visited Spa in the summer of 1613. Apparently he intended to leave England in May with Lord Chandos, Lord Darcy and Lady Lumley, Sir Thomas and Lady Savage, who were making the same journey. As bad luck would have it, a troublesome piece of business kept Southampton in England until the end of June. In late April some fool had left lying around Whitehall Palace a virulent Catholic treatise, entitled *Balaam's Ass*, which maintained the interesting thesis that King James, the British Solomon, was really the Antichrist. Discovery of the book had created an instant furore. Suspicion soon pointed to John Cotton of Soberton in Hampshire as the author. Soberton was one of the manors owned by Southampton, and Cotton was closely linked with Catholic families associated with the Earl. To make matters worse, on June 13th, two days after a proclamation was issued for Cotton's arrest on charges of high treason, the fugitive visited Southampton House. Here, despite the Earl's conversion to Anglicanism, plenty of Cotton's co-religionists were still to be found. Fortunately Cotton very shortly afterwards surrendered himself 'into my Lord of Southampton's hands'. The Earl handed him over to the authorities,[2] then made his delayed departure for the Continent.

Landing at Flushing, Southampton became very much the grand touring English *milord*. Letters from Sir John Throckmorton, the English deputy-governor there, informed Trumbull, the English ambassador at Brussels, that Southampton would visit the latter city 'very privately'. A little while later we find Southampton asking Trumbull to secure permission for him to view the fortifications of Antwerp. After taking the waters at Aachen as well as at Spa, Southampton made a leisurely return to Flushing, where for days a ship of the Royal Navy had been waiting to carry him home to receive King James at Beaulieu. Behind him he left a commission with Sir Thomas Leeds to send cherry-trees for planting in his orchards.

Southampton must have enjoyed his trip, for at the end of March in the following year we find Leeds informing Trumbull, 'My lord of

---

[1] Huntington Library, *Manuscript HA 13684*.

[2] After Cotton had been six years in the Tower, he was found not to have written the offending book. For the Cotton episode see H.M.C., *Ancaster MSS.*, pp. 356–85; also Birch. *Court and Times of James I*, I, 248–9.

Southampton and his lady come this summer to the Spaw.'[1] Southampton does not seem, however, to have had his Bess with him when he arrived on the Continent late in July, taking in Antwerp and Louvain as he moved towards Spa. As a companion he did have with him the magnificent Gray Brydges, fifth Lord Chandos, commonly known as the 'King of the Cots-wolds' because of the sumptuous hospitality in his home there. Arrived at Spa, Southampton was visited by an old comrade in the Irish wars, Sir Griffin Markham, who commanded one of the regiments in the Dutch service. There were exciting developments this August since the famous Spanish general Spinola, endangering the truce in force between the Spaniards and the Dutch, suddenly entered the duchy of Cleves where the succession had for years been disputed by Catholic and Protestant claimants. The Dutch hastily sent forces of their own into the duchy; but, since neither Dutch nor Spanish wanted to end the truce, it became 'the rule of this extraordinary campaign that the hostile armies neither attacked each other nor places occupied by each other's troops, but only made war on neutrals'.[2] Old soldier that he was, Southampton was much interested in these military happenings. Writing to Trumbull on August 20th about his future movements, he noted, 'I think we shall see the Spanish army which I desire much, and then the other [the Dutch] if it be in the field, and so home.'[3] The eccentric Lord Herbert of Cherbury says that he met Southampton that autumn in Prince Maurice's camp in the vicinity of Rees.[4] It seems unlikely that the Earl remained with the Dutch during the long-drawn-out negotiations which led up to the sign-ing of a treaty early in November. Probably he had returned to England by then.

Back home Southampton continued to receive a trickle of dedications and commendatory verses. In 1609 Dr. Christopher Hampton had

[1] H.M.C., *Downshire MSS.*, IV, 351.

[2] Logan Pearsall Smith, *The Life and Letters of Sir Henry Wotton* (Oxford, 1907), I, 137.

[3] *Downshire MSS.*, IV, 499–500.

[4] *Autobiography*, ed. W. H. Dircks (London, 1888), p. 101. It is sometimes stated that Southampton himself served with the Dutch against the Spaniards. I can find no evidence to support this assertion, which seems to have originated with a misinter-pretation by Lee (*D.N.B.* XXI, 1059) of Malone's statement, 'In 1614 we find him with the romantick lord Herbert of Cherbury, at the siege of Rees in the duchy of Cleve, (Shakespeare, Third Variorum ed., XX, 443–4). Southampton seems merely to have been an observer.

Rowse says that Southampton brought 'his own private recruits' (p. 222) over from England with him. He is probably misinterpreting a letter from Flushing in which Throckmorton reported, 'I expect my Lord of Southampton here this day, some of his people and his horses have already come.' H.M.C., *De L'Isle MSS.*, V, 221–2. The reference to Southampton's people almost certainly refers to the servants he had sent ahead with his horses.

dedicated to him two sermons that he had preached before the King at Beaulieu.[1] In the same year Alphonso Ferrabosco, publishing his *Lessons for 1. 2. and 3. Viols*, had dedicated his book 'To the perfection of Honour, My Lord Henry, Earle of South-hampton', declaring 'I made these *Compositions* solely for your Lordship, and doe here professe it'.[2] George Chapman, publishing about the same time his translation of the first twelve books of the *Iliad*,[3] had among his commendatory sonnets one to 'the right valorous, learned, and full sphere of Noblesse, the Earle of South-hampton'. If Chapman addressed other verses to Southampton they have not survived.

This was the time when emblem books, which combined symbolic drawings with interpretive poems, were popular in England. One of these, Henry Peacham's *Minerva Britanna* published in 1611, contained amid its emblems three interlocked garlands of laurel, oak and olive, the impresa of Petrarch's admired Colonna, with whom the accompanying verses compared Southampton as being also 'learned, valiant and wise'.[4]

A dedication of the following year has an interesting Cambridge background. William Crashaw, the eminent Puritan divine, matriculated at St. John's at Easter 1588, and became a fellow of the College in 1593. Later he left Cambridge to become a preacher at the Temple Church in London. In 1613, having married and acquired a son Richard (the future poet), Crashaw lost his position in consequence of his employers, the lawyers of the Temple, 'not enduring women or children to reside amongst us'.[5] It was in the latter year that Crashaw published his *Consilium Quorundam Episcoporum*, a Latin work whose title runs in translation:

> The Recommendations of Certain Bishops
> assembled at Bologna, which were
> presented to Julius III, chief Pontiff,
> concerning means of strengthening
> the Roman church.
> In which are divulged the tricks and
> subtleties of the Romans and not
> a few secrets of the Papal power
> From the library of William Crashaw,
> Bachelor of Theology, Preacher of the Word of God

---

[1] *Two Sermons Preached Before the Kings Most Excellent Majesty in the Church of Beauly in Hampshire* (London, 1609).

[2] Sig. A2r.

[3] Printed under the title of *Homer Prince of Poets*, *v.* sig. Ff 1r. This sonnet, 'In choice of all our Countries Noblest spirits', was reprinted in slightly altered form in *The Whole Works of Homer*.

[4] Sig. E3v.

[5] P. J. Wallis, 'The Library of William Crashawe', *Transactions of the Cambridge Bibliographical Society*, II, 215.

In the Temple of London
Job
The heavens will reveal his iniquity,
And the earth will rise up against him.

The document is in fact a sly burlesque of a conciliar report. Prefaced to it is a lengthy piece of anti-Catholic invective in the form of a dedicatory epistle to the Earl of Southampton.

The dedication of this book cannot have been displeasing to Southampton for a few years later, when Crashaw had to sell his library to pay his debts, that nobleman decided upon a major benefaction. He would buy Crashaw's books and manuscripts and present them to St. John's. Pending the building of a new library at St. John's, the Earl kept in Southampton House the two hundred manuscripts and two thousand books that he had now acquired.[1]

Crashaw was not the only writer of a Puritan tinge to pay his respects to Southampton in 1613, for this year the moralistic George Wither, publishing his *Abuses Stript and Whipt*, not only worked into 'Satyr 10' a compliment to the 'warlike order' that Southampton maintained on the Isle of Wight, but included among his closing 'epigrams' one in which he made an offer to Southampton:

> ... but grace my Rime,
> I will so blaze thy *Hampshire* Springs and *Thee*,
> Thy *Arle*, *Test*, *Stowre* and *Avon* shall share *Fame*
> Either with *Humber*, *Severne*, *Trent* or *Thame*.[2]

There is no evidence that Southampton extended the requested patronage. After all, he was a nobleman with discriminating taste and poor Wither was not much of a poet—during the Civil War, Sir John Denham would save Wither's life with a laughing plea that as long as the latter lived he himself could not be called the worst poet in England.

Nothing reveals more clearly the pattern of Southampton's development than the changing nature of these books dedicated to him—in his younger years erotic poems and frivolous romances; in later life Protestant sermons and polemics, and works of serious scholarship. Among these last must be counted Richard Brathwait's pioneer book on historiography, *The Schollers Medley*, published in 1614. Deservedly admired in its day, it bears in its second edition the more explicit title of *A Survey of History*. A most interesting book it is, defining the scope of history, describing the

[1] For a fuller account of the Earl's gift and the correspondence that attended it, see M. R. James, *A Descriptive Catalogue of the Manuscripts in the Library of St. John's College, Cambridge* (Cambridge, 1913), pp. vii–viii *et passim*.
[2] *Juvenilia: Poems by George Wither*, The Spenser Society (1871), p. 333.

prose style best suited for historians, and setting forth the 'uses and fruits of Histories'. Many a modern historian or biographer would do well to heed Brathwait's injunction to 'prosecute the argument of the Historie without frivolous Ambages, or impertinent circumstances'. Restraining then a powerful impulse to say more about this most attractive work, and one which Southampton himself regarded highly,[1] let us proceed.

Around 1615 the prolix Joshua Sylvester dedicated to Southampton the hundred bland quatrains of his 'first century' of *Memorials of Mortalitie*, a treatise against the fear of death, which he had translated out of the French of Pierre Mathieu. In 1618 Sir Henry Goodyere, who had served with Southampton in Ireland, publishing his mediocre emblem book, *The Mirrour of Majestie*, gave Southampton for an emblem a man half Mars and half Mercury, circled by the motto 'In Utraque Perfectus'. Beneath this emblem he printed a little poem on how Southampton combined military distinction with a love of the arts.[2] When Queen Anne died in 1619, some unknown hack, using the fantastic pen-name of 'James Anne-Son', worked a complimentary reference to Southampton into his *Carolanna*, a poem occasioned by the death of Her Majesty.

Let us return to the chronicle of Southampton's later years. Some time around 1609 the third of his daughters, Elizabeth, was born.[3] In 1611 came Mary, the last of the children, who died at the age of four and is commemorated by a neat little monument in Titchfield church.

Death was beginning to pluck its victims from the ranks of Southampton's own generation. First to go was the valiant Mountjoy, who died in April 1606, leaving no legitimate heir to inherit his recently won earldom of Devonshire. He had scandalized King James a few months earlier by going through a form of marriage with Essex's sister Penelope, now divorced by her husband Lord Rich. As the 'chief mourner' at Devonshire's funeral, Southampton must have been involved in the painful decision not to display Penelope's coat of arms along with that of her 'husband'. A few months later Penelope joined Devonshire in death. Southampton seems to have looked after the interests of the forlorn little family of illegitimate children that they left behind them.[4]

---

[1] For the preceding quotation see *The Schollers Medley* (London, 1614), sig. B2r. The only full-length study of Brathwait is M. W. Black's doctoral dissertation, *Richard Brathwait, An Account of His Life and Works* (Philadelphia, 1928). In 1638 Brathwait, dedicating to Southampton's widow the second edition of the book here under discussion, observed that her late lord did 'highly prize it'. S.T.C. 3583a, sig. A4v.

[2] S.T.C. 11496, sig. E2r. The Goodyeres may long have been family friends. In July 1572 a Henry Goodyere was examined by the authorities at the same time as Southampton's father.

[3] In later life she married Sir Thomas Estcourt.

[4] *S.P. 14/21*, item 4; *Salisbury MSS.*, XIX, 298. The Church of England did not recognize the remarriage of the guilty party in a divorce.

In a letter of November 17th, 1607, the connoisseur Thomas Howard, Earl of Arundel, noted the passing of Southampton's mother:

Old Southampton, I am sure you hear, is dead, and hath left the best of her stuff to her son, and the greatest part to her husband, the most of which I think will be sold, and dispersed into the hands of many men, of which number I would be one. . . .[1]

The dowager countess had made her will the previous April. Reading it, we recall the unhappy events of many years before: the second earl's charge that his wife had been unfaithful, his imprisonment of her in his house, his disinheriting of her daughter if she should ever live under her mother's roof. Only God could know all that was in the countess's mind as she set down at the beginning of her will:

. . . my body I comend to the earthe whereof it was made, and doe directe the same to be interred at Tytchfeilde there to be laied (as neare as may be) unto the body of my honorable and dearlie beloved Lord and husband Henrie late Earle of Southampton. . . .[2]

Her wishes were respected. The parish register at Titchfield records the burial there of 'the Right Honorable marie Countesse of Southampton'.

With the death of his mother Southampton received possession of the dozen manors which had been hers under the terms of her marriage settlement with his father. He received, in addition, numerous legacies set forth in his mother's will—sets of tapestries, 'the pictures in the little Gallerye at Copthall', her scarlet bed with gold lace, her white satin bed, matching furniture to go with these, Turkey carpets, silver basins, ewers, and candlesticks, a diamond ring, and sixteen loose diamonds which she desired her son to mount in a George of gold (the badge of a Knight of the Garter) which he was to wear 'in memorie of me his loving mother'.

It says much for the character of Elizabeth Vernon that the old countess, who had regarded her with hostility when she married her son, now referred to her affectionately as 'my good and loving daughter in law' and left her the double necklace of pearls which she herself had customarily worn. The dowager countess named her 'deare and welbeloved husband Sir William Hervy' as her sole executor and residual legatee, and her 'good and loving frend George Lord Carewe Baron of Clopton' as the overseer of her will.

In her will the old countess left her 'good daughter the Lady Arundell wyfe unto the lord Arundell my Jewell of gold set with dyamondes called a Jesus [a religious medal] if she happen to be living at the time of my decease'. Lady Arundell's death, here so clearly anticipated, did in fact occur a few months before that of her mother. Poor Mary had encountered

---

[1] Lodge, *Illustrations*, III, 209.   [2] P.C.C., Huddleston, 86.

more than her share of crosses during her marriage to Thomas Arundell. King James had dealt graciously with him, in compensation for his disallowed imperial title creating him Baron Arundell of Wardour, but he had remained an irreconcilable Catholic and had soon angered the King by making a forbidden crossing to the Continent. Ironically, Lord Arundell became in his turn just such a heavy father as old Sir Matthew had proved to him. He was furious when, without his consent, in May 1607 his son married a daughter of the Earl of Worcester. Southampton found himself writing a letter to Cecil begging him, once again with the new generation, to be a peacemaker between father and son. The strain of this last family quarrel may have finished off Southampton's invalid sister, for she died a few weeks after this marriage.

Cecil was not to be around much longer to assist with his good offices. In May 1612, now Earl of Salisbury and Lord Treasurer of England, he died miserably, probably of cancer. The little hunchback has often been portrayed as the very type of the cold politician who neither loves nor hates. The picture is somewhat unjust. He had his friendships, even if they were temperate and a little distant, and one of them was with Southampton who had grown up in the house of his father. Himself one of those men who is born old, Cecil no doubt shook his head over the follies of Southampton's younger years, but he seems to have kept a lingering affection for him. When he could help Southampton he did so. We recall that it was Cecil who in 1599 risked the Queen's anger by holding back for five days her order dismissing Southampton from his generalship of the horse, vainly hoping 'time would qualify the sharpness of her humour'.[1] Writing to Cecil the following year, Southampton declared, 'I have still found you kind and friendly unto me',[2] and 'still' in the usage of that day meant 'always' or 'continually'. In the black days after the Essex Rebellion it was Cecil to whom Southampton's wife and mother addressed their pleas, and it was almost certainly he who saved him from the headsman's axe.

After Southampton was released from the Tower, sobered by his ordeal, he seems to have appreciated at last Cecil's sobriety and good sense. Their friendship grew closer. Southampton was one of the little group of friends that Cecil took to Hatfield to help him choose the site for the great house that he was to build there.

In his career at Court Southampton may well have benefited from Cecil's good counsel and support. Certainly he received favours from him along the way. When Southampton's old great-aunt found herself in trouble because of the persecution of the Catholics after the Gunpowder Plot, it was to Cecil that he wrote on her behalf:

[1] *Salisbury MSS.*, IX, 341.
[2] *Cal. S.P. (Ireland), 1600*, p. 329.

> Yet must I now of necessity renew an old suit in the behalf of my poor aunt Katherin Cornwallis, who by your favour has hitherto lived free from trouble for her recusancy, but is now by malice likely to be indicted if you interpose not to help her.

Cecil must have smiled to himself when Southampton came out with his motive for wanting to assist her—'She is an old woman that lives without scandal, and I am in expectation of some good from her.'[1]

Southampton cut a figure at the court of King James, but he was never appointed to any position of real political power. A Knight of the Garter in 1603, he had to wait until April 1619 for the seat on the Privy Council that he eagerly desired. When he at last became a Privy Councillor he found that the Council's membership had become so extended that most of its power had passed to an inner circle of which he was not a member.

It was probably on Cecil's advice that King James established his policy of giving Southampton honours and money but not political power. If Cecil, for all his liking for Southampton, felt that he had still too much of his old impetuosity and emotionality to make a good minister, it was not disloyalty to Southampton but simple fulfilment of his duty to the King to let James know as much. In any event, with the passing of Cecil a new era began for Southampton.

[1] *Salisbury MSS.*, XVIII, 304.

CHAPTER XIV

The Disfavour of King James

IN THE YEARS that followed Cecil's death, Southampton entered into the power struggles at Court. Often he did so with singularly little effect, and sometimes at the cost of temporary loss of the King's favour. Almost immediately he became involved in the manoeuvring as two court factions, the one uncompromisingly Protestant and the other more sympathetic to the Catholics, advanced their candidates for the key offices left vacant by Cecil's death. The first faction was led by the Earls of Southampton and Pembroke, Lord Sheffield, and some of the M.P.s who had played a leading role in King James' first parliament. The other faction, that of the house of Howard, had for its chief tactician the devious old Earl of Northampton, whom we have already noted as possibly responsible for Southampton's arrest back in 1604.[1] The candidates advanced by the Protestant party were Southampton for Lord Treasurer and Sir Henry Neville for Principal Secretary.

Very important in deciding this contest was the King's Scottish favourite, Robert Carr, recently created Viscount Rochester in the English peerage. At first Rochester was on the side of Southampton but later, becoming infatuated with a daughter of Thomas Howard, Earl of Suffolk, he transferred his support to her house. By the late spring of 1613 Southampton could see that he had lost, and withdrew from the fight.

Significantly he chose to travel abroad that summer. In November he wrote to Trumbull at Brussels, 'I have been very seldom at London and then stayed very little'.[2] Southampton was not so stupid as to exhibit pique where it could do him only harm. He took part in the ceremonies when Rochester was made Earl of Somerset on November 4th, and he gratified the King by taking part in the 'general reconcilement' that His Majesty arranged between the two factions at this time. These gestures were not made in vain. Although in 1614 the treasurership went to the Earl of Suffolk, the secretaryship went to Sir Ralph Winwood, whose loyalties were to the Protestant party.

In 1614 when King James summoned his 'Addled Parliament', Southampton was in his place in the House of Lords. Here his growing friendship with the leaders of the popular or 'country' party in the House of Commons made him fight to get the Lords to agree to a joint meeting

[1] v. p. 141 supra.   [2] Downshire MSS., IV, 256.

with the Commons. The King and his ministers strongly opposed any such meeting and Southampton did himself no good in this matter. Sir John Throckmorton, in a letter reporting the King's sudden angry dissolution of this parliament, noted:

> His Majesty is very angry with the lord of Southampton, the lord of Essex, Chandos and divers others. All is out of frame. God put it in again.[1]

In the summer of 1614, while Southampton was on his second visit to Spa, some of his friends of the Protestant faction brought to court a singularly handsome and attractive young man who they hoped would replace Somerset as the royal favourite. He was George Villiers, aged twenty-two, the penniless younger son of a Leicestershire squire. In 1615, after the fall of Somerset, Villiers began a swift advance to power. At the beginning of 1616 King James appointed him his Master of the Horse. In April he made him a Knight of the Garter. In August he created him a viscount, at the beginning of 1617 an earl, and a year later a marquess. As Marquess of Buckingham, Villiers was sure enough of his position to destroy the Howards and their allies as a power in the English Court.

As one would expect from his connection with Villiers' sponsors, Southampton was at the outset in the good graces of the new favourite. In 1617 he was one of the group of English noblemen who accompanied James and Buckingham to Scotland when the King revisited the homeland that he had not seen for fourteen years. We have a vivid little account of how, when King James entered the outer court of Holyrood Palace to be greeted by thirty kneeling young scholars of 'the Colledge off Edenborroughe', he was so pleased by the Latin oration delivered by one of their number that 'he made Pembrughe, Southhampton, Montgomerie ... draw nyer to heir quhat was spok'.[2] Two years later, when Southampton was finally made a member of the Privy Council, it was Buckingham who had secured this advancement for him.

Unfortunately Southampton's relations with Buckingham ceased to be harmonious. The favourite's showering of honours upon his upstart relatives, his growing arrogance in insisting that all the King's favours must come by way of himself, his support for the Spanish ambassador Gondomar in advancing the projected match between Prince Charles and the Infanta, his unwillingness to go as far as the ultra-Protestants wished in aiding the King's son-in-law, the Elector Frederick, against his Hapsburg

---

[1] *Downshire MSS.*, IV, 426. The Essex mentioned here is of course the son of the Essex executed in 1601. King James had restored to him his father's earldom. For a good account of Southampton's role in this dispute which arose out of the Commons' desire to end the King's power to impose import duties without parliamentary consent, see T. L. Moir, *The Addled Parliament* (Oxford, 1958).

[2] H.M.C., *Kenyon MSS.*, p. 20.

enemies—all or any of these things may have accounted for the growing rift between Southampton and the royal favourite.

The bad feeling between the two men was evident to everybody when King James convened his third parliament early in 1621. Judging from the surviving accounts of the debates in the House of Lords, Southampton was again one of the leaders of the House. He was on the committee on customs and privileges. He headed one of the sub-committees that examined witnesses during the impeachment of Bacon. He played a prominent part in the attack against Buckingham's kinsman Sir Giles Mompesson for the latter's ruthless exactions when licensing innkeepers and tavern-owners. Buckingham was ready to sacrifice Mompesson, but even so there was a nasty flare-up in the House of Lords in mid-March with Southampton and his friend Lord Sheffield cutting in on Buckingham and telling him that he kept saying the same thing over and over again. Prince Charles had to intervene to secure a reconciliation.[1]

As the session wore on, in both Lords and Commons the cleavage grew between the 'King's party', always ready to shut off debate in certain areas as encroaching upon the royal prerogative, and the 'country party', which felt that the basic rights of parliament were being jeopardized. In the time of the Commonwealth the Puritan chronicler Arthur Wilson was to recall the parliamentary battles of 1621:

> . . . in both Houses the King had a strong Party, especially in the House of Lords: All the Courtiers, and most of the Bishops, steer'd by his Compass, and the Prince's Presence (who was a constant Member) did cast an Awe among many of them, yet there were some gallant Spirits that aim'd at the publick Liberty, more than their own Interest . . . among which the Principal were, *Henry* Earl of *Oxford*, *Henry* Earl of *Southampton*, *Robert* Earl of *Essex*, *Robert* Earl of *Warwick*, the Lord *Say*, the Lord *Spencer*, and divers others that supported the old *English* Honour, and would not let it fall to the Ground.[2]

Working with this minority in the House of Lords was the group which had established predominance in the House of Commons. Among its leaders were Southampton's friend Sir Edwin Sandys, and Sir Edward Coke, the greatest lawyer of the age. The King, never patient, became choleric when he learned that opposition to his wishes was being organized in Parliament. Reports that Sandys and his friends were meeting Southampton and other lords at Southampton House to co-ordinate their tactics helped to inflame the wrath of His Majesty. In June he abruptly adjourned Parliament.

With Parliament safely in recess, the King and his ministers took reprisals. On June 15th James wrote to the Privy Council, ordering them

---

[1] Camden, *Annals of the Reign of James I* in Kennet's *Complete History*, II, 656.
[2] *The Life and Reign of James the First, King of Great Britain* in Kennet's *Complete History*, II, 736.

TITCHFEILDIÆ . ETC PRÆNOBIL . D° HENRIC WRIOTHESLEY COME SOUTHAMPTON BAR

HENRI SOLI MALY PENSE

The
Right Honourable and most noble HENRY
Wriothsley Earle of Southampton, Baron of
Titchfeild, Knight of tee most nob: Ord: of y̅ Garter.

Simon Passæus sculp: Lō.
A° Dōni 1617.

Are to be sould in Popes head
Ally by Ioh: Sudbury
& Georg Humble.

SOUTHAMPTON IN LATER LIFE
The British Museum

to commit Southampton to the close custody of the Dean of Westminster. At the same time Sir Edwin Sandys was arrested and turned over to the Sheriffs of London.

Examined by a commission headed by the Duke of Lennox, Southampton made a firm denial when queried, if 'his owne conscience did not accuse him of unfaithfulnes to the King in the latter parte of the parliament'. Asked if he had not held meetings or consultations to hinder the King's purposes, he admitted that various M.P.s had kept him informed about what was going on in the Commons, but 'utterly denied that he had ever any desseine or plott in their coming thither'. He conceded that 'unkindness' might exist between him and persons near to the King, but denied having said, 'there would never be a gud Reformacon whyle one [Buckingham] did soe wholy governe the King'. He also denied having said that he disliked attending meetings of the Privy Council since he found 'soe many boyes and base fellowes' there.[1] We do not know what the commission made of these answers. We do know that in July the Earl of Oxford was arrested, apparently for 'too bold speech in behalf of the Earl of Southampton'.[2]

One of the members of the investigating commission was Buckingham's protégé and political adviser John Williams, the Dean of Westminster, who had Southampton as his involuntary guest. A brisk, knowledgeable little Welshman, Williams was in this same month of July 1621 appointed Lord Keeper of the Great Seal, replacing the disgraced Bacon. Williams shared Southampton's own taste for books and learning. Though of a later generation, he had belonged to St. John's, Southampton's own college.[3] The two men now, if not earlier, became good friends. Diligently Williams set himself to clear away the difficulties between Southampton, the angry King and Buckingham. He succeeded. On July 16th Buckingham spent several hours in conversation with Southampton at the deanery. Two days later, Williams took Southampton to Theobalds for a lengthy conference with the King and Buckingham. At the end of this second conference Williams took Southampton to Southampton House in Holborn, dined with him and left him there. Southampton's liberty was not quite complete for he was under instructions to retire to Titchfield and to remain there under the watch of Sir William Parkhurst, who had been serving as his keeper. At the end of August, again thanks to the friendly endeavours of Williams, Parkhurst was given his discharge and Southampton won his complete freedom.

---

[1] S.P. 14/121/224A.   [2] Birch, Court and Times of James I, II, 268.
[3] Several years later Williams was to contribute two-thirds of the cost of the new library built at St. John's in consequence of Southampton's gift of the Crashaw books and manuscripts.

During his rustication Southampton had time to think over the perils of antagonizing the King and Buckingham. From his experience under Elizabeth, he knew only too well the consequences of settled hostility on the part of his sovereign. Increasingly he worried that he might lose his two pensions, the one of £2,000 per annum granted him in 1611 when the Crown had ceased to farm out the custom of the sweet wines, and the other of £1,200 per annum granted in 1619 'in lieu of his land in the New Forest grown useless by the multitude of the deer'.[1] The loss of these pensions would be a devastating blow for Southampton. Williams, writing to Buckingham on November 13th, noted:

> My Lord of S is touch'd with some feare of his two pencions, but relyes all-togeither upon his Majestie's mercy and your Lordship's good mediation. . . .[2]

When Southampton was advised that he would do well not to attend Parliament when it reconvened on November 20th, he took the hint. Absent from the House of Lords, Southampton was not involved in the the flaming finale a few months later when King James, having ripped out with his own hands the offending pages in the journal of the House of Commons, summarily dissolved parliament.

Southampton's political problems with King James in 1621 were inextricably entangled with other problems which faced him as the 'treasurer' [the governor, or president] of the Virginia Company.

A mystery surrounds our earliest evidence of Southampton taking an interest in Virginia. In 1612 William Strachey, writing his *Historie of Travell into Virginia Britania*, declared that a number of years after Sir Walter Raleigh had abandoned his Virginian endeavours, it pleased God so to move the heart of Southampton that:

> . . . having well weyed the greatnes and goodnes of the Cause, he lardgly con-trybuted to the furnishing out of a shippe to be Comaunded by Captayne Bartle-mew Gosnoll and Capt Bartlemew Gilbert and accompanied with divers other Gentlemen, to discover a convenient place for a new Colony to be sent thither who accordingly in March anno 1602 from Falmouth in a Bark of Dartmouth called the Concord sett forward holding a Course for the North-parte of Virginia.[3]

The only difficulty is that, though Gosnold and Gilbert undoubtedly did make a Virginia voyage in 1602, Southampton was at that time a nearly bankrupt prisoner in the Tower of London. One can only wonder if Strachey, even though he had good sources of information, had not made a mistake.

In any event, whether or not as the result of a voyage of reconnaissance

---

[1] For details concerning these pensions see *Cal. S.P.* (*Dom.*), *1611–1618*, p. 40 and p. 154; and *W.P. 577*; *Cal. S.P.* (*Dom.*), *1619–1623*, p. 16 and *W.P. 274*.
[2] *The Fortescue Papers*, ed. S. R. Gardiner, Camden Society (London, 1871), p. 166.
[3] The Hakluyt Society (London, 1953), Second Series, Vol. CIII, pp. 150-1.

made by Gosnold, in March 1605 Southampton and his brother-in-law Arundell sent Captain George Weymouth to found a colony in Virginia.[1]

In mid-July Weymouth returned to England, having discovered a very large river and traded with the Indians. Five of the latter he abducted and brought back to England. According to James Rosier's account of the voyage, Weymouth and his men also brought back the colonists 'we were to leave in the Countrey by their agreement with my Lord the Right Honorable Count Arundell'.[2] Arundell figures so much more prominently than Southampton in Rosier's narration that it seems probable that the whole venture originated in the fertile mind of Arundell, he who in 1596 had planned to sail to the East Indies and open up Bengal, Sumatra and China to English trade. The colonists who returned, apparently in the face of Indian hostility, were almost certainly co-religionists of the fervently Catholic Arundell. The whole voyage may best be regarded as a first attempt to found an American colony that would be an asylum for English Catholics. Probably Southampton's participation was limited to putting up funds out of friendship for his sister's husband.

Although Raleigh in 1605 was a prisoner in the Tower, his rights to Virginia were still valid. He had, in fact, transferred these to a syndicate of London merchants headed by that very wealthy entrepreneur, Sir Thomas Smith. Possibly taking alarm at Weymouth's voyage into what they must have regarded as their own preserve, Smith and his associates the very next year procured from King James a charter setting up two Virginia companies in England: one, based in Plymouth, was given the northern part of that huge ill-defined territory called 'Virginia', and the other, based in London, received the southern part. It may be evidence that the grantees of this charter regarded Arundell and Southampton as interlopers that neither of them was included among the founding members of these companies.

In May 1607 the London company founded Jamestown. Supply expeditions kept the colony alive during the next couple of years, but it was never far from failure. By 1609 Smith and his associates realized that to achieve real success they would have to secure much more capital and send out many more colonists. Accordingly in May of this year they obtained from the King a new grant of incorporation for the 'Treasurer and Company of Adventurers and Planters of the City of London for the

[1] Mrs. Stopes (p. 320) saw the difficulty of accepting Southampton as a backer for Gosnold in 1602. For the 1602 voyage see *A Brief and True Relation of the Discovery of the North Part of Virginia . . . Made This Present Year 1602 by Captain Bartholomew Gosnold . . .* (London, 1602). For further information see W. F. Gookin and P. L. Barbour, *Bartholomew Gosnold* (Hamden, 1963). Barbour (p. 191) seems to have doubts about Southampton's role.

[2] *Purchas His Pilgrimes* (Glasgow, 1907), XVIII, 344.

First Colony in Virginia'. Since the Plymouth company was semi-extinct, this reconstituted London company became known simply as 'The Virginia Company'. Its list of incorporators included 56 London companies and 659 individuals. One of the latter was the Earl of Southampton.[1]

Because of his position, Southampton was a useful acquisition for the Company as were the seven other earls, including Salisbury and Pembroke, who joined it at the same time. We find Southampton almost at once helping to forward the interests of the company. On May 29th, along with Pembroke and the Lords De la Warr, Mounteagle and Lisle, he signed a letter inviting Englishmen resident in the Low Countries to join in the new undertaking. A little while later Southampton was among those signing a letter to the English ambassador at The Hague asking him to commend to the chief English commanders in the Low Countries 'the worthy enterprise of planting Colonies of our Nation in the fruitful and rich country of Virginia'. The writers blamed the disasters so far experienced by the Jamestown colonists on the 'factiousness and insufficiency of the Governors and others in Virginia',[2] and declared that things would go much better under the rule of Lord De la Warr, the newly-appointed governor of the colony. The intent behind these letters is plain. Those directing the Virginia Company must have thought that old soldiers would make good colonists and be able to fight off the Indians.

The spring of 1609 saw the dispatch of the largest 'supply' so far sent to Virginia, some five hundred new colonists sailing in a fleet under the command of Sir Thomas Gates, the Lieutenant-General of the colony. This fleet ran into a hurricane off the West Indies. One ship perished and another, the *Sea Venture*, flying Gates' flag, was reported lost by the ships that finally straggled into Jamestown harbour. The *Sea Venture* had, in fact, been run ashore on one of the Bermuda islands. In May 1610, to the amazement of the colony, Gates and his companions arrived at Jamestown in two little ships, the *Patience* and *Deliverance*, which they had built after their shipwreck. They found that hundreds of the Jamestown colonists had perished during the 'Starving Time' of the past winter, leaving only a pathetic little company of about sixty survivors.

Gates was in the process of abandoning the colony when Lord De la Warr finally arrived from England with a fresh supply fleet just in time to halt the evacuation. From this point the fortunes of Virginia turned slowly upwards. Further expeditions brought hundreds of additional settlers and the colony benefited from strong and capable government. A second settlement was founded at Henrico. In 1614 John Rolfe not only married Pocahontas, bringing an end to the intermittent war with the Indians but,

[1] *Cal. S.P. (Dom.), 1603–1610*, p. 515.
[2] H.M.C., *Buccleuch MSS.*, I, 103.

more important, shipped to England the colony's first four barrels of tobacco. Despite this gradual improvement, in 1616 when the Virginia Company's shareholders were entitled to their first dividend, there were no profits to be distributed.

In April 1619 the ageing Sir Thomas Smith, weary of constant badgering by critics of his administration, declined to stand for re-election as Treasurer. He was succeeded by Southampton's friend, Sir Edwin Sandys. Long active as an assistant to Smith, Sandys at once initiated a policy of greatly increased emigration to Virginia. More than twelve hundred settlers were sent out within a year, doubling the population of the little colony. But unfortunately Sandys became embroiled in a quarrel both with old Sir Thomas Smith and with Robert Rich, Earl of Warwick. Part of the trouble concerned Warwick's privateer, the *Treasurer*. Since Warwick was an important shareholder in the Virginia Company, the *Treasurer* had used Jamestown as one of its bases. Sandys was fearful that if the Spanish once thought the Company was allowing Jamestown to be used for a base for piratical attacks on their commerce, they would wipe out the colony. Accordingly he was determined that the Company should deal so firmly with the *Treasurer* as to make plain that it was in no way conniving in the ship's piracy. Not surprisingly, most of the shareholders backed Sandys. Though Warwick was defeated in the struggle within the Company, he had powerful friends at the court of King James and when a year later Sandys came up for re-election, the King announced that he could not permit him to continue as treasurer. Apart from whatever trouble Warwick had been able to make, King James had no fondness for Sandys whom he remembered as a 'principall man that had withstoode him in Parliment'.[1] He was also most unhappy that the Virginia Company, having found a profitable commodity in tobacco, was shipping an ever-increasing amount of it to England. King James, who years before had written his *Counter-Blaste to Tobacco*, was indignant that under Sandys this 'filthie noveltie' remained the mainstay of the colony's economy.

When the shareohlders found that His Majesty had not only declared Sandys unacceptable but had sent a letter instructing them to choose as their treasurer either old Sir Thomas Smith or one of three other men, they felt that they could not permit such encroachment upon the right of election granted them under their charter. A delegation headed by the Earl of Southampton was sent to remonstrate with the King. After hearing their representations, James said that his message to the Company had been given incorrectly. Acceptance of one of his nominees was optional. But he would not have Sandys.

[1] Chamberlain, *Letters*, II, 305.

The outcome of the whole wrangle was that on June 28th, 1620, the Earl of Southampton was elected Treasurer. In accepting Southampton, King James probably believed that the direction of the Company would pass into new hands. He must have been chagrined when he discovered that such was not the case. Southampton took over Sandys' deputy, John Ferrar, who with his brother Nicholas attended to much of the management of the Company. In the words of one of Nicholas Ferrar's biographers, Southampton 'had a particular friendship with Sir Edwyn Sandys, and took this office conditionally that his friend should continue his advice and assistance in the business of the company'.[1] In short, Southampton proved to be little more than a front for Sandys, who continued to set the policies of the Company.[2]

The shareholders might have fared better if they had accepted one of the King's nominees. James was never a man to trifle with, and when he learned how things were going under Southampton's treasurership he showed his annoyance. In March 1621 he revoked the licence which authorized the Company to hold its Virginia lotteries. Since these lotteries provided much of the income for the development of the colony, the blow was a very serious one. The imprisonment of Southampton and Sandys that summer can be viewed as punishment for their Virginia Company activities as well as for their parliamentary policies. In fact, in November when there was a tumult in the reassembled House of Commons about Sandys' imprisonment, Secretary Calvert 'declared his Imprisonment not to be for anything done in Parliament',[3] probably referring indirectly to his continued management of the Virginia Company's affairs even though forbidden its treasurership.

As we have noted, after imprisonment in the summer of 1621, a chastened Southampton decided to cultivate the favour of James and Buckingham. Besides absenting himself from Parliament, he ceased attending the meetings of the Virginia Company. The King was ready to do his part in closing the rift, and on November 16th the Venetian ambassador wrote to the seigniory that James was seeking to 'conciliate Southampton'.[4] The process of conciliation did not proceed without impediment. Southampton had his share of enemies at Court. Among them was the wily, talented and enormously ingratiating Spanish ambassador Gondomar, whose influence over the ageing King was second only to that of Buckingham. A possibly apocryphal story indicates the way Gondomar

---

[1] P. Peckard, *Memoirs of the Life of Mr. Nicholas Ferrar* (Cambridge, 1790), p. 102.
[2] *v.* R. B. Davis, *George Sandys, Poet-Adventurer* (London, 1955), p. 106, and W. F. Craven, *Dissolution of the Virginia Company* (New York, 1932), p. 145.
[3] Camden, *Annals of James I*, in Kennet's *Complete History*, II, 658.
[4] *Cal. S.P. (Ven.), 1621–1623*, p. 172.

worked to hinder the success of Southampton and the Virginia Company:

> The Marquis of Hamilton and the Earl of Pembroke solemnly affirmed to the
> Earl of Southampton, that they heard Gondomar say to the King, "That it was
> time for him to look to the Virginia courts [meetings of the shareholders] which
> were kept at the Ferrars' house, where too many of his Nobility and Gentry
> resorted to accompany the popular [demogogic] Lord Southampton and the
> dangerous Sandys.[1]

Attacks such as this had their effect. When the shareholders of the Virginia Company convened on May 22nd, 1622, for their annual elections,
they were presented with a message from the King saying that, though he
did not wish to infringe on their rights of election, he would be glad to
have any one of five designated persons elected treasurer of the Company.
Southampton's name was not on the royal list but he was nominated
anyway *in absentia*, along with two of King James' candidates. The ballot
gave Southampton 113 votes, as against a total of 17 for the King's men.[2]
The victory was a costly one for Southampton for the King now struck,
using just the weapon that Southampton had feared the previous year.
On June 8th John Chamberlain wrote from London:

> The earle of Southampton is here about the stopping of his pension out of the
> sweet wines, and other payments graunted him out of the exchequer for the
> damage don him and his tenants by the increase of deere in the new forrest. He
> hath taken the best way and addrest himself to the Lord of Buckingam, from
> whom he hath faire promises.[3]

A month later King James, still fretting that Virginia produced little
except tobacco, wrote to Southampton to 'take speedy order that our
people there use all possible diligence in breeding Silkewormes'. He urged
that 'Silkeworkes' be erected using the directions of John Bonoeil's recent
book on sericulture. Southampton promptly sent to Virginia enough
copies of Bonoeil's book to supply every head of a family with one. He
also dispatched a supply of 'Silke-seede', and a stern letter ordering the
governor to have his colonists promptly undertake the planting both of
mulberry trees and of vines.[4] Such conciliatory moves were not made in
vain. At the end of August Sir Francis Fane, reporting the gossip of the
Court to a friend, wrote:

> My Lord of Sowthampton was with the Kinge privately twoe howers at Alder-
> shott one night after supper, being browght up the back staires by my Lord
> Admirell [Buckingham] whoe only was lockt into the chamber with them; what
> theire discourse was I knowe not, bot theire meetinge and partinge seemed verry
> faire.[5]

---

[1] Peckard, p. 115.
[2] Susan M. Kingsbury, *Records of the Virginia Company of London* (Washington,
1906–35), II, 28–9. Ever since his arrest the previous summer Southampton had been
absent from the Company's meetings.　　　　　　　　　　　　　[3] *Letters*, II, 438.
[4] *Purchas His Pilgrimes*, XIX, 154–7.　　　　[5] H.M.C., *Rutland MSS.*, I, 467.

After this we hear no more of clashes between Southampton and the King and Buckingham.

The Virginia Company was in fact approaching the end of its career. Sir Edwin Sandys and his assistants, in their desire for quick results, had recruited too many unfit persons for settlers. Many of the colonists had died of sickness while being transported to Virginia aboard overcrowded and inadequately provisioned ships. When the survivors came ashore they found that no proper reception arrangements had been made. Some perished in the streets of Jamestown. None of the attempts to promote silk, wine, glass and potash industries had succeeded. Unrealistic orders from England had bedevilled the life of the colony's administrators. Added to all this were events which lay beyond the control of the London office. On Good Friday 1622 the Indians, catching the settlers largely off guard, launched a general massacre which took the lives of more than 350 colonists in a single morning. In January 1623 the colony was ravaged by plague.

At this juncture a tobacco marketing board was set up which would pay, at the expense of an almost bankrupt Virginia Company, very handsome salaries to Sir Edwin Sandys, the board's director, and John Ferrar, his assistant. For years the Earl of Warwick and his friends had been biding their time, and now they struck. One of their number, Alderman Robert Johnson, son-in-law of old Sir Thomas Smith, drafted a 'Humble Petition of Sundry Adventurers and Planters of the Virginia and Summer Ilands Plantations'. He and his friends presented this to the King. The Sandys group hit back at a joint meeting of the Virginia and Bermuda Companies held on May 7th, 1623, when Lord Cavendish arose to read a prepared 'Declaration'. This turned out to be a vicious personal attack on Warwick, Alderman Johnson, Captain Argall and others of the opposite faction.

King James' response was highly sensible. He appointed a royal commission, headed by Sir William Jones, Justice of the Court of Common Pleas, to examine the books of the Virginia Company and report upon its affairs. Southampton was informed that under the circumstances the Company's annual election of officers should be postponed. In October the Privy Council sent a group of commissioners to Virginia to make a first-hand investigation of conditions there. The government had, in fact, already decided to call in the Virginia Company's charter and to issue a new one which would transfer to the Privy Council the real direction of the colony.

Meeting on October 20th, 1623, the shareholders refused to surrender their existing charter, and in November the Crown began proceedings in the Court of King's Bench. In May 1624 the court ruled in favour of the

Crown, the Virginia Company soon after ceased to exist and Virginia became a Crown Colony.

Southampton must have exhibited remarkable skill in his conduct as Treasurer of the Company during these final months, for he managed to retain the good favour both of King James and of the Company's shareholders. On November 19th, 1623, the dying Company granted him twenty shares of land in the colony because he 'hath ever since the eight and twentieth day of June Anno 1620 untill this present performed the place of Treasuror of this Company with singular wisedome providence and care and much Noble paynes and Industrie and with unquestionable integritie'.[1] A week earlier, passing on word of happenings at the court of King James, John Chamberlain had noted that the Earl of Southampton 'is in very goode grace and favor of late'.[2]

In short, Southampton emerged with credit from the adventures and misadventures of the Virginia Company. Also he won a sort of mutilated immortality, for looking at the map of Virginia today, we find his name half preserved for us. The city of Hampton and its adjacent harbour of Hampton Roads took their name originally from what was known in the seventeenth century as the Southampton (or Hampton) River.

The Virginia Company does not provide the whole tale of Southampton's interest in exploration, colonization and overseas trade. He was also a shareholder in the East India Company, to which he was admitted in 1609. Receipts preserved in the Wriothesley Papers show that in 1620 and 1621 he quarterly invested £41 13s. 4d. in additional East India stock.[3] He helped to finance Henry Hudson's fatal last voyage,[4] and in 1613 when Thomas Button was exploring Hudson Bay he named an island promontory Cape Southampton. In the eighteenth century, when explorers found that two islands existed where earlier navigators had believed there was only one, the name of Coats Island was given to that containing Cape Southampton and, somewhat illogically, the name of Southampton Island was transferred to the larger island to the north-west.[5] Thus today, fifteen thousand and seven hundred square miles of Canada help to immortalize Southampton's name.

As 1623 came to its close, Southampton was enjoying life in his house at Titchfield. He was now a man of fifty, a rather older age by seventeenth-century standards than by our own. He had travelled, he had seen the wars, he had endured the vicissitudes of the royal courts of two sovereigns.

---

[1] *W.P. 312.*   [2] *Letters*, II, 522.   [3] *W.P. 969.*
[4] G. M. Asher, *Henry Hudson the Navigator: The Original Documents*, Hakluyt Society (London, 1860), p. 255.
[5] T. H. Manning, 'Some Notes on Southampton Island', *The Geographical Journal*, LXXXVIII (1936), 232.

He had known practically all the educative experiences of life. He was of an age when the vanity of human pomp and circumstance becomes ever more apparent, and correspondingly one values more the serenity of a life undisturbed by clamour and intrigue. In short, Southampton was ready for retirement.

He had long had a taste for the quiet pleasures of his Hampshire domains. Years before, writing to Cecil from Carisbrooke Castle, he had confided that he was 'enough pleased with the quiet life I lead here', though he regretted the absence of his friends who were at the court.[1] The time had come when he could do without the court. In 1619, after Southampton had been created a privy councillor, the Reverend Thomas Lorkin had noted that some further employment would be needed to 'entice him to the court', for he 'seems to prefer a country life'.[2] Now, amid the holiday merriment at Titchfield on the day before Christmas 1623, he wrote to his old friend Sir Thomas Roe at Constantinople:

> ... in this life I have fownd so much quiett & content that I thinke I should hardly ever brooke any other, sure I am I envy none, & shall unwillingly leave this if any occation shall draw mee from it.[3]

The pleasant final years as a Hampshire squire which he seems to be promising himself were not to be. Once more he was to be called to the wars, and when he returned it would be for burial by a broken-hearted Bess in the family vault in Titchfield parish church.

[1] *Salisbury MSS.*, XVII, 423.   [2] Birch, II, 170.   [3] *S.P. 14/151/77.*

CHAPTER XV

Death comes for the Earl

IN 1612 THE Protestant party at Court, headed by Archbishop
Abbot and the Earls of Pembroke and Southampton, rejoiced when
a match was arranged between the King's only daughter, Princess
Elizabeth, and the firmly Protestant Palsgrave Frederick, Elector Palatine
of the Rhine.

On St. Valentine's Day 1613, after a round of fantastically expensive
ceremonies and entertainments, the young Elector married Elizabeth in
the Chapel Royal at Whitehall. Never was the division of the Court more
pronounced than during the weeks preceding and following this marriage.
Joining the pro-Catholic party in pouring contempt upon the bridegroom
was Queen Anne, who thought the match unworthy of her daughter's
position. Prominent among those who rallied about Frederick and Elizabeth was Southampton. When, during the interim between the marriage
and the departure for Germany, King James packed his son-in-law off on
a visit to Cambridge, Southampton was among the courtiers who accompanied him. Back at his old university, Southampton witnessed the plays
staged by the student actors, and heard a learned debate in which young
John Williams of St. John's signally distinguished himself.[1]

At the end of April Frederick and his bride sailed from Margate for the
Continent, where they proceeded by leisurely stages to Frederick's capital
of Heidelberg. Here, established in the Elector's palace high on the hill-
side above the little city, Frederick and Elizabeth settled down for the
five happiest years of their lives.

The quiet years ended in May 1618 when the Protestant lords of
Bohemia, rising in rebellion against their Catholic emperor Matthias,
hurled his deputies through the windows of the Hradschin Palace at
Prague. When the Emperor moved to end the insurrection, Frederick
alone of the three Protestant Electors of the Empire responded to the
rebels' appeals for help. He sent in troops which captured Pilsen and
saved the Protestants from two avenging imperial armies. Soon afterwards the Bohemians invited Frederick to become their king. In September 1619, after weeks of indecision, Frederick accepted. By doing so he
aroused the anger of King James, who abhorred the thought of being

[1] John Hacket, *Scrinia Reserata* (London, 1693), p. 26, and Baker, *History of St.
John's*, I, 201.

dragged into a religious war in central Europe. Moving to Prague, Frederick and Elizabeth set up a royal court there, and commenced the few months of gaiety and festivity which were to win them their names of the Winter King and Queen.

Everybody in Europe knew that Ferdinand of Styria, who had inherited from Matthias the kingdom of Bohemia, would never relinquish the country without a war. In England Frederick's friends, aware of the campaign that he must fight in the coming summer, clamoured for King James to come to the aid of his beleaguered son-in-law. Early in 1620 there were recurrent reports that an army would be raised to aid Frederick, and that its commander would be the Earl of Southampton.[1]

It was practically inevitable that Southampton should be mentioned for this command. For one thing, he was an ardent supporter of Frederick and Elizabeth, and was already raising funds privately for their assistance.[2] For another, the old medieval view still prevailed that the English aristocracy should supply the nation's war leaders. There were at this time no English dukes, and the only marquess, Buckingham, already held the post of Lord Admiral. Of the English earls, none had more experience in war than Southampton. He had served under Essex in the Azores, and under both Essex and Mountjoy in Ireland. During the peaceful years under James I, who gloried in the title of *Rex Pacificus*, Southampton had kept himself informed in military matters, and had been active whenever he had the chance. Hence the enthusiasm with which he applied himself to his captaincy of the Isle of Wight. Hence his desire to view the fortifications of Antwerp in 1613, and to see the Spanish army in the field under Spinola in 1614. Hence the diligence with which, as Lord-Lieutenant, he attended to the annual musters of Hampshire, checking on the arms and powder of the county militia, and prosecuting with perhaps too much zeal those whom he suspected of evading military service.[3]

The military captains who had once turned to Essex as their patron and protector now turned to Southampton. Around 1604 we have an interesting and amusing insight into the bitterness with which some of them competed for the Earl's favour. Captain Barnaby Rich had become allied with Captain Christopher Levens in an obscure quarrel with a Bowyer Worseley. Writing to Cecil, Rich described Worseley as 'given to all manner of licentiousness, a breeder of debates, yet himself a rank coward'. Worseley, he said, 'had a part in that quarrel between the Davers and Longe that was slain', and he added darkly:

> I would the Earl of Southampton did but know something what I could assure him, he would think I loved himself and his honour with more discretion than

[1] *Cal. S.P. (Ven.), 1619–1621*, p. 137 and p. 219.
[2] *Ibid.*, p. 229.   [3] *Acts P.C., 1618–1619*, p. 193.

any pot companion, that will drink a health to his lordship, and then make those braves which might more touch him in honour and credit than I presume to think on.[1]

At times it had seemed that Southampton was about to be given a military command. In 1608 the Venetian ambassador reported that he would probably be sent to Ireland as commander-in-chief there. In 1617 the English merchants, who had been suffering ruinous losses at the hands of the Algerian pirates, asked that four ships of the Royal Navy join their own armed merchantmen and those of the Dutch to clean out Algiers. King James in his reply stipulated that, should a fleet be dispatched, it would have to be under the command of the Earl of Southampton.[2] In the end the proposed expedition never took place, for Gondomar persuaded King James that it would be unfriendly to send English ships in Dutch company into waters so close to Spain.

Now, during the Bohemian crisis, Southampton again lost the chance of a military command. Even though, in the opinion of the Venetian ambassador, more volunteers would follow Southampton to the Continent than would serve under the flag of any other English commander, James with his usual timidity decided that he would be committing himself too deeply if he let a member of his Privy Council command the troops going to aid his son-in-law.[3]

In fact, no English forces went to Frederick's rescue. In September Spinola, storming into the Lower Palatinate, captured Kreuznach, Alzei and Oppenheim. King James talked furiously of entering the war, but it was too late to do anything this year and he knew it. At the end of October, Imperial and Bavarian armies acting skilfully in conjunction overwhelmed Frederick at the Battle of the White Mountain. He and Elizabeth, fleeing from Bohemia, barely managed to reach safety in Brandenburg.

The next year saw James in fatuous pursuit of his scheme to marry Prince Charles to the Spanish Infanta and, in the process, to secure a general European settlement which would restore to Frederick his lost cities in the Palatinate. But people who were aware of realities knew that only direct English military intervention could help Frederick now. Some of the more zealous of his English friends entered into plans for direct action which would completely bypass their increasingly ineffectual monarch. Southampton's participation in such plans, along with his opposition to Buckingham in parliament and his involvement with Sandys

[1] *Salisbury MSS.*, XVI, 321.

[2] *Cal. S.P. (Dom.), 1611–1618*, p. 450. For more on this abortive scheme towards which Southampton was ready to contribute money of his own, see *Cal. S.P. (Ven.), 1615–1617*, p. 496, and *1619–1621*, p. 299. Years earlier Nottingham had appointed Southampton his Vice-Admiral.

[3] *Cal. S.P. (Ven.), 1619–1621*, p. 275; H.M.C., *Supplementary Report on Mar and Kellie MSS.*, p. 100.

in the Virginia Company, lies behind his arrest in June 1621. While he was a prisoner, his examiners quizzed him about his relations with Frederick and Elizabeth. He assured them that he had not plotted to have Parliament vote funds for Frederick which would be sent him directly and not by way of King James and his exchequer.

In the autumn of 1622 final military disaster overtook Frederick. The Duke of Bavaria occupied the Upper Palatinate while Spinola and his Spanish army, striking at the centres of Frederick's remaining power in the Lower Palatinate, took Heidelberg and Mannheim. These new triumphs of Frederick's Catholic enemies raised a fury of frustration and anger in England. King James bent before the storm and sent Endymion Porter to Madrid to tell King Philip that if the latter did not secure the restitution of Heidelberg and Mannheim within seventy days, the English ambassador at Madrid would be recalled and the negotiations for the marriage with the Infanta would be terminated. As Porter left the King's presence, the assembled courtiers shouted 'Bring us war! Bring us war!'

The Spanish reply to Porter's message was to make concessions concerning the marriage terms which seemed far more significant than they really were. James, his son, and his favourite, swallowed the offered bait and persuaded themselves that a marriage with the Infanta and restoration of the Palatinate to Frederick lay just within their grasp. On February 18th, 1623, a heavily disguised Prince Charles and Buckingham left for Spain, determined by personal wooing swiftly to achieve this marriage and this restoration.

In the face of the elaborate formalism of the Spanish court, the personal wooing got nowhere. After months of intricate negotiations, in which King James and Prince Charles made amazing concessions, the Prince and Buckingham returned home to England in October, convinced that the Spanish price was far too high. Behind him in Madrid the Prince left secret instructions cancelling the power of proxy that would have permitted the English ambassador to complete the long-sought marriage with the Infanta.

Back in England, frustrated and disenchanted, Charles and Buckingham decided on war with Spain. In a complete reversal of policy, they took over the leadership of the war party. Only arms, they agreed, could settle the Palatinate problem. England would lead a great crusade against both the Spanish and the Austrian Hapsburgs. A grand alliance would be formed with the Dutch, the Danes, the German Protestant princes, Venice, Savoy and France, all of whom felt threatened by that pernicious dynasty. A parliament was called to finance England's part in the great offensive.

Prince Charles and Buckingham (now the real rulers of England)

decided that in the coming struggle their country's role should be chiefly maritime. Buckingham, as Lord Admiral, would have his chance to harvest glory. The Prince and the Duke (Buckingham had been elevated to this rank in 1623) realized however that they would have to send some English land forces to the Continent to hearten their allies there.

Obviously a first step was to make an alliance with the Dutch, who were already at war with Spain. Envoys arrived from The Hague and negotiated a treaty which required the English to raise four regiments, totalling six thousand men, to serve under the Dutch command. Since these regiments would not be serving together as an English army, it was decided not to appoint an English general.

As soon as these arrangements became known, speculation began as to who would be the colonels of the four English regiments. Southampton seemed a probable choice from the outset, even though some men thought that these colonelcies, to be received from the Dutch and not from the King, were unworthy of earls, being 'so mean places in respect of the countenance our auncient nobilitie was wont to carrie'.[1] Southampton, in fact, proved reluctant to accept a regiment when one was offered to him. As we have seen, he was ready for retirement and he asked that the offered command be given to his elder son, Lord Wriothesley. Even by seventeenth-century standards, however, a boy of nineteen was hardly old enough to command fifteen hundred men in the field, even though he may perhaps have already seen some military service under Sir Horace Vere.[2] Southampton was told that Lord Wriothesley could not have the colonelcy and was pressed by Prince Charles to take it himself. The Prince and Buckingham knew that the recruiting of the six thousand volunteers would be affected by the reputation of the colonels. No name would draw better than Southampton's. In the end he accepted.[3]

Early in June 1624, the Dutch envoys signed the letters patent appointing their colonels:

> Henry Wriothesley, Earl of Southampton
> Henry Vere, Earl of Oxford
> Robert Devereux, Earl of Essex
> Robert Bertie, Lord Willoughby

A week or so later the Privy Council sent letters to the Lord-Lieutenants of the shires instructing them to give every assistance to the officers of the newly appointed colonels as they sought to recruit the six thousand men

---

[1] Chamberlain, *Letters*, II, 562.
[2] On August 14th, 1623, Southampton had written for a passport for his son and four servants to go to the Low Countries with Vere. *Cal. S.P. (Dom.), 1623–1625*, p. 55.
[3] *Cal. S.P. (Ven.), 1623–1625*, p. 333.

needed for the Dutch service. The Privy Council explained that King
James had authorized the raising of the four regiments:

> . . . in regard of his owne interest both for the securitie of his owne dominions
> and the great part his sonne in lawe, his onely daughter and his grandchildren
> have in the preservation of the United Provinces, where they nowe remaine as
> refugees. . . .[1]

While the recruiting officers were going through the shires, to the beat of
drums summoning men to follow the colonels to the war, a troublesome
little problem of precedence arose between Southampton and Oxford.
Fortunately, in an age when such an issue could provoke a major quarrel,
the two earls conducted themselves moderately. For a month the issue was
bandied around, as one person after another evaded involvement in the
issue. At last the King himself had to give the ruling: 'the Earl of Oxford
shall have precedency in all civil and courtly passages and actions, and
the Earl of Southampton in all martial and military passages'.[2]

The books dedicated to Southampton in these last years had all been
sober religious works. In 1623 Abraham Darcie had dedicated to him and
nine other peers his *Preparation to Suffer for the Gospell of Jesus Christ*, a
translation of a work by Du Moulin. This must have been well received
for the next year Darcie made Southampton one of the four dedicatees for
another translation from Du Moulin, *The Teares of Heraclitus: or The
Misery of Mankinde*. Also in 1624 Thomas Ailesbury dedicated to
Southampton his sermon *Paganisme and Papisme*. As a consequence of
Southampton's emergence as a colonel going to the wars, a very different
sort of book appeared honouring him this year. This was Gervase Markham's *Honour in His Perfection*, which in a lengthy subtitle is identified as:

> A Treatise in commendations of the Vertues and
> Renowned Vertuous undertakings of the
> Illustrious and Heroyicall Princes
> Henry Earle of *Oxenford*
> Henry Earle of *Southampton*
> Robert Earle of *Essex*
> and
> The ever praise-worthy and much honoured Lord,
> Robert Bartie, Lord *Willoughby* of *Eresby*
> With a Briefe Cronology of Theirs, and their
> Auncestours Actions[3]

Markham had been brought up at Belvoir, the home of the Earls of
Rutland, and in the wake of the fifth earl he had moved into the circle of
Queen Elizabeth's Earl of Essex. Robert Gittings, in the book in which

[1] *Acts P.C., 1623–1625*, p. 249.
[2] *Cal. S.P. (Dom.), 1623–1625*, p. 311.
[3] *S.T.C. 17361*. I have altered the lineation and punctuation, and corrected 'Bartue'
to 'Bartie'.

he makes a spirited but not too convincing attempt to prove that Markham was the rival poet who figures in Shakespeare's sonnets, describes him as 'the self-appointed laureate of the whole Essex group'.[1] In 1595 he had published commendatory verses to Southampton along with his poem on the death of Sir Richard Grenville.[2] Two years later he had been on the Islands Voyage and had witnessed the knighting of Southampton. Markham, as he notes in *Honour in His Perfection*, had 'lived many yeares where I daily saw this Earle' and had known him 'before the warres, in the warres, and since the warres'.[3] This fact gives authority to the all-too-brief biographical notice of Southampton which Markham gives in this little book, and which has been cited in earlier chapters of the present work.

By the end of July the regiments were ready to embark for the Continent. True, Southampton had encountered problems in getting his men outfitted, and he had been outmanoeuvred in a brave bid to get arms and armour from the Tower of London to make good the deficiencies in deliveries from the armourers of the city. By and large, however, things seem to have been in pretty good shape.

For the senior officers of his regiment Southampton had Sir John Burlacy as his lieutenant-colonel and Sir Jarret Ashley as sergeant-major (modern day 'major'). Heading the list of nine captains were Lord Wriothesley and Lord Mountjoy,[4] the latter despite his bastardy had been given an Irish barony that would perpetuate one of his father's titles. Southampton seems to have attended to the upbringing of this son of his old friend. Back in 1615 he had secured a passport for 'Mountjoy Blount, esquire, to travell beyond the seaes, to attaine the languadges, for three yeres'.[5] For his chaplain Southampton had the Reverend Robert Lane, on leave of absence from St. John's College, Cambridge.

On August 6th Southampton received his passport, and a day or so later he sailed for Holland. Meanwhile the common soldiers were crossing in their transports. On August 16th the Venetian ambassador at The Hague reported that all the English troops had arrived, and he described them as 'in good order and very fine'. A week later Southampton, his fellow colonels, and their officers were conducted by the English ambassador to the Assembly of the States General where they swore their oaths of fealty.[6]

[1] Robert Gittings, *Shakespeare's Rival* (London, 1960), p. 33.
[2] *The Most Honorable Tragedie of Sir Richard Grinvile, Knight.*
[3] Sig. D3r.
[4] The fullest extant list of Southampton's officers, listing not only his captains but his lieutenants and ensigns, is *S.P. 14/168*, ff. 16–17.
[5] *Acts P.C., 1615–1616*, p. 168.
[6] *Cal. S.P. (Ven.), 1623–1625*, p. 422 and p. 429.

This was an age when armies lost more men from sickness than from wounds. In November, Southampton's regiment in its winter quarters at Roosendaal was afflicted by the dreaded fever. Both Southampton and his son caught the contagion. On November 5th young Lord Wriothesley died. The father recovered, and began his long sad journey back to England with the lad's remains.

He was never to complete that journey. On November 10th, 1624, at the age of fifty-one, Henry Wriothesley, third Earl of Southampton, died at Bergen-op-Zoom. The only account that survives of his passing is that of Arthur Wilson, who having recorded the death of the son continues thus:

> ... the drooping Father having overcome the Fever, departed from *Rosendale* with an Intention to bring his Son's Body into *England*, but at *Berghen-op-Zoom* he died of a Lethargy in the View and Presence of the Relator, and were both in one small Bark brought to *Southampton*.[1]

It is hard to know what to make of these mysterious 'lethargies' of which men died in an earlier age. Probably Southampton, exhausted by illness and grief, succumbed to a heart attack.

On November 15th the news of the double tragedy having reached The Hague, Elizabeth, Queen of Bohemia, in her exile there wrote to Southampton's fellow colonel, the young Earl of Essex:

> You may well conceive that the death of the worthie Earle of Southampton did trouble me, which I cannot think but with greef. I have lost in him a most true and faithfull frend, both in him and his sonne.[2]

She added that she had sent letters by Lord Mountjoy to Prince Charles and Buckingham asking that the widowed countess be granted the wardship of her sixteen-year-old younger son Thomas, now the fourth Earl of Southampton.[3]

News of Southampton's death seems to have reached London on November 17th. On that day John Williams, now Bishop of Lincoln, writing from Southampton House whither he had hastened to console the widow, begged Buckingham to extend his 'grace and goodnes towards the most distressed widowe and children of my lord of Southampton'.[4]

---

[1] *The Life and Reign of James the First* in *A Complete History*, II, 789.

[2] H.M.C., *Bath MSS.*, II, 73.

[3] He became Lord Treasurer of England under Charles II, and was noted for his wisdom, humanity and integrity. He left no male heir and so his earldom ended with him. Three of his daughters survived into married life. By his first wife, Rachel de Ruvigny, he was father of Elizabeth, from whom have descended the Dukes of Portland, and of Rachel, from whom have descended the Dukes of Bedford. By his second wife, Elizabeth Leigh, he fathered another daughter Elizabeth, from whom are descended the Dukes of Buccleuch and the Lords Montagu of Beaulieu.

[4] *Harl. MSS. 7000*, f. 164.

Elizabeth was indeed a most distressed widow. Her whole life had centred about her lord, and the double shock of losing both him and their first son left her in utter anguish. Some echo of her grief is found in a letter written to Sir Dudley Carleton on Christmas Eve by Sir John Finett, the Master of Ceremonies at King James' court. After recalling how ever since their student days at Cambridge he and Southampton had maintained their friendship, he continued:

> . . . he hath left a most disconsolat Lady, that wee think wyll not cease lamenting his and her sonns death tyll shee meet them in a better lyfe . . . her patience [power to endure] and strength of mynde have, at her owne request, bene prayed for heer, in divers Churches.[1]

She took her last leave of husband and son on Holy Innocents' Day, 1624, when they were buried in the family vault at Titchfield parish church. It was exactly one year since he had written to Sir Thomas Roe of the 'quiett and content' he found in his Hampshire home.[2]

---

[1] *S.P. 14/177*, f. 1101.

[2] The Inquisition Post Mortem making survey of the estate of the late earl was held on January 12th, 1625. Stopes (p. 474) notes that the first and third pages of the report (*Inq. P.M. 22 James I, Hants* 404/101) are practically illegible. A beautifully clear copy of the first page does in fact survive in *Wards 7/72/120*. This apparently escaped the notice of that indefatigable researcher. Southampton had left no will, but on June 22nd, 1625, his widow was given power to administer his estate. (Somerset House, *Admon. Book, 1623–July 1625*, f. 169).

CHAPTER XVI

Portrait of a Patron

WE HAVE TRACED as best we can the life of Henry, third Earl of Southampton, from that morning in 1573 when his father wrote his letter rejoicing in the birth of his son to that December day in 1624, when his body disappeared into the family vault at Titchfield, rejoining that father in death. We have traced *as best we can*, for the biographer of Southampton is often like a person trying to piece together a jigsaw puzzle from which half the pieces are missing. Frequently one longs for a letter or a witness to fill in the picture. Still, patterns do emerge.

It remains to judge and to evaluate. What sort of man was this Earl of Southampton? Actually a biographer gets the sense of dealing not with one man but with two. One is the profligate unstable young friend of Essex. The other is the grandee of the Jacobean court, 'a leading nobleman, rich and experienced, with considerable influence';[1] the captain of the Isle of Wight whose 'just, affable, and obliging deportment gained him the love of all ranks of people';[2] the treasurer of the Virginia Company whose 'singular wisedome providence and care' and whose 'unquestionable integritie' were recognized in a testimonial from the Company; the loving husband whose first thought when arrested in 1621 was to ask permission to write to his countess breaking the bad news, 'in regard his lady was much subject unto sudden grief and passion'.[3] The great divide which separates the youthful Southampton from the Southampton of later years is the period of his imprisonment in the Tower. Writing just when that dark interim was beginning, Cecil declared, 'I grieve for the young Earl of Southampton.'[4] The *young* Earl of Southampton! After his imprisonment one never hears that phrase again. He had crossed a great watershed and had left his youth behind him.

It is chiefly with the young Earl of Southampton that we are concerned in this book, for it was the young Earl of Southampton who, in 1593, became the patron of William Shakespeare. Before trying to present the

[1] *Cal. S.P. (Ven.), 1619–1621*, p. 275.
[2] Malone quoting unpublished Oglander memoirs, Third Variorum ed. of Shakespeare, XX, 443.
[3] Birch, II, 259.
[4] *Cal. S.P. (Dom.), 1598–1601*, p. 598.

portrait of this young lord we must deal with two problems. The first concerns Southampton's place amid the religious differences which sundered his society. He began as a devout little boy, so ardently Roman Catholic that he refused even to attend the services of the Church of England. He ended as the Protestant stalwart to whom Thomas Ailesbury dedicated a sermon full of abuse of Rome as 'this Jezabel', and with a central thesis that 'Papall Rome at this day out-bids the Pagan for Idols'.[1] We must try to establish the point at which Southampton broke with the Catholicism of his family and crossed into the Protestant world.

Southampton's conversion has usually been placed in the reign of James I. Three pieces of evidence have supported this dating. One is the declaration by Dr. Peckard, an eighteenth-century Cambridge don, who declared flatly, 'This Earl . . . had been converted from Popery by Sir Edwin Sandys.'[2] Since the friendship with Sandys, as far as we know, dates from the reign of James, it seemed logical to put Southampton's conversion some time after 1603. Peckard however is an unreliable writer. Judging from the Virginia Company's own records, his account of Southampton's election to the Company's treasurership in 1620 is incorrect in various details. A piece of evidence that apparently indicates that Southampton was a Roman Catholic even after 1603 is a document cited by Mrs. Stopes,[3] as showing that around 1604 Southampton was one of the recusants whose fines were granted to Lady Walsingham. When Mrs. Stopes wrote this passage, however, she was completely confused about the nature of the document in question. Actually it lists Southampton not as one of Lady Walsingham's recusants but as one of the persons who, along with her, were granted recusants.[4] It thus becomes evidence of Southampton's Protestantism and not of his Catholicism. The final evidence is that supplied by Scaramelli, the secretary of the Venetian embassy, who reported in May 1603:

> . . . old Howard [Lord Henry Howard, soon to become Earl of Northampton] who has lately been appointed to the Council, and Southampton, who are both Catholics, declare that God has touched their hearts, and that the example of their King has more weight with them than the disputes of theologians. They have become Protestants, and go to church in the train of the King.[5]

[1] *Paganisme and Papisme*, sig. B2r.
[2] Peckard, p. 102.
[3] Stopes, p. 295.
[4] *S.P. 14/11*, ff. 57r–59r. Since various of the recipients are Scottish, the list clearly belongs to the reign of James I. The recusants granted to Southampton are Andrew Bendlosse, Austen Belson, Edward Gage of Wormesley, John Shelley, Edward Gage of Bentley, William Copley, Sir John Carrell the younger, Thomas Hoord. Another copy of this list for Southampton is noted in *Cal. S.P. (Dom.), 1598–1601*, p. 524, where it is conjecturally assigned to 1600.
[5] *Cal. S.P. (Ven.), 1603–1607*, p. 42.

But Scaramelli was wrong about Howard, who certainly remained a Catholic even if a secret one. And he was probably wrong about Southampton, whose very genuine Protestantism seems to have started much earlier.

Turning to the evidence of Southampton's Protestantism we note that Powell, dedicating his *Welch Bait* to the Earl in 1603, had in the book references to 'the tyranny of Rome', which certainly would have been unacceptable to anyone who was a Catholic. Further evidence of Southampton s Protestantism in 1603 can be found in Sir William Browne's recommendation to his patronage, in June of that year, of a Venetian who had fled Italy 'for religion'.[1] Looking back into Elizabeth's reign for Southampton's switch in religion we may note he was probably a Protestant at the time of Essex's Rebellion. After the failure of the uprising, the government investigated very thoroughly the background of all the principal conspirators. Endeavouring to make the plot appear to be a Catholic one, it established the Catholicism of Essex's stepfather, Sir Christopher Blount, of Sir Charles Danvers and of Sir John Davies. But no evidence was turned up which identified Southampton as a Catholic. The one single tie between Southampton and the Catholics was supplied by a Valentine Thomas who testified that Thomas Wright,[2] a seminary priest, had told him that Southampton was 'well given', meaning nothing more than that he was friendly towards Catholics. At Southampton's trial, Sir Edward Coke, as usual mingling facts with unproven allegations, did accuse Southampton of being a Catholic. Presumably he felt that since the Earl came of a notoriously Catholic family he could try the accusation and see how it went. As we noted earlier, Southampton firmly denied the allegation and Coke let the matter drop.

Reaching back beyond 1600 for the date of Southampton's switch in faith, one finds one's attention drawn to the events of 1598. Essex himself was a Protestant, even a bit of a Puritan, and among his secretaries was Henry Cuffe, at one time Greek Orator at the University of Oxford, who was remarkable for the intensity of his Puritan convictions. Sir Henry Wotton, also at one time a secretary to Essex, tells us that once when Essex dismissed Cuffe (apparently in the fall of 1600), it was Southampton who interceded for Cuffe and secured his reappointment.[3] We have seen that Southampton's Catholic brother-in-law Thomas Arundell was vehement against Cuffe in his letter to Cecil of February 15th, 1601, identifying him as a Puritan scholar and noting that he had done no good for

[1] H.M.C., *De L'Isle MSS.*, III, 32.
[2] See p. 125, footnote 1. He may well be the same Thomas Wright who dedicated to Southampton his *Passions of the Mind* (see page 139 *supra*).
[3] *Reliquiae Wottonianae* (London, 1672), p. 181.

Southampton while studying Aristotle's *Politics* with him in Paris. This Paris episode almost certainly dates back to the summer of 1598.[1] The suggestion must be made that Arundell was more upset by Cuffe's moulding of Southampton's religious views than by his shaping his political philosophy.

Weighing what evidence we have, we may make the following statement of probabilities. Burghley apparently got the boy earl in time to start an effective brainwashing where his youthful Catholicism was concerned. The process begun in Cecil House was continued at St. John's College. (Southampton's lifelong affection for his college would hardly accord with years spent clinging there to his Catholic faith amid the aggressively Protestant spirit of St. John's.) After setting up for life on his own, Southampton for some while probably concealed from his intensely Catholic family the degree of his alienation from their faith,[2] but probably in 1598 following his marriage to Elizabeth Vernon, he made known to his family his transfer of allegiance to Anglicanism. His Catholic kin blamed the trouble on the pernicious Puritan Cuffe. Arundell, regarding Southampton as a renegade, began that extended estrangement which he mentioned in 1601 in his letter to Cecil.

We may be confident that Southampton postponed as long as possible any declaration to his family of his conversion to Anglicanism. In Elizabethan England great houses such as Cowdray and Titchfield were strongholds of Catholicism, bases from which priests operated, circulating clandestinely from one such house to another as they moved about the country ministering to those of the Old Religion. Southampton's father had been intensely Catholic. According to Mrs. Stopes, he had not permitted non-Catholics to be tenants in his houses.[3] The trusted stewards whom Southampton inherited from his father, Gage and Chamberlain, must both have been Catholics, like all the servants or retainers who had served the family in his father's time. His great-aunt Anne Pound was the mother of Thomas Pound, an 'approved scholastic' of the Society of Jesus who spent the last years of Elizabeth's reign imprisoned for his faith. His aunt Mary had taken for her second husband one of the Shelleys of Michelgrove, a notably Catholic family. A report of April 1580 naming,

[1] For evidence that Cuffe was in Paris in July and September 1598, see *Salisbury MSS.*, XIV, 63 and VIII, 353. For Southampton's presence in Paris at that time see pp. 70–3 *supra*.

[2] It is worth noting that Southampton's contemporary at St. John's, Thomas Nashe, has some anti-papal passages in his *Unfortunate Traveller* which he dedicated to Southampton in 1594—the bandit Esdras is 'authorized by the Pope because he had assisted him in some murders'; Zadok curses the Pope 'with all his sin-absolved whores and oil-greased priests'.

[3] Stopes, p. 20.

shire by shire, the English Catholic refugees in France, listed under Hampshire:

3 Shelleys
2 Writhesleys[1]

Southampton's mother, a devout Catholic until her dying day, had been brought up by her stepmother, the Viscountess Montagu, who was a notable and saintly figure in the tight little society of English Catholic aristocracy. Southampton's cousin Anthony Maria Browne, second Viscount Montagu, was so vehement a Catholic that he stunned the House of Lords in 1604 with a speech in which he not only defended his own religion but denigrated the Church of England, saying:

That we had been misled to forsake the Religion of our Fathers, and to follow some light Persons, of late Time sprung up, that were of unsound Doctrine and evil Life. . . .[2]

The defection of Southampton, head of one of the great Catholic families, would be a serious blow to the Old Religion. It would alienate him from many of his own kin who were suffering grievously because of their determination to preserve their faith. The English Catholics must generally have regarded Southampton with contempt as a turncoat. Little wonder if he did, by subterfuge and evasion, postpone for years the moment of final breach, coming out into the open only when marriage brought him into the Protestant family of Essex.

A streak of evasiveness ran through Southampton's character. In his earliest years he had lived in the atmosphere of concealment, equivocation and secrecy which was essential for Catholics of his father's kind. After he had passed into the Protestant world of Cecil House and St. John's, protective evasion probably kept his family from realizing that they were losing him. Although Southampton had a spontaneity of feeling and an engaging impulsiveness of manner, he did at times show a sly secretiveness. Of this latter trait, even in later life, we have the unequivocal testimony of Arthur Wilson, who knew him personally, and in the main admired him: 'He carried his business closely and slily', says Wilson.[3] There seems little reason to doubt that Southampton had early learned to banish candour from certain regions of his life.

A last word about Southampton and the Catholics. After the break became apparent to everyone, Southampton did not dismiss his Catholic servants or banish his Catholic kin from Southampton House. He seems to have dealt with them in as friendly and tolerant a way as possible, even

[1] *Cal. S.P. (Foreign) Elizabeth, 1579–1580*, p. 250.
[2] *Lords Journals*, II, 328.
[3] Wilson, II, 736.

though at the cost of such an occasional embarrassment as befell in January 1605 when John Chamberlain reported:

> Eight or ten dayes since there was above two hundredeth pounds worth of popish bookes taken about Southampton house and burned in Poules Churchyard.[1]

When Southampton could do a good turn for his former co-religionists by the discreet use of his influence, or by taking nominal possession of estates that Catholic families such as the Uvedales and Philpots[2] had forfeited to the law, he did so. He seems to have become a useful middleman between Catholics and the Protestant government, trusted by both.

Inadequate as is the evidence concerning Southampton's change in religion, it is copious compared with that dealing with a second problematic area in his life, that of the homosexuality which may have marked his earlier years.

A case of sorts can be made to indicate homosexuality. The argument would run that the young boy Southampton, convinced that his mother had betrayed his father, reacted so violently against her as to be left for years with a distrust of women. It would be further argued that the exclusively masculine society of St. John's into which he entered at the age of twelve, turned him towards persons of his own sex for love. His unwillingness to marry would be viewed as part of a homosexual's aversion to women. Something might be made of the fact that neither of his closest friends, Sir Charles and Sir Henry Danvers, ever married. Thomas Nashe might be made to give some not very convincing evidence. Nashe, who was at St. John's in Southampton's time, published in 1592 his *Pierce Penilesse His Supplication to the Devil*. This book ends with a fulsome dedication to that 'matchlesse image of Honor, and magnificent rewarder of vertue, *Joves Eagle-borne Ganimed*, thrice-noble *Amyntas*'.[3] To Sir Sidney Lee, Amyntas was 'beyond doubt' Southampton.[4] A 'ganymede', however, was an Elizabethan slang word for a homosexual. It might be suggested that Nashe, a mad wag, was indulging in a dangerous 'in' joke. Finally, it might be noted that when Southampton was in Ireland, for months away from his wife, he may have had a homosexual relationship with one Piers Edmonds, an officer in Essex's army. The sole evidence here is a passage in an informer's letter, sent to Cecil after the collapse of the Essex Rebellion:

> I do mervell allso what becam of pearse edmones [wanted for participation in the rebellion] called captane pearse, or captaine edmones, the earle of essex man, borne in strand neare me, one which has had many rewards & preferments by the

---

[1] *Letters*, I, 202. See also the case of John Cotton, p. 146 *supra*.
[2] V.C.H., *Hampshire*, IV, 385.
[3] Nashe, *Works*, ed. McKerrow, I, 243.
[4] *A Life of William Shakespeare* (New York, 1927), p. 665.

earle essex, his villany I have often complaind of, he dweles in london, he was corporall generall of the horse in Ierland under the earle of Sowthamton, he eate & drancke at his table and lay in his tente, the earle of Sowthamton gave him a horse, which edmonds refused a 100 markes for him, the earle sowthamton would cole and huge [embrace and hug] him in his armes and play wantonly with him.[1]

At this point the possible evidence comes to an end. It all adds up to one thing: nothing would be less surprising than to learn that during certain periods of his early life Southampton passed through homosexual phases but, until better evidence is found, only a fool will declare that he did.

Leaving behind these uncertain matters, let us make our appraisal of the young Earl of Southampton. An indictment of his flaws can be easily drawn. He lacked stability. Lady Bridget Manners, declining in 1594 to consider either the Earl of Southampton or the Earl of Bedford as a husband, remarked 'they be so yonge and fantastycall and woulde be so caryed awaye'.[2] Queen Elizabeth had some reason for her pithy character-ization of Southampton in 1599 as 'one whose counsel can be of little, and experience of less use'. To his stepfather Heneage he was 'an unkind and injurious son-in-law'.[3]

There was plenty about young Southampton to exasperate his elders. He was slapdash and careless. (Characteristically he hardly ever took time to date his letters, thereby creating problems for his later biographers.) He could be selfish and unkind, seducing Elizabeth Vernon and then leav-ing her amid her tears. At times he was moody and petulant. All beholders could see when he was 'full of Discontentments'. He was hot-tempered and sudden in quarrel—ready to duel with Northumberland, brawling with Ambrose Willoughby, pestering his mother about her relations with Sir William Harvey, and involved in a long feud with Lord Grey. The years were to chasten that hot temper, but even in later life it would still blaze forth. In April 1610, when Southampton quarrelled with the youthful Earl of Montgomery during a tennis match, 'the racketts flew about theyre eares' and only the King's intervention kept Southampton from settling the matter with rapiers.[4]

The youthful Southampton could be intolerably stiff-necked. Sir Charles Danvers reveals a lot when, writing to him in Ireland about his lost generalship of the horse, he urged him to write a submissive letter to the Queen using 'your own pen in such style as is no less fit for this time than contrary to your disposition'. He frankly told his friend that the Queen's hostility was 'as much grounded upon the sternness of your carriage as upon the foundation of any other offence'.[5]

[1] *Cecil Papers*, 83, 62.   [2] *Rutland MSS.*, I, 321.
[3] *Salisbury MSS.*, V, 277.
[4] Chamberlain, I, 298; *Downshire MSS.*, II, 280.
[5] *Salisbury MSS.*, IX, 246.

Finally there is that prodigality which we so often have had occasion to note. The young earl was bent on living like a lord. He poured forth money upon his luxuries, his pleasures, his pastimes. He was a gamester who relished the excitement of high stakes. Surviving, in fantastically exaggerated form in an old ballad, is a story of how he bet 'seven good thousand pound' on his ability to outleap those competing in a match with him.[1] Within four years of attaining his majority he had so dissipated his fortune as to have to sell land, turn over the administration of his debt-encumbered estate to the family's old men of business, and retreat to the Continent. When he came back it just was not in his character to live quietly and modestly. He revealed quite a lot at his trial when he declared that, coming to Essex House on the morning of the rebellion, 'I had not above ten or twelve men attending me, which was but my usual Company'.[2]

But having categorized all the follies and vices of the young earl, we have still to explain why he attracted people as he did, and bound them to himself and his fortunes. Even as a young boy he must have had something singularly attractive about him. When Southampton was only fifteen, his brother-in-law, writing to Burghley, noted that 'Your Lordship doth love him' and added, for himself, 'My love and care of this young Earl enticeth me.'[3] William Camden, who as a master at Westminster School had learned to appraise boys and young men, seems to have had a decided liking for young Southampton. Mountjoy, the conqueror of Ireland, trying to get for him the governorship of Connaught, wrote, 'I can name no man that I love better than the Earl of Southampton.'[4] Cecil at Southampton's trial could speak of 'all the love and friendship that hath been betwixt us'. Sir Charles Danvers, after the Essex Rebellion, could declare that his chief motive for joining in it had been 'the great obligation of love and duty' that bound him to Southampton.[5] We are forced to the conclusion that, despite all his faults and follies, Southampton was a young man of quite singular charm and attractiveness.

Part of that attraction derived from the fact that young Southampton was an exceptionally handsome man. Part of his striking appearance seems to have been a particular brilliance of the eyes. We note it in the early picture of him at Worksop. It may have been an inherited feature in his

---

[1] *Roxburghe Ballads*, VIII, 135-7. The scene is laid in the court of King James, apparently after the death of Prince Henry, but mention of Essex and St. Lawrence seems to indicate that the original exploit and the large bet belong back in the time of Elizabeth when Southampton was a young man.

[2] Hargrave, *State Trials*, I, 202.

[3] *Salisbury MSS.*, III, 365.

[4] *Cal. S.P. (Ireland), 1600*, p. 223.

[5] *Cal. S.P. (Dom.), 1598-1601*, p. 571.

family, for the portrait of his grandfather at Beaulieu shows even more markedly the same bright intense gaze. Barnabe Barnes in his sonnet to the young earl dwells upon those eyes:

> Vouchsafe, right virtuous Lord! with gracious eyes,
> (Those heavenly lamps which give the Muses light,
> Which give and take, in course, that holy fire)
> To view my Muse with your judicial sight. . . .[1]

Gervase Markham, in his sonnet extolling Southampton, mentions the eyes also:

> Thou glorious Laurell of the Muses hill,
> Whose eyes doth crowne the most victorius pen. . . .[2]

Markham mentions also something else, Southampton's dulcet speech. He tells us that he is an 'eares-inchaunting man' and, speaking of the harshness of his own verse, makes a petition:

> Vouchsafe to sweet it with thy blessed tong[ue],
> Whose wel tun'd sound stills musick in the sphears.

Southampton's charm was more than physical. He did have virtues to outweigh his taints. He was passionately loyal to his friends, as befitted a man whose family motto was '*Ung par tout, tout par ung*'.[3] If he caused Elizabeth Vernon great sorrow at first, he did finally marry her and not leave her an object of scorn, as Pembroke a few years later was to leave Mary Fitton. Elizabeth's kinship with Essex may finally have induced Southampton to marry her, but every consideration of Elizabethan common sense demanded that he repair his ruined fortunes by taking some rich heiress, not penniless Elizabeth, for his countess. Moreover, there seems to have been from the beginning a basic generosity of spirit in Southampton and, as the years passed and he outgrew the excesses of his youth, this became more and more apparent. Various of his benefactions we have noted earlier.

For a just appreciation of Southampton we need to know the philosophy which he quite deliberately accepted, and realize the programme of action that he early adopted. Our best means of understanding both this philosophy and this programme is to see Southampton as a member of the Sidney–Essex group.

Anybody with even the flimsiest knowledge of English literature and English history knows that Sir Philip Sidney epitomized in himself the

[1] Sir Sidney Lee ed., *Elizabethan Sonnets* (New York, n.d.), I, 314–15.
[2] *The Most Honorable Tragedie of Sir Richard Grinvile, Knight* (London, 1595), sig. A4r.
[3] *Add. MS. 5504*, f. 92. See also B. W. Greenfield, 'The Wriothesley Tomb in Titchfield Church', Hampshire Field Club, *Papers and Proceedings*, 1889, p. 71.

whole Renaissance ideal of the *homo universalis*, scholar and statesman, soldier and poet. What is not so widely realized is that Essex and those about him were the conscious continuators of the Sidney ideal. Not for nothing did Sidney bequeath his best sword to his 'beloved and much honoured Lord, the Earl of Essex'.[1] It has very properly been observed that 'Essex was Sidney's successor as "Patron of Learning and Cheval-rie"'. Thus the group that assembled about Essex were conscious of themselves as heirs of the Sidney tradition. This group included Sidney's younger brother Robert, a valued friend of Southampton, Sidney's widow who became Essex's wife, and Sidney's daughter who by marrying the Earl of Rutland brought him closer into the group. Also in the circle was Essex's sister Penelope, who almost certainly had been Sidney's 'Stella'; Charles Blount, Lord Mountjoy, who became her lover; and Sir Henry Danvers who, as Sidney's page, had walked in his funeral procession. When Southampton married Essex's cousin Elizabeth Vernon, he made even closer his association with this group.

They made up a brilliant and gifted little company. With reason they saw themselves as the wave of the future, the new generation destined to take over from the old men, Burghley, Buckhurst, Egerton and the rest who surrounded the ageing Queen. But a fatal flaw in Essex frustrated those hopes, and power passed to Burghley's son, little crook-backed Robert Cecil whom, like the Emperor Justinian, no man could remember having ever been young.

Southampton sought to realize in his own person the Renaissance ideal epitomized by Sir Philip Sidney. We see how well he succeeded when, reading Francis Beale's lament after his death, we encounter the lines:

> I can no more in this lugubrious Verse:
> Reader depart, and looke on Sidneys Herse.[2]

Like Sidney, Southampton set himself to combine the military life and the humanistic. Everybody who knew him seems to have been aware of his twofold ideal:

> The height of armes and artes in one aspiring,
> Valor with grace, with valor grace attiring. . . .

Thus John Florio in the dedicatory sonnet he prefaced to his *Worlde of Wordes*.

> Incomprehensible is the height of your spirit, both in heroical resolution and matters of conceit. . . .

[1] G. B. Harrison, *The Life and Death of Robert Devereux, Earl of Essex* (New York [1937]), p. 33.
[2] *The Teares of the Isle of Wight*, reprinted in Malone's 'Memoir', *Shakespeare*, 1821 ed., XX, 452.

Thus Thomas Nashe, dedicating to Southampton his *Unfortunate Travel-ler*. Camden proved right in his assessment of the young Southampton:

> He, in his youth, fortifies his noble descent with the defence of humane studies and knowledge of the art of war, so that at a riper age he may pour forth fruits for his country and his sovereign.[1]

Of Southampton's military interests and achievements we have already taken sufficient note. We have seen his courage as a cavalry commander in the field. We know that the Flemish physician Baldwin Hamey was right in describing Southampton as 'a man of bold mind and reckless of danger'.[2] He was indeed, as a Venetian ambassador said, one of the bravest and noblest cavaliers of the English nation.[3]

It is the other side of his character that we must treat now—his love for learning, and his encouragement of poets and musicians,[4] and of scholars be they historians, lexicographers or translators. Probably Southampton's love of learning was instilled in him by Burghley at Cecil House. This attachment to learning was an essential part of Southampton, not an affectation. How many young lords would combine as pleasures in Paris gambling at the gaming tables and reading Aristotle with a Puritan scholar?

Some of Southampton's benefactions in support of learning are still on record. His munificent gift to St. John's library we noted earlier. His widow used a significant phrase in her letter when she sent the Crashaw books down to Cambridge after the new library had been built and was ready to receive them. Speaking of her son, who had followed his father to St. John's, she said, 'I hope he will therein imitate his noble Father for his love to learning and to you.'[5] Oxford as well as Cambridge benefited from Southampton's generosity. In 1605 he contributed to the setting up of the Bodleian Library. In a much humbler sphere we find him in 1619 helping with the maintenance of the grammar school at Newport on the Isle of Wight. As for Southampton's benefactions to individuals, these ranged from the assistance he gave John Minsheu, deep in his heroic labours in bringing out a comparative dictionary for eleven languages,[6]

---

[1] *Britannia* (London, 1600), sig. Q8v (trans.).

[2] *Hamey the Stranger*, p. 76.

[3] *Cal. S.P. (Ven.), 1623–1625*, p. 501.

[4] We noted earlier Ferrabosco's dedication to Southampton of his airs for the viol. We may add that in 1607 Tobias Hume included in his *Poetical Musicke* a piece entitled, 'The Earl of Southamptons favoret'.

[5] R. W. Goulding, *Wriothesley Portraits*, Walpole Society (Oxford, 1920), p. 33.

[6] Lodge, *Portraits*, III, 163. For Minsheu's special presentation copy of his work given to Southampton (now in the Library of University College, London), see F. B. Williams, 'Scholarly Publication in Shakespeare's Day: A Leading Case', *Joseph Quincy Adams: Memorial Studies* (Washington, 1948), p. 764.

to encouragement for a bright young Welsh undergraduate at Cambridge:

> . . . Robin [Wynn] at Cambridge did so well in his acting that my Lord of
> Southampton, who was present, sent for him and graced him exceedingly, taking
> notice whose son he was, and sent afterwards for him to come to his house [at
> Shelford] within three miles of Cambridge.[1]

Let us turn from the scholars to the poets. In 1594 Thomas Nashe
declared to Southampton, 'A dere lover and cherisher you are, as well of
the lovers of Poets, as of Poets themselves'.[2] Thirty years later Sir John
Beaumont, remembering how Southampton had encouraged him with his
'Crowne of Thornes', and writing an elegy in his honour, declared:

> I keep that glory last, which is the best;
> The love of learning, which he oft exprest
> By conversation, and respect to those
> Who had a name in arts, in verse or prose.
> Shall ever I forget, with what delight,
> He on my simple lines would cast his sight?
>
> . . .   .
>
> Now since his death how can I ever look,
> Without some tears, upon that orphan book?[3]

Finally, one last word about Southampton's prodigality in his favours
to those to whom he gave his patronage. This bears a somewhat altered
aspect when we see it as part of the Renaissance-Sidney ideal. Not for
nothing does our word 'generous' derive from the Latin *generosus*,
designating one of noble birth. A lord who was truly noble was expected
to pour forth bounty. Southampton in his youthful prodigality may have
allowed that bounty far to outstrip his means, but we can respect the ideal.

And now, before turning from Southampton, the patron, to Shakespeare whose patron he was, we may pause for a moment to look at the
portrait of the young earl preserved for us in the home of his descendant,
the Duke of Portland. Here he stands, magnificent in white silk doublet
and gold-encrusted purple trunks and knee breeches, with white hose
fastened with purple garters, black rosetted shoes on his feet and flower-
embroidered gauntlets on his hands. On his right is his helmet with its
white plumes, on his left his cuirass. About his neck, richly damascened
with gold, is his red leather gorget.

Our attention lingers upon his face. Down the left side hangs the long

---

[1] Letter of May 22nd, 1612, *Calendar of the Wynn Papers* (Aberystwyth, 1926), p. 95.

[2] Dedication to *The Unfortunate Traveller* (London, 1594), sig. A2v.

[3] The poem is reprinted in its entirety in Malone's 'Memoir', *Shakespeare*, 1821, ed.
XX, 448–50.

On 'The Crowne of Thornes' see B. H. Newdigate, 'Sir John Beaumont's "The
Crowne of Thornes"', *Review of English Studies*, XVIII (1942), 284–90, and Ruth
Wallerstein, 'Sir John Beaumont's *Crowne of Thornes*, A Report', *Journal of English
and Germanic Philology*, LIII (1954), 410–34.

tress of hair in the fashion he affected along with other gallants of the Court. The rest is brushed back, exposing the high forehead. A pensive expression marks the long delicate face. The lips are slightly pursed, hinting at tensions within. But the clear eyes gaze out firmly yet thoughtfully.

Here, regarding the centuries, is Henry Wriothesley, third Earl of Southampton, sole patron ever acknowledged by the greatest poet, perhaps, that our world will ever know.

THE POET AND THE PATRON

CHAPTER I

Enter William Shakespeare

D R. JOHNSON once observed that the province of the conjecturer
is perilous and difficult, but he added 'the peril must not be
avoided or the difficulty refused'. In this second part of our book,
as we seek to trace the relationship between Shakespeare and his patron,
we shall often lack evidence and be forced back upon conjecture. But we
offer our readers this double assurance: we will endeavour to limit ourselves to those conjectures which seem to have some real likelihood, and
we will keep before us Johnson's warning that conjecture must never be
'wantonly nor licentiously indulged'.[1]

Much of the generally accepted early biography of William Shakespeare rests on little more than probability. Though he was christened in
Holy Trinity Church, Stratford-upon-Avon, on April 26th, 1564, nobody
knows when he was born. However, since he died on April 23rd (St.
George's Day) in 1616, symmetry and patriotism have established April
23rd, 1564, as the traditional birthday of William Shakespeare. The date
is probably reasonably close. Probability likewise favours Stratford-upon-
Avon as the place of Shakespeare's birth, and is on the side of the millions
of tourists who, visiting the 'Birthplace', his father's house in Henley
Street, have inspected the empty cradle placed in one of the rooms there
by the Shakespeare Birthplace Trust. But the poet's mother could have
had her birthpangs come upon her prematurely while visiting Warwick, or
Coventry, or Wilmcote.

Shakespeare's mother came from a Catholic family, the Ardens, and his
father, John Shakespeare, may have been a covert Catholic. The 'Old
Religion' was still strong in Warwickshire and Shakespeare, like the Earl
of Southampton, may have spent his earliest years in a Catholic household.

Since John Shakespeare, a glover and dealer in hides and grain, was a
leading citizen of Stratford, his son William probably went to the local
grammar school. However, since no school registers survive from this
period, there is no proof that he did. If young Shakespeare attended
Stratford Grammar School, he was probably taken away a year or so
before the completion of his studies, his father having suffered some sort

[1] D. Nichol Smith, ed., *Eighteenth Century Essays on Shakespeare* (Glasgow, 1903),
pp. 153-5.

of financial disaster and needing either his son's services at home, or whatever wages the lad could earn.[1]

On November 27th, 1582, the episcopal registry of the diocese of Worcester issued a special licence for the marriage of William Shakespeare and Anne Hathaway. The parish register at Stratford records, on May 26th, 1583, the baptism of Susanna, daughter of William Shakespeare. It would appear, then, that Shakespeare had married a pregnant bride, an occurrence not unusual in the England of Elizabeth I, or of Elizabeth II. The register also records, on February 2nd, 1585, the baptism of 'Hamnet & Judeth sonne and daughter to William Shakspere'. Probably it was after the arrival of the twins that William Shakespeare left Stratford.

There follow the so-called 'lost years' for which we have no information. Writers have speculated that Shakespeare was at this time a lawyer's clerk, an apothecary, a seaman, a soldier, a visitor to Italy, a player with a travelling company, and a retainer in a noble house. About 1681 an old actor told John Aubrey that Shakespeare 'had been in his younger yeares a Schoolmaster in the Countrey'.

The mists begin to clear in 1592. Early in September that year there died in squalid circumstances Robert Greene, a Master of Arts of Cambridge and Oxford, who in his poverty had become a hack writer of pamphlets, romances and plays. Behind him he left some miscellaneous pieces which appeared in a little book entitled *Greenes Groats-worth of Witte*, seen through the press by a fellow hack, Henry Chettle. Among the contents of this book was an open letter addressed by Greene to other impoverished university men who had turned playwrights for the London professional stage. After inveighing bitterly against the actors for the way they had dealt with him, Greene warned these 'University Wits' to expect no better treatment, especially since one of these actors had set himself up as a playwright and was plagiarizing from their plays:

> Yes trust them not: for there is an upstart Crow, beautified with our feathers, that with his *Tygers hart wrapt in a Players hyde*, supposes he is as well able to bombast out a blanke verse as the best of you: and beeing an absolute *Johannes fac totum*, is in his owne conceit the onely Shake-scene in a countrey.[2]

Since the phrase about the 'Tygers hart' is very close to a line in Shakespeare's *Henry VI, Part Three* ('O tiger's heart wrapt in a woman's hide', I, iv, 137), and since 'Shake-scene' is a play on Shakespeare's name, we have

---

[1] Nicholas Rowe's account, in 1709, of how 'the narrowness of his Circumstances' forced Shakespeare's father to take his son prematurely out of school fits in with the surviving evidence of his financial troubles around 1577. See Chambers, *William Shakespeare* (Oxford, 1930), II, 264, and I, 14–15.

[2] Chambers, op. cit., II, 188. Not all scholars believe Greene was charging Shakespeare with plagiarism. J. A. Lavin reviews this controversy in the introduction to his edition of Greene's *James IV* (London, 1967), pp. x–xi.

WILLIAM SHAKESPEARE
(from the Droeshout engraving)

no difficulty in identifying Greene's target. The *Groats-worth of Witte*, in short, yields us the invaluable information that by September 1592 William Shakespeare, an actor turned playwright, had achieved sufficient reputation to arouse the hostility of an established dramatist. Amid the repercussions following publication of Greene's bitter letter, we find the first indications of a possible friendship between Shakespeare and the Earl of Southampton.

We have no evidence as to when, where, or under what circumstances William Shakespeare first met the Earl of Southampton. We have only conjectures[1]—that William Harvey, not yet a knight, first introduced Shakespeare to Southampton; that the office was performed by Sir Thomas Heneage, whose official duties brought him into contact with the actors; that Shakespeare was engaged in 1591 as Southampton's tutor; that Shakespeare sought out Southampton because he wanted him to use his influence with the Earl of Essex to get him a coat of arms; that Shakespeare with a company of players acted at Cowdray and Titchfield during the royal progress of 1591. Developing this last idea, Austen K. Gray argued that Shakespeare's company presented *Love's Labour's Lost* at Titchfield on the afternoon of September 2nd, 1591.[2] Unfortunately, the remarkably full account of the royal entertainment at Cowdray makes no mention of a play or actors. Likewise, there is no evidence of a play or actors at Titchfield.

If the present writer must add his own guess as to where and when Shakespeare and Southampton first met, he would suggest a backstage meeting in a London playhouse sometime in 1591–92. The person who first presented Shakespeare to the Earl may have been Sir George Carew, whose marriage in 1580 to a Clopton heiress had made him a great man around Stratford. The number of books (mostly military) that were dedicated to him show that he had some interest in literature. He could be expected to take an interest in a Stratford man with a mounting reputation in London. Carew was long a friend of Southampton and his mother.[3]

Let us return to the publication of *Greenes Groats-worth of Witte* in the

---

[1] For these theories see Barbara Mackenzie, *Shakespeare's Sonnets: Their Relation to His Life* (Cape Town, 1946), p. 2; Nathan Drake, *Shakespeare and His Times* (London, 1817), II, 2; W. Schrickx, 'Solar Symbolism and Related Imagery in Shakespeare', *Revue Belge de Philologie et d'Histoire*, XXIX (1951), 115; Herbert Howarth, 'Shakespeare's Gentleness', *Shakespeare Survey 14* (Cambridge, 1961), p. 91; Arthur Acheson, *Shakespeare's Lost Years in London, 1586–1592* (London, 1920), pp. 36–7.

[2] 'The Secret of *Love's Labour's Lost*', *PMLA*, XXXIX (1924), 581–611.

[3] (p. 151 *supra*.) Sir George was created Baron Carew of Clopton in May 1609, and Earl of Totnes in February 1626. About 1610 he became the first High Steward of Stratford-upon-Avon. He lies buried, not far from Shakespeare, in Stratford parish church. For an undated letter from Southampton to Carew see *Cecil Papers*, 167, 141.

autumn of 1592. Apparently the word got around that the attack upon
Shakespeare had been written by Thomas Nashe, another of the University Wits. Nashe lost no time in denying this charge. About mid-October,
in an epistle prefaced to his *Pierce Penilesse*, he declared:

> Other news I am advertised of, that a scald trivial lying pamphlet, cald *Greens
> groats-worth of wit*, is given out to be my doing. God never have care of my soule,
> but utterly renounce me, if the least word or sillable in it proceeded from my pen,
> or if I were any way privie to the writing or printing of it.[1]

The vehemence of Nashe's language suggests that he was badly worried
by the suspicion that had fallen upon him. Both Nashe and Shakespeare
were soon to dedicate works to the Earl of Southampton, and probably
the two were already moving in the young Earl's circle. Presumably Nashe
feared that Southampton, angered by this attack upon a playwright whom
he admired, would become hostile if he once believed Nashe its author.
The next move was up to Chettle since the offending book had been
entered in the Stationers' Register 'uppon the perill of Henrye Chettle'.[2]
In December Chettle prefaced his own *Kind-Harts Dreame* with an epistle
in which he not only declared that Nashe was in no way responsible for the
attack in the *Groats-worth of Witte* but made his own apology to Shakespeare:

> I am as sory as if the originall fault had beene my fault, because my selfe have
> seene his demeanor no lesse civill than he exelent in the qualitie he professes.

Then Chettle added a significant comment:

> Besides, divers of worship have reported his uprightnes of dealing, which argues
> his honesty. . . .[3]

'Divers of worship' suggests persons of rank and position. It seems a good
guess that the youthful Earl of Southampton was among those in the
playgoing crowd who had rallied to the defence of Shakespeare.

Greene's attack came when Shakespeare, without employment in the
playhouses, needed the help of a patron. The previous June, because of
a riot by the London apprentices, the Privy Council had closed all the
theatres until Michaelmas. Then, before this period ended, plague broke
out and the players were ordered not to resume performances until the
end of December. The playhouses reopened briefly in January 1593 but,
the plague flaring up again, were closed at the end of the month. While
the plague ravaged the capital, the acting companies, at the end of their
tether financially, reduced their strength and went on tour in the provinces. Not until June 1594 did the theatrical life of London resume its
normal pace. Faced in February 1593 with this renewed closure of the

---

[1] Nashe, *Works*, ed. McKerrow, I, 154.   [2] Arber, *Transcripts*, II, 620.
[3] Chambers, *William Shakespeare*, II, 189.

theatres, William Shakespeare apparently decided against demotion to the
wearing and dismal life of a touring player and, remaining in London, set
about establishing himself as a man of letters. He began writing *Venus and
Adonis*.

In a fine essay Miss Muriel Bradbrook has argued that Shakespeare's
poem is in part a retort to the attack against him as 'an upstart Crow,
beautified with our feathers'. Greene's words had bitten deeply and left
their mark on Shakespeare's sensibilities. (Years later, unconsciously con-
ditioned to that 'beautified', he had Polonius, commenting upon Hamlet's
love letter, declare: 'Beautified is a vile phrase'.) Now he would show what
he could do as a writer. Not a play this time (nobody yet thought of the
scripts supplied for the players as being 'literature'), but a superb Ovidian
poem. But here let us quote Miss Bradbrook:

> After extracting an apology from Chettle, Shakespeare went on to safeguard his
> reputation with a work whose elegance and modishness was recognized within the
> walls of Greene's own college and university. . . . *Venus and Adonis*, sumptuous
> and splendidly assured, was designed not to answer Greene, but to obliterate the
> impression he had tried to make.[1]

Thus it was that William Shakespeare sat down and began to write:

> Even as the sun with purple-colored face
> Had ta'en his last leave of the weeping morn,
> Rose-cheeked Adonis hied him to the chase.
> Hunting he loved, but love he laughed to scorn.
>   Sick-thoughted Venus makes amain unto him,
>   And like a bold-faced suitor 'gins to woo him.

Shakespeare's major source, it has long been known, was Golding's translation of Ovid's *Metamorphoses*, but another source has so far gone undetected. Intending to dedicate his poem to the Earl of Southampton,
Shakespeare was aware of Southampton's fight against marriage to Lady
Elizabeth Vere, and he remembered how the Earl's feelings had been hurt
several years earlier by John Clapham and his mocking *Narcissus*.[2] In this
poem Shakespeare would apply balm to the wounds inflicted by Clapham.
Not Venus and Narcissus this time, but Venus and Adonis! No overt
identification of course. Southampton would not be the Adonis of this
poem to the extent he had been the Narcissus of the former. Still, a few
things could be discreetly said excusing his lordship's aversion to marriage.

> Hunting he loved, but love he laughed to scorn.

No suggestion here of self-love. The unresponsive young man is simply
not yet ripe for love. Young Adonis cautions Venus, 'Before I know

---

[1] 'Beasts and Gods: Greene's *Groats-worth of Witte* and the Social Purpose of *Venus
and Adonis*', *Shakespeare Survey 15*, p. 68.
[2] *v.* pp. 33–34 *supra*.

myself, seek not to know me'. Knowing how Southampton had begged old
Burghley for more time before taking a bride, Shakespeare, writing this
line, could envisage his patron giving an approving nod.

The text of *Venus and Adonis* supplies evidence that Shakespeare knew
Clapham's poem. The basic pattern is the same: the meeting with Venus,
the departure of the young man, Venus's lamentation, and the final meta-
morphosis—in Clapham's poem into a narcissus, in Shakespeare's into
an anemone. Narcissus himself briefly reappears in *Venus and Adonis*:

> Narcissus so himself himself forsook,
> And died to kiss his shadow in the brook.
>
> (lines 161–162)

We have, also, the interesting matter of Adonis' horse. Source-hunters
have wondered where Shakespeare got that horse which, as a fine con-
trasting element in the poem, breaks free from its tether and gallops off in
sexual pursuit of the mare. Ovid mentions no horse ridden by Adonis.
Geoffrey Bullough has suggested, very tentatively, that the 'breeding
jennet may owe a little to Virgil's *Georgic* III',[1] but it is unlikely that
Shakespeare knew the *Georgics*. A much more likely source would seem
to be *Narcissus*, especially since the wild steed which runs off with Narcissus in the earlier poem is given the name of 'Libido'.

Venus and Adonis is a fine poem and a notable piece of Renaissance
literary art. It is also, in places, erotic. Shakespeare, aware of his patron's
taste for highly-spiced passages, saw to it that his poem would not dis-
appoint in this respect. Venus offers herself to Adonis in terms of a land
which he may possess, declaring:

> I'll be a park, and thou shalt be my deer.
> Feed where thou wilt, on mountain or in dale.
>   Graze on my lips, and if those hills be dry,
>   Stray lower, where the pleasant fountains lie.
>
> Within this limit is relief enough,
> Sweet bottom-grass and high delightful plain,
> Round rising hillocks, brakes obscure and rough,
> To shelter thee from tempest and from rain.
>
> (lines 231–238)

Shakespeare's contemporaries were aware of the wanton aspect of the
poem. John Davies of Hereford primly said of *Venus and Adonis*:

> Fine wit is shew'n therein; but finer 'twere
> If not attired in such bawdy Geare.

A character in a Middleton play includes the poem in a list of 'wanton
pamphlets'. And Thomas Freeman noted:

---

[1] *Narrative and Dramatic Sources of Shakespeare* (London, 1957), I, 163–4.

> Who list read lust there's *Venus* and *Adonis*
> True modell of a most lascivious leatcher.[1]

All of which makes it a little interesting that *Venus and Adonis* was personally licensed for printing by the Archbishop of Canterbury. We may have lost a good story concerning Archbishop Whitgift's licence. Could it be that Southampton, meeting His Grace at Whitehall Palace, mischievously asked him to sign for the book, assuring him there was 'no offence in it ?'[2]

Venus and Adonis probably came from the press in May or June 1593. The printer, Richard Field, had produced an attractive little book printed in handsome large type. The title page bore a proud motto taken from Ovid:

> Vilia miretur vulgus: mihi flavus Apollo
> Pocula Castalia plena ministret aqua.

> (Let the common people marvel at mean objects;
> may golden-haired Apollo provide me with cups
> full from the Castalian spring.)

On the next page comes the dedication:

> To the Right Honorable Henrie Wriothesley,
> Earle of Southampton, and Baron of
> Titchfield

> Right Honourable, I know not how I shall offend in dedicating my unpolisht lines to your Lordship, nor how the worlde will censure mee for choosing so strong a proppe to support so weake a burthen, onelye if your Honour seeme but pleased, I account my selfe highly praised, and vowe to take advantage of all idle houres, till I have honoured you with some graver labour. But if the first heire of my invention prove deformed, I shall be sorie it had so noble a god-father: and

---

[1] *The Shakespeare Allusion Book* (London, 1932), I, 189, 220 and 245.

[2] *Venus and Adonis* was entered on April 18th, 1593, 'under th[e h]andes of the Archbisshop of Canterbury and master warden Stirrop' (Arber, *Transcripts*, II, 630). A number of persons, including Whitgift's secretaries Murgatroyd and Hartwell, were authorized to license books for printing. Greg (*Licensers for the Press to 1640*, Oxford, 1962, pp. 18–20) lists 162 books for which Whitgift signed personally between 1584 and 1604. The great majority of these, as one would expect, are religious or devotional. In 1587 Whitgift licensed an edition of Boccaccio's *Decameron*, but this was in the original Italian and its usefulness in encouraging young gentlemen to study the language may have weighed with the archbishop. In 1593, along with such works as *The Lawes of Ecclesiastical Polity* and *De imperandi aucthoritate et Christiana obediencia*, Whitgift licensed both Nashe's *Christs Teares over Jerusalem* and his *Unfortunate Traveller*, but Nashe was known and liked by Whitgift, who had him as his guest at Croydon in the latter half of 1592. Perhaps it was Nashe who brought Shakespeare around to Whitgift to secure the archbishop's signature for his poem. There may have been some repercussions after the licensing of *Venus and Adonis*. When Marlowe's *Hero and Leander* was entered a few months later it was, exceptionally, signed for by both the wardens of the Stationers' Company as well as by Murgatroyd, and it was specifically noted as 'an amorous poem' (Arber, II, 636). It should, of course, be remembered that the chief purposes of Elizabethan censorship were political and theological.

never after eare so barren a land, for feare it yeeld me still so bad a harvest, I leave it to your Honourable survey, and your Honor to your hearts content, which I wish may alwaies answere your owne wish, and the worlds hopefull expectation.

Your Honors in all dutie,

William Shakespeare

Shakespeare had made his first real bid for literary status.

That bid succeeded magnificently. The richness, the freshness, the daring sensuality and literary elegance of *Venus and Adonis* secured immediate success for the poem. In the next ten years it went through ten editions. In 1598 when Francis Meres made survey of Shakespeare's works, he put *Venus and Adonis* at the head of the list. A little later Gabriel Harvey noted, 'The younger sort takes much delight in Shakespeares Venus & Adonis.' Apparently the youthful Earl of Southampton took much delight in it also. He may well have shown that delight by taking Shakespeare into his household, just as at one time he took into his service the less distinguished poet and playwright Thomas Heywood.[1]

During the months that followed, Shakespeare set to work on a longer and more ambitious poem, *Lucrece*. This is set in a very different world from the fresh countryside and open skies of *Venus and Adonis*. Commenting on how the imagery of *Lucrece* derives from courtly life, Muir and O'Loughlin have noted:

> Heraldic imagery and that connected with page-boys, servitors, rich fabrics and paintings come naturally to a middle-class provincial newly introduced to the splendours of a nobleman's town mansion.[2]

Lucrece was entered in the Stationers' Register on May 9th, 1594. Published shortly thereafter, it bore a dedication to Southampton eloquently indicative of a much closer relationship than had existed when Shakespeare had offered his lord *Venus and Adonis*:

> The love I dedicate to your Lordship is without end. . . . The warrant I have of your Honourable disposition, not the worth of my untutord Lines makes it assured of acceptance. What I have done is yours, what I have to doe is yours, being part in all I have, devoted yours.

Speaking of the overflowing affection in these lines, Nichol Smith declared, 'There is no other dedication like this in Elizabethan literature.'[3]

Venus and Adonis and *Lucrece* are 'companion studies—one of female

---

[1] Heywood in his *Funeral Elegie upon the Death of King James* (London, 1625) digresses to praise also the memory of Southampton:

'. . . as in dutie bound,

Because his servant once.'   Sig. B5v.

[2] *The Voyage to Illyria* (London, 1937), pp. 57–8.

[3] *Shakespeare's England* (Oxford, 1916), II, 201.

lust and boyish coldness, the other of male lust and womanly chastity'.[1] We have no way of knowing what suggested to Shakespeare the theme for his second poem. It is worth noting however that Nashe, in his *Unfortunate Traveller* dedicated to Southampton the previous year, has a notable rape and lamentation passage. Perhaps Shakespeare, hearing Southampton praise this part of his competitor's work, decided to show what he could do in verse with such a subject. Lucrece's outcries about her 'poor soul's pollution' and her 'compelled stain' may owe something to ravished Heraclide's lamentations upon being 'tyranously polluted' and upon her 'compelled offence'.[2] At this time Nashe and Shakespeare, both seeking Southampton's favour, presumably kept a sharp eye on each other's writing. Nashe's dedicatory sonnets to his scandalous *Choise of Valentines* may owe something to Shakespeare's dedication to *Venus and Adonis*.[3]

No work of Shakespeare's is more alien to modern feeling, both aesthetic and ethical, than *Lucrece*. Listening to modern critics stigmatize the poem as crude, vulgar, tedious, morbid, and immature, one would conclude that Shakespeare's contemporaries must have been sadly disappointed in what had followed the brilliant success of *Venus and Adonis*. In fact *Lucrece* went through four editions in six years. With it Shakespeare increased his reputation. Those who had been shocked by the eroticism of *Venus and Adonis* felt that Shakespeare had redeemed himself with this second poem. Gabriel Harvey, having noted the special enthusiasm that young men had for *Venus and Adonis*, went on to add, 'But his Lucrece, & his tragedie of Hamlet, Prince of Denmarke, have it in them, to please the wiser sort', and Thomas Freeman even while condemning Shakespeare's earlier poem for its lust remarked, 'Who loves chaste life, there's *Lucrece* for a Teacher'.

The Elizabethans valued *Lucrece* for more than its chastity. In a masterly essay E. P. Kuhl has shown us how for Shakespeare 'this theme of Tarquin becomes a vehicle for his own views on kingship—lust, tyranny,

---

[1] Edward Dowden, *Shakspere: A Critical Study of his Mind and Art* (London, 1892), pp. 49–50.

[2] *Lucrece*, lines 1157 and 1708; Nashe, *Works*, ed. McKerrow, II, 293.

[3] Cf. Nashe's   Accept of it Dear Lord in gentle gree
                  And *better lynes* ere long shall *honor thee*
                . . .   . . .
                  My mynde once purg'd of such lascivious witt,
                  With purifide words, and hallowed verse
                  Thy praises in large volumes shall rehearce,
                  That better maie thy *graver* view befitt.

and Shakespeare's '. . . if your honour seem but pleased, I account myself highly praised, and vow to take advantage of all idle hours, till I have *honoured* you with some *graver* labour. (My italics.)

Of course Shakespeare may have been the borrower, but one rather doubts it.

statecraft, justice, the laws that govern political life—precisely the problems that absorbed the contemporary Elizabethan mind'. And he concludes:

> Perhaps we can glimpse a new relationship between the poet and his patron. Southampton, young in years, unmarried, eager to serve his country, in need of sage counsel, is addressed, delightfully, by an ardent patriot and poet.[1]

Shakespeare may have begun by pandering a bit to Southampton's taste for erotica but now, secure in his friendship, he is trying to lead the young aristocrat into the paths that he ought to follow.

[1] 'Shakespeare's *Rape of Lucrece*', *Philological Quarterly*, XX (July 1941), 359.

The First Sonnets

IN 1609 THE London bookseller Thomas Thorpe published a quarto entitled *Shake-speares Sonnets*, and bearing the declaration 'Never before Imprinted'. These sonnets, unlike most Elizabethan sonnet collections, do not constitute a 'cycle' for they are not a sequence of poems addressed to one particular person or exploring one particular relationship. Though many of the sonnets in the 1609 quarto appear to be addressed to the same handsome young man, a discernible group is addressed to the famous 'Dark Lady' and some may have been addressed to other persons. A few are addressed by the poet to himself. The two final sonnets are mere literary exercises, being free translations of a poem originally written in Greek in the fifth century A.D. Dover Wilson, hitting upon a felicitous term, has spoken of Thorpe's little book as a 'portfolio' of poems.[1]

These sonnets were composed over a number of years. One, as we shall see, was demonstrably written in 1603. Two were printed in slightly different form in *The Passionate Pilgrim* in 1599. And the earliest of them were written in 1593–94 (probably in those months of 1593 which followed the writing of *Venus and Adonis*).[2]

The remarkable vogue of the sonnet in England in the mid-1590s resulted from the publication in 1591 of Sir Philip Sidney's cycle *Astrophel and Stella*, in which Sidney in splendid poetry had traced the progress of his love for Penelope Devereux, Essex's sister, who later became Lady Rich. This work received at once the attention that it merited. Inspired by Sidney, the poets of England turned to show what they could do with the sonnet. In 1593 no less than four cycles came from the printing presses: Thomas Watson's *The Teares of Fancie*, Barnabe Barnes' *Parthenophil and Parthenophe*, Thomas Lodge's *Phillis*, and Giles Fletcher's *Licia*. By the next year three more cycles were ready for publication.

---

[1] ed. *The Sonnets* (Cambridge, 1966), p. xxxiv.

[2] Among those who support 1593–4 are Sir Sidney Lee (*Life of Shakespeare*, p. 89), Joseph Quincy Adams (*A Life of William Shakespeare*, Boston, 1923, p. 163), J. A. Fort (*A Time Scheme for Shakespeare's Sonnets*, London, 1929, p. 21), E. K. Chambers (*William Shakespeare*, I, 564–5), T. W. Baldwin (*On the Literary Genetics of Shakespeare's Poems and Sonnets*, Urbana, 1950, p. 344), G. Bullough (*Narrative and Dramatic Sources of Shakespeare*, I, 164).

It seems almost inevitable that Shakespeare, having completed his *Venus and Adonis*, would seek further laurels by entering the competition in sonnet writing. Obviously he was interested in the sonnet form at this time: after the theatres reopened in mid-1594, new plays by Shakespeare that were presented (*Love's Labour's Lost, Two Gentlemen of Verona, Romeo and Juliet*) contained sonnets as part of their poetic ornamentation. What of other sonnets that he had written while the theatres were closed? Some at least of these survive. They are the opening poems in Thorpe's quarto of 1609—a cycle of seventeen sonnets addressed to the Earl of Southampton and urging that young lord to marry.

Let us recall the situation that prompted Shakespeare to choose this theme. Knowledgeable people, taking note in 1593 of the dedication of *Venus and Adonis*, must have felt that Shakespeare had been acute in his choice of a patron. Not only was Southampton a young lord with a genuine interest in literature who would shortly inherit a very sizeable estate, he was also the ward and protégé of Lord Treasurer Burghley, and his good looks had so obviously won the interest of Queen Elizabeth that he stood a good chance of taking over Essex's place as the royal favourite. Nobody could guess that Southampton would run through his fortune in short order and incur the lasting distrust and dislike of his sovereign. The one thing that cast something of a shadow over the glittering prospect for Southampton in 1593 was his continuing avoidance of marriage to Lady Elizabeth Vere. Burghley was keeping the match open for him. But if the young earl persisted in his refusal he would be burdened with a fine so heavy as to impair his finances for years. He would also expose himself to the ill-will of Burghley, and perhaps of the Queen herself, in whose hands lay the key to the dazzling career at Court which seemingly lay before him. Little wonder if all those who had hitched their fortunes to South-ampton's star, including Shakespeare, did all they could to persuade the young man to marry Lady Elizabeth. Since Southampton had declared that his aversion was not to the lady so much as to marriage itself, Shake-speare's tactic, once he was sure of Southampton's goodwill, was to write poems urging the principle of marrying and begetting an heir.

Sonnet 1

From fairest creatures we desire increase,
That thereby beauty's rose might never die,
But as the riper should by time decrease,
His tender heir might bear his memory.
But thou, contracted to thine own bright eyes,
Feed'st thy light's flame with self-substantial fuel,
Making a famine where abundance lies,
Thyself thy foe, to thy sweet self too cruel.
Thou that art now the world's fresh ornament
And only herald to the gaudy spring,

> Within thine own bud buriest thy content
> And, tender churl, makest waste in niggarding.
> Pity the world, or else this glutton be,
> To eat the world's due, by the grave and thee.

The next sixteen sonnets develop this marriage-procreation theme and are linked among themselves by skilful repetitions of words and images. Repetition of 'winter' and 'distilled' joins Sonnets 5 and 6:

> But flowers *distilled*, though they with *winter* meet,
> Leese but their show. Their substance still lives sweet.
> > (Sonnet 5: 13–14)

> Then let not *winter's* ragged hand deface
> In thee thy summer, ere thou be *distilled*.
> > (Sonnet 6: 1–2)

Similar repetition of 'war' and 'Time' links Sonnets 15 and 16:

> And all in *war* with *Time* for love of you,
> As he takes from you, I engraft you new.
> > (Sonnet 15: 13–14)

> But wherefore do not you a mightier way
> Make *war* upon this bloody tyrant, *Time*?
> > (Sonnet 16: 1–2)

Because of this double bond, in theme and imagery, the integrity of Sonnets 1–17 as a self-contained sequence has been generally recognized. Even those who have teased their brains trying to rearrange Shakespeare's sonnets have usually recognized the group as an entity and have left it undisturbed.

Good evidence assigns these seventeen sonnets to 1593–94. Style alone marks them as early work. Except for an occasional awkwardness, the lines move with a rather mechanical regularity. They are rich in conceits, but lack the profundity of the great sonnets that will come later. Shakespeare has still a long way to travel before he can write Sonnet 116 ('Let me not to the marriage of true minds'), or Sonnet 129 ('The expense of spirit in a waste of shame'). Looking for verbal parallels, we find these seventeen sonnets chiefly echo the plays and other poems that Shakespeare was writing around 1593–94.[1]

---

[1] Shakespeare's amazing retentiveness of images and phrases makes arguments based on parallel passages decidedly tricky. After all, 'Go to thy cold bed and warm thee' in *The Taming of the Shrew* (Ind., i, 9–10) reappears more than ten years later in *King Lear* (III, iv, 48) without a word altered. And the jewels that fill the sockets of the dead man's skull at the bottom of the ocean, first mentioned in *Richard III* (I, iv, 27–9), are to be found twenty years later in Ariel's sea lament in *The Tempest*.

Something, however, must be conceded to cumulative evidence. The counts of parallels made independently by Conrad and Davis (*v.* H. E. Rollins ed., *The Sonnets*, Philadelphia, 1944, II, 64–5), show the greatest number of sonnet parallels are in *Lucrece, Venus and Adonis, Love's Labour's Lost* and *Romeo and Juliet*, though precedence within the group varies. Roderick Eagle, the Baconian (*The Secrets of the Shakespeare*

Particularly interesting are the links between Sonnets 1–17 and *Venus and Adonis*. Shakespeare again and again put into the mouth of Venus arguments which recur in his sonnets urging Southampton to wed. Venus declares:

> Beauty within itself should not be wasted.
> Fair flowers that are not gathered in their prime
> Rot and consume themselves in little time.
>
> (lines 130–132)

Sonnet 1 picks up that theme:

> From fairest creatures we desire increase,
> That thereby beauty's rose might never die. . . .

Venus instructs Adonis:

> By law of nature thou art bound to breed,
> That thine may live when thou thyself art dead. . . .
>
> (lines 171–172)

Shakespeare instructs Southampton:

> She [Nature] carved thee for her seal, and meant thereby
> Thou shouldst print more, not let that copy die.
>
> (Sonnet 11: 13–14)

Venus asks Adonis:

> What is thy body but a swallowing grave,
> Seeming to bury that posterity
> Which by the rights of time thou needs must have,
> If thou destroy them not in dark obscurity?
>
> (lines 757–760)

Shakespeare asks Southampton:

> . . . who is he so fond will be the tomb
> Of his self-love, to stop posterity?
>
> (Sonnet 3: 7–8)

Sonnets, London, 1965, p. 65) making a table of the parallels he found in the first 136 sonnets, came out with the same four works at the head of his list.

Since the sonnets were written over a number of years, what we really need is a breakdown that will show chronologically the blocks of sonnets in which significant predominances of parallels are to be found. The present writer, having over the years assembled his own list of parallels, plotted their occurrence on a graph, with the sonnets in numerical order running along the upper edge and Shakespeare's other works in chronological order running down the left side. A glance at the completed chart showed that while no discernible pattern could be detected for Sonnets 53–126 and 142–54, the parallels for Sonnets 1–52 and 127–41 were predominantly to works written between 1593 and 1596 with *Love's Labour's Lost*, *Lucrece*, *Venus and Adonis*, and *Romeo and Juliet* once more heading the list.

Joseph Quincy Adams, working from his own collection of parallels 'in thought, imagery, and phraseology' found it virtually certain that Shakespeare began writing his sonnets around 1594 (*Life of Shakespeare*, p. 163).

Venus, championing procreation, brings in an analogy:

> Foul cankering rust the hidden treasure frets,
> But gold that's put to use more gold begets.
>
> (lines 767–768)

Shakespeare, urging Southampton to get a wife with child, uses the same images of treasure and interest:

> Make sweet some vial, treasure thou some place
> With beauty's treasure ere it be self-killed.
> That use is not forbidden usury,
> Which happies those that pay the willing loan.
>
> (Sonnet 6: 3–6)

Venus laments of dead Adonis:

> . . . true sweet beauty lived and died with him.
>
> (line 1080)

Shakespeare declares that if Southampton does not wed and beget:

> . . . I prognosticate:
> Thy end is truth's and beauty's doom and date.
>
> (Sonnet 14: 13–14)

In fact Shakespeare, writing *Venus and Adonis*, was already so concerned lest Southampton wreck his career by refusing to marry Lady Elizabeth Vere that, while writing the sort of Ovidian poem popular at this period, he kept slipping into the mouth of Venus the arguments for marriage which he would shortly present more directly in his sonnets.

Something must be said of the evidence that points to the Earl of Southampton as the recipient of Sonnets 1–17. The descriptions of the young friend as 'now the world's fresh ornament' (1:9) and as 'the lovely gaze where every eye doth dwell' (5:2) well describe a dazzling young nobleman at Queen Elizabeth's court. Moreover, the language of these sonnets is consistently aristocratic. Mention is made of the 'herald to the gaudy spring' (1:10), 'youth's proud livery' (2:3), and 'bounteous largesse' (4:6). The friend is told that his 'presence' is 'gracious and kind' (10:11), and he is urged to beget a 'tender heir' (1:4). Likening the begetting of this heir to the maintenance of a lovely habitation, Shakespeare asks:

> Who lets so fair a house fall to decay,
> Which husbandry in honour might uphold . . .?
>
> (13: 9–10)

Here we have a second meaning: the responsibility of a young lord to ensure the continuance of the honourable house from which he has descended.

Finally we must note one passage that seems to point directly to Southampton:

> You had a father. Let your son say so.
>
> (13: 14)

You *had* a father! That unequivocal past tense can be accounted for by the death, years earlier, of Southampton's father.

In summary we may say that the date of the first seventeen sonnets,[1] their relationship with *Venus and Adonis* and *Lucrece* (the two poems openly dedicated to Southampton), and the evidence within their own text make it evident that these sonnets were addressed to the same young nobleman. Though Southampton persisted to the end in his refusal to marry Lady Elizabeth Vere, it was not for want of urging of marriage by William Shakespeare.

---

[1] Sonnets 18 and 19 shift to a different but allied subject, the perpetuation of the friend's beauty not through the begetting of a son but through the immortalization provided by Shakespeare in his poetry. The transition is prepared for at the end of Sonnet 15:

> And all in war with Time for love of you,
> As he takes from you, I engraft you new.

For this reason, many critics take the first bloc in the *Sonnets* to consist of Sonnets 1–19 (e.g. Hilton Landry, *Interpretations of Shakespeare's Sonnets*, Berkeley, 1963, diagram facing p. 130).

If Sonnets 1–17 (or 1–19) had reached us alone and not as part of the conglomerate of the 1609 quarto, their date and purpose would have been universally recognized long ago.

A Play for Lord Southampton and his Friends

DURING THE TWO YEARS or so when the London playhouses were closed, William Shakespeare's writing was not limited to two narrative poems and a short sonnet cycle. Apparently at this time he also wrote *Love's Labour's Lost* for private production before Southampton and his friends. The play is full of topical allusions and coterie jokes, most of which now lie beyond recognition. Sufficient are identifiable, however, to relate the play to its original audience, one which surely included the Earl of Southampton, who may well have commissioned the play.[1]

Looking closely at *Love's Labour's Lost*, we cannot help but wonder if the King of Navarre and his friends, who unexpectedly find themselves unable to resist the charms of the ladies of France, may not be based to some extent on Southampton and the young gallants who were his friends. Certainly the King, in his initial aversion to marriage and his enthusiasm for studies, duplicates two of the most notable characteristics of the young earl. If in this play Shakespeare is gently teasing his friend and patron, he is careful to supply him with compliments also—the Princess of France describes young Navarre as:

> the sole inheritor
> Of all perfections that a man may owe . . . .
>
> (II, i, 5-6)

In return for a tribute such as this, Southampton could excuse a little twitting. But in truth the evidence is not strong enough for us to insist upon a parallel here. For real links with Southampton and his circle we must turn to the persons whom Shakespeare caricatures in his play. Let us begin with Sir Walter Raleigh, who is one of the two people who constitute Don Adriano de Armado.

Raleigh, since his first coming to the English Court as a captain fresh from service in Ireland, had been a notably military figure among Elizabeth's courtiers, a role accentuated by his appointment as Captain of the

---

[1] I find no evidence to support Ivor Brown's surmise (*Shakespeare*, London, 1949, p. 159) that Southampton was the original author of *L.L.L.*, or Janet Spens' belief ('Notes on *Love's Labour's Lost*', *Review of English Studies*, VII (1931), 333) that Shakespeare originally played the part of the King and the Earl of Essex that of Berowne.

Queen's Guard. Late in the 1580s Raleigh and Essex became bitter rivals for Elizabeth's favours. In 1590 Essex's marriage gave Raleigh the lead for a while, but in 1592 the latter, having gotten with child Elizabeth Throckmorton, one of the maids of honour, married her and in the process completely lost the royal favour. Imprisoned in the Tower for a few months, he turned to poetry in an attempt to move an unrelenting Queen. In 1594, still forbidden access to the Queen, Raleigh was continuing to work hard to regain her esteem. He had given good service in Parliament the previous year and now, supported by Lord Admiral Howard and Sir Robert Cecil, was planning to send a fleet to Guiana.

Such was the background when Shakespeare, for the delectation of Southampton, Essex and their friends, presented Raleigh as the fantastic Spaniard in *Love's Labour's Lost*. That Armado was originally Raleigh there can be no doubt. He is both Raleigh the military man and Raleigh the poet:

> Adieu, valour! Rust, rapier! Be still, drum! For your manager is in love—yea, he loveth. Assist me, some extemporal god of rhyme, for I am sure I shall turn sonnet. Devise, wit; write, pen; for I am for whole volumes in folio.
>
> (I, ii, 187–191)

Allusion is made to 'The Lie', the verse satire (already well known) in which Raleigh gives 'the world the lie'. Speaking of Raleigh-Armado the King quips:

> I protest I love to hear him lie
> And I will use him for my minstrelsy.
>
> (I, i, 176–177)

'Minstrel' was hardly a status word; Raleigh the poet was being notably downgraded. Even Raleigh's broad Devonshire accent is ridiculed:

> *Armado* [To *Moth*]: Chirrah!
> *Holofernes:* Quare chirrah, not sirrah?
> *Armado:* Men of peace, well encountered.
> *Holofernes:* Most military sir, salutation.
>
> (V, i, 35–38)

And Southampton and his friends must have laughed when Raleigh's gallant gesture in spreading his cloak to protect Queen Elizabeth's foot from the mud became matter for a bawdy jest:[1]

> *Armado:* I do adore thy sweet Grace's slipper.
> *Boyet* [Aside to *Dumain*]: Loves her by the foot.
> *Dumain* [Aside to *Boyet*]: He may not by the yard.
>
> (V, ii, 674–676)

---

[1] On this reference to Raleigh and his cloak, see Walter Oakeshott, *The Queen and the Poet* (London, 1960), pp. 22–3. For much of the above I am indebted to Oakeshott's extended presentation of the Armado-Raleigh case. For a defence of the historicity of Fuller's account (c. 1662) of the Raleigh cloak story, see W. M. Wallace, *Raleigh* (Princeton, 1959), p. 21.

If we accept the braggard Armado as being the arrogant Raleigh, we must equate Jaquenetta, the country wench whom Don Armado gets in the family way, with Raleigh's Elizabeth Throckmorton though the fun gets rather rough here:

> *Armado*: Callest thou my love 'hobbyhorse'? [Elizabethan slang for a prostitute]
> *Moth*: No, master, the hobbyhorse is but a colt, and your love perhaps a hackney [a horse for common hire].

(III, i, 30–32)

It may have been a paying-off of an old score. According to Miss Yates in her study of *Love's Labour's Lost*, Raleigh's friends had been less than complimentary towards Essex's sisters.[1]

Don Adriano de Armado may have started life as a caricature of Raleigh, but he underwent a somewhat startling change a few years later. Although *Love's Labour's Lost* was probably written in the opening months of 1594, our earliest edition of the play is a quarto published in 1598. This is entitled *A Pleasant Conceited Comedie Called, Loves Labors Lost. As it was presented before her Highnes this last Christmas. Newly corrected and augmented. By W. Shakespere.* The command performance here referred to was almost certainly given at Christmas 1597. Proof positive that Shakespeare had newly augmented the play comes from J. W. Lever, who has demonstrated that the song 'When daisies pied' must have been written after the publication of Gerard's *Herball*[2] in 1597. Another change that Shakespeare made at this time concerns Don Armado.

By the latter part of 1597 circumstances were very different from what they had been four years earlier. Raleigh and Essex had effected a reconciliation before sailing on the Islands Voyage and, despite a flare-up during that expedition, were no longer the enemies they had been once and were to become again. Raleigh, back in the Queen's favour, was once more exercising his office of Captain of the Guard. Under the altered circumstances, Shakespeare's company could hardly present before the Queen a play which heaped merciless ridicule on one of her leading courtiers. Something had to be done about Don Armado. The obvious thing was to supply new lines which would make it plain that somebody other than Raleigh was being burlesqued. Accordingly, in the play as it has reached us, the very first we hear of Don Armado comes in a speech by the King of Navarre in the opening scene:

[1] *A Study of 'Love's Labour's Lost'* (Cambridge, 1936), p. 149 *et passim*.

[2] 'Three Notes on Shakespeare's Plants', *The Review of English Studies* (N.S.), III (January 1952), 119–20.

> Our Court, you know, is haunted
> With a refined traveler of Spain—
> A man in all the world's new fashion planted
> That hath a mint of phrases in his brain;
> One whom the music of his own vain tongue
> Doth ravish like enchanting harmony;
> A man of complements. . . .
>
> (I, i, 163–169)

Who is this 'refined traveler of Spain', this 'man of complements'? He is our old acquaintance Antonio Perez, the renegade Spanish secretary of state sent to England by Henri IV in 1594, who had been enthusiastically received by Essex and who, publishing his *Relations*, had presented copies to Essex and Southampton along with fulsome letters of compliment. By 1596 he had become completely discredited in England and when he made a brief second visit to England in that year Essex received him very coldly. Here was a person Shakespeare could safely guy, knowing that his butt would be recognized and his satire appreciated by everybody in the audience. Revising his play, probably through oversight he left in enough of the original Armado for us to see that he must have been Raleigh, but added new ingredients so that Don Armado becomes, amazingly, two utterly different persons—a blustering arrogant military man of the old Plautine *miles gloriosus* sort who is a caricature of Raleigh, and a sycophantic elderly Spanish courtier who is a caricature of Antonio Perez. Some of the Perez additions are easily spotted. Among these are the passages which emphasize the age of Don Armado:

> *Moth*: And I [call you Armado], tough senior, as an appertinent title to your old time, which we may name tough.
>
> (I, ii, 17–18)

> *Armado*: Now, by the salt wave of the Mediterraneum, a sweet touch, a quick venue of wit—snip, snap, quick and home! It rejoiceth my intellect—true wit!
> *Moth*: Offered by a child to an old man, which is wit-old.
>
> (V, i, 61–66)

Armado's letter read by the King of Navarre is to be seen as a burlesque of the fantastically elaborated letters of compliment that Perez sent with copies of his *Relations* to most of the dignitaries at the English court:

> Great deputy, the welkin's vice-gerent, and sole dominator of Navarre, my soul's earth's god, and body's fostering patron.
>
> (I, i, 221–223)

When Perez boasts how the King of Navarre will please 'sometime to lean upon my poor shoulder, and with his royal finger, thus, dally with my excrement, with my mustachio' (V, i, 107–9), we probably have echoes of Perez boasting in the English court of the close friendship which did in fact exist between him and Henri IV.

One passage in *Love's Labour's Lost* cinches the Armado-Perez identification. The nom-de-plume under which Perez published his *Relations* was
'Rafael Peregrino', and in his letters of compliment to the English courtiers he constantly played upon 'peregrine' in its meanings of 'traveller' and
'wanderer'. Typical is a letter sent to Essex, apparently in June 1594:

> *Raphael Peregrino* auctor desse libro me ha pedido que se le presente à Vuestra
> Excellençia de su parte. . . . Quiça se ha fiado en el nombre sabiendo que Vuestra
> Excellençia es amparo de *peregrinos* de la Fortuna. Quiça tambien ha temido por
> el nombre de *peregrino* a los perseguidores de *peregrinos*. . . . Vuestra Excellençia
> no me tenga por adulador en nombrar le para moverle tantas vezes el nombre de
> *Peregrino*. . . . Però permitame que de firmado de mi nombre que soy su *Peregrino*.[1]

Shakespeare never uses the noun 'peregrine'. Only once does he use the
adjective 'peregrinate'. This word comes, in a fashion calculated to concentrate attention upon it, when Holofernes and Nathaniel are discussing
Armado:

> *Holofernes:* . . . He is too picked, too spruce, too affected, too odd, as it were, too
>   peregrinate, as I may call it.
> *Nathaniel:* A most singular and choice epithet.

(V, i, 14-17)

The Armado-Perez identification, like the Armado-Raleigh identification, has been advanced before.[2] But these have been viewed as rival
theories, nobody apparently having realized that both are true.

Holofernes, the pedant, may have undergone a change similar to that
of Don Armado, starting as George Chapman and ending as John Florio.

Around 1593 that strange, misanthropic visionary George Chapman
was looking for a patron. He had one glittering prize for any noble lord
who would subsidize him while he worked at his cumbersome verses. This
was the dedication of the first English translation of Homer, on which
Chapman must by this time have been well started. Southampton, with
his interest in Greek,[3] must have impressed Chapman as a logical person
to approach. Thus Chapman would have been drawn into a contest with
William Shakespeare for the young earl's patronage. In any event, when
at the beginning of 1594 Chapman published two pretentious bad poems
under the collective title of *The Shadow of Night*,[4] he used the opportunity to attack Shakespeare. The latter had prefaced his *Venus and Adonis*

---

[1] Antonio Perez, *Obras* (Geneva, 1631), p. 530. My italics. The preceding letter, also
to Essex, is dated '16 Iun. 1594'.

[2] The Perez identification was first made by Martin Hume in his *Spanish Influence
on English Literature* (London, 1905), pp. 268-73. The most extended presentation of
the case is that of Robert Gittings in his *Shakespeare's Rival* (London, 1960), pp. 56-60.

[3] *v.* p. 130 *supra*.

[4] This little book was entered on the last day of December 1593 (Arber, *Transcripts*,
II, 642). I take it to have been published very soon thereafter. Obviously all this has
an important bearing on our dating of *L.L.L.*

with a ringing quotation from Ovid to the effect that Apollo could minister to him beakers filled at the Castalian spring. *Venus and Adonis* itself has been described as 'the supreme example of what may be termed the Elizabethan "fleshly school of poetry"'.[1] These things being so, it is not hard to recognize Chapman's target when he declared:

> Presume not then, ye flesh-confounded souls,
> That cannot bear the full Castalian bowls,
> Which sever mounting spirits from their senses,
> To look in this deep fount for thy pretences.[2]

In his twin poems, Chapman deplored the degeneration of mankind and lauded, in suitably obscure verse, the eternal night which reigned before man and his world were created. In laboured conceits Chapman developed a thesis that, symbolically at least, night is both fairer than day and more congenial to intellect. According to Chapman, intellectual pursuits are vastly to be preferred to love.

Smarting under Chapman's attack on *Venus and Adonis*, Shakespeare in *Love's Labour's Lost* gave him his come-uppance for the portentous nonsense in his *The Shadow of Night*. Chapman had declared:

> No pen can any thing eternall wright,
> That is not steept in humor of the Night.
> ('Hymnus in Noctem', 376–377)

Shakespeare retorted:

> Never durst poet touch a pen to write
> Until his ink were tempered with Love's sighs.
> (IV, iii, 346–347)

Punning on Chapman's name, Shakespeare had his Princess of France declare:

> Beauty is bought by judgment of the eye,
> Not uttered by base sale of chapmen's tongues.
> (II, i, 15–16)

Chapman had called upon 'nimble and aspiring wits' to:

> ... consecrate with me to sacred Night
> Your whole endevours, and detest the light.
> ('Hymnus in Noctem', 372–373)

Rhapsodically he had apostrophized Night:

> ... thou (great Mistresse of heavens gloomie racke)
> Art blacke in face, and glitterst in thy heart.
> ('Hymnus in Noctem', 226–227)

---

[1] J. Dover Wilson, *The Essential Shakespeare* (Cambridge, 1932), p. 55.

[2] *Poems*, ed. Phyllis B. Bartlett (New York, 1941), p. 34; ('The Shadow of Night: Hymnus in Cynthiam', lines 162–5). This thrust at Shakespeare has been noted by J. Middleton Murry (*Shakespeare*, London, 1936, pp. 36–7), and by J. A. K. Thomson (*Shakespeare and the Classics*, London, 1952, pp. 175–6).

Shakespeare's retort, spoken by his King of Navarre, is pithy:

> Black is the badge of Hell,
> The hue of dungeons and the school of night. . . .
>
> (IV, iii, 254–255)

In 1903 Arthur Acheson theorized that this 'school of night' referred to a little group of speculative thinkers associated with Raleigh and referred to elsewhere as Raleigh's 'school of atheism'. Acheson saw *Love's Labour's Lost* as part of a battle between two literary factions, one supporting Essex and headed by Shakespeare, the other championing Raleigh and headed by Chapman. Acheson's view was taken up with enthusiasm for some time,[1] but unfortunately no direct link has ever been found between Chapman and Raleigh. Recently Millar MacLure has found 'no satisfying substance' in all these conjectures about Chapman's membership in a literary coterie around Raleigh. In 1941 E. A. Strathmann demonstrated that 'school of night' may very well be a misreading for 'suit of night'.[2]

In a sense *Love's Labour's Lost*, with its demonstration of how Navarre and his friends having met the ladies of France desert their ideal of an 'academe' from which women are excluded, is a mocking refutation of Chapman's thesis of the pre-eminence of contemplation and study. In a play so slanted and containing such detectable retorts to Chapman, one might reasonably look for a caricature of that unhappy man. Holofernes may at one time have represented Chapman or, more probably, Raleigh's friend Thomas Harriot[3] the mathematician. But Gittings is surely right in his hypothesis that during the revision of 1597 Shakespeare made over Holofernes in the image of John Florio.[4]

John Florio, we saw earlier, was Southampton's Italian tutor in 1594. Although according to his own account he lived for some years in Southampton's 'pay and patronage', he may not have been a favourite with the young earl. Frances Yates has surmised that Burghley placed Florio in the young man's household to spy upon him, Southampton subsequently 'distrusting Florio whilst fearing to get rid of him'.[5] When Shakespeare first entered Southampton's circle he may have been impressed for a while by 'resolute John Florio', as the latter liked to style himself. But

---

[1] See Acheson, *Shakespeare and the Rival Poet* (London, 1903); *Love's Labour's Lost*, New Cambridge ed., pp. xlvii–lii; and Muriel Bradbrook, *The School of Night* (Cambridge, 1936).

[2] MacLure, *George Chapman* (Toronto, 1966), p. 10; Strathmann, 'The Textual Evidence for "The School of Night"', *Modern Language Notes*, LVI (1941), 176–86.

[3] *Love's Labour's Lost*, ed. J. Dover Wilson (Cambridge, 1962), pp. xv–xix. As Wilson points out, the name Holofernes comes from Rabelais, where he is tutor to Gargantua, and a Gargantua-Raleigh linkage fits in as part of the scorn directed against Raleigh in this play.

[4] *Shakespeare's Rival* (London, 1960), p. 79.

[5] *John Florio* (Cambridge, 1934), p. 218.

Florio, arrogant towards his equals and inferiors though sycophantic towards the young lords by whom he made his living, was not a man of whom Shakespeare would make a friend. Certainly Florio's view of English as a mongrel language of little use, and his contempt for English plays as lacking 'decorum', being 'neither right comedies, nor right tragedies',[1] could be guaranteed sooner or later to cause friction between him and Shakespeare.

The evidence identifying Holofernes with Florio is conclusive.[2] We are given Florio's pomposity, his infatuation with fine language, and his larding of conversation with proverbs and moralizings. Florio the dictionary-maker stands behind Holofernes the addict to strings of synonyms:

> The deer was, as you know, *sanguis*, in blood; ripe as the pomewater, who now hangeth like a jewel in the ear of *caelo*, the sky, the welkin, the heaven, and anon falleth like a crab on the face of *terra*, the soil, the land, the earth.
>
> (IV, ii, 3–7)

In 1591 Florio had announced that he would 'shortly send into the world an exquisite Italian and English Dictionary'. Florio entered this, with a dedication to Southampton, in the Stationers' Register early in 1596. When the book was finally published in 1598 it included among its definitions:

> Cielo, *heaven, the skie, the firmament or welkin* . . .
> Terra, . . . *earth, countrie, province, region, land, soile*[3]

Presumably Shakespeare had seen this dictionary, Florio's *Worlde of Wordes*, while it was being used in manuscript by his student Southampton.

Another of Florio's works contributed something to *Love's Labour's Lost*. Wickedly Shakespeare put on the lips of Holofernes some Italian to be found in Florio's *Second Fruits*:[4]

> Ah, good old Mantuan! I may speak of thee as the traveller doth of Venice:
> *Venetia, Venetia,*
> *Chi non ti vede non ti pretia.*
>
> (IV, ii, 97–100)

Finally, when revising his play in 1597, Shakespeare worked in a reference both to the fees that Florio was charging as a foreign language teacher,

---

[1] *Florios Second Frutes* (London, 1591), sig. D4r.

[2] Warburton, in 1747, was the first to report the true identity of 'Holofernes'. He was followed by Charles Armitage Brown in 1838. Modern writers who have supported the identification include Yates, Gittings, and the editor of the New Arden edition of *L.L.L.*

[3] *A Worlde of Wordes* (London, 1598), sigs. F6v and Mm5r. For more of Holofernes' list of synonyms see V, i, 96–8.

[4] *S.T.C. 11097*, sig. P1v.

and to his current labours translating Montaigne. Armado asks Holofernes:

> Do you not educate youth at the charge house on the top of the mountain?
>
> (V, i, 86–87)

A 'charge house' is a school that charges fees; the 'mountain' is a pun on Montaigne.[1] It is not surprising that Florio, stung by the mockery of Shakespeare and the actors, in 1598 struck back at 'Aristophanes *and his comedians*' who '*make plaies, and scowre their mouthes on* Socrates'.[2]

Before leaving *Love's Labour's Lost* and all its puzzling quips and allusions, a word must be said about some other possible identifications. 'Moth' may well be a good-humoured representation of witty Tom Nashe.[3] Various writers have noted a distinct resemblance between the Dark Lady of Shakespeare's sonnets, fascinating and promiscuous, and Rosaline of whom Berowne remarks:

> . . . among three, to love the worst of all,
> A whitely wanton with a velvet brow,
> With two pitch balls stuck in her face for eyes—
> Aye, and, by Heaven, one that will do the deed
> Though Argus were her eunuch and her guard.
> And I to sigh for her!
>
> (III, i, 197–202)

It would however be naïve to argue that Berowne is therefore Shakespeare himself. Berowne with his life, his wit and his abundant flow of words belongs to a group that includes Mercutio, Gratiano, and Benedick. Possibly behind them all stands some clever young man in Southampton's circle—perhaps Sir Charles or Sir Henry Danvers—but we shall never know.

[1] Florio's translation of Montaigne's *Essays*, published in 1603, was entered in the Stationers' Register in 1600. Yates finds evidence (*Florio*, p. 213) that Florio had already gone some distance with his translation in 1598.

For the pronunciation of 'Montaigne', note that in 1595 Florio's competitor Edward Aggas had entered in the Register his 'Essais of Michaell Lord of Mountene'. A contemporary Bishop of London was referred to with almost equal frequency as 'George Mountain' and 'George Montaigne'.

[2] Florio's address to his readers prefaced to his *Worlde of Wordes*, reprinted as Appendix I of Yates' *Florio*.

[3] R. David, *Love's Labour's Lost* (New Arden ed.), pp. xxxix–xlii.

Shakespeare, Southampton and 'Avisa'

EARLY IN SEPTEMBER 1594 there was entered in the Stationers' Register 'WILLOBYE his avisa or the true picture of a modest maid and of a chas[t]e and Constant wife'.[1] The book, published in the next few months, consisted of dialogues in which the chaste Avisa, in mediocre verse, rejects her would-be seducers. The first of her triumphs, before her marriage, is over an unnamed 'Noble man'. After she has married and become the hostess of the St. George Inn, she overcomes the blandishments of 'Caveleiro'; of 'D.B. A French man'; of 'Dydimus Harco. Anglo-Germanus'; and lastly of 'H.W.' A preface signed by 'Hadrian Dorrell' (probably an alias for Henry Willoughby, the Oxford student who wrote the poem) points to the possibility that 'though the matter be handled poetically, yet there is some thing under these fained names and showes that hath bene done truely'.[2] Contemporaries must have found hidden meanings behind the poem's bland repetitive moralizings, for *Willobie His Avisa* went through five editions in fifteen years, even though the authorities tried to suppress it in 1599.

The unriddling of *Avisa* has a particular interest for Shakespeareans because of the passage presenting H.W. to the book's readers:

Henrico Willobego. Italo-Hispalensis
H.W. being sodenly infected with the contagion of a fantasticall fit, at the first sight of A, pyneth a while in secret griefe, at length not able any longer to indure the burning heate of so fervent a humour, bewrayeth the secresy of his disease unto his familiar frend W.S. who not long before had tryed the curtesy of the like passion, and was now newly recovered of the like infection; yet finding his frend let bloud in the same vaine, he took pleasure for a tyme to see him bleed, & in steed of stopping the issue, he inlargeth the wound, with the sharpe rasor of a willing conceit, perswading him that he thought it a matter very easy to be compassed, & no doubt with payne, diligence & some cost in time to be obtayned. Thus this miserable comforter comforting his frend with an impossibilitie, eyther for that he now would secretly laugh at his frends folly, that had given occasion not long before unto others to laugh at his owne, or because he would see whether an other could play his part better then himselfe, & in vewing a far off the course of this loving Comedy, he determined to see whether it would sort to a happier end for this new actor, then it did for the old player. But at length this Comedy was like to have growen to a Tragedy, by the weake & feeble estate that H.W. was brought unto, by a desperate vewe of an impossibility of obtaining his purpose. . . .[3]

[1] Arber, *Transcripts*, II, 659.
[2] *Willobie His Avisa 1594*, ed. G. B. Harrison, Bodley Head Quartos (London, 1926), p. 9.   [3] Ibid., pp. 115–16.

With these initials 'W.S.', and the cluster of references to 'actor', 'player', and 'Comedy', the theory was inevitably advanced that W.S. must be William Shakespeare himself—especially since commendatory verses prefaced to *Avisa* mention 'Shake-speare paints poore Lucrece rape', and so supply our earliest reference to Shakespeare's recently published poem.[1]

Building on these foundations Arthur Acheson, using arguments which became increasingly convoluted and fantastic, equated Avisa with the Dark Lady of the sonnets. He maintained that both were portraits of one Anne Sachfeilde who, he declared, became the mistress of Shakespeare and Southampton.[2] G. B. Harrison, publishing in 1926 his facsimile edition of *Avisa*, rejected like everybody else Acheson's preposterous ideas about Avisa. Encouraged however by 'Hadrian Dorrell's' statement that H.W. was not necessarily Henry Willoughby, he supported the identification with Henry Wriothesley, Earl of Southampton. Harrison argued that *Avisa* was an attack launched against Southampton by Raleigh's friends who had mistakenly identified the ravisher Tarquin in *Lucrece* as a portrait of their chief. Muriel Bradbrook in her book *The School of Night* also viewed *Avisa* as emanating from the Raleigh camp. All this was undercut, however, first by Leslie Hotson and then by Tucker Brooke, who decided against identifying H.W. with Southampton.[3] Brooke was not unfriendly to the identification of 'Caveleiro' with Raleigh's neighbour and enemy, Sir Ralph Horsey. However, it is difficult to see why a very tepid, veiled attack on this Dorsetshire worthy should send *Avisa* into repeated editions and provoke an order suppressing it. Obviously something bigger must have been involved.

In proposing a new solution to the *Avisa* riddle, the present writer begins with what seems the obvious starting-point, the identity of Avisa herself. The key to this question is surely supplied by the phrase with which Avisa signs her verse epistles informing her would-be seducers of

---

[1] Chambers (*William Shakespeare*, I, 569) thought he detected significant Shakespeare parallels in a couplet spoken by W.S.:

> She is no Saynt, She is no Nonne,
> I thinke in tyme she may be wonne.

[2] *Shakespeare's Sonnet Story* (London, 1922) pp. 120–56 *et passim*. For a demolition of Acheson see Chambers, *William Shakespeare*, I, 569–76.

Almost as absurd as Acheson is Pauline K. Angell who, in her 'Light on the Dark Lady', *PMLA*, LII (September 1937), 652–74, makes Avisa and the Dark Lady representations of the Countess of Oxford, and has Southampton take her home at the end of afternoon performances in the playhouses and use the opportunity to cuckold his brother earl.

[3] See Hotson's chapter 'Willobie His Avisa' in *I, William Shakespeare* (London, 1937), and Brooke's astringent 'Willobie's Avisa' in *Essays in Honor of Albert Feuillerat* (New Haven, 1943), pp. 93–102.

her continued refusal to accept their 'filthy' propositions. These epistles are signed:

Alway the same
Avisa[1]

'Always the same' translated into Latin becomes *Semper eadem*, the motto of Elizabeth I. Remembering the paeans of praise raised in honour of the chastity of Eliza, the Virgin Queen, it seems unnecessary to look farther for 'Avisa'.

Significantly the later editions of *Avisa* include an 'Apologie' which, though saying nothing about the identity of Avisa's wooers, goes to great lengths to emphasize that the poet had no original for Avisa herself:

> To this fained *Individuum* he gave this fained name *Avisa* . . . it is Chastity it selfe, not any woman in the world. . . . *A'visa* should signifie (by this) as much as *Non visa*, that is: Such a woman as was never seene.[2]

This 'apologie' is dated 'this 30 of June 1569', a typographical error, as Hotson has demonstrated, for 1599.[3] Significantly, then, this disingenuous disclaimer was drafted only a few weeks after the banning of *Avisa* on June 3rd, 1599. Its author must have been seeking to persuade the authorities to lift their injunction, assuring them that there had been no *lèse-majesté*, and declaring by implication that the poet had neither presented the Queen as the hostess of an inn nor had commented upon those seeking her favours. The 'apologie' apparently failed to convince. The next surviving edition of *Avisa* was not published until the reign of James I.[4]

Once 'Avisa' is identified as Elizabeth, the other pieces of the puzzle begin to fall into place. Avisa's marriage which makes her mistress of 'yonder house where hanges the badge of Englands Saint' refers to her accession to the throne. The unnamed nobleman who had wooed her before she became Queen is Leicester. The foreign suitors, 'D.B. A French man' and 'Dydimus Harco. Anglo-Germanus', may refer either to foreign suitors such as the Duke of Anjou, or to English courtiers who sought to ingratiate themselves with Elizabeth. Interest centres, of course, on the last of the ineffectual seducers, H.W. Although he is only one of five, far more of the poem is devoted to him than to any of the others. Who is he?

A glance at Elizabeth's court in mid-1594 supplies us with the answer. Southampton was among the foremost of the contenders for royal favour. The previous year he had reportedly been nominated for the Order of

---

[1] See Cantos XXXII, XLI, XLIII, LXII, LXXIV. In the first of these it is given as 'Alwaies the same'.

[2] *Avisa*, pp. 239–43.　　　　　　　　　　[3] *I, William Shakespeare*, pp. 69–70.

[4] In 1594 clever young Henry Willoughby must have known that he was playing a dangerous game. Hence, although he could not deny himself the pleasure of seeing his name attached to his poem, he used the elaborate pretence that 'Hadrian Dorrell' had caused it to be published without his knowledge or consent.

the Garter. Not until 1595, when his attentions to Elizabeth Vernon became obvious, did he forfeit the Queen's affection. The 'H.W.' who was seeking Avisa's favour in 1594 can only have been Henry Wriothesley, Earl of Southampton.

It is impossible to decipher all the clues in *Avisa*.[1] Two of them, besides the use of his initials, point to Southampton. The first consists of the Italian tags such as 'Chi la dura, la Vince', 'Felice chi puo', 'Chi cerca trova', which close H.W.'s epistle to Avisa. These poke fun at Southampton's Italianate affectations. The major clue, however, consists of the allusions to Shakespeare, who only recently had dedicated two very popular poems to Southampton. At the outset we have the mention of Shakespeare put into the commendatory verses. Then, many pages later, comes the theatre analogy with W.S., the old player, urging on H.W., a new actor in this comedy.

It is impossible to tell how literally we should interpret Willoughby's allegory. Close transposition of the Henrico Willobego passage would give us something like the following: William Shakespeare has suffered some rebuff from the Queen (refusal of an office?). Now he is strongly urging his close friend the Earl of Southampton to seek to become her favourite. He knows, however, that such hopes are unrealistic. Shakespeare gives his advice because he is something of a hypocrite in his friendship with the young earl and will rather enjoy seeing him suffer. Meanwhile, encouraged by Shakespeare, Southampton is getting into financial difficulties as he tries, through lavish expenditure, to become preeminent among Elizabeth's courtiers.

It is idle to speculate about what lay behind *Avisa* with its presentation of the young rake Southampton as trying to seduce (metaphorically) the Queen. The poem may represent the next round after *Love's Labour's Lost* in a continuing literary battle.[2] Perhaps we should not be too confident that the poem was really written by Willoughby. Arthur Acheson and G. B. Harrison have both believed the author to be Matthew Roydon, a friend of Raleigh and Chapman. Before taking leave of young Willoughby, we may note that he has another Shakespearean connection. He was related, through marriage, to Thomas Russell, one of the overseers of Shakespeare's will.[3]

---

[1] The reference to the goddesses having framed Avisa
>   At wester side of Albions Ile,
>   Where Austine pitcht his Monkish tent'

may refer to Elizabeth's Welsh origins. The theory that links this passage with Cerne Abbas, where St. Augustine was reputed to have founded an abbey, calls for antiquarian knowledge that few if any of *Avisa's* readers would have possessed.

[2] Bradbrook, *The School of Night*, pp. 168–71.

[3] Hotson, *I, William Shakespeare*, pp. 68–9.

Shakespeare Returns to the Public Stage

WHEN, IN 1709, Nicholas Rowe published his edition of Shakespeare, he included with it 'Some Account of the Life of William Shakespeare'. Here Rowe gives us the following information about Shakespeare's relations with his patron:

> He had the Honour to meet with many great and uncommon Marks of Favour and Friendship from the Earl of *Southampton*, famous in the Histories of that Time for his Friendship to the unfortunate Earl of Essex. . . . There is one instance so singular in the Magnificence of this Patron of *Shakespear's*, that if I had not been assur'd that the Story was handed down by Sir *William D'Avenant*, who was probably very well acquainted with his Affairs, I should not have ventur'd to have inserted, that my Lord *Southampton*, at one time, gave him a thousand Pounds, to enable him to go through with a Purchase which he heard he had a mind to.[1]

Among scholars there has been an almost universal agreement that Rowe's figure is exaggerated (his £1,000 would be at least £20,000 today), and an almost equal readiness to believe that Rowe does preserve for us the memory of some munificent gift given to Shakespeare by his patron.[2]

The most likely of the many surmises concerning the occasion for this gift is that of Dover Wilson,[3] who linked it with Shakespeare becoming a founding member of the Lord Chamberlain's company of players in 1594. Some capital was undoubtedly needed for the setting up of the new company, and Southampton may have contributed Shakespeare's share.

A special circumstance may have had something to do with the offering of this gift. Shakespeare may not have particularly enjoyed the life of a playwright and actor at one of the public playhouses. We must not overlook his exclamation in Sonnet 3 against Fortune:

> The guilty goddess . . .
> That did not better for my life provide
> Than public means which public manners breeds.

Perhaps he had hoped he would be able to remain indefinitely a subsidized man of letters in the Earl's entourage. Southampton's gift of

---

[1] Chambers, *William Shakespeare*, II, 266–7.

[2] I am obliged to Professor A. C. Hamilton for pointing out that A. K. Gray's story about Southampton giving money to Spenser (*PMLA*, XXXIX, 594) is only a distorted version of an apocryphal tale about Spenser and Sidney. The earliest version of the Sidney-Spenser story is to be found in the life of Spenser in the 1679 folio edition of his works. [3] *The Essential Shakespeare* (Cambridge, 1932), pp. 66–7.

money may have been intended to soothe hurt feelings when Shakespeare learned that his earl would no longer support him now that the plague was finally abating and the playhouses were reopening.

The first we hear of the Lord Chamberlain's Men is in June 1594 when, together with the Lord Admiral's Men, they were putting on plays at Henslowe's theatre at Newington Butts. Among the plays offered in this month was one dealing with the taming of a shrew. This may very well have been Shakespeare's *The Taming of the Shrew*.

Let us briefly view Shakespeare's position as a playwright once the London theatres had resumed playing. The plays which he had previously written consisted of four rather crude English history plays (the *Henry VI* trilogy and *Richard III*), a Senecan melodrama (*Titus Andronicus*) and the Plautine *Comedy of Errors*. In none of these do we find the slightest evidence of a Southampton connection. Now, in 1594–95 he starts writing plays of a different kind, 'a series of plays with Italian settings, which were something of a new departure in English drama',[1] and in these for the first time we have discernible links with the Earl of Southampton.

The Taming of the Shrew seems to be the earliest of these Italian comedies. It is not an original play for behind it lies the older *The Taming of a Shrew*,[2] a knockabout farce garnished in its romantic scenes with pseudo-Marlovian verse. Both plays begin with inductions in which the drunken Christopher Sly is the butt of a practical joke by an unnamed 'Lord'. Shakespeare, however, takes over hardly more than a couple of phrases from the earlier induction and more than doubles its length. To give a fuller portrait of Sly, he provides him with a background from his own native Warwickshire: 'Am not I Christopher Sly, old Sly's son of Burton Heath?' (Shakespeare had an aunt at Barton-on-the-Heath, sixteen miles from Stratford.) 'Ask Marian Hacket, the fat ale-wife of Wincot, if she know me not.' (The parish register shows that Hackets dwelt in the tiny village of Wincot, four miles from Stratford.)

Shakespeare also gives a larger role to the Lord, and here he seems to have drawn upon more recent experience. In his instructions concerning the drunken Sly, Shakespeare's Lord declares:

> Carry him gently to my fairest chamber
> And hang it round with all my wanton pictures.
> Balm his foul head in warm distilled waters
> And burn sweet wood to make the lodging sweet.
> Procure me music ready when he wakes,
> To make a dulcet and a heavenly sound;
> And if he chance to speak, be ready straight

[1] Chambers, *William Shakespeare*, I, 61.
[2] I am not among those who believe that *A Shrew* is a 'bad quarto' of *The Shrew*.

> And with a low submissive reverence
> Say, 'What is it your Honour will command?'
> Let one attend him with a silver basin
> Full of rose water and bestrewed with flowers;
> Another bear the ewer, the third a diaper,
> And say, 'Will't please your lordship cool your hands?'
> Some one be ready with a costly suit,
> And ask him what apparel he will wear.
>
> (Ind., i, 46–60)

'All my wanton pictures!' We have no mention of these in the earlier induction. They seem to point directly at Southampton and his early taste for erotica. Probably the whole passage portrays the sybaritic life of Shakespeare's dandified young patron.

Shakespeare gives us something else not in the original, the passage in which with gracious affability the Lord greets the players who have arrived at his house:

> *Servant:* An't please your Honour, players [are come]
>   That offer service to your Lordship.
> *Lord:* Bid them come near.
>   *Enter Players*
>   Now, fellows, you are welcome.
> *Players:* We thank your Honour.
> *Lord:* Do you intend to stay with me tonight?
> *A Player:* So please your lordship to accept our duty.
> *Lord:* With all my heart. This fellow I remember,
>   Since once he played a farmer's eldest son.
>   'Twas where you wooed the gentlewoman so well.
>   I have forgot your name, but, sure, that part
>   Was aptly fitted and naturally performed.
>
> (Ind., i, 77–87)

All this is remarkably similar to Prince Hamlet's reception of the players at Elsinore. Hamlet likewise recognizes individual players ('Welcome, good friends. Oh, my old friend! Why, thy face is valanced since I saw thee last.'); recalls appreciatively particular performances ('an excellent play, well digested in the scenes'); and orders that the players be well entertained ('. . . will you see the players well bestowed? Do you hear, let them be well used . . .'). Hamlet's counsel to the actors, 'Suit the action to the word, the word to the action, with this special observance, that you o'erstep not the modesty of nature', tallies perfectly with the taste of the earlier Lord for parts 'aptly fitted and naturally performed'. Behind both scenes may lie the taste of the Earl of Southampton. What has variously been called Hamlet's or Shakespeare's advice to the players may be Southampton's also.

Did Shakespeare, writing these two scenes of aristocrats welcoming players, draw upon recollections of Southampton greeting players at

Titchfield? Is there any evidence that Shakespeare himself ever visited Titchfield? In 1925 a letter in *The Times Literary Supplement*[1] announced that the name of Gobbo, the clown in *The Merchant of Venice*, is to be found in the Titchfield parish register. Unfortunately this information is incorrect. The present writer, searching for Shakespearean names, has transcribed the Titchfield parish register from its beginnings in 1587 to the burial entry for Southampton in 1624. There are no Gobbos. The names misread as 'Gobbo' were Holte and Hobbes.

If this writer must sadly demolish this piece of evidence, he can offer another in its stead. Elizabethan lords did sometimes have plays performed in their country mansions. In 1596, for example, Sir John Harington had a professional London company come up to his house in Rutlandshire to put on a private performance.[2] Earlier the Duke of Norfolk had maintained a playhouse at his palatial country mansion at Kenninghall. There is evidence that Southampton similarly had a private theatre at Titchfield. The plans of Titchfield, dated 1737, which survive as part of the Wriothesley Papers, show a large room on the upper level, to the left of the main entrance (see Plate XI), and this is plainly labelled 'Play house room'.[3] Since no major structural changes had been made to Titchfield House since the third Earl's time, custom had probably kept this name attached to the room ever since the days when Shakespeare's patron welcomed players to his home. A local tradition that *Romeo and Juliet* was performed at the great house by Shakespeare's company[4] is too late to have any authority, though it may just possibly have grown out of early recollections of plays at Titchfield House.[5]

Returning to *The Taming of the Shrew*, let us look at the play staged for the entertainment of Christopher Sly. In the old *Taming of a Shrew* this play within the play takes place in Athens. Thither comes the son of the Duke of Cestus to study with his friend Polidor, and here the two young men fall in love with the two younger daughters of old Alphonso. Shakespeare takes over the plot pretty much verbatim, but makes everything Italian. The scene is now the university city of Padua. Here we meet

[1] Lillian Gilchrist Thompson, 'The Name of Gobbo', *T.L.S.*, September 17th, 1925, p. 600.

[2] G. Ungerer, 'An Unrecorded Elizabethan Performance of *Titus Andronicus*', *Shakespeare Survey 14*, pp. 102–9.

[3] *W.P. 1557.*

[4] See the little guide to St. Peter's Church sold at the door there. Those who place faith in such traditions would do well to read Lord Raglan's chapter on 'Local Tradition' in *The Hero* (London, 1936).

The parish guide is incorrect in claiming that Shakespeare's fellow actor, Beeston, was a Titchfield man. No Beestons are listed in the register during this period.

[5] Titchfield House and Titchfield Abbey were commonly used alternative names for Place House.

Baptista Minola, Petruchio of Verona, Lucentio of Pisa and the rest. Moreover, for the first time Shakespeare begins using Italian:

> Petruchio: Signior Hortensio, come you to part the fray? 'Con tutto il core ben trovato', may I say.
> Hortensio: Alla nostra casa ben venuto, molto honorato signor mio Petruchio.
>
> (I, ii, 23–26)

And we have a thin sprinkling of other Italian words.

Looking for a reason why Shakespeare has suddenly taken an Italianate turn, we recall the strong Italian interests of the Southampton circle. We remember how the young earl's friend, Sir Charles Danvers, imported books from Italy, and we remember that in 1594, about the time that this play was written, John Florio was Southampton's Italian tutor. We feel no surprise when Mario Praz informs us:

> It is from Florio's manuals for the study of Italian, entitled *First* and *Second Fruites* that come the Italian sentences which occur in I, ii of *The Taming of the Shrew*. . . . The expression found in *The Taming of the Shrew*, I, i, 'Lombardy, the pleasant garden of great Italy' is similar to Florio's 'La Lombardia è il giardino del mondo' in the *Second Fruites*.[1]

Some brief comment must be made on two other Shakespeare plays that belong to this Italianate period around 1594–95, *Romeo and Juliet* and *The Two Gentlemen of Verona*. No references to Southampton are to be found in *Romeo and Juliet*. A theory that the play was produced before Queen Elizabeth to make her favourable to a match between Southampton and Elizabeth Vernon is mere romantic moonshine.[2] It is idle to try to link old Montague with Southampton's grandfather, Viscount Montagu —Shakespeare found 'Montegewe' in his source, Brooke's *Romeus and Juliet*. Admitting failure to find anything germane to our quest in *Romeo and Juliet*, we may pass to *The Two Gentlemen of Verona*, a play written at much the same period. Here we find passages which can at least give rise to interesting surmises.

Two things stand out in the opening act of *The Two Gentlemen of Verona*: the heavy emphasis on the importance of foreign travel as part of the education of young gentlemen (though Valentine and Proteus only travel from Verona to Milan), and the repeated statements about young Valentine being with the Emperor (though he never ventures to the imperial court but remains with the Duke of Milan). Both discrepancies may possibly be accounted for by events in Southampton's circle late in 1594 and early in 1595.

After Southampton came of age in October 1594 and took over direction of his own affairs, he might be expected to consider rounding out his education with travel on the Continent. Two special circumstances would

---

[1] 'Shakespeare's Italy', *Shakespeare Survey 7*, p. 105.
[2] Acheson, *Shakespeare's Sonnet Story*, p. 223.

PLACE HOUSE (TITCHFIELD ABBEY) IN 1733
('The 'Playhouse room' is on the second storey, to the left of the main entrance)
The Hampshire Record Office

favour foreign travel at this time. First his close friends, Sir Charles and Sir Henry Danvers, were already on the Continent, assisted thither by Southampton after the murder of Henry Long. Secondly, Southampton had the example provided by his brother-in-law, Thomas Arundell, who set out in 1595 to serve the Emperor. It may then be of some significance that Shakespeare, in *The Two Gentlemen*, provides strenuous arguments why young gentlemen should travel.

> Home-keeping youth have ever homely wits.
> (I, i, 2)

> . . . let him spend his time no more at home,
> Which would be great impeachment to his age
> In having known no travel in his youth.
> (I, iii, 14–16)

> . . . he cannot be a perfect man,
> Not being tried and tutored in the world.
> (I, iii, 20–21)

On the basis of these lines, one might expect Shakespeare to be among those advising Southampton to travel.

And what of the Emperor's court? Although in the first scene of the play Valentine tells Proteus that he is going to Milan, two scenes later Proteus's father is informed:

> . . . youthful Valentine
> Attends the Emperor in his royal Court.
> (I, iii, 26–27)

The father thereupon decides to send his son likewise 'to the Emperor's Court' (I, iii, 38), being resolved that he shall spend some time 'with Valentinus in the Emperor's Court' (I, iii, 67). Now Shakespeare must have known that though the imperial court might have been in Vienna or Prague, it could not be in Milan. And when Proteus joins Valentine the two young gentlemen are at the court of the Duke of Milan, and we have no mention at all of the Emperor. How are we to account for the discrepancy?

Looking for an answer, we may recall that *The Two Gentlemen* is in some ways a carelessly written play. Amazing slips occur. Speed, in Milan, bids Launce 'welcome to Padua' (II, v, 1). The Duke of Milan, unquestionably in his capital, remarks, 'There is a lady in Verona here' (III, i, 81).[1] It may be part of this confusion that Shakespeare, his mind running on possible plans for Southampton to travel with Arundell, spoke inadvertently of his Veronese gentlemen going to the Emperor's court. We must remember, however, that no documents show that Southampton at this time was contemplating travel on the Continent. In the absence of

---

[1] It is only fair to Shakespeare to note that some critics attribute these errors to mutilations and adaptations of the text before it was printed in the First Folio.

any such evidence, we would do well to resist temptation and not urge acceptance of what must remain only an interesting surmise.

If the customary dating of *The Two Gentlemen of Verona* is right in assigning it to either 1594 or 1595, the play may well have been written after the flight to France of Sir Charles and Sir Henry Danvers, outlaws in consequence of their murder of Henry Long. Things being so, we would do well to look closely at the outlaws led by Valentine. These are among the most gentlemanly outlaws in all literature. Valentine's speech to the Duke on behalf of his outlaw friends is just such an apologia as the Danvers' friends repeatedly made when seeking a pardon that would permit the brothers to return safely to England:

> These banished men . . .
> Are men endued with worthy qualities.
> Forgive them what they have committed here,
> And let them be recalled from their exile.
> They are reformed, civil, full of good,
> And fit for great employment, worthy lord.
>
> (V, iv, 152–157)

Gentlemanly outlaws, though none appear in the known literary sources for this play, are among the stock in trade of romance writers. But we must admit the possibility that Shakespeare, writing this passage, was mindful of his patron's outlawed friends.

Part of the evidence that Shakespeare rather carelessly threw together *The Two Gentlemen of Verona* is the abrupt way in which he winds things up at the end. Valentine's beloved friend Proteus has shown himself 'subtle, perjured, false, disloyal'. He has just laid violent hands on Valentine's love, Silvia, unmistakably intending to rape her, when Valentine and his outlaws come to her rescue. What follows is amazing:

> *Valentine:*   . . . Oh, time most accurst,
>   'Mongst all foes that a friend should be the worst!
> *Proteus:* My shame and guilt confounds me.
>   Forgive me, Valentine. If hearty sorrow
>   Be a sufficient ransom for offense,
>   I tender 't here. I do as truly suffer
>   As e'er I did commit.
> *Valentine:*   Then I am paid,
>   And once again I do receive thee honest.
>   Who by repentance is not satisfied
>   Is nor of Heaven nor earth, for these are pleased.
>   By penitence the Eternal's wrath's appeased.
>   And, that my love may appear plain and free,
>   All that was mine in Silvia I give thee.
>
> (V, iv, 71–83)

Some critics have viewed this fantastic ending simply as part of the huddle of surprise developments with which Shakespeare will at times end

a comedy. They have argued that wc must not look for too much realism in a romance. Others have invoked the Renaissance cult of friendship which made loyalty to a friend count for more than the love that a man bears for a woman. Even when all concessions are made, it is difficult to stretch these answers to account for Valentine's amazing forgiveness. But this resolution, inexplicable as far as logic of character is concerned, may become more understandable if we see it as a sudden overflow from something deeply distressing in Shakespeare's own life. For the evidence here, we must turn to the further sonnets that Shakespeare was writing at this time.

CHAPTER VI

The Unfaithful Friend and the Sonnets

IN 1827 William Wordsworth said of the sonnet:

> ... with this key
> Shakespeare unlocked his heart.

Years later Browning retorted:

> Did Shakespeare? If so, the less Shakespeare he.

and resolutely looked the other way. Despite Browning, the main emphasis of nineteenth-century criticism fell upon the essentially autobiographical nature of the sonnets. Edward Dowden likened Shakespeare to Whitman in his revelation of himself in his poetry,[1] and proposed as a motto for Shakespeare's sonnets Whitman's lines:

> Come, I will take you down underneath this impassive exterior,—
> I will tell you what to say of me;
> Publish my name, and hang up my picture as that of the tenderest lover.

Enthusiasts of the autobiographical school were given a cooling card at the turn of the century when Sir Sidney Lee demonstrated that generally the Elizabethan sonneteers were writing literary exercises on standard Renaissance themes, utilizing a body of literary conventions and received ideas. Lee could find small grounds for treating Shakespeare's sonnets as autobiographical. The counter-attack was soon forthcoming. It was headed by H. C. Beeching, who observed that the sonnet had been used to convey personal emotion from the time of Michaelangelo with his sonnets on his love for Tommaso Cavalieri, to that of Rossetti with his sonnets to his wife. The counter-attack was largely successful. The position generally held today is that Shakespeare's sonnets are basically autobiographical though they may employ at times the language of convention and share in the artifice which is inseparable from art. J. W. Lever, in the standard book on the Elizabethan sonnet, has observed:

> Doubtless Shakespeare, like all good poets, found enough experience in his own life to supply him with the material he needed. We may be equally sure that as a literary artist working through the sonnet medium, he selected, adapted, and reshaped experience as judiciously as did every other great sonnet poet.[2]

[1] *Shakspere: His Mind and Art*, (London, 1892), p. 402.
[2] *The Elizabethan Love Sonnet* (London, 1956), pp. 163–4.

228

Noting that a major break comes at the end of Sonnet 126, many scholars view the sonnets as consisting of two blocs. The first of these, Sonnets 1–126, is concerned chiefly with the friend. The second, Sonnets 127–54, is more miscellaneous and contains all the sonnets addressed to the Dark Lady. Having found no significant Southampton clues in the second bloc, we need concern ourselves only with Sonnets 1–126. The first seventeen or nineteen of these, we have seen, were addressed to Southampton in 1593–94. Picking up the thread with Sonnet 20, we may now note what evidence authorizes us to think that many of these succeeding sonnets were also addressed to Southampton.

Sonnet 20 has been stigmatized as 'notorious', but there is no need for the pejorative word. At the time of writing this poem, Shakespeare found himself deeply involved emotionally with a young man. Almost inevitably he asked himself if this love might not have a homosexual basis. In Sonnet 20, which not uncharacteristically combines bawdy levity with a basic seriousness, he concludes that his love is not homosexual:

> But since she [Nature] pricked thee out for women's pleasure,
> Mine be thy love, and thy love's use their treasure.

As we move forward from Sonnet 20 a story of sorts begins to emerge. Sonnets which hymn the young friend's beauty and the poet's love are followed by ones dealing with an estrangement between poet and friend:

> Even so my sun one early morn did shine
> With all-triumphant splendour on my brow.
> But out, alack! he was but one hour mine,
> The region cloud hath masked him from me now.
>   Yet him for this my love no whit disdaineth;
>   Suns of the world may stain when heaven's sun staineth.
>   (Sonnet 33: 9–14)

We are given no hint as to the cause of the alienation. The fault however lies with the friend who, weeping, professes contrition and wins the poet's instant forgiveness:

> Ah, but those tears are pearl which thy love sheds,
> And they are rich and ransom all ill deeds.
>   (Sonnet 34: 13–14)

Sonnet 35 shows the poet experiencing self-contempt at his over-readiness to forgive the friend's 'sensual fault'. The language here is consistent with the theft of a mistress, an event clearly referred to in Sonnet 40. Here, in lines so parallel to Valentine's amazing surrender of Silvia to Proteus as to make Geoffrey Bullough speculate that *The Two Gentlemen* may have been 'written as a gesture of renewed friendship to

Shakespeare's own betrayer',[1] the poet surrenders his woman and all that he holds precious to the 'lascivious grace' of his friend:

> Take all my loves, my love, yea, take them all.

Such is the cry which opens Sonnet 40, though the anguish springs not from loss of the woman so much as from discovery of the friend's treachery. Succeeding sonnets show Shakespeare hunting for excuses for the unfaithful friend. These range from the rather commonplace:

> Beauteous thou art, therefore to be assailed.
> And when a woman woos, what woman's son
> Will sourly leave her till she have prevailed?
>
> (Sonnet 41: 6–8)

to the laboured literary conceits of:

> Loving offenders, thus I will excuse ye:
> Thou dost love her because thou know'st I love her,
> And for my sake even so doth she abuse me,
> Suffering my friend for my sake to approve [experience] her.
>
> (Sonnet 42: 5–8)

The sensual fault having been forgiven, other sonnets celebrate the beauty and worth of the friend, and passionately declare Shakespeare's love for him. Running intermittently through these sonnets are feelings of unworthiness which haunt the poet.

Since Shakespeare has this inner doubt of his own worth, the shock is great when he finds another poet taking his place in his friend's regard. Feelings of insecurity engulf Shakespeare as he contemplates loss of the friend who had done so much to aid him:

> Oh, how I faint when I of you do write,
> Knowing a better spirit doth use your name,
> And in the praise thereof spends all his might,
> To make me tongue-tied, speaking of your fame!
>   . . .   .
>   . . . I am a worthless boat,
> He of tall building and of goodly pride.
>   Then if he thrive and I be cast away,
>   The worst was this: my love was my decay.
>
> (Sonnet 80)

At the end, Shakespeare refuses to continue a contest in flattery:

> Farewell! Thou art too dear for my possessing,
> And like enough thou know'st thy estimate.
>
> (Sonnet 87: 1–2)

With the friend drifting away from him, Shakespeare abates the tortuous process of rationalization by which he had blinded himself to the young

---

[1] *Narrative and Dramatic Sources*, I, 210–11.

man's vices. The facing of the facts had begun earlier with Shakespeare questioning his friend's choice of company:

> Ah, wherefore with infection should he live
> And with his presence grace impiety,
> That sin by him advantage should achieve
> And lace itself with his society?
>
> (Sonnet 67: 1–4)

Now he comes closer and closer to direct criticism. The flower image so often attached to the friend acquires a different emphasis:

> The summer's flower is to the summer sweet,
> Though to itself it only live and die,
> But if that flower with base infection meet,
> The basest weed outbraves his dignity.
>   For sweetest things turn sourest by their deeds;
>   Lilies that fester smell far worse than weeds.
>
> (Sonnet 94: 9–14)

Lilies that fester smell far worse than weeds! That biting last line lingered in Shakespeare's mind. He repeated it verbatim in *Edward III* (II, i, 451). And since *Edward III* was published in 1596 we are supplied with a *terminus ante quem* for Shakespeare's disillusion with the friend.[1]

Sonnet 95 continues the mounting criticism:

> How sweet and lovely dost thou make the shame
> Which, like a canker in the fragrant rose,
> Doth spot the beauty of thy budding name!
> Oh, in what sweets dost thou thy sins enclose!

The poem ends with a quiet warning against the consequence of continued debauchery:

> Take heed, dear heart, of this large privilege;
> The hardest knife ill-used doth lose his edge.

These criticisms are continued in Sonnet 96 ('Some say thy fault is youth, some wantonness'). Then suddenly we come to a break in the *Sonnets*.

---

[1] Although *Edward III* is one of the apocryphal plays, Shakespeare's authorship of the 'countess scenes', including II, i, has been generally recognized. (See Kenneth Muir's 'A Reconsideration of *Edward III*' in *Shakespeare Survey* 6.)

The crucial question is that of priority. I think it demonstrable that the line was originally written as part of the sonnet. It is merely one of a mechanical series of antitheses in *Edward III*, but it is an organic part of Sonnet 94. Not only do we have the preparatory thirteenth line, but we find 'summer's flower' and 'flower' in lines 9 and 11 leading up to 'lilies' in the crystallizing final line. Similarly 'die' and 'infection' anticipate 'fester'; and 'weed' in line 12 contributes a final repetitive emphasis to 'weeds'. We may note that this passage in Sonnet 94 is a further development of 'to thy fair flower add the rank smell of weeds' (Sonnet 69, 12).

For possible origins of the image in Greene and Lodge see Lever, *The Elizabethan Love Sonnet*, p. 220.

Nothing in mood or diction links Sonnet 96 to the closely related trio that follow it. Probably the mounting distaste and disappointment with which Shakespeare was viewing his handsome young male friend had led to some sort of a break between them.

The break was not final, for we find Shakespeare returning to hymn the friend, and to offer excuses for the period when he had submitted no poetic tributes (Sonnets 100 and 109). Seeking to re-establish the former relationship, Shakespeare pleads the precedent that once (cf. Sonnet 33) the friend had turned away from him:

> That you were once unkind befriends me now,
> And for that sorrow which I then did feel
> Needs must I under my transgression bow. . . .
>   (Sonnet 120: 1–3)

As we approach the major division between Sonnets 1–126 and 127–54, we find Shakespeare again declaring his love for his friend.

Having thus briefly reviewed the 'sonnet story', let us turn to the identity of the persons who figure in Sonnets 20–126—the stolen mistress, the rival poet, and the friend. The stolen mistress may very well be the 'Dark Lady' addressed in various of the sonnets which follow Sonnet 126. However, since nobody has turned up any real clues to the identity of the Dark Lady, we have no indication as to who this stolen mistress may have been.

We fare better with the rival poet. Years ago Sir Sidney Lee made out a plausible case for Barnabe Barnes being that rival.[1] Others have advanced claims on behalf of Samuel Daniel, Michael Drayton, Gervase Markham, and Edmund Spenser. Nevertheless it seems clear that the rival poet was George Chapman, the pedantic obscurantist who was one of Shakespeare's targets in *Love's Labour's Lost*. The identification with Chapman, first proposed by William Minto,[2] has been greatly strengthened by subsequent realization that Shakespeare's gibe that his rival depends upon an 'affable familiar ghost/Which nightly gulls him with intelligence' (Sonnet 86) refers to Chapman's fantastic claim to be inspired by the spirit of Homer, which came to him on a hill close to his native Hitchin.[3]

Although Chapman in his *Shadow of Night* had taunted Shakespeare with the sensuality of *Venus and Adonis*, he later decided to show what he himself could do in the erotic line. Nothing was less appropriate for Chapman's ponderous Muse, and the best that even Chapman's editor

---

[1] *Life of Shakespeare*, pp. 202–3.
[2] *Characteristics of the English Poets from Chaucer to Shirley*, 2nd ed. (Edinburgh, 1885), pp. 221–3.
[3] J. A. K. Thomson, *Shakespeare and the Classics* (London, 1952), pp. 162–76.

can say of his 'Ovid's Banquet of Sense' is that it 'proves that Chapman was susceptible to at least an academic interest in bodily sensation'.[1] Published with 'Ovid's Banquet' in 1595 was another poem, 'The Amorous Zodiack', in which portions of the mistress's body are likened to various houses of the Zodiac. Shakespeare's Sonnet 21, which contains the first mention of the rival poet, is a contemptuous dismissal of Chapman and this poem.[2]

> So is it not with me as with that Muse
> Stirred by a painted beauty to his verse,
> Who Heaven itself for ornament doth use
> And every fair with his fair doth rehearse. . . .
>> (Sonnet 21: 1–4)

The sonnet ends with a submerged pun upon Chapman's name:

> Let them say more that like of hearsay well.
> I will not praise that purpose not to sell.

The gibe becomes apparent once we recall Shakespeare's line in *Love's Labour's Lost* about the 'base sale of chapmen's tongues'.

No doubt Chapman caused Shakespeare much uneasiness but in the end Essex, not Southampton, became Chapman's patron. Chapman's *Seven Books of Iliad*, published in 1598, were dedicated to Essex.

With the rival poet identified as Chapman, we come to the final question: is the friend who figures so prominently in Sonnets 20–126 that same Henry Wriothesley, Earl of Southampton, who was the recipient of the opening sonnets? Was Nathan Drake correct when in 1817 he launched the Southamptonite hypothesis, declaring:

> If we may be allowed, in our turn, to conjecture, we would fix upon LORD SOUTHAMPTON as the subject of Shakspeare's sonnets, from the first to hundredth and twenty-sixth, inclusive.[3]

Reading these sonnets, we pick up a surprising amount of information about the friend. He is considerably younger than the poet, who addresses him as 'sweet boy' (Sonnet 108: 5), and 'my lovely boy' (126: 1). His beauty is a frequent theme and we are told that his good looks have almost a feminine delicacy—he has 'A woman's face with Nature's own hand painted' (20: 1). If we may judge from Sonnet 36 this friend must be of very conspicuous rank:

> Nor [mayest] thou with public kindness honour me,
> Unless thou take that honour from thy name.
>> (lines 11–12)

[1] *Poems*, ed. Bartlett, p. 5.
[2] This point was first made by Arthur Acheson (*Shakespeare's Sonnet Story*, pp. 310–13). Acheson may be right also when he sees a gibe at Shakespeare in Chapman's 'A Coronet for his Mistresse Philosophie' (Ibid., 136–8).
[3] *Shakespeare and His Times* (London, 1817), II, 62.

The 'honour' of the friend's name may be a quibble upon 'The Right Honourable Henry Wriothesley, Earl of Southampton'. Shakespeare may also be playing upon an actual title in Sonnet 26 when he salutes the friend as 'Lord of my love'. Somewhat less likely is the claim that the rose images repeatedly applied to the friend play upon 'Rosely' as a pronunciation of Southampton's name.[1] As would befit a nobleman, this friend is generous in his gifts and rewards; Shakespeare likens his bounty to the 'foison of the year' (53: 9) and, possibly with reference to Southampton's famous gift of £1,000, puns upon the friend's 'dear purchased right' to his attention (117: 6). We learn that because of his liberality many other poets have sought the friend for their patron:

> . . . every alien pen hath got my use
> And under thee their poesy disperse.
>> (Sonnet 78: 3–4)

We learn other things. At one point the friend must have travelled beyond the sea, for Shakespeare, lamenting the killing thought that 'so much of earth and water' separates them, declares that his thoughts will leap 'both sea and land' to go where the friend has gone (44: 7–12). Moreover, the friend is seriously flawed. He has a 'sensual fault' (35: 9) and twice Shakespeare, not mincing matters, describes him as 'lascivious'. He is also something of a Narcissist:

> You to your beauteous blessings add a curse,
> Being fond on praise, which makes your praises worse.
>> (Sonnet 84: 13–14)

Adding it all up, we have a young lord with striking but somewhat effeminate good looks, a patron of literature who is notably generous in his rewards, a person who at least on one occasion has been away from England, one who is lascivious and narcissistic. It all adds up to a good description of Southampton during the 1590s.

Additional passages point more directly towards Southampton. In Sonnet 99, for example, Shakespeare declares 'buds of marjoram had stol'n thy hair'. According to H. C. Hart, 'dark auburn . . . would be the nearest approach to marjoram in the colour of hair'.[2] A glance at the frontispiece of this book will show that 'dark auburn' perfectly describes the colour of Southampton's hair. Commenting upon the friend's illicit relationships with women, Shakespeare speaks of 'wilful taste of what thyself refusest' (40: 8), a mystifying phrase until we realize its meaning that

---

[1] Supporters of this theory make much of the fact that *Rose* is capitalized and italicized in Sonnet 1 in Thorpe's 1609 quarto. On the pronunciation of 'Wriothesley' see p. 3, footnote 3.

[2] Cited by Beeching who, writing with half-opened marjoram before him, described the colour as similar to 'brown madder' (ed. *Sonnets*, p. 110).

though the friend uses women he will not marry one. Southampton's libidinous taste, along with his refusal to marry, links him with the person referred to here. Other clues point to Southampton. Thus, critic after critic has noted the striking parallel in wording between Sonnet 26 and Shakespeare's dedication of *Lucrece* to Southampton. Moving on to Sonnet 53, we find the friend being identified with Adonis:

> Describe Adonis, and the counterfeit
> Is poorly imitated after you.

Since, as we noted earlier, one of Shakespeare's purposes in writing *Venus and Adonis* was to draw a Southampton-Adonis parallel, this becomes one more piece of evidence that Southampton and the sonnet friend are the same person.

A parallel, which apparently has gone undetected, links Sonnet 106 and Chapman's *Seven Books of Iliad*. Chapman in his dedicatory epistle to Essex saluted him as 'most true Achilles (whom by sacred *prophecie* Homere did but *prefigure*)'.[1] Shakespeare, it would seem, wrote Sonnet 106 as something of a compensatory piece for Southampton. True, Shakespeare can make no reference to Homer but, borrowing the italicized words, he assures Southampton that when he is quarrying for material for his English history plays he finds him prefigured there:

> When in the chronicle of wasted time
> I see descriptions of the fairest wights,
> And beauty making beautiful old rhyme
> In praise of ladies dead and lovely knights,
> Then, in the blazon of sweet beauty's best,
> Of hand, of foot, of lip, of eye, of brow,
> I see their antique pen would have expressed
> Even such a beauty as you master now.
> So all their praises are but *prophecies*
> Of this our time, all you *prefiguring*. . . .
> (Sonnet 106: 1–10)

Finally we must consider the way in which Shakespeare addresses his friend as if the latter were his literary mentor and patron. He emphasizes how ignorant and unpolished he was before benefiting from the friend's educating influence:

> But thou art all my art, and dost advance
> As high as learning my rude ignorance.
> (Sonnet 78: 13–14)

The lines can only refer to how Shakespeare, with no more education than a provincial grammar school could supply, had attained a new literary

---

[1] *S.T.C. 13632*, sig. A4r. My italics.

sophistication once he came into Southampton's circle. In Sonnet 103 Shakespeare assures the friend:

> . . . to no other pass my verses tend
> Than of your graces and your gifts to tell . . . .

In other words, the friend is the only person that Shakespeare praises in his writing. The lines would be a crude lie if addressed to anyone other than Southampton.

When we add to all this evidence the strong probability that Shakespeare, having addressed his earliest sonnets to Southampton, would direct later ones to him also, and add the fact[1] that Sonnet 107 was addressed to Southampton upon his release from the Tower, we are pretty much forced to the conclusion that, if the discernible episodes in Sonnets 20–126 do all refer to the same person, that person must have been Southampton.

One piece of hitherto unnoticed evidence seems to indicate that some of Southampton's contemporaries knew that he was the friend charged with disloyalty by Shakespeare. The evidence consists of the four lines of verse praising Southampton, set at the head of Powell's *Welch Bayte* dedicated to the Earl in 1603.[2] The last two lines read:

> The grey-eyde morne in noontide clowdes may steepe,
> But traytor and his name shall never meete.

The 'grey-eyde morne' comes from *Romeo and Juliet* (II, iii, 1). This first Shakespearean image alerts us to the one which follows. The early morn which lost its brightness in 'noontide clowdes' was the metaphor that Shakespeare used in Sonnet 33 for his friend's act of desertion:

> Even so my sun one early morn did shine
> With all-triumphant splendour on my brow;
> But out, alack! he was but one hour mine,
> The region cloud hath mask'd him from me now.
>
> (lines 9–12)

Primarily the author of the *Welch Bayte* lines was refuting the charge that, politically, Southampton had been a traitor to his sovereign. But for those who caught the allusion he was also repudiating the charge, implicit in various of Shakespeare's sonnets, that, personally, he had betrayed the poet as well.

Let Southampton be identified as the sonnet Friend, and a flood of light is cast upon the basic relationship between poet and patron. To most contemporaries who were aware of the connection, it probably seemed a squalid association between a libertine young aristocrat and a player with

---

[1] *v.* pp. 254–55 *infra.*   [2] *v.* p. 138 *supra.*

a homosexual bias. Shakespeare himself was aware of how sordid the whole affair must appear. In one of the sonnets he despairingly declares that so much scandal is being created by their association that it must be broken off completely if young Southampton's reputation is to be saved:

Sonnet 36
Let me confess that we two must be twain,
Although our undivided loves are one.
So shall those blots that do with me remain,
Without thy help, by me be borne alone.
In our two loves there is but one respect,
Though in our lives a separable spite,
Which, though it alter not love's sole effect,
Yet doth it steal sweet hours from love's delight.
I may not evermore acknowledge thee,
Lest my bewailed guilt should do thee shame;
Nor thou with public kindness honour me,
Unless thou take that honour from thy name.
But do not so. I love thee in such sort
As thou being mine, mine is thy good report.

What was it that made Shakespeare think that Southampton would lose honour if he showed 'public kindness' to him? It must have been more than social inequality. Elizabethan lords could be on a friendly footing with actors and not lose honour. Years later the Earl of Pembroke would have seen nothing dishonourable in his admission that, Burbage having recently died, he had deliberately excused himself from seeing a play—'I being tender-harted could not endure to see so soone after the loss of my old acquaintance Burbadg.'[1] Shakespeare's references to 'blots', 'bewailed guilt', and 'shame' have to refer to more than a difference in social background. One is forced to suspect that some element of homosexuality lay at the root of the trouble. It is hard to think of anything else that would elicit from Shakespeare his cry:

My name be buried where my body is,
And live no more to shame nor me nor you.
(Sonnet 72: 11–12)

It is one thing to see a relationship of this kind with the eyes of society, with the eyes of outsiders. It is something else to see it through the eyes of the principals. Of Southampton's feelings we have small indication other than that Shakespeare found him gracious and kind. Certainly with his feeling for literature he must have appreciated Shakespeare as a poet. Almost certainly he felt affection for him. Beyond this we can say nothing. For Shakespeare the record lies before us in the sonnets. The love which he felt for Southampton may well have been the most intense emotion of his life.

[1] E. K. Chambers, *The Elizabethan Stage* (Oxford, 1923), II, 308.

Sonnet 29

When in disgrace with fortune and men's eyes
I all alone beweep my outcast state,
And trouble deaf Heaven with my bootless cries,
And look upon myself and curse my fate,
Wishing me like to one more rich in hope,
Featured like him, like him with friends possessed,
Desiring this man's art and that man's scope,
With what I most enjoy contented least—
Yet in these thoughts myself almost despising,
Haply I think on thee, and then my state,
Like to the lark at break of day arising
From sullen earth, sings hymns at Heaven's gate.
   For thy sweet love remembered such wealth brings
   That then I scorn to change my state with kings.

The same thought is repeated in the succeeding sonnet:

  . . . if the while I think on thee, dear friend,
All losses are restored and sorrows end.
                    (Sonnet 30: 13–14)

It is easy to see why C. S. Lewis declared:

In certain senses of the word 'love', Shakespeare is not so much our best as our only love poet.[1]

John Middleton Murry with splendid insight has analysed the quality of the Shakespeare-Southampton friendship in its earliest phases:

Probably each was captivated by the other. The young aristocrat was as yet sufficiently unspoiled to respond to Shakespeare's natural charm and genius; and the situation was sufficiently new and unexpected for Shakespeare to be dazzled by the relation. I have seen the same thing happen in the case of the only poet I ever knew whose native genius was remotely comparable to Shakespeare's, and I have witnessed the same eagerness to discover virtues where no virtues were, and to translate condescension into true esteem. The position of his patron-friend would merely add intensity to Shakespeare's love. It would appear to him as evidence of his friend's regard for him that it made light of the vast difference in rank. He would see in Southampton the aristocrat by birth and fortune who recognized in Shakespeare the aristocrat by nature and genius. And this motion of the soul would be the more overwhelming in Shakespeare, precisely because he was conscious that his original motive in seeking Southampton's patronage had been economic necessity. . . . The very reluctance with which he had turned to patronage inclined him to invest the particular relation into which he entered with a dignity that was illusory.[2]

'A dignity that was illusory'. Illusory indeed, like so many of the loves of men. In time, after the double shock of Southampton's theft of his mistress, and his equal affability towards another poet, Shakespeare began to

---

[1] C. S. Lewis, *English Literature in the Sixteenth Century excluding Drama* (Oxford, 1954), p. 505.
[2] *Shakespeare* (New York, 1936), pp. 74–6.

WILLIAM SHAKESPEARE: THE CHANDOS PORTRAIT
National Portrait Gallery

recognize certain realities. The criticisms became stronger until, finally, the glittering lord was informed:

> Lilies that fester smell far worse than weeds.

But was Southampton ever so informed? Many of the sonnets may have been written for the private discharge of anguished love and disappointment. It is as difficult to conceive of some of these sonnets being handed to the Earl of Southampton as it is to imagine some of the Dark Lady sonnets being given to that lady. Had Southampton seen all these sonnets, he might well have been amazed at the intensity of the feelings that he had inspired. Probably Shakespeare put many of his sonnets away in some private drawer.

We have seen that Shakespeare's love for young Southampton may have been the greatest emotional experience of his life. The consequent bitterness when he found that love betrayed may have left him emotionally marked for life. For evidence of that trauma we must resume our study of the plays.

CHAPTER VII

The Unfaithful Friend and the Plays

'YOU INVENT FICTION,' said Hemingway, 'but what you invent it out of is what counts. True fiction must come from everything you've ever known, ever seen, ever felt, ever learned.'[1] 'Out of my great sorrows I make my little songs,' said Heine. Behind *Samson Agonistes* lie Milton's blindness and the disappointment of all his hopes for the government of England. Most writers of real intensity write out of an excited condition of the complex and emotional organism that is man. The work becomes an extension of the man. The work is the man.

Surely Shakespeare, working in 'the quick forge and working-house of thought', wrote out of all that he had ever known, ever seen, ever felt, ever learned. Occasionally the overflow from actual experience signals its presence. Into the Illyria of *Twelfth Night* slips an approving comment on an inn close to the Globe Theatre.

> In the south suburbs, at the Elephant,
> Is best to lodge.
>
> (III, iii, 39–40)

Into *The Taming of the Shrew*, as we have noted, come the names of Warwickshire hamlets and their inhabitants.

A number of Shakespeare's plays seem, in their writing, to have activated that part of his consciousness concerned with Southampton's unfaithfulness. *Richard II* may be one of these plays. Miss Mahood has pointed out how close the parallel is between the description of the king on the walls of Flint Castle and that of the estranged friend given in Sonnet 30.[2] Something of Southampton may be present in handsome, poetical Richard, unreliable, self-indulgent, and dependent upon flatterers. This is mere speculation, however, and we would be most unwise to assert any connection here.

Before turning to those plays to which the Southampton relationship does seem to have contributed something, we must say a few words about *A Midsummer Night's Dream*. No evidence supports the theory that this was written for the marriage of Southampton's mother to Sir Thomas Heneage. Shakespeare would hardly have been such a tactless blunderer

---

[1] A. E. Hotchner, *Papa Hemingway* (Toronto, 1967), p. 112.
[2] 'Love's Confined Doom', *Shakespeare Survey 15*, pp. 50–1.

as to put in a play written for that occasion lines which could be taken as a palpable hit at the bride:

> . . . a dowager,
> Long withering out a young man's revenue.
>
> (I, i, 5–6)

Probably the courtly wedding for which *The Dream* was written was that of the Earl of Derby when he married Southampton's rejected Lady Elizabeth Vere. Derby was one of Southampton's friends, and perhaps Southampton had something to do with Shakespeare being asked to write the play.

If *A Midsummer Night's Dream* has little or nothing for us, the situation changes when we come to *The Merchant of Venice*. Here, in the story of Antonio and Bassanio, we may very well have a reflection of the Shakespeare-Southampton relationship.

For most people *The Merchant of Venice* is a romantic tale of Bassanio's wooing of witty Portia, of the choice of the caskets, of the villainous money-lender Shylock, and of the trick by which Portia frustrates him. Most people give hardly a thought to Antonio and are startled when told that he gives the play its title.[1] That Shakespeare named his play after Antonio, 'that royal merchant', suggests that though he gave his audience a boy-and-girl love story, his own interest may have been less in Bassanio and Portia than in Bassanio and Antonio. View the play from this somewhat unexpected vantage-point and what do we find?

The play begins with Antonio. He speaks the opening lines and immediately sets a question to engage our attention:

> *Antonio :* In sooth, I know not why I am so sad.
>   It wearies me, you say it wearies you;
>   But how I caught it, found it, or came by it,
>   What stuff 'tis made of, whereof it is born,
>   I am to learn.
>
> (I, i, 1–5)

An answer is proposed but rejected—this is not love melancholy. When Salarino asks if he is in love, Antonio, who seems to be uninterested in women, gives a deprecatory 'Fie, fie!' However, we soon get an inkling of the cause of Antonio's sorrow. He is deeply involved emotionally with a glittering young prodigal, Bassanio, and that young gentleman has recently informed him that he intends to court a young lady. With signal unselfishness, Antonio agrees to furnish his extravagant friend with money with which to go a-wooing Portia in Belmont:

---

[1] It is a common misconception that Shylock is the merchant. The word 'merchant' is never applied to Shylock, being reserved for Antonio. 'Which is the merchant here, and which the Jew?' (IV, i, 174).

> You know me well, and herein spend but time
> To wind about my love with circumstance.
> And out of doubt you do me now more wrong
> In making question of my uttermost
> Than if you had made waste of all I have.
> Then do but say to me what I should do. . . .
>
> (I, i, 153–158)

Because his capital is all tied up in ventures abroad, Antonio cannot supply the needed funds himself, so he stands security for Bassanio when the latter borrows three thousand ducats from old Shylock. Shylock attaches a condition to this loan: if the money is not repaid within three months, he is to have a pound of Antonio's flesh, cut from wherever he chooses. Even the heedless Bassanio has misgivings about Shylock's pretence that this forfeit is but 'a merry sport' and not to be taken seriously. Subsequently Salarino gives an account of Bassanio's parting from Antonio:

> . . . his eye being big with tears,
> Turning his face, he put his hand behind him,
> And with affection wondrous sensible
> He wrung Bassanio's hand; and so they parted.
>
> (II, viii, 46–49)

In Belmont, Bassanio chooses the right casket and receives from Portia a ring in token of his victory:

> This house, these servants, and this same myself
> Are yours, my lord. I give them with this ring,
> Which when you part from, lose, or give away,
> Let it presage the ruin of your love. . . .
>
> (III, ii, 172–175)

Hardly has the ring been received when Salerio arrives with news that Antonio, having failed to repay the three thousand ducats within the allotted time, must die. With him Salerio brings Antonio's letter which tells Bassanio:

> . . . all debts are cleared between you and I, if I might but see you at my death. Notwithstanding, use your pleasure. If your love do not persuade you to come, let not my letter.
>
> (III, ii, 321–324)

Summoned thus in the name of love, Bassanio instantly weds and, not waiting for the consummation of the wedding night, heads for Venice and Antonio.

Portia, left behind in Belmont, approves of her husband's devotion to his friend, but nevertheless is given a somewhat unnecessary speech by Lorenzo who expatiates on the 'godlike amity' that joins Bassanio with Antonio. He tells her 'how dear a lover' Bassanio has in Antonio.

Obviously Shakespeare is now manoeuvring his play towards the old

theme of the conflicting claims of love for one's woman and love for one's friend, a situation which can very easily slip over into a pitting of hetero-sexual versus homosexual love. Shakespeare's characters seem to cross into the latter area.

Antonio, on the threshold of death, speaking to Bassanio instructs him to present his commendations to his wife, but then continues:

> Say how I loved you, speak me fair in death;
> And, when the tale is told, bid her be judge
> Whether Bassanio had not once a love.
>
> (IV, i, 275–277)

'Whether Bassanio had not *once* a love.' There is a note of triumph in that 'once'. Bassanio's answering speech confirms that triumph. He assures Antonio that where the latter's life is concerned Portia, and everything else, is expendable:

> Antonio, I am married to a wife
> Which is as dear to me as life itself,
> But life itself, my wife, and all the world,
> Are not with me esteemed above thy life.
> I would lose all, aye, sacrifice them all
> Here to this devil, to deliver you.
>
> (IV, i, 282–287)

Writing these lines, Shakespeare knew of course that Portia, disguised as the young lawyer sent by Bellario, was on hand to hear the speech. Plenty of points were being scored against the female.

The victory of Antonio should by now have been sufficiently estab-lished, but even more is to follow. Bassanio, bent on rewarding the young lawyer who has saved his friend, urges him to accept a reward. Portia mischievously says that the only reward she will take is the ring so recently given to Bassanio. He protests that he will procure for her any other ring, no matter how costly, but not this ring which was given to him by his wife. 'Well, peace be with you!' says the young lawyer and departs. But then follows a remarkable passage. Antonio speaks up:

> My Lord Bassanio, let him have the ring.
> Let his deservings and my love withal
> Be valued 'gainst your wife's commandment.
>
> (IV, i, 449–451)

We have seen earlier mentions of Antonio's *love*. Now it is directly pitted against the *commandment* of the wife. There is no excuse for Antonio's request: the issue is no longer his life, and he has heard Bassanio declare what the ring means to him. Moreover the young lawyer, who has already departed, plainly was not much upset at being refused the ring. But Antonio intervenes. Invoking, not for the first time, the love between himself and Bassanio, he asks him to surrender the ring.

Bassanio's response is interesting. Without a word of expostulation he immediately says:

> Go, Gratiano, run and overtake him.
> Give him the ring. . . .
>
> (IV, i, 452–453)

A singular demonstration once more of love for a man triumphing over that for a woman. The Antonio-Bassanio story really ends here, though later we find the victor Antonio being presented to Portia, now in her own person, as part of the 'happy ending' of the play.

If any play of Shakespeare's may be taken to have a submerged homosexual element within it, surely *The Merchant of Venice*, with these multiple victories of Antonio over Portia, is that play. Using a different approach, Nevill Coghill has observed, 'To make credible the turn in the plot by which Antonio must show himself willing to offer a pound of his flesh for the convenience of a friend, nothing less than a high homosexual affection, worthy of the *Symposium*, would poetically suffice. . . .'[1]

The usual date assigned to *The Merchant of Venice* is 1596–97. In February 1597 the Earl of Southampton, through his extravagances, was so far into debt that he had to turn over his estate to administration by attorneys. The traditional course for a bachelor English earl on the verge of bankruptcy was marriage to a wealthy heiress. Southampton's advisers must have urged this remedy upon him. One sees a parallel emerging between Southampton and Bassanio who, likewise gifted and attractive, 'a scholar and a soldier', and encumbered with debts, seeks to salvage his fortunes by marrying a wealthy wife. As for Antonio, be begins to resemble Shakespeare himself, loving the young gallant, ready to see him wed, but unable to surrender his love.[2] The ring episode with Bassanio and Antonio becomes, in short, something of a wish fulfilment for Shakespeare's yearning still to possess Southampton's love even though encouraging him to wed an heiress.

All this may seem tenuous speculation, but one thing about Antonio does tie in, quite remarkably, with the Shakespeare of the sonnets. When, just before the trial begins, Bassanio seeks to encourage Antonio, the latter breaks forth:

---

[1] 'The Basis of Shakespearian Comedy' in *Shakespeare Criticism 1935–60,* Anne Ridler ed. (London, 1963), p. 212.

[2] Shakespeare had become capable of that surrender when he wrote the superb sonnet, 'Let me not to the marriage of true minds/Admit impediment'. This is an unspoken response to the priest's words when reading the banns before a marriage, 'If any of you know cause or just impediment why these two persons should not be joined together in holy matrimony ye are to declare it'. Various critics have sought to relate this sonnet to the marriage of Southampton and Elizabeth Vernon.

> I am a tainted wether of the flock,
> Meetest for death. The weakest kind of fruit
> Drops earliest to the ground, and so let me.
>
> (IV, i, 114–116)

The vehemence of this statement of inadequacy and guilt comes home to us when we think for a moment about that phrase, 'a tainted wether'—it means literally a diseased castrated sheep. Very similar statements of guilt and inadequacy occur in the sonnets. Patrick Cruttwell has noted how 'self-disgust, self-contempt, self-reproach', so often mark Shakespeare's introspection there.[1] That key word 'tainted', applied to Antonio, lurks in Shakespeare's self-denunciations in the sonnets:

> With mine own weakness being best acquainted,
> Upon thy part I can set down a story
> Of faults concealed, wherein I am *attainted*,
> That thou in losing me shalt win much glory.
>
> (Sonnet 88: 5–8)

We recall Shakespeare speaking in Sonnet 36 of the 'blots' that remain with him, and his cry to the friend:

> My name be buried where my body is,
> And live no more to shame nor me nor you.
>
> (Sonnet 72: 11–12)

There is something of Shakespeare in the sombre figure of Antonio. Suffering with those heightened sensitivities which mark a poet, Shakespeare discharged part of his pain into *The Merchant of Venice*.

Evidence of the continuance of the tie between Shakespeare and Southampton is provided by the poet's coat of arms. This was given, nominally to Shakespeare's father, on October 20th, 1596. The grant from the College of Arms describes the new arms as:

> Gould, on a Bend Sables, a Speare of the first steeled argent. And for his creast or cognizaunce a falcon his winges displayed Argent standing on a wrethe of his coullers: suppo[rting] a Speare Gould steeled as aforesaid sett uppon a helmett with mantelles & tasselles as hath ben accustomed. . . .[2]

There is probably a special significance to the silver falcon supporting the spear on the Shakespeare crest. The Southampton arms consisted of 'Azure a Cross Or between four Falcons Argent'. It seems likely that, as late as October 1596, Shakespeare wished his arms to declare his allegiance to the Earl of Southampton.

Between 1596 and 1598 Shakespeare was at work on the two parts of *Henry IV*. William Empson[3] is probably right in seeing Shakespeare

---

[1] *The Shakespearean Moment* (London, 1954), p. 9.

[2] Chambers, *William Shakespeare*, II, 19.

[3] *Some Versions of Pastoral* (London, 1935), pp. 104–7.

and Southampton behind Falstaff and Prince Hal. Without resorting to such weak arguments as making Fall-staff an ironic counterpun on Shake-speare, or belabouring the fact that both prince and earl are Henries, one may note certain parallels. There is the divergence in rank and age. There is the fact that Hal values Falstaff chiefly as a source of entertainment. The play-acting scene at the Boar's Head, in which Hal and Falstaff in turn take the role of Henry IV, may relate in some dim way to Shakespeare's awareness of himself as an actor and of Southampton as a devotee of the theatre. The rejection of Falstaff at the end of *Henry IV, Part Two*, may either foreshadow or reflect a Shakespeare-Southampton separation that was bound shortly to come, if it had not already occurred. Hal's rejection of Falstaff is mirrored when, in Sonnet 49, Shakespeare dreads the day:

> . . . when thou shalt strangely pass,
> And scarcely greet me with that sun, thine eye,
> When love, converted from the thing it was,
> Shall reasons find of settled gravity. . . .

One phrase here, 'the thing it was', is practically identical with words spoken by the new king, Henry V. 'Presume not that I am the thing I was,' he tells Falstaff. Sonnet 87 ends with a rueful couplet which could be Falstaff's final word on the friendship that had been:

> Thus have I had thee, as a dream doth flatter,
> In sleep a king, but waking no such matter.

Little wonder that Miss Mahood, noting these and other parallels, concluded that the relationship between the poet and his friend in the sonnets 'seems closely to parallel that of the Prince of Wales and his reprobate old companion'.[1]

For a tragic sounding of the anguish of betrayal comparable to that in the sonnets, we must turn not to the *Henry IV* plays but to *Henry V* written in 1599. It is not merely that Falstaff dies, his heart 'fracted and corroborate' by the King's aloofness. Henry himself gives an agonized statement of what betrayal by a friend can do to a man:

> What shall I say to thee, Lord Scroop? Thou cruel,
> Ingrateful, savage, and inhuman creature!
> Thou that didst bear the key of all my counsels,
> That knew'st the very bottom of my soul,
> That almost mightst have coined me into gold
> Wouldst thou have practiced on me for thy use . . .?
> (II, ii, 94–99)

So Henry begins, strangely echoing the flesh-bond signed by Antonio when he speaks of the coining of a man's body into gold for his friend.

---

[1] 'Love's Confined Doom', *Shakespeare Survey 15*, p. 57. See also J. C. Maxwell, *Notes and Queries*, CCVIII, 352.

On and on the tremendous denunciatory speech continues, far beyond the needs of so minor an episode within the play.

During the years that follow *Henry V*, betrayal becomes a central, almost compulsive theme in Shakespeare's plays. In *Julius Caesar* we have Caesar betrayed by Brutus—'Then burst his mighty heart'. In *Twelfth Night* we have the anguish of Antonio when he believes himself betrayed by Sebastian:

> This youth that you see here
> I snatched one half out of the jaws of death,
> Relieved him with such sanctity of love,
> And to his image, which methought did promise
> Most venerable worth, did I devotion.
>
> . . .   .
>
> But oh, how vile an idol proves this god!
> Thou hast, Sebastian, done good feature shame.
> In nature there's no blemish but the mind;
> None can be called deformed but the unkind.
>
> (III, iv, 393–402)

Parallel is Duke Orsino's bitterness at the supposed treachery of Cesario. *Hamlet*, it has been remarked, is 'a tissue of betrayals'. *Othello* centres around the betrayal of Othello by Iago, which entails the betrayal of Desdemona by Othello. *Macbeth* is full of betrayal; Macbeth knows that Duncan comes to his house 'in double trust'. *King Lear* deals with betrayal of kin by kin. *Timon* deals with friendship betrayed on a gigantic scale. There are more betrayals in *Troilus and Cressida* than that of Troilus by Cressida. Betrayal is one of the central tragic facts for Shakespeare. And it may well be that Henry, Earl of Southampton, and a woman whose name we shall never know, taught Shakespeare the meaning of betrayal.

Shakespeare and the Essex Rebellion

SOUTHAMPTON'S FEW surviving letters make no mention of Shakespeare and contain no allusion to any Shakespearean play or character. However his wife, writing to him in Ireland in 1599, has an interesting reference to 'Sir John Falstaff'. To a letter dated July 8th, the Countess added a postscript:

> all the nues I can send you that I thinke wil make you mery is that I reade in a letter from London that sir John falstaf is by his m^{rs} dame pintpot made father of a godly [goodly?] milers [miller's] thum a boy thats all heade and veri litel body, but this is a secrit.[1]

For years scholars speculated as to who this 'sir John falstaf' might be. Lee thought it might be Shakespeare who had fathered the strangely proportioned child. Chambers made a guess that Henry Brooke, Lord Cobham, was the man. Finally Leslie Hotson broke the Countess's code and, pointing out that a 'miller's thumb' was at one time a common name for a small fish with a big head known also as a 'cob', demonstrated that Cobham was indeed the man.[2] With this puzzle solved, Hotson could also explicate the earliest known allusion to Falstaff. This was made by Sir Robert Cecil during his journey to France with Southampton in February 1598. In a letter to Essex, Cecil wrote: 'I pray you commend me allso to Alex. Ratcliff and tell him for newes his sister is maryed to S^r Jo. Falstaff.'[3] The sister was Margaret Radcliffe, one of Elizabeth's favourite maids of honour. In fact, she never married Lord Cobham or anybody else.

It is hardly surprising that 'Falstaff' became a nickname for Cobham. When in 1596 Shakespeare wrote *Henry IV, Part One*, he gave his fat knight the name of Sir John Oldcastle, a Lollard who had served in the Welsh campaigns of Henry IV and who had figured in the old play *The Famous Victories of Henry V*. Apparently Cobham or his father,[4] being

---

[1] *Cecil Papers*, 101/16.

[2] *Shakespeare's Sonnets Dated* (London, 1949), p. 156.

[3] Ibid., pp. 147–8.

[4] William Brooke, Lord Cobham, was Lord Chamberlain from July 22nd, 1596, until he died on March 5th, 1597, and was succeeded in his baronage by his son, Henry Brooke, the Lord Cobham, with whom we are concerned. As Lord Chamberlain, the father had for a subordinate the Master of the Revels, who attended to the licensing of plays. Hence he could easily have required that some other name be used instead of Oldcastle's.

descendants of Oldcastle, took exception to Shakespeare's portrayal of their ancestor. The consequence of all this was that Shakespeare changed his character to 'Sir John Falstaff', though leaving in the play a few telltale indications of the original name. Once Oldcastle had been renamed Falstaff, it became an obvious jest for courtiers to nickname Cobham 'Falstaff'.

Cobham became an inveterate enemy of Essex and Southampton. When Shakespeare wrote *The Merry Wives of Windsor* for the Garter festivities of May 1597, the two earls may have put him up to the mischievous trick of having the jealous husband Ford take the name of Brook when visiting Falstaff in disguise. Henry Brooke, Lord Cobham, must have struck back, for in the First Folio text of the play 'Brook' has been changed to 'Broom'. Probably the whole Essex-Southampton circle joyously encouraged Shakespeare in the game of Brooke-baiting.

Moving in the orbit of the Earls of Essex and Southampton, Shakespeare must have seen much of the military captains who, late in 1598 and early in 1599, frequented Essex House hoping for appointments in the coming campaign against the Irish rebels. There he would hear debates between officers who in their rival military manuals championed the opposing 'ancient' and 'modern' theories of warfare.[1] It was only natural that Shakespeare, writing *Henry V* in the spring of 1599 and looking around for a comic element to take the place of the deceased Falstaff, should bring in Captain Fluellen and the three other captains, and make Fluellen argue vehemently for the 'disciplines of the pristine wars of the Romans'. There may have been a special comic effect to all this, for it has been suggested that Fluellen is based upon the valiant Welsh captain Sir Roger Williams, a close friend to Essex and an ardent champion of the modern school, who had died only a few years before.[2] The fact that Shakespeare gives the name 'Williams' to one of the common soldiers at Agincourt may indicate that memories of Sir Roger Williams were active in his mind while working on this play.

Shakespeare may have become disillusioned about Southampton, but this does not mean that he made his altered feelings evident to the Earl himself, and surrendered the entrée into the Essex circle that Southampton had secured for him. Near the end of *Henry V* Shakespeare, after telling how the Londoners welcomed Henry home after Agincourt, turns to praise Essex:

[1] On these 'book-writing captains', see Paul A. Jorgensen, *Shakespeare's Military World* (Berkeley, 1956), pp. 76 *et passim*.

[2] John Dover Wilson, 'Martin Marprelate and Shakespeare's Fluellen', *The Library*, Third Series, III (1912), 113–51. For a counter claim that Fluellen represents Ludovic Lloyd, see J. H. Walter, *Henry V*, New Arden ed. (London, 1954), p. xxxiii. Bullough, *Narrative and Dramatic Sources*, IV, 372, opts for Williams.

> . . . by a lower but loving likelihood,
> Were now the general of our loving empress,
> As in good time he may, from Ireland coming,
> Bringing rebellion broached on his sword,
> How many would the peaceful city quit
> To welcome him!
>
> (V, Pro., 29–34)

A link of some sort between Shakespeare's company and the Essexians may be indicated by an event just before Essex's disastrous rebellion. Some of the conspirators wanted to prepare the Londoners psychologically for their intended coup. Hence several days before the rebellion Lord Mounteagle, Sir Charles Percy, and some friends called on the Lord Chamberlain's company and asked them to 'have the play of the deposyng and kyllyng of Kyng Rychard the second to be played the Saterday next'. When the players protested that *Richard II* was an old play that would not draw, the Essexians offered to subsidize the performance to the extent of forty shillings. A bargain was struck, the money was paid, and on Saturday, February 7th, *Richard II* was played at the Globe with Sir Charles Percy, Lord Mounteagle, Sir Christopher Blount, Sir Gelly Merrick, and Captain Thomas Lee among the audience.[1] After the failure of the rebellion, the circumstances surrounding this special performance were carefully scrutinized by the authorities. Augustine Phillips, a veteran member of the Lord Chamberlain's company, was questioned but he seems to have convinced his interrogators that he and his fellows had no fore-knowledge of the rebellion.

What appearance did the world possess for Shakespeare after the sentences of death or imprisonment that followed Essex's rebellion? Essex, the brilliant and debonair, was rotting in an unmarked grave. So was the scholar-soldier Sir Charles Danvers who, because of the love that he bore to Southampton, had joined in the rebellion. Southampton, an ailing prisoner kept incommunicado in the Tower, was as good as dead. We need not be surprised if Shakespeare despaired and the world seemed to him indeed 'weary, stale, flat, and unprofitable'. Out of his grief and desolation, he wrote for Essex and those who had perished with him the greatest threnody in our language.

A curious incident supplied Shakespeare with the occasion for writing this lament. One of the oddities of Elizabethan literature is a volume of mediocre verse by one Robert Chester entitled *Love's Martyr: Or, Rosalin's Complaint. Allegorically shadowing the truth of Love, in the constant Fate of the Phoenix and the Turtle.* Also in this volume in 1601 were a number of short poems, including one by Shakespeare, likewise on the Phoenix and Turtle theme and 'consecrated . . . to the love and merite

---

[1] For the documents see Chambers, *William Shakespeare*, II, 324–7.

of the true-noble Knight, Sir John Salisburie'. For a great many years scholars tried, with varying degrees of implausibility, to fit the poems in *Love's Martyr* to the known facts about Salusbury, a Welsh gentleman with a complicated love life. A minor figure at the court of Queen Elizabeth, he had been knighted not long after the Essex Rebellion. Only in 1965 did William Matchett show that *Love's Martyr* was originally written in 1599 to commend Essex (the turtle-dove) to Queen Elizabeth (the phoenix), and that it was published by Edward Blount for sale to those loyal to Essex's memory. The authorities, of course, would not for a minute have permitted the publication of a book extolling the recently executed traitor. For this reason Chester invoked the name of his sometime patron, Sir John Salusbury, 'as a shield for the treasonable nature of his volume'.[1] There was a nice irony to using Salusbury as a blind— Captain Owen Salusbury, who perished in the defence of Essex House, had been Sir John's kinsman and enemy. Such was the nature of the volume to which Shakespeare contributed his poem.

Shakespeare's 'The Phoenix and the Turtle' is a tremendously evocative poem. Its syntax is compacted; its lines are hauntingly ambiguous; and its meaning is protean in the various guises it was required of necessity to wear. Matchett in a masterpiece of sensitive exegesis has analysed 'The Phoenix and the Turtle' stanza by stanza. Following his pattern, let us set forth in briefer and therefore less adequate manner the contents of the poem.

For the frame of 'The Phoenix and the Turtle' Shakespeare has taken the bird fable, so frequently used for purposes of allegory. The poem falls into three sections. The first, the summons, sees an unidentified 'bird of lowdest lay' serving as a herald to call together all chaste and gentle birds for a ceremony commemorating the dead Phoenix and the Dove, its love, which had earlier perished in a mutual flame. Only one foul bird of 'tyrant wing' is permitted to attend these solemn rites. This is 'the Eagle, feath'red King'. The symbolic company of birds having assembled, an anthem is sung lamenting:

> Love and Constancie is dead,
> *Phoenix* and the *Turtle* fled. . . .

Metaphysical stanzas, strangely similar to Donne's poetry, develop the paradox that love makes one out of two. The anthem ends with Reason, which at first is confounded and appalled by something beyond its comprehension, finally perceiving that Love has an overriding reason of its own. Thus enlightened, Reason offers the threnody for the Phoenix and the Dove which ends the poem:

---

[1] William H. Matchett, *The Phoenix and the Turtle* (The Hague, 1965), p. 142.

Beautie, Truth, and Raritie,
Grace in all simplicitie,
Here enclosde, in cinders lie.

Death is now the *Phoenix* nest,
And the *Turtles* loyall brest,
To eternitie doth rest.

. . .   . . .

Truth may seeme, but cannot be,
Beautie bragge, but tis not she,
Truth and Beautie buried be.

To this urne let those repaire,
That are either true or faire,
For these dead Birds, sigh a prayer.

The poem ends on the authentic note of tragedy. In this world Truth and Beauty no longer exist in their perfect state. Those who partake to a lesser degree of these qualities which have died with the Phoenix and Turtle can only mourn. The closing line has a leaden bleakness.

Who is represented by the Phoenix and who by the Dove? Matchett decided that Shakespeare had maintained the identity set forth in Chester's original poem, and hence the Phoenix is Queen Elizabeth and the Turtle is Essex. But there are two objections to this interpretation. One, which Matchett noted, is that Queen Elizabeth was still alive in 1601, whereas Shakespeare's poem emphasizes the death of both the Phoenix and the Turtle. The other objection is that surely Shakespeare, who in 1603 did not mourn in verse the death of Elizabeth, would never have allowed himself to praise her in 1601. Elizabeth is present, indeed, in the poem but she, having ordered the deaths of Essex and his friends, is now the Eagle with the 'tyrant wing'. As for the Phoenix and the Turtle, one of them certainly symbolizes Essex. The other may be Sir Christopher Blount, or Captain Owen Salusbury, or Sir Charles Danvers. Or it may be Southampton, doomed to a living death in the Tower. Or it may represent all of them. What of Reason which, confounded at first, sings at the last the 'Threnos' which closes the poem? Here we have Shakespeare's comment in retrospect upon the Essex Rebellion: look at the rebellion with cool common sense and what a lunatic venture it was; but look at it not in terms of reason but of love, the love that bound Essex and his friends, and what a different aspect it must bear. Reason itself, illuminated, sings their requiem. The enlightenment of Reason is only a slight palliative. Shakespeare, looking back on the Essex group, of which Southampton and himself had been a part, sees a brilliant and gifted company of friends overwhelmed in disaster. 'Truth and Beauty buried be.'

The shock of the Essex catastrophe seems to have been devastating in its effects upon Shakespeare. A world from which truth and beauty have

departed becomes the world of *Hamlet*; 'things rank and gross in nature possess it merely'. It is the world of *Troilus and Cressida* of which Una Ellis-Fermor has said, 'The dark night of the soul comes down upon the unilluminated wreckage of the universe of vision.'[1]

Undoubtedly the literary scene was darkening over in the last few years of Elizabeth's reign, and Shakespeare was moving in the same direction as his contemporaries. Still it is worth observing that the period of Shakespeare's profoundest tragedies and of his cynical, jaundiced problem comedies does follow close upon the Essex catastrophe.

---

[1] *The Frontiers of Drama* (London, 1945), pp. 71–2. The view has sometimes been expressed that Achilles, sulking in his tent, represents Essex, who at times petulantly retreated from the court; that Patroclus, his 'masculine whore', is Southampton; and that the foul-mouthed Thersites is Essex's secretary Cuffe. Although initially I was inclined to accept, in part, this interpretation of the play, the further I went with this study, the more improbable this theory appeared to me. Any overtones which do appear are accidental or incidental.

CHAPTER IX

Shakespeare and Southampton in the Jacobean Age

ON APRIL 10TH, 1603, the Earl of Southampton was released from the Tower on the orders of James I, and it soon became obvious that the new monarch was bent on showering his favour upon him. Men of letters once more sought Southampton's patronage. Among them was Shakespeare who, in the following sonnet, congratulated Southampton upon his release:

Sonnet 107

Not mine own fears, nor the prophetic soul
Of the wide world dreaming on things to come,
Can yet the lease of my true love control,
Supposed as forfeit to a confined doom.
The mortal moon hath her eclipse endured,
And the sad augurs mock their own presage.
Incertainties now crown themselves assured,
And peace proclaims olives of endless age.
Now with the drops of this most balmy time
My love looks fresh, and Death to me subscribes,
Since, spite of him, I'll live in this poor rhyme
While he insults o'er dull and speechless tribes.
 And thou in this shalt find thy monument,
 When tyrants' crests and tombs of brass are spent.

The interested reader can find elsewhere the mass of evidence which has firmly established the dating of this sonnet.[1] It may be useful, however, to restate the poem's contents, making explicit the topical allusions which are

[1] This sonnet was first assigned to 1603 by an unidentified J.R. in 1848. Sir Sidney Lee found that in Sonnet 107 'plain reference is made to Queen Elizabeth's death' and examined some of the evidence (*Life of Shakespeare*, p. 91 and pp. 226–7). H. C. Beeching, although a Pembrokian, declared, '. . . the only sonnet that can be dated with absolute certainty from internal evidence (107) belongs to 1603' (ed. *Sonnets*, p. xxiv). Dover Wilson, even after crossing to the Pembroke camp, has continued to recognize that Sonnet 107 dates from 1603. The fullest setting forth of the evidence for 1603 will be found in Garrett Mattingly's 'The Date of Shakespeare's Sonnet CVII', *PMLA*, XLVIII (1933), 705–21. Mattingly has been supported by Mark Eccles, *T.L.S.* (February 15th, 1934), p. 108, and by Alfred Harbage in his 'Dating Shakespeare's Sonnets', *Shakespeare Quarterly*, I (1950), 57–63.
Rereading Sonnet 107 in another connection, at the time when I was writing my chapter on the accession of James I for *Jacobean Pageant*, I had a sudden complete conviction that the sonnet belonged to 1603, almost as if it had the date visibly branded upon it. Professor G. B. Harrison, who once assigned the sonnet to 1596, tells me in a letter that he had the same conviction of the rightness of 1603 when he came back to the sonnet after working on his first *Jacobean Journal*.

implicit in the sonnet. This is what Shakespeare had to say to Southampton upon his release from imprisonment:

> I myself in my fears had thought, like everybody else, that the future held nothing for you beyond continued confinement in the Tower. But now Queen Elizabeth, so often likened to Cynthia, the virgin goddess of the moon, has finally been eclipsed by death. Since she had no acknowledged heir, pessimists had feared that her passing would bring a disastrous civil war, but now even they mock their earlier dismal prophecy. With the peaceful accession of King James, feelings of uncertainty give way to feelings of security. Our new King, dedicated to peace, brings us an unending era of peace and prosperity. The refreshing showers of this pleasant spring give new vigour to my love for you. Poor though my verse may be, it forces death to submit to me. I shall attain a literary immortality denied to the inarticulate masses. And this poetry of mine will provide you with a monument which will keep you remembered when elaborate tombs, like that to be raised for our late tyrannic Queen, have disappeared.

We have no way of knowing how Southampton responded to Shakespeare when he presented him with the sonnet. One thing, however, suggests that the newly-released Southampton received Shakespeare graciously. When, on May 19th, 1603, the Lord Chamberlain's players became the King's Men, the royal licence conferring their new status recited the names of the members of the company. Second on the list was William Shakespeare. Lawrence Fletcher, whose name preceded his, had been a 'comediane serviteur' to King James in Scotland and so probably had a special role in securing the royal appointment. But the fact that Shakespeare was named ahead of Burbage, Phillips, and the rest suggests that Southampton may also have helped to obtain the royal patronage for Shakespeare's company.

A little light on Shakespeare and Southampton is cast by a letter written to Cecil by Sir Walter Cope in 1604:

> . . . Burbage is come, and says there is no new play that the Queen [Anne] has not seen; but they have revived an old one called *Love's Labour Lost*, which for wit and mirth he says will please her exceedingly. And this is appointed to be played to-morrow night at my Lord of Southampton's unless you send a writ to remove the *corpus cum causa* to your house in the Strand.[1]

The passage is an interesting one. It ties in with the idea that *Love's Labour's Lost* was originally commissioned for Southampton's entertainment, and it shows that in 1604 Southampton was on good terms with Shakespeare's company and, presumably, with Shakespeare.

Around 1603–4 Shakespeare wrote *All's Well that Ends Well*. Described by one critic as 'an unpleasant play with an unpleasant hero', *All's Well* tells how the young Count of Rousillon, forced by the King of France to marry Helena, scorns her love and leaves her to go to the wars in Italy, where she reclaims him by changing places in the night with the girl

---

[1] *Salisbury MSS.*, XVI, 415.

whom he had sought to seduce. Writing this play, Shakespeare, perhaps partly unconsciously, drew upon his memories of the youthful Southampton when portraying Rousillon. The parallels are so numerous and striking as to admit little doubt:

   (i) Both Rousillon and Southampton are earls. In earlier comedies such as *Much Ado* and *Twelfth Night*, Shakespeare consistently calls his counts 'counts'. Twice in this play Shakespeare slips and calls Bertram an 'Earl' (III, v, 12 and 19).

  (ii) Both these earls are royal wards.

 (iii) Both these royal wards fight against marriages which have been arranged for them.

 (iv) Each goes travelling outside his own country, leaving behind a loving and distressed young lady.

  (v) In Italy Bertram is appointed General of the Horse, just as Southampton was in Ireland.

 (vi) The same stiff-necked pride which marked Southampton is exhibited by Bertram, that 'proud scornful boy' (II, iii, 158) and 'rash and unbridled boy' (III, ii, 30).

(vii) Bertram, 'that lascivious young boy' (IV, iii, 333), is given the same licentious character as Southampton with his 'lascivious grace' (Sonnet 40: 13).

Once we see Bertram as a portrayal of Southampton, we catch glimpses of other parallels. Shakespeare must often have viewed with jealous distaste the military captains who thronged around Southampton. His dislike of them shows itself in the cowardly braggart Parolles, who is blamed for leading Bertram astray. It would be idle to seek a specific identification of Parolles as Captain Piers Edmonds or Bowyer Worseley.[1] Parolles, however, probably owes something to various Elizabethan military men besides the Plautine *miles gloriosus*. We must not push likelihood too far when looking for parallels. The widowed Countess of Rousillon, with her cool aristocratic poise, shares nothing but her widowhood with Southampton's volatile and excitable mother.

What of Helena who, conscious of her social inferiority, still persists in loving her young lord despite all that is shameful and unattractive about him? Shakespeare may have identified himself to some extent with her. As Dover Wilson has noted, when Helena makes her speech on Rousillon being a bright particular star beyond her orbit, she 'exactly defines the social relationship between Shakespeare and his patron'.[2] If we may judge anything from the sonnets, there was something feminine in his love for Southampton. A bi-sexual Shakespeare could feel close to

---

[1] *v.* pp. 181 and 168 *supra.*
[2] *The Essential Shakespeare* (Cambridge, 1932), p. 59.

Helena. It is worth noting that when Helena writes a letter to her earl, it takes the form of a sonnet (III, iv, 4–17).

Critics have been too ready to castigate Helena for her love for a 'worthless' young man. Young men who appear worthless may occasionally have an unexpected amount of good in them. By 1604 Shakespeare had the evidence that such was the case with Southampton. The self-indulgent profligate of earlier years, lascivious and unreliable, proud and rash, had settled down to a useful life; he had become a constant and loving husband, and an ornament of the English court. He was diligent in his duties in Parliament and attentive to the improvement of his estates. 'All's well that ends well' had proved true ultimately for Southampton, and why not for Bertram-Southampton also?

King Lear (1605) has several interesting connections with Southampton's circle. One of these concerns Sir William Harvey who, after the death of Southampton's mother in 1607, took for his second wife Cordell or Cordelia Annesley,[1] one of the three daughters of Brian Annesley, for thirty years a gentleman pensioner to Queen Elizabeth. In his old age Annesley's mind began to fail. Two of his daughters, Christian, Lady Sandys (wife of the bellicose Lord Sandys involved in the Essex Rebellion) and Lady Grace Wildgoose, thereupon petitioned to have their old father declared insane and the administration of his estate turned over to Lady Wildgoose's husband. Cordell Annesley opposed their suit and in October 1603 sent a moving letter to Cecil on behalf of her 'poor aged and daily dying father', urging that he should not be 'begged for a lunatic, whose many years service to her late Majesty deserved a better agnomination'. She asked that, if her father must be put under guardianship, it should be under his old friend Sir James Croft, 'who from love of him and his children will take charge of him and his estate, without intention of benefit to himself'.[2] We do not know the outcome of this struggle between Cordell Annesley and her two sisters. We do know that when old Brian Annesley died in 1604 Lady Wildgoose contested his will but lost her case. Sir William Harvey was an overseer of that will.

With the Sandys and Harvey connections of the Annesley family, Cordell's struggle on behalf of her old father must have been well known in the circle around Southampton. Many of its members, seeing *King Lear*, would have sensed a parallel between Goneril and Regan and Ladies Sandys and Wildgoose, and between Cordell and Cordelia. They may

---

[1] The Annesley element in *King Lear* was first discovered by G. M. Young (see his essay 'Shakespeare and the Termers' in *Today and Yesterday*, London, 1948). Sir Gyles Isham in 'The Prototypes of King Lear and His Daughters', *Notes and Queries*, CXCIX (1954), 150–1, added the information that Cordell's name was given as Cordelia both when she was married and when she was buried.

[2] *Salisbury MSS.*, XV, 266.

have spotted a play on the Wildgoose name when the Fool, commenting on the alliance between Regan and Goneril, exclaimed, 'Winter's not gone yet if the wild geese fly that way' (II, iv, 46). Shakespeare must have been powerfully moved by the story of old Brian Annesley and his troubles amid his senility. Kenneth Muir has pointed out that in none of the many earlier versions of the Lear story available for Shakespeare does Lear go mad.[1]

In one of his mad speeches Lear uses a striking simile: 'I will die bravely, like a smug bridegroom' (IV, vi, 202). We encounter the same image a few years later in *Antony and Cleopatra* when Antony declares, 'I will be a bridegroom in my death' (IV, xiv, 99–100). Earlier, in *Measure for Measure*, we find Claudio saying:

> If I must die,
> I will encounter darkness as a bride,
> And hug it in mine arms.
>
> (III, i, 83–85)

Haunted though Shakespeare was by this image, he makes no use of it before 1604, the probable date of *Measure for Measure*. Probably he had picked it up while reading the account of how Sir Charles Danvers had died 'rather like a Bridegrome, then [than] a prisoner appointed for death'.[2]

Coming to Shakespeare's final plays, we find little or nothing to associate them with Southampton. The reason may have been a final rift between the two men in consequence of the publication of Shakespeare's sonnets.

On May 20th, 1609, Thomas Thorpe, bookseller, entered in the Stationers' Register, 'a Booke called Shakespeares sonnettes'.[3] When the book appeared it was prefaced by Thorpe's famous dedication, 'To the onlie begetter of these insuing sonnets Mr. W.H.' An intermittent controversy has long dragged on as to whether the 'only begetter' was the person who inspired the writing of these sonnets, or the person who secured them for Thorpe. Elizabethan linguistic usage decidedly favours the former interpretation.[4] Since Southampton was demonstrably the recipient of Sonnet 107, virtually certainly the recipient of Sonnets 1–17, and probably the recipient of most of the remainder of Sonnets 1–126, it would seem to follow that Mr. W.H. is 'Wriothesley, Henry', Southamp-

---

[1] *King Lear* (New Arden ed.), p. xliii.

[2] Stow, *Annals* (London, 1631), sig. Xxx Ir. Earlier editions of the *Annals* merely record Danvers' execution. Howes in his 1631 augmentation of Stow presumably incorporated a 1601 news-letter account of Sir Charles' execution. We cannot be absolutely certain that the phrase did not originate with Shakespeare. However, the fact that Shakespeare did not use this image before 1604 strongly suggests he took it over from a news-letter.

[3] Arber, *Transcripts*, III, 410.

[4] W. G. Ingram and T. Redpath, ed., *Shakespeare's Sonnets* (New York, 1965), p. 3.

ton himself. Nobody who has read F. B. Williams' useful little article[1]
on how the Elizabethans would, upon occasion, deliberately scramble
initials will see any reason for disagreeing with Chambers' view that
there was nothing very unusual 'either in the inversion of initials or in the
suppression of an actual or courtesy title'.[2]

Thorpe's motive for disguising the identity of his dedicatee is not hard
to surmise. Probably he was apprehensive that Southampton would be
angered by the publication of poems relating so closely to the scandals of
his youth. A conciliatory dedication might moderate that anger, yet an
open dedication to Southampton would indicate to all the world that his
were the faults which marred Shakespeare's much-loved friend. A veiled
dedication, intelligible only to those who already knew the Shakespeare-
Southampton story, probably seemed the best solution.

To reduce further the perils of his venture, Thorpe seems to have done
a little editing. Earlier we noted the mounting criticism against the friend
in Sonnets 94–96. In the first two of these the closing couplet is used for a
final thrust. Sonnet 94 ends with a warning:

> For sweetest things turn sourest by their deeds;
> Lilies that fester smell far worse than weeds.

Sonnet 95 ends with another warning:

> Take heed, dear heart, of this large privilege;
> The hardest knife ill-used doth lose his edge.

But Sonnet 96, after comments upon the friend's 'wantonness', 'faults'
and 'errors', ends with a couplet which simply does not relate to the
preceding twelve lines:

> But do not so. I love thee in such sort
> As thou being mine, mine is thy good report.

This ending, in fact, was borrowed from Sonnet 36. Presumably Thorpe
found the original ending of Sonnet 96 more bitter in its denunciations
than anything that had appeared up to this point. Judging the lines too
dangerous to print, he struck them out and lifted the final couplet from
Sonnet 36 to make up the necessary number of lines.[3] He may have suppressed entirely other sonnets which he found too apparent in their references to Southampton and too slanderous in their implications.

Thorpe's precautions seem to have been only partly successful. Dover
Wilson, noting that *Shakespeare's Sonnets* went into no second edition

---

[1] 'An Initiation in Initials', *Studies in Bibliography*, IX (1957), 163–78.

[2] *William Shakespeare*, I, 156.

[3] This explanation has not, to my knowledge, been suggested before. Malone in
the eighteenth century was the first to note that the concluding couplet of Sonnet 96
also ends Sonnet 36.

after 1609 (though Drayton's sonnets, already six times printed, went into three more editions after that date), accepted a solution proposed earlier by F. Mathew: 'no sooner did it [the book] appear in the bookshops and its contents become known than the printer was ordered by authority to discontinue further issues'.[1] Certainly Southampton, a grandee in the Jacobean court, was in a position to secure such an injunction. If after the publication of the *Sonnets* Southampton withdrew his favour from Shakespeare once and for all, we can understand why Condell and Heminge, publishing the Shakespeare First Folio in 1623, dedicated it not to Southampton but to the Earls of Pembroke and Montgomery, who had also extended favour to Shakespeare but had never withdrawn it.[2]

Coming to the vexed question of just how Shakespeare's sonnets reached Thorpe in 1609, we must remember two things. The first is that, although Shakespeare was so popular an author in his own lifetime that unscrupulous publishers used his name to sell works not of his authorship, only two of his sonnets other than those in the plays had escaped into print before 1609. The other thing to remember is the amazing range of Thorpe's collection. Thorpe had secured early sonnets dating back to 1593–94 and a sonnet written in 1603, sonnets written on various occasions and under the stress of a variety of emotions, sonnets addressed to a mistress and sonnets that were mere literary exercises. He had secured better texts for the two sonnets (138 and 144) already in print, and he had obtained others so personal that Dover Wilson is probably right in calling them 'secret or private'. Moreover, along with these one hundred and fifty-four sonnets, Thorpe had secured a hitherto unpublished early poem by Shakespeare. Entitled 'A Lover's Complaint', this has special interest for us since it has been claimed that the lamenting shepherdess represents Elizabeth Vernon, and that the young man with 'browny locks' who has seduced her portrays Southampton.[3] How had Thorpe obtained this very comprehensive collection, this decidedly valuable literary property?

Theories that Thorpe had obtained his material from Southampton, or from Sir William Harvey who had inherited it from Southampton's mother, or from the Dark Lady who in middle age was desperate for money, are all alike incompatible with the nature of the collection. The mind boggles at the idea of Shakespeare turning over all these poems to

[1] ed. *The Sonnets*, p. xlii.

[2] I see no evidence that William Herbert, Earl of Pembroke, is the friend mentioned in Sonnets 1–126. The Pembrokian case requires far too late a dating for Sonnets 1–17. Pembroke may be one of the Wills mentioned in Sonnets 134–6, but it would seem an amazing coincidence that got Shakespeare entangled in the love lives of two earls.

[3] These identifications, first proposed by the Comtesse de Chambrun, were accepted by J. A. Fort in his 'The Story Contained in the Second Series of Shakespeare's Sonnets', *Review of English Studies*, III (1927), 406–7.

any one of these persons. Southampton would have been angered by some of the poems, and the Dark Lady would have deeply resented others. The alternative is that the collection passed more or less directly from Shakespeare to Thorpe. This explanation, which fits the fact that Thorpe had an excellent uncorrupted text for the poems, occurred to J. A. Fort, who found it, however, 'an unwelcome thought' and declined to pursue it further.[1]

Even if a gentlemanly schoolmaster at Winchester College found unwelcome the idea that Shakespeare could betray personal relationships by selling poems in which the Dark Lady and Southampton figured at times so ignobly, the possibility should be explored.

The fact that the *Sonnets* were published in 1609 may be significant. Shakespeare's mother died in the autumn of 1608. With her death the family house on Henley Street passed into Shakespeare's possession. Inevitably the settlement of her estate would bring Shakespeare back to Stratford. The unusually full stage directions in *Coriolanus*, written around this time, may indicate that Shakespeare worked on the play while in Stratford and attached these uncharacteristically detailed directions because he knew that he would not be in London to supervise the play's production. There is some evidence that he was already contemplating retirement to Stratford. In September 1609 Thomas Greene, Shakespeare's cousin who had been living at New Place, wrote that unexpectedly he would be able to remain there a year longer. Greene's news suggests that earlier he had been told to move out since Shakespeare himself would be coming to live at New Place. If Shakespeare were preparing for retirement in 1609, a connection with the publication of the sonnets at once suggests itself. Going through his effects with a move in mind, Shakespeare might well have come across the sonnets, perhaps at the back of some drawer where over the years he had stuck them away, never intending most of them for any eyes other than his own. Perhaps he threw them aside for burning, and some servant or acquaintance, seeing them discarded and knowing them marketable, picked them up and sold them to Thorpe.

But could Shakespeare ever have brought himself to throw away the sonnets? Leafing over the manuscript pages he would have had his attention caught by passages here and there:

> Shall I compare thee to a summer's day?
> Thou art more lovely and more temperate.
>   . . .   . . .
>   Love is not love
> Which alters when it alteration finds,
> Or bends with the remover to remove.
>   . . .   . . .

[1] Ibid., III, 414.

> So shalt thou feed on Death, that feeds on men,
> And Death once dead, there's no more dying then.

Shakespeare was a supreme connoisseur of our language. He needed no Professor of English to tell him that this was great poetry.

> Time doth transfix the flourish set on youth
> And delves the parallels in beauty's brow,
> Feeds on the rarities of nature's truth,
> And nothing stands but for his scythe to mow.

Time had always been the great enemy, the appalling bringer-on of oblivion. Against Time he had mustered the force of his poetry:

> And yet to times in hope my verse shall stand,
> Praising thy worth, despite his cruel hand.

In such a situation would Shakespeare have let Time have its victory, either by sending his poems to the flames, or by taking them back to Stratford half-knowing they would some day perish ingloriously there, perhaps as papers under some woman's pies? Would he not more probably perform the last act of literary paternity and see that somehow these poems reached the press? His unprinted plays belonged to his company—it lay with his fellow actors whether or not these plays survived—but here the responsibility was his alone. Little wonder if Shakespeare gathered up the poems and resolved that one way or another they should reach a printer.

Two pieces of evidence indicate that Shakespeare himself may have arranged the publication of the *Sonnets*. At some indeterminable date after the publication of Alexander's sonnet cycle *Aurora* in 1604, William Drummond of Hawthornden made mention of 'Sir *William Alexander* and *Shakespear*, who have lately published their Works'.[1] Our second piece of evidence is provided by another contemporary poet, Thomas Heywood, who about this time was involved in a quarrel with the printer William Jaggard. In 1599 Jaggard had published *The Passionate Pilgrim*, a collection of verse which he had attributed entirely to Shakespeare though most of its poems were not by him. In 1612 Jaggard had the audacity to bring out an augmented third edition which he still represented as being entirely Shakespeare's. Among the new contents were pieces from Thomas Heywood's *Troia Britannica*. In his *Apology for Actors*, Heywood protested against Jaggard's sharp practice, which might leave people thinking that Heywood had stolen from Shakespeare. Referring apparently to Shakespeare's own poems, including Sonnets 138 and 144 which had appeared in the various editions of *The Passionate Pilgrim*, Heywood noted that Shakespeare 'to doe himselfe right, hath since published them

---

[1] *The Works of William Drummond of Hawthornden* (Edinburgh, 1711), p. 226.

in his owne name'.[1] Heywood's account of what had happened is far from clear, but he may be telling us that Shakespeare himself was responsible for the 1609 volume.[2]

One thing mitigates against the idea that Shakespeare supplied Thorpe with his copy. This concerns the very nature of the collection. Though some of the sonnets are as fine as anything in our literature, others are laboured, obscure and unsatisfactory. As for 'A Lover's Complaint', its latest editor has dismissed it as a 'poem of very little merit'.[3] If Shakespeare had sent the 1609 poems to Thorpe, he would probably have suppressed those poems which mature judgment would have told him were unsatisfactory.

A last possibility remains, that the poems were stolen. Some servant may have purloined them. Or perhaps somebody who had the use of Shakespeare's chambers while the poet was in Stratford discovered the manuscripts and unscrupulously sold them to Thorpe. Either of these explanations is likely enough. But one can imagine the cold look of disbelief with which Southampton would have received such excuses. Stories of this sort were too often used as a pretence to protect an author.

After 1609 very little links Shakespeare's work in any way with Southampton. We noted earlier how in 1610 the Virginia Company received news of the amazing survival of Sir Thomas Gates and his company after their ship the *Sea Venture* had run ashore on one of the Bermuda Islands. The news aroused great public interest when it reached London; but the Virginia Company, believing their management of affairs was not shown in an entirely favourable light in William Strachey's account sent from Virginia, kept it out of print while using parts of it in their own *True Declaration of the Estate of the Colonie in Virginia*, which they entered for publication late in 1610. Nevertheless, although Strachey's account was not printed until after Shakespeare's death in 1616, he somehow had access to a manuscript copy of it when writing *The Tempest*.[4] Because of Southampton's prominent role in the management of the Virginia Company, one might expect that Shakespeare had been shown a copy of the Strachey letter by the Earl. Leslie Hotson has pointed out, however, that Sir Dudley Digges was probably the person who let Shakespeare see Strachey's letter.[5]

The last of Shakespeare's dramatic writing is to be found in *Henry VIII*. It is still a matter of controversy whether or not Shakespeare wrote the

[1] *An Apology for Actors* (London, 1612), sig. G4r.
[2] Such is the view of Muir and O'Loughlin, *The Voyage to Illyria*, p. 14.
[3] J. C. Maxwell, ed., *The Poems* (New Cambridge Shakespeare), p. xxxv.
[4] C. M. Gayley, *Shakespeare and the Founders of Liberty in America* (New York, 1917), pp. 40–76.
[5] *I, William Shakespeare*, pp. 224–6.

whole of this play. One thing is certain: the trial of Buckingham (II, i) is remarkably parallel to the trial of Essex in 1601. Both trials were held in Westminster Hall, both accused lords desired to be personally confronted by the witnesses against them, both the accused peers were loved by the commoners, both were betrayed by men to whom they had given the utmost confidence, both left with the axe blade turned towards them, and both travelled by water back to the Tower after being found guilty. Although all these details concerning Buckingham's trial were to be found in Holinshed's *Chronicle*, they must inevitably have awakened in Shakespeare powerful recollections of Essex and Southampton. Further on in the play we come to Wolsey's great speech of counsel to Thomas Cromwell:

> Say, Wolsey, that once trod the ways of glory
> And sounded all the depths and shoals of honour,
> Found thee a way, out of his wreck, to rise in—
> A sure and safe one, though thy master missed it.
>
> (III, ii, 435–438)

That image of the safely marked channel that can save a man from shipwreck had been used earlier by Essex in his letter of good counsel[1] sent to Southampton in the autumn of 1599:

> . . . I have staked and bounded all the ways of pleasure to you and left them as sea marks for you to keep the channel of religious virtue.[2]

William Shakespeare died on April 23rd, 1616. A few weeks earlier he had made his will. In it he left one final evidence of his connection with the Southampton circle. As an overseer of his will Shakespeare named 'Thomas Russell Esquier'. This Thomas Russell was a half-brother of that Sir Maurice Berkeley who travelled to France with Southampton in 1598, served with him on the Council of Queen Anne, was arrested with him during the mysterious affair in 1604, was his ally in Parliament and associate in the Virginia Company. Another of Thomas Russell's half-brothers was married to Elizabeth Neville, daughter of that Sir Henry Neville who shared Southampton's imprisonment after the failure of the Essex Rebellion, and was likewise arrested with the Earl in 1604.[3] Many of Southampton's friends were probably Shakespeare's friends also.

---

[1] *v.* p. 96 *supra.*

[2] *A Collection of Scarce and Valuable Tracts* [The Somers Tracts], 2nd ed. (London, 1809), I, 504. The verbal echoes in 'sounded – bounded' and the repeated 'the ways of' seems to me conclusive evidence when added to the other similarities.

[3] Hotson, *I, William Shakespeare*, p. 152 and p. 102.

A Summing-up

I N his little handbook to Shakespeare, G. E. Bentley has an admirable cautionary statement:

> In spite of the thousands of pages that have been written on the Earl of Southampton as the poet's patron, the only *facts* so far established are Shakespeare's dedication of two long poems to him in 1593 and 1594.[1]

Earlier the reader was advised that in Part Two he would be offered probabilities, not certainties. Confining ourselves to what has seemed likely, we have had to exclude from our survey vast provinces of possibility. Thus, Shakespeare may have had momentary recollections of Southampton and Elizabeth Vernon when he had Claudio get Juliet with child in *Measure for Measure*, but hundreds of thousands of young men have been similarly caught and we have no grounds for making Claudio a portrait of Southampton. Sir John Peyton, Keeper of the Tower of London during Southampton's imprisonment there, was a kindly man— Cuffe before his execution made a special bequest of £100 to him, in testimony of the 'kynde favours and Chrestian comfortes'[2] he had shown him—but this does not necessarily make Peyton the model for the kindly provost in *Measure for Measure*. Shakespeare may have been thinking of Essex on the scaffold when he wrote of the rebel Thane of Cawdor that nothing in his life became him like the leaving of it, but many men besides Essex have met the sentence of death with courage and dignity.[3] Southampton was present at Oxford, carrying the sword of state before the King, when James I was treated to a little entertainment in August 1605 in which three 'sibyls' saluted the King's ancestor Banquo as 'no king, but to be the father of many kings', but this is no evidence that Southampton consequently suggested to Shakespeare the writing of *Macbeth*. Lord Timon, attended by poet, painter and jeweller, and pouring forth his money, may well incorporate elements of the youthful extravagance of Southampton, but plenty of young lords have lived beyond their means

---

[1] *Shakespeare: A Biographical Handbook* (New Haven, 1961), p. 155.

[2] Bruce, *Correspondence of James VI*, p. 192.

[3] For more substantial evidence of Essex's presence in *Hamlet*, see Edward S. Le Comte, 'The Ending of *Hamlet* as a Farewell to Essex', *ELH, A Journal of English Literary History*, XVII (1950), 87-114.

and one is hardly justified in embarking on a thesis that Timon is South-ampton.

We have taken little if any account of thousands of pages of criticism in which passing references to springtime, to roses and cankers, to storms, to stars and eclipses, have been made reasons for assigning particular sonnets to a particular year, month or day, so that at last their writers have produced fantastic, detailed schedules for the writing of the poems. We have had to pass over such charming fancies as that of Walter Thomson who declared that the more unsatisfactory of Shakespeare's sonnets were written by the Earl of Southampton and that in 1609 the two friends published their sonnets jointly as begotten by Mr. W[illiam Shakespeare]. H[enry Wriothesley].[1]

Though dealing so often with conjectures, we have hoped that our readers would find 'a constant and cumulative probability in their favour', to borrow a phrase from William Archer. Now that our task is completed, something may be said by way of summary. Emancipating ourselves, for a few final minutes, from all those warning uses of 'probably', 'apparently', 'might' and 'may' which scholarly conscience requires, let us for succinct-ness use the language of fact to summarize what has seemed probable.

By the latter half of 1592 Shakespeare had attracted the attention of the young Earl of Southampton, who joined in his defence at the time of Greene's attack. With the theatres closed, Shakespeare turned to non-dramatic writing. When in 1593 he dedicated his *Venus and Adonis* to Southampton, the young Earl was so pleased with the work that he took Shakespeare into his household. While Southampton's 'servant', Shake-speare wrote his *Lucrece* (also dedicated to Southampton), the earliest of his sonnets (in which he urged his patron to marry), and *Love's Labour's Lost* (a coterie play written for the entertainment of the Southampton circle).

With the reopening of the London playhouses in mid-1594 Shakespeare left Southampton's service, receiving on this occasion a very generous gift of money.

By the beginning of 1595 the bloom was off the Shakespeare-Southampton relationship. This had acquired a homosexual tinge, though it 'did not necessarily include paederasty in any lurid sense'.[2] Shakespeare's increas-ing awareness of George Chapman as a rival claimant for Southampton's literary patronage, and his discovery that Southampton had stolen his mistress, were now causing Shakespeare much unhappiness. By now, however, he was too deeply involved emotionally to make a break with

---

[1] *The Sonnets of William Shakespeare and Henry Wriothesley, Third Earl of Southamp-ton* (Oxford, 1938), p. 82.

[2] Ingram and Redpath, ed. *Sonnets*, p. xi.

Southampton, and for some time he contrived by various rationalizings to
blind himself to the very serious flaws in his patron. Ultimately he was
unable to avoid the truth any longer and, in sonnets which he never
showed him, he became increasingly critical of his patron. Southampton's
extensive absences from England in 1598 and 1599 coincided with a period
when Shakespeare felt intensely a break in the friendship between
Southampton and himself.

Although Shakespeare was no longer on terms of intimate friendship
with Southampton at the time of the Essex Rebellion, he had over the
years formed a number of continuing friendships with other members of
the Essex group. When *Love's Martyr* was published as a crypto-tribute
to the dead Essex, Shakespeare contributed to the volume his own
threnody, 'The Phoenix and the Turtle'.

With the accession of James I and the emergence of Southampton as
one of the persons particularly enjoying his favour, Shakespeare sought to
renew his friendship with the Earl, addressing Sonnet 107 to him when
he was released from the Tower. The two men were on terms of reasonable affability until 1609 when Southampton, holding Shakespeare
responsible for the publication of his sonnets, many of which reflected
unfavourably upon the Earl, terminated their friendship.

Such appears to be the general pattern of the Shakespeare-Southampton relationship. No doubt it is in part incorrect, but the errors probably
lie chiefly in the relative dating of events. The main thesis—that Shakespeare was very powerfully attracted to Southampton and that, in consequence, over a number of years he went through a series of profound
emotional experiences both joyful and agonizing—does seem to be supported by 'a constant and cumulative probability' when we review all the
evidence.

Patrick Cruttwell in a fine essay has observed, 'Many of the Sonnets,
in fact, are not love-poems at all; they are poems about an all-embracing
disturbance of which love was only the starting-point.'[1] A whole nexus of
Shakespeare's central formative experiences of life relates intimately to
his connection with the Earl of Southampton. Again and again an overflow
from these experiences becomes part of the substance of his plays. Just
how profoundly Southampton influenced Shakespeare's view of man and
the world, and consequently his tragic vision, lies beyond possible
definition. What does seem clear is that, in a sense extending far beyond
financial aid during the lean years of 1593 and 1594, Southampton contributed to the process by which Shakespeare became Shakespeare.

In this book we have had to concern ourselves chiefly with the dark and

[1] 'A Reading of the Sonnets', *Hudson Review*, V (1953), 550. This essay is reprinted
in part in Cruttwell's *The Shakespearean Moment* (London, 1954).

troubled parts of Shakespeare's life. Only occasionally have we been able to make passing reference to what Coleridge so fittingly called the 'angelic' part of him. That Shakespeare should at times have experienced inadequacy, shame and guilt must never cause us to forget that he was Shakespeare. The spots on the sun do not obscure its brightness. In the very fact of Shakespeare's moods of despair lies hope for those lesser souls that are the rest of us. As for the third Earl of Southampton, though he was flawed more deeply than his poet, he rose to noble things.

> They say best men are molded out of faults,
> And, for the most, become much more the better
> For being a little bad.
>
> (*Measure for Measure*, V, i, 444–446)

INDEX

Aachen, 146
Abbot, George, Archbishop of Canterbury, 167
Abbot's Worthy, 5
Acheson, Arthur, 213, 219
Aclint, 91
Acuna, Diego Sarmiento de, Conde de Gondomar, 155, 162–3, 169
Adam of Greenwich, 16
Adams, Joseph Quincy, 38
Adare, 83
Aderton, Captain, 104
Ailesbury, Thomas, 172, 177
Aldeburgh, 51
Aldershot, 163
Alexander, Sir William, 262
Alton, 20
Alvey, John, 29
Anderson, Sir Edmund, 121
Angell, Pauline K., 217 n.
Angers, 69
Angra, 60, 64, 65
Anne, Queen, 136–7, 140, 141, 142, 150, 167
'Anne-Son, James', 150
Annesley, Brian, 257–8
Annesley, Cordell, 257
Antwerp, 146, 147
Ardee, 91
Ardolph, 91
Argall, Capt. Samuel, 164
Aristotle, 130
Arklow, 85–6, 93
Armagh, 76
Arundell, Blanche (b. Somerset), Lady Arundell, 152
Arundell, Mary (b. Wriothesley), Lady Arundell, 12, 17, 19, 27, 43, 50, 52, 59, 151–2
Arundell, Sir Matthew, 6 n., 27, 41 n., 50–1, 52, 59, 152
Arundell, Thomas, Lord Arundell of Wardour, 27, 43, 45 n., 50–3, 59, 129–

130; English peerage 152, 159, 178–9, 183, 225
Arundell, Thomas, 2nd Lord Arundell, 152
Ascham, Roger, 5
Ashley, Sir Jarret, 173
Askeaton, 83
Ashton, Abdy, 119
Askew, Anne, 5
Athy, 80
Audley, Lord. *See* Tuchet.
Azores. *See* Islands Voyage.

Bacon, Anthony, 58
Bacon, Sir Francis, Lord Verulam, Viscount St. Alban, 121, 124, 137, 157
Bacon, Sir Nicholas, 26
Bagenal, Sir Henry, 76
Balaam's Ass, 146
Bald Head, 45
Balliboy, 83
Ballyknockan, 81
Barnes, Barnabe, 38, 184, 201, 232
Barton-on-the-Heath, 221
Basilden, 142
Basse, Humphrey, 69
Baynham, Sir Edmund, 109
Beale, Francis, 185
Beaulieu, 5, 20, 21, 59, 136, 144–5, 146, 184
Beaumaris, 78
Beaumont, Comte de, 141, 142
Beaumont, Sir John, 187
Bedford, Earl of. *See* Russell.
Beecher, Alderman, 9
Beeching, H. C., 228
Bellaclynthe, 91
Bellingham, Mr., 86
Bellingham, John, 47
Belson, Austen, 177 n.
Bendlosse, Andrew, 177 n.
Bentley, G. E., 265
Bergen-op-Zoom, 174

269